THE RENAISSANCE OF FEELING

History of Emotions

Series Editor:

Peter N. Stearns, University Professor in the Department of History at George Mason University, USA, and Susan J. Matt, Presidential Distinguished Professor of History at Weber State University, USA.

Editorial Board:

Rob Boddice, Senior Research Fellow, Academy of Finland Centre of Excellence in the History of Experiences, Tampere University, Finland
Charles Zika, University of Melbourne & Chief Investigator for the Australian Research Council's Centre for the History of Emotions, Australia
Pia Campeggiani, University of Bologna, Italy
Angelika Messner, Kiel University, Germany
Javier Moscoso, Centro de Ciencias Humanas y Sociales, Madrid, Spain

The History of Emotions offers a new and vital approach to the study of the past. The field is predicated on the idea that human feelings change over time and they are the product of culture as well as of biology. Bloomsbury's History of Emotions series seeks to publish state-of-the-art scholarship on the history of human feelings and emotional experience from antiquity to the present day, and across all seven continents. With a commitment to a greater thematic, geographical and chronological breadth, and a deep commitment to interdisciplinary approaches, it will offer new and innovative titles with convey the rich diversity of emotional cultures.

Published:

Fear in the German Speaking World, 1600-2000, edited by Thomas Kehoe and Michael Pickering
Feelings and Work in Modern History, edited by Agnes Arnold-Forster and Alison Moulds
Feeling Dis-Ease in Modern History, edited by Rob Boddice and Bettina Hitzer
Emotional Histories in the Fight to End Prostitution, by Michele Renee Greer
Emotions and Migration in Argentina at the Turn of the 20th Century, by María Bjerg
Emotions in the Ottoman Empire, by Nil Tekgül
The Business of Emotion in Modern History, edited by Andrew Popp and Mandy Cooper

Forthcoming:

Revolutionary Emotions in Cold War Egypt, by Christiane-Marie Abu Sarah
Emotions and the Letter, edited by Katie Barclay and Diana G. Barnes

THE RENAISSANCE OF FEELING

Erasmus and Emotion

Kirk Essary

BLOOMSBURY ACADEMIC
LONDON • NEW YORK • OXFORD • NEW DELHI • SYDNEY

BLOOMSBURY ACADEMIC

Bloomsbury Publishing Plc, 50 Bedford Square, London, WC1B 3DP, UK
Bloomsbury Publishing Inc, 1385 Broadway, New York, NY 10018, USA
Bloomsbury Publishing Ireland, 29 Earlsfort Terrace, Dublin 2, D02 AY28, Ireland

BLOOMSBURY, BLOOMSBURY ACADEMIC and the Diana logo are trademarks of Bloomsbury Publishing Plc

First published in Great Britain 2024
Paperback edition published 2025

Copyright © Kirk Essary, 2024

Kirk Essary has asserted his right under the Copyright, Designs and Patents Act, 1988, to be identified as Author of this work.

For legal purposes the Acknowledgments on p. vii constitute an extension of this copyright page.

Cover image: Woodcut initial by Hans Holbein the Younger, from Desiderius Erasmus, *Enarratio Psalmi trigesimi octavi*. Basileae: Hieronymum Frobenium, 1532, fol. a3. Universitätsbibliothek Basel, FL VII 12:2

All rights reserved. No part of this publication may be: i) reproduced or transmitted in any form, electronic or mechanical, including photocopying, recording or by means of any information storage or retrieval system without prior permission in writing from the publishers; or ii) used or reproduced in any way for the training, development or operation of artificial intelligence (AI) technologies, including generative AI technologies. The rights holders expressly reserve this publication from the text and data mining exception as per Article 4(3) of the Digital Single Market Directive (EU) 2019/790.

Bloomsbury Publishing Plc does not have any control over, or responsibility for, any third-party websites referred to or in this book. All internet addresses given in this book were correct at the time of going to press. The author and publisher regret any inconvenience caused if addresses have changed or sites have ceased to exist, but can accept no responsibility for any such changes.

A catalogue record for this book is available from the British Library.

A catalog record for this book is available from the Library of Congress.

ISBN: HB: 978-1-3502-6979-8
PB: 978-1-3502-6982-8
ePDF: 978-1-3502-6980-4
eBook: 978-1-3502-6981-1

Series: History of Emotions

Typeset by Deanta Global Publishing Services, Chennai, India

For product safety related questions contact productsafety@bloomsbury.com.

To find out more about our authors and books visit www.bloomsbury.com and sign up for our newsletters.

CONTENTS

Acknowledgments	vii
Abbreviations of Works Frequently Cited	ix

Chapter 1
INTRODUCTION: ERASMUS AND THE INTELLECTUAL HISTORY OF EMOTION 1
    A Humanist Emotional Style 3
    Religion and Emotion in the Renaissance 9
    Erasmus's Emotional Lexicons 17
    Overview of Chapters 21

Chapter 2
COMIC AND TRAGIC FEELINGS: THE EMOTIONS OF CLASSICAL LITERATURE 25
    Ethos, *Pathos*, and the Epic Emotions 28
    Mythopoeia and Mythopatheia 33
    Tragicomic Emotions in (Ps.-)Ovid's *Nux* 40

Chapter 3
BIND THIS PROTEUS: TRANSFORMING THE ANCIENT PHILOSOPHY OF FEELING 49
    Unbridled Emotions in the *Enchiridion* 52
    Fearing Death in the *De taedio Iesu* 60
    Emotion between Body and Soul 66
    Foolish Feeling 70

Chapter 4
BIBLICAL EMOTIONS I: AFFECTIVE THEOLOGY AND THE NEW TESTAMENT 77
    Paratextual Passions 78
    Pauline Passions 87
    Arguing about *Affectus* 95
    The Pauline Psalms and Intertextual Emotion 100

Chapter 5
BIBLICAL EMOTIONS II: STOMACHS, STRINGS, AND SYNECDOCHE IN
THE PSALMS   107
    Our Stomach Is Our *Affectus*: Organ and Emotion in the Psalms   110
    Feeling Harmony in Psalm 38   116
    "Anything Metaphorical is Ambiguous": Divine Feelings as
        Synecdoche in Psalm 2   125

Chapter 6
PASSIONATE PREACHING: AFFECTIVE RHETORIC IN THE PULPIT   133
    Affective Adages and Emotional Expression   135
    Emotion in the *Ecclesiastes*   141
    Wise Hearts and Minds on Fire   144
    Affective vs. Affected Rhetoric   153

Chapter 7
EPISTOLARY EMOTIONS: AUTHENTICITY, EXILE, AND CONSOLATION   163
    Performative or Constitutive Emotions?   165
    Emotions in Exile: From Basel to Freiburg, 1528–30   172
    A Burdensome Consoler   178

Chapter 8
"ALWAYS BREATHING TRAGEDY": LUTHER AND THE VIOLENT
EMOTIONS   187
    Lutheran Angers   188
    θυμὸς ἀγήνορ: The *Purgatio* of 1534   195

EPILOGUE: "PHILISTINES FOAMING AT THE MOUTH"   203

Bibliography   211
Index   219

ACKNOWLEDGMENTS

I began thinking seriously about a longer project on Erasmus and emotion sometime around 2017, in what seems like a lifetime ago, while working as a postdoc for the Australia Research Council Centre of Excellence for the History of Emotions (CHE). CHE afforded me with extraordinary opportunities for research collaboration (first as a research fellow and later as director), including dozens of national and international conferences and symposia, as well as a barrage of international experts on emotion visiting Australia—this book benefited greatly from all the conversations, interactions, and friendships that arose out of my time with CHE. Thanks especially to Merridee Bailey, Jenny Clement, and Paul Megna, who have provided meaningful feedback on something written that ended up in the chapters that follow, and I'm very grateful to Paul for our discussions on regular walks through Kings Park in search for beer.

Several colleagues at the University of Western Australia have been supportive in a variety of ways relevant to the project: special thanks to Susan Broomhall, Andrew Lynch, Bob White, Chris Mallan, Yasmin Haskell, Paul Gibbard, and Jacqueline Van Gent. CHE, again, comprised the most supportive and energetic group of scholars one could dream of; for their collaboration and support I am ever grateful to Charlotte Rose-Millar, Robin MacDonald, Michael Barbezat, Kathryn Prince, Katie Barclay, Peter Holbrook, Charles Zika, Michael Champion, Juanita Feros Ruys, Giovanni Tarantino, Gordon Raeburn, Kenneth Chong, and Kimberley-Joy Knight. Many thanks to Clare Davidson for digging up many of the emotional *Adagia* that appear throughout. I am also indebted, for their scholarly support—whether in the form of passing along texts, colloquializing over Erasmiana, reading related work, or otherwise—to Brian Cummings, Eric MacPhail, Naama Cohen-Hanegbi, Reinier Leushuis, Thomas Dixon, Matthew Champion, Miri Rubin, Richard Meek, Jane Rickard, John Corrigan, Jan Bloemendal, Bill Regier, Riemer Faber, Cameron Jeffrey, Don Lavigne, and François Dupuigrenet-Desroussilles. Maddie Holder and Megan Harris from Bloomsbury helped shepherd the text through the press and indulged (or endured) my tardiness with the final draft—I thank them for that.

I owe the biggest debt to my partner Dalina and our daughter Luna for all their love and support—I couldn't have finished the book without them. Dalina also kindly touched up the image used for the cover, which is a woodcut initial designed by Hans Holbein the Younger of Democritus (the laughing philosopher) and Heraclitus (the weeping philosopher), names reversed, from Erasmus's *Enarratio Psalmi trigesimi octavi* (Basel: Froben, 1532).

Parts of the following previously published articles have been reworked and integrated into various places in this book, and credit to Brill for allowing the material to appear again here: Kirk Essary, "Fiery Heart and Fiery Tongue: Emotion in Erasmus' *Ecclesiastes*," *Erasmus Studies* 36:1 (2016), 5–34; Kirk Essary, "Annotating the Affections: The Philology of Feeling in Erasmus' New Testament and Its Reception in Early Modern Dictionaries," *Erasmus Studies* 37:2 (2017), 193–216; and Kirk Essary, "Protean Passions: Erasmus, Emotion, and Classical Myth," *Erasmus Studies* 40:2 (2020).

ABBREVIATIONS OF WORKS FREQUENTLY CITED

Allen   *Opus Epistolarum Des. Erasmi Roterodami* ed P. S. Allen, H. M Allen, and H. W Garrod (Oxford, 1906–58) 11 vols.
ASD   *Opera omnia Desiderii Erasmi* (Amsterdam, 1969–). References are to volume and page number.
CWE   *Collected Works of Erasmus* (Toronto, 1974–). References are to volume and page number.
Ep   Epistles of Erasmus, from CWE when translated (unless otherwise indicated), or from Allen. References by letter number are to Allen (which CWE also uses).
LB   *Desiderii Erasmi Roterodami opera omnia*, ed. J. Leclerc (Leiden, 1703–06), 10 vols.
PG   *Patrologiae Graeca*, ed. J.-P. Migne (Paris, 1844–65).
PL   *Patrologiae Latina*, ed. J.-P. Migne (Paris, 1844–56).

Chapter 1

INTRODUCTION

ERASMUS AND THE INTELLECTUAL HISTORY OF EMOTION

In his last major work, the *Ecclesiastes* of 1535—ostensibly a preaching manual, but in truth a multivolume treatise on everything possibly related to Christian pedagogy—Erasmus of Rotterdam (c. 1466–1536) offers a partial description of the rich archive of literary resources, both pagan and biblical, that one might invoke when attempting to elicit tears from an audience:

> We see that sometimes spectators burst into tears not only at tragedies but at comedies as well if their characters are moral. But if this happens in stories that we know are artistically contrived, how much more will it be regular practice in those that are true and undoubted and thus pertinent to us. This class of emotions [that is, the calmer ἤθη, as opposed to the more violent πάθη] holds absolute sway in comedies, though it frequently occurs in tragedies too, especially Greek; Homer is felicitous in treating it, especially in the *Odyssey*, from which it is thought New Comedy was derived. Yet you could find its sharp barbs in Sacred Scripture as well, for instance in the story that is told at Genesis 42 and some following chapters, likewise in the parable of the prodigal son returning to his senses in Luke—indeed, a comedy of some elegance could be woven from it.[1]

Erasmus here illustrates the diverse confluence of classical and biblical source material that he is wont to reference when writing about emotion—a topic of interest that appears in all his works. In this case, Erasmus is elaborating on a distinction (one we will return to repeatedly in the chapters that follow) between the calm and violent emotions, which the Roman rhetorician Quintilian, loosely following Aristotle, had divided between the *ethē* and *pathē* respectively. Erasmus, like Quintilian, ascribes these two categories of emotion fluidly to the literary genres of tragedy and comedy, but also finds that they appear in both the Old and New Testaments. Other references to writers from antiquity (some famous, others less so) follow closely behind the passage quoted above, so that in the space of a

---

1. Erasmus, *Ecclesiastes*, in the *Collected Works of Erasmus* (henceforth cited as "CWE"), 68: 793–4.

page Erasmus recalls Quintilian (and Aristotle), Homer, Moses, Luke, Euripides, Virgil, Augustine, Macrobius, Pliny the Elder, and Aulus Gellius, and glances at Aristophanes.[2] This is vintage Erasmus, undeniably encyclopedic.[3] It is also indicative of a distinctive approach to writing about emotion that is only possible in an author with Erasmus's Christian-humanist bona fides, a representative (if extraordinary) example of describing feeling in the renaissance. It is the purpose of this book to further describe, contextualize, and exposit the complex and at times contradictory discourses of feeling that converge in and emerge out of Erasmus's extensive corpus.

The history of emotions has rapidly expanded as a distinctive subdiscipline in historical and literary studies, providing scholars and students fresh perspectives on a wide range of cultures of feeling from the past.[4] But many lacunae remain to be filled, and details to be fleshed out. If Thomas Aquinas and William Shakespeare have multiple volumes dedicated to unpacking the significance of emotion in their works and those of their contemporaries, several important and influential *longue durée* studies from the new history of emotions leap right over the sixteenth century.[5] And yet, when scholars have focused on the so-called renaissance, their work has uncovered distinct approaches to affectivity. This is unsurprising, perhaps, given the various cultural shifts attendant to the European invention of print, the rise and spread of humanism in the universities with its renewed focus on classical sources and the study of languages, as well as the religious

---

2. See CWE 68:792, and on Aristophanes, note 374.

3. On Erasmus's penchant for copiousness and polymathy, see Brian Cummings, "Encyclopaedic Erasmus," *Renaissance Studies* 28, no. 2 (2014): 183–204.

4. The vast bibliography has far outgrown a manageable footnote, but for a few recent overviews of the discipline and guides to relevant approaches, see Katie Barclay, "State of the Field: The History of Emotions," *History* 106 (2021): 456–66; Jan Plamper, *The History of Emotions: An Introduction* (Oxford: Oxford University Press, 2017); Katie Barclay, *The History of Emotions: A Student Guide to Methods and Sources* (Bloomsbury, 2020); Bob Boddice, *The History of Emotions* (Manchester University Press, 2018); Barbara Rosenwein, *Generations of Feeling: A History of Emotions, 600–1700* (Cambridge: Cambridge University Press, 2016); Susan Broomhall and Andrew Lynch (eds.), *The Routledge History of Emotions in Europe: 1100–1700* (London: Routledge, 2017); also *A Cultural History of Emotions* (6 vols.), edited by Susan Broomhall, Jane Davidson, and Andrew Lynch (Bloomsbury, 2022).

5. Barbara Rosenwein's *Generations of Feeling* (cited in the note above), an excellent work from a preeminent figure in the field, represents a microcosm of broader trends in that it moves from a chapter on Jean Gerson to one on seventeenth-century English melancholy. See also Thomas Dixon, *From Passions to Emotions: The Creation of a Secular Psychological Category* (Cambridge: Cambridge University Press, 2004), whose highly influential book moves from Aquinas to Descartes. There is, of course, a plethora of work out there that also glosses over the medieval period as well; see, e.g., Daniel Gross, *The Secret History of Emotions: From Aristotle's Rhetoric to Modern Brain Science* (Chicago: University of Chicago Press, 2006).

reformations of the sixteenth century.[6] From the perspective of Erasmus studies specifically, the importance of affectivity to his thought has long been recognized, but there has until now been no monograph devoted to the subject. This book attempts to fill that gap by examining the ways in which the renowned and highly influential Christian humanist defined, described, prescribed, and proscribed emotion and affectivity. In Erasmus's writings, classical, biblical, medieval, and humanist approaches are brought together to form a complex and multilayered set of emotional discourses, usually aimed at striking a balance between cultivating the virtuous (often religious) emotions and taming the unruly and disruptive ones.

A Humanist Emotional Style

Erasmus's corpus is significant in that it marks a culmination of humanistic learning in the northern renaissance, and is shaped by (and, in some accounts, gives rise to) the Protestant Reformations. Few thinkers from any period have had the command of such a wide range of sources from classical and biblical antiquity, much less the ability to translate those sources into digestible pedagogical treatises, entertaining colloquia, irresistible literary satire, and scathing (but somehow only occasionally tedious) religious diatribe. It is virtually impossible to understate Erasmus's vast influence, even if it is often difficult to trace it. For even though Erasmus was widely recognized during his own lifetime as perhaps Europe's most monumental intellectual figure, and although his works were printed more often and more widely than anyone else's before Martin Luther arrived on the scene, his refusal to play partisan in a divided Christendom resulted in a substantially decreasing acknowledgment of his influence by both Protestants and Catholics in the decades after his death. When one looks, however, one finds Erasmus

---

6. See, for example, Susan Karant-Nunn, *The Reformation of Feeling* (Oxford, 2010); Elena Carrera, "The Emotions in Sixteenth-Century Spanish Spirituality," *Journal of Religious History* 3 (2007): 235–52; idem, "Anger and the Mind-Body Connection in Medieval and Early Modern Medicine," in *Emotions and Health, 1200–1700* (Leiden and Boston: Brill, 2013), 95–146; Brian Cummings and Freya Sierhuis (eds.), *Passions and Subjectivity in Early Modern Culture* (Ashgate, 2013); Richard Strier, "Against the Rule of Reason," in *Reading the Early Modern Passions*, ed. Gail Kern Paster (University of Pennsylvania Press, 2004); Susan Broomhall, *Early Modern Emotions: An Introduction* (Routledge, 2016); idem (ed.), *Gender and Emotions in Medieval and Early Modern Europe* (Routledge, 2015); Karl Enenkel and Anita Traninger (eds.), *Discourses of Anger in the Early Modern Period* (Leiden: Brill, 2015); Luisanna Sardu, "How Gaspara Stampa Challenged Classical Tradition and Conventional Notions of Women's Anger," *Emotions: History, Culture, Society* 3 (2019): 24–46; Giovanni Tarantino and Charles Zika (eds.), *Feeling Exclusion: Religious Conflict, Exile, and Emotions in Early Modern Europe* (London: Routledge, 2019); and the special issue on Erasmus and emotion in *Erasmus Studies* 40, no. 2 (2020).

everywhere.⁷ The purpose of this book is not, however, to demonstrate the legacy of Erasmus's writings about emotion, but to illuminate the ways in which he was a critical figure in participating in and shaping a humanist discourse of feeling. This discourse (or set of discourses) arose in part out of the new world of print, and on account of the sheer accessibility of a larger library of texts which that world made possible.

The increasing prevalence of "rediscovered" ancient philosophical, literary, and rhetorical works, and the printing, editing, and translation of biblical and other ancient religious texts from the late fifteenth to the mid-sixteenth century, inevitably led to a reconsideration and often a redescription of human emotion and affectivity in light of re-readings of those texts. Erasmus was, for much of his lifetime, at the very center of this world of texts, both as a creator and as a consumer. He went to extraordinary lengths to edit and publish new editions and translations of works from Greco-Roman antiquity (including the Bible and church fathers), and he incorporated and reshaped the ideas from these texts into his own literary, pedagogical, and theological productions, which were in turn widely published and translated across Europe during the sixteenth and seventeenth centuries. Given the widely read nature of his corpus, the intellectual, religious, and literary history of emotions in Europe remains incomplete without a consideration of the subject from the perspective of Erasmus's works.

Moreover, while scholars of early modern Europe have learned—or at least some of them have learned—from their patient medievalist colleagues that one must always be wary of arguing for significant cultural shifts or brand new ideas in the so-called renaissance, humanists consciously mined a variegated range of texts, some of which, like Quintilian's *Institutio oratoria* or the New Testament in Greek, simply were not widely available until the fifteenth or sixteenth century.⁸ And these texts had an indelible impact on conceptions of emotion and affectivity in certain circles, and on Erasmus's thought in particular. So, even though my aim is not to argue that a radical transformation in the European understanding the emotions took place during the early modern period, it takes seriously the key

---

7. While there is plenty of work yet to be done on the reception of Erasmus, see, for example, Bruce Mansfield, *Phoenix of His Age: Interpretations of Erasmus, 1550–1750* (Toronto: University of Toronto Press, 1979); idem, *Man on His Own: Interpretations of Erasmus, 1750–1920* (Toronto: University of Toronto Press, 1993); idem, *Erasmus in the Twentieth Century* (Toronto: University of Toronto Press, 2003); Karl Enenkel (ed.), *The Reception of Erasmus in the Early Modern Period* (Leiden: Brill, 2013); Kirk Essary, *Erasmus and Calvin on the Foolishness of God: Reason and Emotion in the Christian Philosophy* (Toronto: University of Toronto Press, 2017).

8. Quintilian's text circulated in part before Poggio Bracciolini found a complete manuscript version at St. Gall, but the partial texts were missing Book 6, which contains the most germane material on rhetoric and emotion. See further Rita Copeland, *Emotion and the History of Rhetoric in the Middle Ages* (Oxford: Oxford University Press, 2022), 5 and notes.

contention of the new history of emotions, namely that emotions themselves, or at least how they are described and ethically adjudicated, do change over time in response to various cultural inputs.[9] Additionally, as Benno Gammerl has suggested, understanding how emotions were described and understood in the past should be an important aspect of history of emotions scholarship. He asks:

> What did they [i.e., past actors] perceive of as emotions or feelings or sentiments or affects? Obviously, words and their meanings vary across times and settings. . . . Did actors think of emotions rather as mental or corporeal occurrences, as spontaneous reflexes or as enduring attitudes, as irrational or as sensible? And how did they distinguish emotions from ideas, interests, beliefs and other sorts of phenomena?[10]

Answering such questions about any thinker or group allows us to appreciate continuity as well as to delineate difference when carrying out comparative work. Tracing how Erasmus writes about emotion with reference to works and ideas from classical and biblical antiquity, and how the proliferation of works from and about the Greco-Roman world, lastingly shaped Erasmus's ideas about feeling, allows us to situate him in a longer intellectual history of feeling. We are able then to discern in Erasmus something like a humanist—or, probably more accurately, Christian humanist—emotional *style* that differs from other conceptualizations of and discourses about emotion.[11]

In order to fully appreciate Erasmus's emotional style, it is necessary to read widely across his variegated corpus. Erasmus did not write a treatise *de ira*, for example, as did Seneca in antiquity or Johann Weyer in the sixteenth century. For that matter, he did not write systematically (at least at length) on any aspect

---

9. It is a commonplace in history of emotions scholarship that emotions are not experienced in the same way across time, place, and circumstance but, rather, are experiential phenomena determined in significant ways by cultural inputs. The clearest argument for this position, to my mind, remains Martha Nussbaum's, in *Upheavals of Thought: The Intelligence of Emotions* (Cambridge: Cambridge University Press, 2001), esp. 139–73. Nussbaum's account is based on her argument that emotions are "cognitive/evaluative," with the implication that "If we hold that beliefs about what is important and valuable play a central role in emotions, we can readily see how those beliefs can be powerfully shaped by social norms as well as by an individual history; and we can also see how changing social norms can change emotional life" (ibid., 142). One needn't (as Nussbaum points out) adhere to the cognitive/evaluative model, however, in order to maintain a (soft or hard) social constructionist view of emotional experience.

10. Benno Gammerl, "Emotional Styles—Concepts and Challenges," *Rethinking History* 16, no. 2 (2012): 162.

11. For the original conceptualization of emotional styles, see Peter N. Stearns and Carol Z. Stearns, "Emotionology: Clarifying the History of Emotions and Emotional Standards," *American Historical Review* 90 (1985): 813–36.

of faculty psychology, as did Aristotle in the *De anima* or Erasmus's humanist contemporaries Juan Luis Vives and Philip Melanchthon.[12] While Erasmus does deploy some ideas and heuristics about emotions and affectivity consistently, what makes Erasmus's approach simultaneously so vibrant and also so frustrating is his refusal to write in formal terms, to adhere to scholastic or otherwise rigorous philosophical norms. That is, of course, deliberate. Erasmus routinely eschewed formalisms, and he did so for affective reasons: they were frigid (a favorite pejorative) and lifeless. As George McClure put it some time ago, we should not underestimate "the psychological dimension of the rhetorical revolt" against scholastic method, a revolt Erasmus very actively participated in and which is deep with affective resonance.[13] Avoiding technical and formal approaches, Erasmus writes about emotion not only from different perspectives—theological, philosophical, medical, literary, rhetorical—but also in different genres. In doing so, he provided a distinctive, if not unique, Christian humanist model of affectivity.

Utilizing such a variety of ostensibly competing discourses about feeling afforded Erasmus (consciously nor not) the ability to better grasp the protean nature of emotional experience itself. As Richard Meek and Erin Sullivan write, with regard to Shakespeare's use of figurative language to explain feeling in *Richard III*, "While there are many ways to describe what such emotional experience might be like, there is no single or straightforward way of explaining what it actually is."[14] Thus writers like Shakespeare, and Erasmus before him, resorted to an assortment of descriptive and prescriptive tactics. What Meek and Sullivan call the "diversity and even mystery of early modern emotional experience, especially as it related to the understanding of the self," combined with the extraordinary arsenal of sources Erasmus had at his disposal, mean that his works are not tied together by a singular framework for understanding feeling but are laden with multiple discursive structures, interwoven and intertextual. This feature of Erasmus's corpus is constitutive of the variegated arsenal he deploys—Homeric, Platonist, Aristotelian, Stoic, Virgilian, Ovidian, Ciceronian, Pauline, Quintilianic, Galenic, Origenist, Augustinian, Cistercian, and even Thomistic descriptions of feeling all together shape Erasmus's emotional style.

We might also usefully refer to this confluence of sources, following recent scholarship, as constitutive of various "structures of feeling." For example, in

---

12. On Vives, see Carlos Norena, *Juan Luis Vives and the Emotions* (Carbondale: University of Southern Illinois Press, 1980), and Kaarlo Havu, *Juan Luis Vives: Politics, Rhetoric, and Emotion* (London: Routledge, 2022); on Melanchthon, see Simeon Zahl, "On the Affective Salience of Doctrines," *Modern Theology* 31, no. 3 (2015): 428–44; and idem, *The Holy Spirit and Christian Experience* (Oxford: Oxford University Press, 2020), esp. ch. 3.

13. *Sorrow and Consolation in Italian Humanism* (Princeton: Princeton University Press, 1991), 157.

14. Richard Meek and Erin Sullivan, *The Renaissance of Emotion: Understanding Affect in Shakespeare and His Contemporaries* (Manchester: University of Manchester Press, 2015), 3.

describing the "form of ethical life" that derives from medieval trends of affective piety, Holly Crocker writes that "Christ's suffering offers a new structure of feeling, a different way of understanding what it means to be human."[15] Even if Erasmus was not as keen as some of his medieval predecessors to emphasize Christ's physical suffering as a way of restructuring feeling, by documenting the significance of emotions (theologically-oriented or otherwise) in Erasmus's works, we are able to more fully appreciate how he understood what it means to be human. His approach to emotion also helps us to think through questions of periodization, for, as Barbara Rosenwein puts it, "Although there are other ways to bridge the medieval/early modern divide, the study of emotions has unusually good potential to knit together the two sides and yet point up their differences."[16] Erasmus is important for such a knitting project precisely because he sits somewhat awkwardly in the middle of these two constructed temporalities (confounding their rigidity), and because he is self-consciously pitting his own methods against those of some of his medieval predecessors while at the same time tacitly appropriating other forms of affective theology from the same period.

By illuminating the classical, biblical, patristic, and medieval features of Erasmus's writings on feeling, we also begin to uncover a specifically Christian-humanist "emotional community"—defined by Barbara Rosenwein as a "group in which people adhere to the same norms of expression and value—or devalue—the same or related emotions."[17] Indeed, Lisa Jardine had effectively argued (before Rosenwein developed this helpful heuristic) that Erasmus himself attempted to create such a community via the rhetorical and political strategies of his correspondence, with some implication that it was more ideal than real. Jardine writes, for example, that the "northern humanist 'world of learning'" was constructed by Erasmus, as "seductively vivid and emotionally charged" and as "carefully controlled and programmed as the Metsys panel or Holbein painting."[18] Jardine's insights help us to see just how important rhetorical strategies can be for producing and perpetuating emotional norms, regardless of whether these norms were always strictly adhered to. By bringing earlier Erasmus scholarship into

---

15. Holly Crocker, "Medieval Affects Now," *Exemplaria* 29, no. 1 (2017): 85.

16. *Generations of Feeling*, 252. For a substantive overview of medieval philosophies and theologies of emotion, see Simo Knuuttila, *Emotions in Ancient and Medieval Philosophy* (Oxford: Oxford University Press, 2004).

17. A caveat is in order insofar as I'm only—primarily—focusing on the works of a single author, and thus such concepts (style, community) are inherently limited in this work. Nevertheless, they are useful heuristic devices that do helpful work, especially to the extent that we can take Erasmus's works as at least in some meaningful sense as representative of the sixteenth-century *respublica litterarum*. Future research might very well further confirm or indeed reject such an extrapolation.

18. Lisa Jardine, *Erasmus, Man of Letters: The Construction of Charisma in Print* (Princeton: Princeton University Press, 1993), 148.

conversation with recent work on the history of emotions, we can further clarify the affective valences of Erasmus's works in a broader humanist context.

The reader might be wondering what Erasmus's *writings about* emotion may have had to do with his *actual* emotions—or whether an intellectual history of emotions is germane to a history of the phenomenology or experience of emotions. How does one, in other words, bridge the gap between described feelings and felt feelings? Various solutions to this problem have been proposed, and it is as much an epistemological matter as it is a psychological or historical one. There is no way to fully comprehend a past actor's (or a contemporary actor's) feelings, and certainly no iron-clad guarantee that a discursive framework for emotion in a didactic, literary, or theological work bears any actual reflection of how anyone felt at a given time. Nonetheless, there are good reasons, I think, to believe that what one says, or thinks, about emotion in descriptive terms has some bearing on the feeling process itself—that is, that discourses around and conceptualizations of emotion are integral aspects of the phenomenon of feeling. We learn, to some extent at least, to describe, explain, and signal our feelings from cultural inputs (whether literary, philosophical, rhetorical, musical, or otherwise), and if those inputs change over time, so does some aspect of our feelings. From this perspective, explanations of emotion, philosophies of feeling, discursive practices, and descriptions of affectivity are all worthy of the study of emotional life; understanding them tells us something about how emotions were and are experienced.

Another way of putting it is that a full account of emotion includes intellectual and cognitive content, along with physiological and embodied phenomena. As Martha Nussbaum writes, "the fact of language does change emotion," and "a person who does not know the emotional 'grammar' of his or her society cannot be assumed to have the same emotional life as one who does know this 'grammar'. To be able to articulate one's emotions is *eo ipso* to have a different emotional life."[19] By extension, varied articulations of emotional experience also imply different experiences, however slight. Emotional experience partially comprises the narratives, tropes, terms, and gestures familiar as forms of emotional expression. Relatedly, Catherine Peyroux argues that the meaning of an emotion "is located in the particular social framework in which it is generated and expressed. Whatever the immediate felt experience or physiological component of emotions, feelings are 'cultural acquisitions' intelligible only in the context in which they occur."[20] Thus it is important to pay close attention to the language used to describe particular emotions, but also to the narratives and scripts employed in describing or prescribing modes of affectivity.[21] I take all of the above as applicable to the textual

---

19. *Upheavals of Thought*, 149.

20. Peyroux, "Gertrude's *furor*," in *Religion and Emotion: Approaches and Interpretations*, ed. John Corrigan (Oxford: Oxford University Press, 2004), 310.

21. It is important to pay close attention to original languages of feeling for another reason as well, as articulated by Barbara Rosenwein, in order to construct "the building blocks of a new history of the emotions based not on the presentist and Anglophone biases

resources that Erasmus marshals in order to give expression to the multifaceted nature of emotional life.

One learns how to feel, and different individuals and communities learn how to feel differently. Erasmus learned how to feel, at least in part, by reading books, and he taught how to feel by writing them. To paraphrase Holly Crocker again, Erasmus uses "texts to produce feelings that consolidate a specific form of the self."[22] This does not mean that Erasmus's emotions, or those of other premodern Christian readers and writers, are reducible to discursive structures, but rather that insofar as emotions are also cognitive phenomena, they are heavily shaped by such discursive structures—and, in the case of Erasmus at any rate, discursive structures are all we've got (and he wouldn't have it any other way). In what remains of this introduction, I will provide a bit more background on two aspects of Erasmus's thought that will feature throughout this book: religious feeling and the language of emotion.

Religion and Emotion in the Renaissance

Erasmus argues repeatedly that theology itself is, or ought to be, intrinsically emotional, and that Christian perfection itself happens through the emotions (*affectus*). It is more affective than intellective.[23] As Dominic Baker-Smith has written, "The distinction between outward acts and inner disposition or *affectus* lies at the heart of Erasmus's critique of contemporary religious practice, from the early days of the *Enchiridion* down to the final expositions of the psalms."[24] Moreover, while emotion preoccupied Erasmus from his earliest writings to his latest, it is also clear that some developments occur. Brian Cummings has argued for an "affective turn" in Erasmus's career, represented in his biblical hermeneutics as laid out in the theological treatise, the *Ratio*, of 1519.[25] As will be seen, Erasmus's extensive exegetical works, on both the New and Old Testaments, constitute a deeply affective enterprise that differs in meaningful ways from his earlier works, even if some common themes recur throughout his career. At the same time, religious concerns pervade Erasmus's whole corpus, which means that even in the chapters of this book that focus on emotion in classical literature and ancient

---

of modern emotion studies but on the words as they were really used in the past" ("Emotion Words," in *Le sujet des émotions au Moyen Âge*, ed. Piroska Nagy and Damien Boquet [Beauchesne, 2008], 106).

22. Crocker, "Medieval Affects Now," 87.

23. See *Ratio* (Vessey et al.), 124; *Paraclesis* (in *Novum instrumentum omne* [Basel: Froben, 1516], fol. aaa4.

24. CWE 65: xvi.

25. Brian Cummings, "Erasmus, Sacred Literature, and Literary Theory," in *Erasmus on Literature: His* Ratio *or "System" of 1518/19*, ed. Mark Vessey (Toronto: University of Toronto Press, 2021), 61.

philosophy, the religious significance of emotion is always fundamental. We might ask, as well, what Erasmus's relationship is to historical affective theologies in the Christian traditions that precede him, in light of recent research on emotion in patristic and medieval Christianity.

Erasmus, who advocated for an approach to Christian pedagogy that engaged and reformed the emotions by teaching which emotions should be cultivated and how, argued further that his theological method itself engaged the emotions more successfully than rival approaches—that is, that the precepts of theology should be taught in such a way that they move the Christian reader (or auditor).[26] Theology must be transformative. Here it is perhaps useful to make a distinction between a meta-theological claim, which considers the *form* of theological discourse vis-à-vis its affective purchase (or lack thereof), and the kinds of affective practices *qua* "intimate scripts" that Sarah McNamer and others have studied so carefully as forms of medieval affective meditation (although both are relevant to Erasmus's writings). Such scripts, McNamer suggests, are often constitutive of what William Reddy has called "emotives," or first-person utterances that do a certain amount of cultural work in terms of producing emotional norms in their readers. They are "mechanisms for the production of emotion."[27] The goal of Christian thinkers advocating what Charles Trinkaus long ago called *theologia rhetorica* (a distinctively humanist rhetorical theology) was to convince theologians and preachers to produce similarly intimate scripts of one sort or another—whether in the form of theological treatises, biblical commentaries, or sermons.

It is therefore necessary to simultaneously examine the affective-theological rationale behind such scripts (or behind advocating for them) in the works of Erasmus, while illuminating the scripts themselves. If the *telos* of an intimate script in the context of medieval affective meditation is to produce a certain kind of affective disposition, or to induce particular emotions, we should add that the *telos* of Erasmus's affective theology is also to teach *by means of* emotion. It is to inculcate something akin to what Katie Barclay, in her recent study of early modern *caritas*, has referred to as an "emotional ethic," while also engaging the emotions in order to impart wisdom.[28] Parsing all this out in Erasmus's works can be difficult, for he often writes as though emotion is not, religiously speaking, an end in itself, but is rather a key mechanism for the production of faith and wisdom. If he denounces scholastics like Thomas Aquinas for producing theologies that lack feeling, he had no problems with the Peripatetic conception of emotions as "goads to virtue." At other times, however, it is clear that *affectus* was also more than a means to an end

---

26. Or, as the case may be, to be more pedagogically effective because of its operation on the affections.

27. Sarah McNamer, *Affective Meditation and the Invention of Medieval Compassion* (University of Pennsylvania Press, 2010), 12.

28. Katie Barclay, *Caritas: Neighbourly Love and the Early Modern Self* (Oxford: Oxford University Press, 2021), passim.

for Erasmus, that an emotionally rich version of Christian experience, and even a deeply affective form of Christian knowledge, is the goal of true theology.

Some recent studies of Augustine's thoughts on emotion in theology provide a helpful comparative model for thinking about Erasmus. For example, James K. A. Smith has argued for a "deconstruction of Augustine" which pits the Bishop of Hippo's platonizing critique of the pernicious affective effects of drama in the *Confessions* against a love-centered Incarnational theology in order to disabuse us of a caricature of Augustine as a "dry scholastic."[29] As Smith shows, Augustine's rejection of rhetoric and the theatre does not derive from a rejection of the emotions *in se*, but of their misplaced use in these arenas: the emotions are aroused for their own sake—as ends in themselves—and not put to use for knowing or loving God.[30] While Smith's purpose is to delineate (or "retrieve") a working affective theology from a deconstructed Augustine, rather than to trace the significance of emotions in the history of theology, his suggestion that one can construct a Christian epistemology from Augustine's aesthetics that "understands the mode of *affectivity* as a means of 'knowing' that is as fundamental—and perhaps more primordial—than the ratiocinative or intellectual" reflects an important aspect of Augustinianism that is also reflected in the writings of early modern humanists and religious reformers.

Debora Shuger has demonstrated this most clearly in relation to an early modern humanist context: "The polarization of reason and passion, and hence of philosophy and rhetoric, does not seem to have been central to Renaissance thought."[31] This is vitally important for understanding Erasmus's anthropology in general, even though he does occasionally express such a polarization in his works. At the same time, Erasmus goes farther than Augustine in integrating emotion into the very center of religious life. As Jonathan Teubner has recently written of Augustine's approach to religious affectivity, "affections are both necessary and necessarily a failure."[32] For Erasmus they are necessary and not necessarily a failure—indeed, their failure would signal doom for his spiritual project. Erasmus repeatedly writes, in various formulations, that theology is about engaging the emotions more than it is about rational forms of religious knowledge and discourse. In his 1518 letter to Paul Volz, which prefaced a new edition of the *Enchiridion* (originally published in 1503, and one of Erasmus's most influential

---

29. James K. A. Smith, "Redeeming the Affections: Deconstructing Augustine's Critique of Theatre," in *The Spirit, the Affections, and the Christian Tradition*, ed. Dale Coulter and Amos Yong (University of Notre Dame Press, 2016).

30. See ibid., 46–7.

31. Debora Shuger, "The Philosophical Foundations of Sacred Rhetoric," in *Religion and Emotion: Approaches and Interpretations*, ed. John Corrigan (Oxford: Oxford University Press, 2004), 120.

32. Jonathan Teubner, "The Failure of *Affectus*: *Affectiones* and *constantiae* in Augustine of Hippo," in *Before Emotion: The Language of Feeling, 400–1800*, ed. Juanita Feros Ruys, Michael Champion, and Kirk Essary (London: Routledge, 2019), 9.

and widely published works), Erasmus writes that the pursuit of perfection in Christ has nothing to do with one's profession, or way of life (*genus vitae*), but that "*in affectibus est Christi perfectio*"—the perfection of Christ lies *in the emotions*.[33] It is worth reiterating that this line comes in a prefatory letter to the *Enchiridion*, a work where Erasmus is also most assiduously critical of the sinful emotions.[34] As will become clear especially in Chapter 5, on his engagement with the Psalms, *affectus* comes to serve as the lynchpin of religious subjectivity in Erasmus's thought.

The striking features of affectivity in some of Erasmus's writings necessitate slight modifications to earlier narratives of emotion in the context of early modern humanism as well. For example, in his article on the "two faces of humanism" in the renaissance (the Stoic and the Augustinian), William Bouwsma emphasized the significance of the will for the latter:

> The will, in this view, is seen to take its direction not from reason but from the affections, which are in turn not merely the disorderly impulses of the treacherous body but expressions of the energy and quality of the heart, that mysterious organ which is the center of the personality, the source of its unity and its ultimate worth. The affections, therefore, are intrinsically neither good nor evil but the essential resources of the personality; and since they make possible man's beatitude and glory as well as his depravity, they are, in Augustinian humanism, treated with particular respect.[35]

This would not be a bad generalized account of the religious emotions as explicated by Erasmus, but it requires a qualification: outside of his dispute with Luther, Erasmus does not very often refer to the will (*voluntas*) as a particular faculty of the soul.[36] In some ways the *affectus* itself (or themselves) takes on the role of the will for Erasmus as the "organ" that might be either depraved or sanctified (this is even explicit at times, as in the *Hyperaspistes 2*, the second installment of Erasmus's response to Luther's *On the Bondage of the Will*[37]). Invoking what Monique Scheer

---

33. Allen Ep 858, ll. 330–1.

34. See further Chapter 3.

35. William Bouwsma, "The Two Faces of Humanism: Stoicism and Augustinianism in Renaissance Thought," in *Itinerarium Italicum: The Profile of the Italian Renaissance in the Mirror of Its European Transformations*, ed. Heiko Oberman and Thomas Brady (Leiden: Brill, 1975).

36. This is one of many ways in which Erasmus rejects scholastic determinations about emotion; as Knuuttila notes, Franciscan thought after Scotus discussed the emotions primarily as movements tied to the will (see *Emotions in Ancient and Medieval Philosophy*, 268–70).

37. See CWE 77:594 and cf. Chapter 4 on emotions in the New Testament, where Erasmus does refer to *affectus* as "in ea parte animi, quae dicitur voluntas" in his dispute with Titelmans.

has called "topographies of emotion," we are able to recognize that for Erasmus the *affectus* often serves to displace the *voluntas* as well as the *intellectus* as the locus of meaningful religious activity—and it is the interior and psychological, not corporeal, *affectus* that matters most.[38] But if this is a responsible extrapolation, and one part and parcel with Erasmus's extensive use of classical sources (he also almost never uses the common Thomistic distinction—rooted though it is in ancient philosophy—between concupiscible and irascible appetites[39]), it is not always so simple: in general Erasmus's descriptions of psychological faculties, and of emotions as situated in relation to them, is far from systematic, in line with his preference for literary variety against dry formalism.[40]

As a rule, Erasmus maintains the generalization throughout his corpus that an emotion can be legitimate or illegitimate depending on its object, but he also privileges *affectus* more generally as a key spiritual faculty. As Jacques Chomarat put it, Erasmus legitimizes or saves the emotions by ascribing to them this ambiguity.[41] Throughout all of Erasmus's work, there is a simultaneous criticism of the earthly and sinful emotions and an exaltation of the pious, virtuous, emotions of the heart. Erasmus himself describes this relationship succinctly in his recalling to Pieter Gillis a dispute with Francis Titelmans in 1530 over the legitimacy of using the term *affectus* to describe a virtuous disposition in his New Testament translation: "just as in a human being there are two kinds of will, one good, one bad, so there are two kinds of *affectus*, good and bad, spiritual and carnal."[42] And yet that still does not quite get at the full significance of emotion in his religious

---

38. See Monique Scheer, "Topographies of Emotion," in *Emotional Lexicons*, ed. Ute Frevert et al. (Oxford: Oxford University Press, 2014), 32–61.

39. Knuuttila notes that Suarez abandoned the distinction in the sixteenth century as well, citing P. King, "Late Scholastic Theories of the Passions: Controversies in the Thomist Tradition," in *Emotions and Choice from Boethius to Descartes*, ed. Henrik Lagerlund and Mikko Yrjonsuri (Springer, 2002), 229–58.

40. We never find in Erasmus's works a sober, precise, and consistent description of the role of affectivity—either in the practice of rhetoric or theology, or in terms of faculty psychology—as we find, for example, in Erasmus's contemporary, Juan Luis Vives's *De ratione dicendi*, which when compared with Erasmus's malleable treatments of feeling reads almost as a scholastic treatise (see, e.g., the section in Juan Luis Vives, "De movendis affectibus," in *De ratione dicendi*, ed. Walker (Leiden: Brill, 2018), 249ff.

41. "Ainsi donc il y a dans les passions une ambiguïté, une plasticité; la rigidité du schéma dualiste s'assouplit . . . De plus, comme les analyses du chapitre V elle a pour effet de légitimer, de sauver les *affectus*; selon qu'ils sont orientés vers la chair ou vers l'esprit les mêmes *affectus* appellent des jugements opposés" (Jacques Chomarat, *Grammaire et Rhetorique Chez Erasme*, 2 vols [Paris: Les Belles Lettres, 1981], 60–1).

42. Verum ut in homine duplex est voluntas pia et impia, ita scire debebat esse duplices affectus, bonos et malos, spirituales et carnales (Allen Ep 2260).

thought.⁴³ As early as the *Enchiridion* of 1503 the *affectus* had already taken on a central role for Erasmus as the key to religious transformation, and—despite first appearances—not only because the emotions need to be tamed or ordered properly. Alec Ryrie's gloss on early modern Protestant approaches to emotion is apt: "They went beyond the medieval, scholastic view of emotions as appetites to be bridled, and even beyond the Aristotelian view of passions to be brought into harmony with the higher faculties. Certainly the affections had to be disciplined, but they ought not to be restrained: rather, the point was to direct and to heighten them."⁴⁴ Not only would this be accurate for Erasmus as well, but many of the Protestants described by Ryrie would have read Erasmus's works closely.⁴⁵

Erasmus's hermeneutics also heavily informs his affective theology, as Dominic Baker-Smith notes:

> Erasmus's lifelong distrust of literalism, whether in the handling of signs, of ceremonies, or of words, was the natural consequence of his rhetorical formation: it is the literal reading that excludes affectivity or, as we might put it, the subjective response. It was precisely his concern to allow full scope to the affective layer in religious language that made his interventions in the religious disputes of the 1520s and 30s often appear soft-centred, giving the term "Erasmian" its regrettably gelatinous character.⁴⁶

This is another way in which the concept of an "emotional style" is readily applicable to an Erasmian mode insofar as it might be used to delineate a specifically humanist set of emotional norms, or at least of an evaluation of emotional dispositions.⁴⁷ At a very basic level, Erasmus often positions himself in one religious group or against another in affective terms—against, for example, the frigidity of the scholastics, or the violent temperament of the Lutherans—and teasing out the details of these formulations is key to this project. The humanist rejection of scholastic method might, for example, be thought of as a countercultural movement, whereby the perceived regnant approach to theological discourse was challenged precisely because it lacked sufficient affective movement. When Erasmus does mention

---

43. "Toute l'oeuvre d'Erasme est à la fois condamnation du monde, du corps, de l'ici-bas, des passions terrestres et charnelles—et d'autre part exaltation du sentiment, du coeur, de l'amour" (Chomarat, *Grammaire et Rhetorique Chez Erasme*, 61).

44. Alec Ryrie, *Being Protestant in Reformation Britain* (Oxford: Oxford University Press, 2013), 18–19.

45. See Essary, *Erasmus and Calvin on the Foolishness of God*, esp. ch. 5.

46. Dominic Baker-Smith, "*Tranquillitas Animi*: Erasmus and the Quest for Spiritual Reassurance, 1533–43," in *Erasmus and the Renaissance Republic of Letters*, ed. Stephen Ryle (Brepols, 2014), 384.

47. See further Monique Scheer, "Are Emotions a Kind of Practice and Is That What Makes Them Have A History? A Bourdieuian Approach to Understanding Emotion," *History and Theory* 51, no. 2 (2012): 217; Gammerl, "Emotional Styles," 161–75.

scholastic theologians, it is often to criticize them. Thomas Aquinas, who admittedly receives less abuse than Duns Scotus, is nevertheless denounced as ἀπαθής (unemotional) for his writing style—he teaches but does not move.[48] After all, Erasmus argued that a renovation in theology was necessary because it had languished under an emotional regime that lacked fervor.

As he writes in the dedicatory epistle to his *Paraphrase of John*, "Although, to speak openly, in no centuries have men been lacking to pay the gospel the honour that is its due; but all the same in these last four hundred years its energy in most hearts has grown cold."[49] While many aspects of classical rhetoric were appreciated and employed by Christian humanists, they also conceived of (in the words of Erasmus) a "new method of teaching" that took seriously the notion that the modes of discourse and narrative structures found in the original biblical texts were representative of divine revelation: God not only revealed theological truths to humans through scripture but also offered a discursive model in the biblical writers for doing theology.[50] As Erasmus puts it in his *Sermon on the Child Jesus*, it is the Holy Spirit whose "living and efficacious discourse pierces deeper than any two-edged sword, reaching right to the inmost recesses of the heart."[51] The idea that humanists criticized scholastics for their lack of attention to the emotions is, of course, not new. But tools from the history of emotions provide the means to be more precise in analyzing the emotional significance of that criticism, to historicize it in a new way.

Erasmus has a specific brand of scholastic theology in mind when he rejects the whole medieval theological tradition as having gone too cold in his *Paraphrase of John*, but his relationship to the robust affective theologies of the Middle Ages is more complicated.[52] R. W. Southern long ago pointed to an Anselmian affective theology that gave rise to Cistercian versions of something similar, a view which has been challenged in meaningful ways by historians of emotion such as Sarah McNamer, who argues that the medieval theological praxis which is often referred to as "affective piety" had its roots in women's writings and practices

---

48. In the *Ciceronianus*; ASD I-2, 661.

49. CWE 46:10; Froben, 1532: Quanquam, ut ingenue fatear, nullis seculis defuerunt, apud quos Evangelio suus constiterit honos, sed tamen his annis quadringentis vigor illius apud plerosque refrixerat.

50. For an argument that something similar was at work in Abelard, see Peter von Moos, "Literary Aesthetics in the Latin Middle Ages: The Rhetorical Theology of Peter Abelard," in *Rhetoric and Renewal in the Latin West 1100–1540*, ed. C. Mews, C. J. Nederman, and R. M. Thomson (Brepols, 2003), 81–98.

51. *De concio puero Iesu*, CWE 29:56; ASD V-7, 171: "cuius sermo vivus et efficax penetrantior est quovis gladio ancipiti, ad intimos etiam cordis recessus penetrans."

52. I have attempted to outline some aspects of this relationship elsewhere: see Kirk Essary, "Rhetorical Theology and the History of Emotions," in *The Routledge History of Emotions in Europe: 1100–1700*, ed. Susan Broomhall and Andrew Lynch (Routledge, 2019).

developed around feelings of compassion for Christ's suffering.⁵³ Heiko Oberman similarly described the "Franciscan Middle Ages" as involving an especially "anti-speculative, affective thrust."⁵⁴ More recently, Damien Boquet's study of Aelred of Rivaulx's *anthropologie affective* analyzes the importance of the role of the heart in medieval Cistercian thought, a topic explored in a more general nature by Eric Jager, who considers the "pectoral psychology" of the Middle Ages to be an Augustinian relic.⁵⁵ Indeed, Piroska Nagy has provided a helpful overview of a whole cluster of emotional theologies in the Middle Ages, not necessarily all emerging out of the same traditions, which provides a rich, but complicated, background for considering Erasmus's thought.⁵⁶

Erasmus was not only an Augustinian canon regular but was also partly educated in a setting associated with the *devotio moderna*. His relationship to both traditions is complicated, given that he left the monastery, routinely attacks the hypocrisy of monks, and says little by way of appreciation or otherwise for the Brethren of Common Life. Cornelis Augustijn has written, for example, regarding the *devotio moderna*, that "emotional life reached its fulfilment in a new way, not in the depths of an intense mysticism but in the withdrawal from life in the world to the serenity of a hidden communing with God . . . Erasmus's own experience of it was entirely negative."⁵⁷ While it is true that Erasmus became strongly critical of isolated monks and advocated for moderated rather than excessive feeling, his demonstrable dependence on Augustine and the echoes of Bernard of Clairvaux (two favorites of the *devotio*) in his affective theology might rather indicate at least

---

53. McNamer, *Affective Meditation and the Invention of Medieval Compassion*. See also Elizabeth Dreyer, "The Transformative Role of Emotion in the Middle Ages," in *The Spirit, the Affections, and the Christian Tradition*, ed. Dale Coulter and Amos Yong (University of Notre Dame Press, 2016); and E. Jost, "Spirituality in the Late Middle Ages: Affective Piety and the Pricke of Conscience," in *Mental Health, Spirituality, and Religion in the Middle Ages and Early Modern Age*, ed. Albrecht Classen (Berlin, DE: Deguyter, 2014).

54. Heiko Oberman, "The Reorientation of the Fourteenth Century," in *Studi sul XIV secolo in memoria di Anneliese Maier*, ed. A. Maierù and A. Paravicini Bagliani (Rome: Raccolta di Studi e Testi, 1982), 514.

55. See Damien Boquet, *L'Ordre de l'affecte au Moyen Âge* (Caen: CRAHM, 2005); Eric Jager, *The Book of the Heart* (Chicago: University of Chicago Press, 2000).

56. Piroska Nagy, "Émotions de Dieu au Moyen Âge," in *Émotions de Dieu: Attributions et Appropriations Chrétiennes (XVIe-XVIIIe Siècle)*, ed. Bernat et al. (Brepols, 2019). See also Knuuttila, *Emotions in Ancient and Medieval Philosophy*; Lagerlund and Yrjönsuuri (eds.), *Emotions and Choice from Boethius to Descartes*; D. Boquet and P. Nagy, *Sensible Moyen Âge* (Paris: Le Seuil, 2015); and Rosenwein, *Generations of Feeling*; and Naama Cohen-Hanegbi, *Caring for the Living Soul: Emotions, Medicine and Penance in the Late Medieval Mediterranean* (Leiden: Brill, 2017).

57. Augustijn, *Erasmus: His Life, Works, and Influence* (Toronto, 1991), 15.

some positive influence.[58] At the same time, while Erasmus very often deploys the terms *affectus* and *pietas* alongside one another in his theological writings, the medieval theological tendencies described by scholars as "affective piety" share little in common with his thought. Erasmus's deep suspicion of materiality and the body, and his distrust of affectation and excessive emotionalism, leave little room in his writings for an appreciation of the highly emotive and ecstatic practices associated with Christ's bodily suffering. It might be helpful, in fact, to think of Erasmus's affective theology as an attempt to navigate between two dominant strands of late medieval Christian theology and practice: overly intellectual scholasticism on the one hand, and a type of affective piety, on the other, which "utilized the passions of pathos and disgust" to induce commiseration.[59] Examining Erasmus's theological writings with questions about emotion at the forefront will permit us to clarify his relationship to earlier as well as then-contemporary Christian traditions while simultaneously expanding on the extensive body of work on Erasmus's religious thought.

Erasmus's Emotional Lexicons

Scholarship on emotion in multiple disciplines, including not only history and literature, but also anthropology and linguistics, has highlighted the importance of tracing emotional vocabularies while also emphasizing the difficulty of translating emotion terms.[60] Studying the language of feeling is important not only for the

---

58. On the emotions and the *Devotio Moderna*, see Mathilde Van Dijk, "The *Devotio Moderna*, the Emotions and the Search for Dutchness," *BMGN: Low Countries Historical Review* 129, no. 2 (2014): 20–41.

59. Jost, "Spirituality in the Late Middle Ages," 391. "Affective piety" might be conceived in a broader manner than this, of course. See the helpful suggestions by Paul Megna for broadening out the category to incorporate other affective dispositions in "Dreadful Devotion," in *The Routledge History of Emotions in Europe, 1100–1700* (Routledge, 2019), 72–90. Erasmus's approach also differs notably from that of some other sixteenth-century Catholics, as is clear from Erasmus's own denunciations of contemporary theologians and overly dramatic preachers, as well as in comparison with the traditions studied by Susan Karant-Nunn in her illuminating book *The Reformation of Feeling* (Oxford: Oxford University Press, 2010), especially the first chapter.

60. For the clearest recent assessment of the pitfalls of translating emotional language and of what Cliff Goddard calls "terminological ethnocentrism," see Thomas Dixon, "What Is the History of Anger a History Of?" *Emotions: History, Society Culture* 4 (2020): 1–39. See also Anna Wierzbicka, "The 'History of Emotions' and the Future of Emotion Research," *Emotion Review* 2 (2010): 269–73; Douglas Cairns and Laura Fulkerson (eds.), *Emotions Between Greece and Rome. BICS Supplement* 125 (University of London, 2015), introduction; Frevert et al., *Emotional Lexicons*; Kirk Essary, "Passions, Affections, or Emotions? On the Ambiguity of 16th-Century Terminology," *Emotion Review* 9 (2017):

fundamental purposes of tracing linguistic usage but also because such language is one determinative factor in delineating different emotional communities, as well as for understanding how emotions are conceived of or experienced by a particular person or group. To quote Monique Scheer, "If naming emotions makes them available to experience, then charting changes in naming means writing a history of feeling in the fullest sense."[61] It is also a fruitful way of doing reception history. For example, when Erasmus, in the *Enchiridion*, quotes a litany of emotion words verbatim from Marsilio Ficino's Latin translation of Plato's *Timaeus*, he is at least tacitly endorsing a certain mode of describing affectivity. When he ceases to use much of the same emotional vocabulary in later works, it tells us that he has moved on somehow, that he has extended or modified his emotional lexicon (and, perhaps, that he got better at reading Greek). When he criticizes the Vulgate's use of the word *passio* (emotion, passion) as a neologism, or when he advocates repeatedly for *mansuetudo* (mildness) instead of *ferocia* (harshness or ferocity), he is articulating a commitment to a kind of Christian humanist usage, with ethical implications, which potentially resonates for other speakers and writers in his emotional community. Indeed, Erasmus's glosses of certain emotion terms in his New Testament scholarship often made their way into Latin and Greek dictionaries, with some entries remaining in editions centuries later—an example of his lasting influence.[62] Attending closely, then, to the range of terms and phrases Erasmus uses when describing emotions gives us a more accurate perspective on meaning while mitigating inevitable anachronistic generalization.

Terms denoting specific emotions raise particular difficulties, such as translating *ira* or *stomachus* always and everywhere as "anger," especially if we are operating on the assumption that emotions change over time and in varied cultural contexts. Anger in the twenty-first century is not exactly or always the same thing as *ira* in the sixteenth; *stomachus* might mean something like anger, as we will see in Erasmus's denunciations of Luther, but it might also stand in as an organ of affective piety, as we will see in his Psalms commentaries.[63] At the same time, as important as charting emotional lexicons can be, an overly strict focus on discreet terms can be limiting, as F. Scott Spencer has written in a recent introduction to a volume on emotions in biblical literature: it might result in "atomistic analyses

---

367–74; also *Before Emotion*; Rosenwein, "Emotion Words," 94–106; Merridee Bailey, "Early English Dictionaries and the History of Meekness," *Philological Quarterly* 98, no. 3 (2019): 243–72, has demonstrated the fruitfulness of cross-linguistic comparison of words associated with "meekness," how the emotional force shifts across language cultures and over time.

61. Scheer, "Are Emotions a Kind of Practice and Is that What Makes Them Have a History?" 214.

62. See Kirk Essary, "Annotating the Affections: The Philology of Feeling in Erasmus' New Testament and Its Reception in Early Modern Dictionaries," *Erasmus Studies* 37, no. 2 (2017): 193–216.

63. Dixon, "What Is the History of Anger a History Of?," 1–39.

of emotion words, incidents, or experiences decoupled from wider literary (and social-cultural) contexts."[64] Spencer provides the apt example of the biblical book of Lamentations, which, he writes, "fits the elegiacal mold, however many times it actually uses the word *grief* and related terms."[65] This is helpful to keep in mind when reading Erasmus, for not only is genre at times determinative of his emotional tone and style, he also deploys a rhetorical copiousness and eschews formalism, which has the result that too much focus on a given term would be misleading.

Some terms, however, such as the Latin *affectus* (emotion, feeling, disposition) require close analysis. General categories denoting emotion or feeling, or definitions of what constituted an emotion, were contested in the early modern period and are contested now, meaning that no easy definition is possible. Brian Cummings has recently reminded us that *affectus* (far and away Erasmus's preferred term for "emotion" and the full range of affective dispositions) is one of the most difficult terms to render from Latin antiquity.[66] Erasmus uses the term *affectus* to describe what most English speakers would call "emotions" (cognitive-affective movements similar or identical to what we call anger, grief, sadness, joy, hope, and the like) but also for other habituated dispositions that our English term does not entail (e.g., drunkenness).[67] Manfred Hoffmann writes that "Erasmus uses the concept *affectus* in three ways, as the divine (or author's) attraction in the word, as natural human affection in general, and as a moral disposition of human beings within the (Stoic) framework of virtues and vices."[68] This is true but ultimately not specific or detailed enough to exhaust the richness of Erasmus's usage, and one motivation of this book is to provide just such detail. Erasmus occasionally, but less frequently, uses *affectiones*, or *motus animi*, but he explicitly eschews *passiones* as an unnecessary late-antique invention.[69] At times, especially when describing sinful or worldly or

---

64. F. Scott Spencer (ed.), *Mixed Feelings and Vexed Passions: Exploring Emotions in Biblical Literature* (SBL Press, 2017), 17.

65. Ibid., 17.

66. Cummings, "Erasmus, Sacred Literature, and Literary Theory," 60.

67. This, of course, is already to beg the question to some extent, and one might legitimately wonder what constitutes an emotion (either for "us" or for a particular group in history). I'll take the easy road here and suggest that the purpose of this book is to flesh out what Erasmus considers to be the essence and significance of *affectus*, but also the significance of affectivity more generally. Whether his concerns and definitions are always commensurate with those of late modern subjects will also be considered, implicitly and explicitly, throughout the book.

68. Manfred Hoffmann, "Erasmus on Language and Interpretation," *Moreana* 28 (1991): 18n41.

69. Although he does use *passiones* to describe the emotions of Christ in the early work, *De taedio Iesu* (see ASD V-7, 242). For a more detailed look at Erasmus's usage in the wider context of humanist usage of *affectus* and *affectio*, see Kirk Essary, "The Renaissance of *affectus*? Biblical humanism and Latin style," in *Before Emotion: The Language of Feeling,*

bodily emotions, desires, and related vices, Erasmus uses the terms *cupiditates, perturbationes,* or (worse) *morbi animi*.[70]

Erasmus's usage and opinions were not necessarily normative, as his dispute over these terms with Francis Titelmans in 1529 demonstrates (see further our chapter on the New Testament), but there is at the same time a rich classical as well as medieval monastic and scholastic tradition of using *affectus* in various ways, which allows us to align Erasmus with some writers who came before him.[71] Future research will, ideally, continue to illuminate further connections in the emotional lexicons of this period. Erasmus's strong rejection of *passio*, noted previously, is a departure from much of the Christian tradition, including the Vulgate, and would seem to stem from Erasmus's debts to fifteenth-century Italian humanism: Lorenzo Valla had earlier criticized Poggio Bracciolini for using the term despite his professed allegiance to Cicero.[72] This is noteworthy, especially given Thomas Dixon's influential claim that "the heart of Christian affective psychology" from Augustine until the Enlightenment rests in a distinction between the virtuous

---

400–1800, ed. Juanita Feros Ruys, Michael Champion, and Kirk Essary (Routledge, 2019), 156–69.

70. See, for example, Allen Ep 2443 to Sadoleto, line 374, or *Ennaratio in psalmum 22* (LB V 339A).

71. See the essays in *Before Emotion: The Language of Feeling, 400-1800*.

72. See Lorenzo Valla, *Antidoti in Pogium*, Lib. III; *Opera Omnia*, I, ed. Eugenio Garin (Torino: Bottega d'Erasmo, 1962), 517. Relatedly, Jean Gerson wrote a treatise entitled *De passionibus animae*, which had some influence on sixteenth-century lexicons. For instance, a lexicon published by Johann Altenstaig in 1517, contains an entry for *passiones spirituales*, which cites Gerson, among other scholastics: "dicuntur spirituales affectiones, et haec magis attendendae sunt animae ad denotionem vocatae quam sensuales ... Ecce habemus inspiritu passiones xi. principales, Amorem, concupiscentiam, delectationem, odium, fugam, tristitiam, spem, desperationem, audaciam, metum, iram vel zelum. Et differunt passiones animales et spirituales. Nam animales ut sunt tales, versantur circa rationem commodi vel incommodi. Spirituales vero ad rationem solius iusti vel iniusti respiciunt. Gers. ubi supra. Et passiones spirituales immittuntur frequenter ab angelo Dei bono, quamvis crebro perturbentur ab immisionibus per angelos malos factis" (*Lexicon theologicum complectus vocabulorum descriptiones* [Altensteig, 1517], *ad loc.*).

Meanwhile, one of several Latin lexicons published under the name of Calepino point to the use of *passio* by the *neoterici auctoribus ecclesiasticis*, while the entry for *affectus* invokes Cicero and Augustine (see the 1512 Basel edition, *ad loc.*). Some early modern dictionaries, like Robert Estienne's *Dictionariolum puerorum* (London, 1552), lack an entry for *passio* altogether. I have discussed these matters in more detail elsewhere, with reference to the relevant scholarship: Essary, "Passions, Affections, or Emotions? On the Ambiguity of Sixteenth-Century Terminology."

religious *affectus* and the unruly and sinful *passiones animae*, and that until the eighteenth century this distinction was maintained with general regularity.[73]

In a perfect world we could simply leave all these terms untranslated from their original languages. I have nevertheless endeavored, in most cases, to render them into their English equivalents. Despite some acknowledged slippage between the English terms, I primarily use the terms *emotion, feeling, affective disposition* and, less often, *affection* throughout this book, more or less interchangeably, to translate Erasmus's *affectus*, for those terms come closest to his meaning. "Affect" in English, ostensibly convenient as a cognate, brings serious baggage from the critical approach "affect studies," which is rather different from the history of emotions, and so I avoid the term.[74] "Passions" is borderline arcane and, as mentioned, Erasmus rejects its Latin cognate (but the keen-eyed reader will have already noticed that I couldn't resist its alliterative allure for some chapter headings). To avoid ambiguity, I have provided the relevant Latin or Greek emotion terms where relevant either in parentheses or in the footnotes.

Overview of Chapters

Erasmus consciously developed his philosophy of feeling first and foremost by engaging with the authors from Greco-Roman antiquity and from the Bible (both Old and New Testaments). Thus, a key approach of the chapters that follow is one of reception history: a close examination of how Erasmus received and transformed ideas about emotion from earlier periods. Which writers or figures from antiquity most influenced his opinions about how emotions ought to be regulated, for example, or how they ought to be inflamed? What categories or definitions of emotion did Erasmus borrow from the Greco-Roman world, and how did he shape them to his own purposes? How, in other words, did Erasmus's understanding of feeling derive from his humanist learning, and how, in turn, did he contribute to the formation or perpetuation of a humanist emotional style? Although distinguishing between genre and discipline can be misleading when reading a figure like Erasmus, I have nevertheless chosen to carve up the chapters according, roughly, to themes associated with genre or discipline: literature, philosophy, religion, and rhetoric.

Tracing the classical literary sources Erasmus used to understand and explain emotion is the purpose of Chapter 2, "Comic and Tragic Feeling: The Emotions of Classical Literature." There we will see how Erasmus deployed Greco-Roman

---

73. Dixon, *From Passions to Emotions*, 61.

74. For a helpful critique of affect studies from the perspective of the historical semantics of emotion, with specific reference to the long history of the Latin word *affectus*, see Michael Champion, "From *affectus* to Affect Theory and Back Again," in *Before Emotion: The Language of Feeling, 400–1800*, ed. Juanita Feros Ruys, Michael Champion, and Kirk Essary (Routledge, 2019), 240–56.

literary tropes, categories, and specific myths in order to explain human feeling. Erasmus builds a scaffolding for describing emotion out of the narratives, characters, and epithets from the works of Homer, Virgil, and Ovid. In addition to characters and tropes, generic (as in, from genre) categories from the ancient world also play a fundamental role in Erasmus's taxonomy of emotion. In this, Erasmus is following Quintilian, who had effectively developed his own theory of emotions by mapping the *ethē* and *pathē* of Aristotle's rhetorical theory onto the emotions inherent in the genres of comedy and tragedy respectively, which Quintilian argues derive from Homer's epics. Erasmus marshals this framework repeatedly, beginning with the *De copia* of 1512, by invoking the language of the calm and violent emotions, or a gentle versus vehement rhetorical style, or by using literary figures from comedy, tragedy, or epic as *exempla* for emotional expression. Classical literature provides a substantial basis for describing emotion in other ways as well, across Erasmus's corpus, as we will see from pedagogical works like the *De ratione studii*, to the monumental collection of *Adagia*, to his religious polemics, and in his underrated commentary on Ovid's *Nux*.

The purpose of Chapter 3, "Bind This Proteus: Transforming the Ancient Philosophy of Feeling," is to examine Erasmus's use of Greco-Roman philosophies in his conceptualization of emotion. The chapter focuses on the *Enchiridion*, the *De taedio Iesu*, and the *Praise of Folly*. Erasmus engaged often with the various schools of ancient philosophy on questions related to the legitimacy of emotional feeling and expression, and, especially, of their relation to and effects on reason. He often used clichés and tropes to dismiss the Stoic doctrine of *apatheia* as un-Christian, for example, but he also referenced Plato's works to denigrate the passions as inhibitors of unfettered rational thought and action. When he mentions Aristotle on emotion, it is always in a positive evaluation of the idea that emotions are useful for cultivating virtue. If such generalizations and caricatures serve a rhetorical purpose for Erasmus in didactic works like the *Enchiridion*, they also undermine easy generalizations about Erasmus's own attitude toward affectivity. He cannot, in other words, be easily enlisted into one of the ancient philosophical schools on this question; rather, in borrowing from each of them in constructing his (ultimately unsystematic) philosophy of feeling, Erasmus reveals his malleable approach to philosophical sources.

While the religious emotions are not at all absent in the second and third chapters, they are brought to the forefront in the chapters that follow. In Chapter 4, "Biblical Emotions I: Affective Theology and the New Testament," we see Erasmus develop the substance of his affective Christian theology in the context of his exegetical and philological work on the New Testament. The chapter begins with a consideration of the importance of affectivity in Erasmus's theological method, with a focus on the *Ratio seu methodus theologiae* of 1519; it moves on to show how Erasmus imagines Paul (after Jesus) to be a model of Christian emotional life by examining the *Annotations* and *Paraphrases* of his epistles. Chapter 5, "Biblical Emotions II: Stomachs, Strings, and Synecdoche in the Psalms," demonstrates how Erasmus's exegesis of the psalter represents the most deeply affective expression of his theology, while also considering the intractable exegetical issues that arise from thinking about God's emotions. Chapter 6, "Passionate Preaching: Affective Rhetoric in the Pulpit," examines the role of rhetoric and emotion in Erasmus's writings about teaching and preaching, with a focus on the *Ecclesiastes*, his manual for preachers and his last major work. Before publishing the *Ecclesiastes* in 1535, Erasmus had developed a series of overlapping images across various works, including the *Adagia* and *Ciceronianus*, of the relationship between the voice, the tongue, and the heart in order to argue for a kind of affective authenticity as necessary for true persuasion to take place. In the *Ecclesiastes* he brings these ideas together with a litany of ancient rhetorical, literary, and biblical models to present his most extensive analysis of the importance of emotion in Christian life.

The final two chapters and the epilogue contextualize Erasmus's feelings about the rise of Protestantism, which impacted Erasmus's life directly in multiple ways: on an intellectual and religious level, because he got caught up in the bewildering array of debates that attended Luther's challenges; and on a more mundane level because Erasmus's adopted hometown of Basel turned Protestant, forcing him into exile. Chapter 7, "Epistolary Emotions: Authenticity, Exile, and Consolation," reconsiders scholarship around the affective nature of Erasmus's correspondence before turning to two case studies to explore: (1) his anxieties about leaving Basel after it turned Protestant, and (2) his writing of and theorizing about letters of consolation. Chapter 8, "'Always Breathing Tragedy': Luther and the Violent Emotions," reinterprets the relationship between Erasmus and Luther from the perspective of Erasmus's attribution of various anger-like emotions to the German Reformer (in contrast to his own ideals of moderation). The epilogue extends this analysis by considering Erasmus's use of the trope of the tragic emotions as a heuristic for explaining the violence of the religious reformations more generally. Taken together, we see how Erasmus was emotionally affected by the religious and political movements of the last decade and a half of his life, as well as how his assiduous commitment to arguing for moderation (emotional and otherwise) never waned.

Chapter 2

COMIC AND TRAGIC FEELINGS

THE EMOTIONS OF CLASSICAL LITERATURE

In *De copia*, Erasmus's very popular treatise on a copious style, first published in 1512 (and printed in roughly thirty editions per decade for over fifty years[1]), he writes, "When we use an anecdote which cannot possibly be believed, it will be best, unless we are being humorous, to preface it by saying that those wise old men of long ago did not invent stories like this for no good reason, nor was it for nothing that they have been current by general consensus for so many centuries."[2] This can be appreciated as a justification for Erasmus's own extensive invocation, translation, and transformation of anecdotes from classical literature into a vast array of contexts: philosophical, literary, rhetorical, theological. It is also the basis for a tradition that invokes mythology to elicit and to explain emotions.[3] A prime example comes in the *Enchiridion*, where Erasmus asks: "What is so protean as the emotions and desires of the foolish? Are not the words of the learned poet

---

1. Figure taken from Peter Mack, "Quintilian in Northern Europe during the Renaissance, 1479–1620," in *The Oxford Handbook to Quintilian*, ed. Marc Van Der Poel et al. (Oxford: Oxford University Press, 2022), 385.

2. *De Copia*; CWE 24:610. See also the *Enchiridion*, CWE 66:68–9, for explicit examples of allegorizing myths both biblical and pagan, since otherwise, according to Erasmus, the "carnal" sense is unhelpful.

3. There is, of course, a long-standing tradition of an allegorical understanding of Greek poetry (dating at least to the sixth century BCE), and Erasmus is but a participant in a lengthy history of appropriating classical literature to pedagogical or broadly philosophical ends. My purpose here is to understand the ways in which this appropriation comes to bear specifically on Erasmus's understanding of the emotions. On Cicero's use of Greek and Roman drama to teach emotional regulation in the *Tusculan Disputations*, see Ruth Rothaus Caston, "*Pacuvius hoc melius quam Sophocles*: Cicero's Use of Drama in the Treatment of the Emotions," in *Emotions Between Greece and Rome*, ed. Douglas Cairns and Laura Fulkerson (London: Bulletin of the Institute of Classical Studies Supplements, 2015), 129–49. For an introduction to the complex literary reception of Homer and poetry in antiquity, see *The Cambridge History of Literary Criticism Volume 1: Classical Criticism* (ed. George Kennedy; Cambridge: Cambridge University Press, 1989).

perfectly appropriate to describe how they are dragged into bestial lust, wild anger, venomous envy, and other monstrous vices?" He continues, quoting Virgil's *Georgics*: "'Of various beasts he takes the differing shapes/ Now like a bristly boar, or deadly tiger, / Now scaly snake or tawny lioness / Or crackling sound of fire.'"[4] This is, in fact, useful as an analogy for Erasmus's own shape-shifting approach to the emotions, which is protean in its difficulty to adequately and neatly summarize, as well as multiform in its discursive approach. We can only hope to follow his caveat in this and subsequent chapters to gain a better hold on his understanding of emotion: "Be sure to remember the lines that follow: 'The more new forms and shapes you see him take / The more draw tight the tautened bonds.'" Erasmus is not only adept at alluding to classical myths for the purpose of illustrating various truisms regarding affective experience, but he is also an advocate for the tactic, instructing his readers in the process. Before considering further specific examples, more can be said about Erasmus's program of reviving classical literary modes—including proverbial wisdom but also biblical literature—as constitutive of affective discourse.

While for Erasmus multiple competing discourses (the philosophical, theological, literary, and scientific, for example) all contribute to his understanding and expression of affectivity, Greco-Roman epic, tragedy, and comedy would seem to contribute a lion's share. Of course, Erasmus's prescriptions to study classical literature are well known, appearing as they do in his heavily influential pedagogical works, and it will not come as a surprise to anyone who has read him that he mined Greco-Roman literary texts in order to explicate his thoughts about human feeling. In his introduction to the *Adagia*, for example, Erasmus explains at least half-seriously that proverbs (most of which are taken from Greek and Roman literature) "belong to the science of philosophy" (*pertinere scientiam philosophiae*), and "should be looked into, not in sluggish or careless fashion, but closely and deeply."[5] In the *De pueris instituendis*, a manual on teaching children, he writes, "young children should be taught brief, pointed aphorisms, which include almost all proverbs and sayings of famous men, and which used to be the only means whereby moral truths were passed on to the common people."[6] A proverb, moreover, Erasmus quotes Quintilian as saying, is nothing more than a myth writ small (*fabella brevior*),[7] and thus "protean passions," though not technically an adage,

---

4. CWE 66:50, modified. LB V 18C: Quid autem tam Proteus, quam adfectus et cupiditatus stultorum, quae eum eos nunc in belluinam libidinem, nunc in iram ferinam, nunc in venenatam invidiam, nunc in alia atque alia vitiorum portenta trahunt, nonne pulcre quadrat, quod eruditissimus Poeta dixit: *Tum variae illudent species, atque ora ferarum. / Fiet enim subito sus horridus, atraque tigris, / Squamosusque draco, et fulva cervice leana. / Aut acrem flamma sonitum dabit*. Hic vero memento quod sequitur: *Sed quanto ille magis formas se vertet in omnes, / Tanto nate magis contende tenacia vincla*.

5. CWE 31:14.

6. CWE 26:336.

7. See his introduction to the *Adages*, CWE 31:8.

picks out a recognizable form of gnomic wisdom that tells us something about the conception of emotions lying behind it. As a medium of expressing something about emotion, then, we can think of the reception of classical proverbial wisdom (or classical models and tropes rendered into proverbial wisdom) as instrumental to Erasmus's approach.

In this way Erasmus regularly translates emotional experience into what Jessica Wolfe has helpfully described as "mythographic shorthand."[8] Wolfe's chapter on Erasmus and the discourse of strife details extensively how Erasmus and his colleagues expressed their opinions about strife and how to regulate it via a seemingly endless series of Homeric allusions. There Homer's epics become a prominent framework within which Erasmus negotiates his ethics of discord (and concord), especially in the *Adagia*, and a similar approach to Erasmus's use of myth in his writings about emotion is equally fruitful. Cora Fox's work on Ovid and emotion in Renaissance England provides another helpful way of thinking through Erasmus's use of classical literature and emotion: she writes, for example, that "Ovidianism served as a code for emotional expression in the period, and it participated in scripting not just private experiences of the self but public uses of emotional rhetoric."[9] While Erasmus uses many literary sources in addition to Ovid, we will see that this is an apt description of his approach as well. The poets, after all, as Erasmus wrote to Luther, "know human emotions [*affectus hominis*] most deeply and depict them most skilfully."[10]

The purpose of this chapter, then, is to evaluate the manner in which Erasmus likewise employs and advocates employing examples, tropes, metaphors, and allegories from classical literature in order to explain emotion, but also to clarify how he interprets the emotions of classical literature by translating them into a Christian humanist context. In doing so, it will foreground the classical literary context of Erasmus's thoughts about, for example, what constitutes affectivity, or how emotions might be employed in the service of persuasion and pedagogy, or how emotions ought to be regulated in everyday life. The overall aim is to place Erasmus into the conversation as a representative of a key way of understanding the emotions in a humanist context by considering three aspects of Erasmus's mythologization of feeling: first, his adaptation of Quintilian's taxonomy of emotions as either tragic or comic, which will serve as a key framework for his understanding of feeling throughout his life; second, his use of classical literature to explore and explain the emotions in works such as the *De copia*, *Adagia*, and *Moria*; third, the analysis of emotion and rhetoric in his commentary on the Ovidian poem, the *Nux*. This will give the reader a broad overview of the ways in which Erasmus received classical literature and transformed it into contemporary emotional meaning.

---

8. Jessica Wolfe, *Homer and the Question of Strife from Erasmus to Hobbes* (Toronto: University of Toronto Press, 2015), 5.
9. *Ovid and the Politics of Emotion* (Palgrave MacMillan, 2009), 2.
10. CWE 77:592.

Ethos, Pathos, *and the Epic Emotions*

The generic categories of comedy and tragedy play a fundamental role in Erasmus's descriptions of affectivity, linked as they were, in Greek and Roman manuals of rhetoric, to the calm and violent emotions, respectively. The first extensive instance of Erasmus deploying this categorization comes in the *De copia*, his influential style manual. Erasmus taxonomizes feeling by distinguishing between the stronger or more violent (e.g., *vehementiores*) and the calmer or more moderate (e.g., *moderatiores*) emotions, and ultimately identifies the violent emotions with tragedy and the calmer ones with comedy. Quintilian's adaptation of Aristotle is the ultimate source for this distinction, but Aristotle's *Rhetoric* itself also had a distinctive afterlife in the early modern period with respect to thought on emotions.[11] In explaining this distinction—which is also mapped onto the division of the Greek rhetorical categories *pathos* and *ethos*—Erasmus himself invokes not only Quintilian, but also Cicero and Aristotle:[12]

> The more violent emotions, which the Greeks call πάθη are to be discovered in Homer's *Iliad* and in tragedy; the calmer ones, which are pleasant rather than disturbing, are supplied by Homer's *Odyssey* and by comedy. Yet ἤθη, which is what the Greeks call the emotions of comedy, are often interspersed in the *Iliad* and Greek tragedy. Latin tragedy makes rather sparing use of them.[13]

Erasmus conceives of affectivity in literary terms, and he expands this particular Quintilianesque reading of Aristotle[14] into a regularly employed lens through which to assess not only affectivity, but eventually the Europe-wide events that constituted the religious reformations of the sixteenth century.[15] It is a particular instance of

---

11. This has been explicated neatly (albeit without reference to Erasmus) by Lawrence D. Green, "Aristotle's *Rhetoric* and Renaissance Views of the Emotions," in *Renaissance Rhetoric*, ed. Peter Mack (Palgrave MacMillan, 1993), 1–26.

12. For Aristotle, see *Rhetoric* II, xii–xvii on *ethē*; and II i–xi on *pathē*, as well as *Nic. Eth.* 1105b19–1106a13. For Quintilian, see *Inst.* VI.2.8–9. For a distinction between *habitus* and *affectio* in Cicero, see *De Inventione* I.25 and for Cicero's discussion of *ethē* and *pathē*, see *De Oratore* 37.128; also relevant is *Tusc. Disp.* IV.10, and *De Orat.* 38–44.216.

13. CWE 24:654. Quin et poetae in hoc genere miri sunt. Vehementiores, quos Graeci *pathe* vocant, suppeditant Ilias Homeri ac tragoediae; moderatiores illos, qui delectant potius quam perturbant, subministrat Odyssea Homeri, et comoediae. Quanquam in Iliade Graecorumque tragoediis saepe miscentur *ethe* (sic enim Graeci vocant affectus comicos); Latinorum tragoedia parcius hoc genere utitur (ASD I-6, 276).

14. For Aristotle's own discussion of the *Iliad* and *Odyssey* in the *Poetics* as works indicative of *pathetikon* and *ethikon* (or of suffering and character) respectively, see *Poetics*, ch. 24.

15. Erasmus makes the same distinction, with reference to Quintilian, explaining the adage *Tragicum malum* (Adag. IV iii 40; see LB II 1014C, and CWE 36:27), in the *Ratio*

a wider trend in Quintilian's reception, which, as Peter Mack has recently shown, reached its culmination during Erasmus's lifetime and was widespread especially among humanists in northern Europe.[16] Erasmus maintains and develops this particular distinction in several ways, and with varying examples, throughout his later career, although, as Manfred Hoffmann noted and as we will explore further below, the binary nature of the taxonomy is ultimately insufficient for Erasmus, who needed a third category to cover some emotions, such as *caritas*, that fall into both camps, or the affections between family and friends that fall into neither.[17] Indeed, earlier in the *De copia*, describing the "common affections" (*communes affectus*) Erasmus had given several examples of affectivity that would count as neither comic nor tragic: a father's love for his children, a citizen's for their country, and "all the others discussed in detail by Aristotle in his *Rhetoric*."[18]

Regarding the tragicomic binary, though, the Erasmus passage quoted earlier is a paraphrase of Quintilian's *Institutio oratoria*, and he was not the first or last to put it to use.[19] The delineation between the emotions of tragedy and comedy had already appeared in the third book of Agricola's *De inventione dialectica* (1479), and the division of emotions into calm and violent types remained a fairly prominent way of classifying emotions up to David Hume, even making its way into early

---

(Holborn, 187), and in the *Ecclesiastes* (CWE 68:794). See also the adage "All men must either act tragedies or go mad" (III ii 54; CWE 34: 245–6), where Erasmus recalls from Lucian a story about the people of Abdera who went mad for weeks after seeing Euripides's plays performed ("the basis of tragedy is violent emotion").

16. Mack, "Quintilian in Northern Europe during the Renaissance, 1479–1620," 379–98. See also Blandine Perona, "Imagination et rhétorique dans l'Ecclesiastes: Érasme lecteur de Quintilien," *Camenae* 8 (2010): 1–13.

17. See Manfred Hoffmann, *Rhetoric and Theology: The Hermeneutics of Erasmus* (Toronto: University of Toronto Press, 1994), 204. One might note that familial affections do not include what is described in *Adage* II ii 94, *Odium novercale*, or "stepmotherly hatred", which Erasmus describes as innate and "a sort of predestined and irreconcilable hatred for stepchildren" (CWE 34, ad loc.).

18. CWE 24:584.

19. Compare Quintilian, from *Inst.* VI.2.9-10: "The more cautious writers have preferred to give the sense of the term rather than to translate it into Latin. They therefore explain *pathos* as describing the more violent emotions and *ethos* as designating those which are calm and gentle: in the one case the passions are violent, in the other subdued, the former command and disturb, the latter persuade and induce a feeling of goodwill. Some add that *ethos* is continuous, while *pathos* is momentary" (*Institutio oratoria* [trans. H. E. Butler; Loeb Classical Library (1922), ad loc.], modified; emphasis in original) (Cautiores voluntatem complecti quam nomina interpretari maluerunt. Adfectus igitur hos concitatos, illos mites atque compositos esse dixerunt: in altero vehementes motus, in altero lenes, denique hos imperare, illos persuadere, hos ad perturbationem, illos ad benivolentiam praevalere. X. Adiciunt quidam ethos perpetuum, pathos temporale esse).

modern Greek-to-Latin dictionaries.[20] But similar ideas are, as indicated, hinted at in Aristotle and Cicero.[21] What Erasmus takes from Quintilian specifically (and what Quintilian seems to have invented out of the prior tradition) is the notion of *ethē kai pathē* as substantive types of emotion (*affectus*), rather than as modes of oratory or rhetoric relevant to emotional movement (although Erasmus notes that Quintilian has taken some liberties[22]). It is a fine distinction, but an important one. The *ethē* described here are, as sometimes elsewhere in Erasmus's corpus, similar to *natura animi* and *habitus animi*—that is, not (only) emotions themselves, but affective dispositions or habits.[23] As Betty Knott points out in the *apparatus criticus* to the *De copia* in the Amsterdam edition, "the former term [i.e. *ethos*] indicated normal moderate human reactions (often determined by characteristic traits, such as irascibility); the latter [*pathos*], specific and stronger emotional responses to some particular situation, e.g. Achilles' grief at the death of Patroclus."[24] There is a spectrum of affectivity that Erasmus found easier to organize and describe with recourse to classical precedent, specifically in literary-rhetorical terms.

Importantly, Erasmus found in Quintilian what Virginia Cox writes about Italian humanists like Lorenzo Valla (whom Erasmus is, of course, also consciously indebted to), who utilized the Roman rhetorician's work in an anti-scholastic

---

20. See Kirk Essary and Yasmin Haskell, "Calm and Violent Passions: The Genealogy of a Distinction from Quintilian to Hume," *Erudition and the Republic of Letters* 3, no. 1 (2017): 55–81. Re dictionaries, the entry for the Greek term *pathos* in the *Lexicon graeco-latinum, seu Thesaurus linguae graecae*, ed. Bude et al. (Geneva: Jean Crespin, 1554), reads "passio, molestia, affectio, noxa qua quid afficitur, clades, interitus, desyderium, plaga, afflictio, *diathesis*, aerumna, languor, affectus perturbatur: nam *ethos* affectus est mitis, res, accidens . . ." (ad loc.). For similar ideas in Juan Luis Vives, see Lorenzo Casini, "Emotions in Renaissance Humanism," in *Emotions and Choice from Boethius to Descartes*, ed. Henrik Lagerlund and Mikko Yrjonsuri (Dordrecht: Kluwer, 2002), 212.

21. Cicero, *Orat.* 37.128, for example, reads: Duo restant enim, quae bene tractata ab oratore admirabilem eloquentiam faciunt. Quorum alterum est, quod Graeci *ethikon* vocant, ad naturas et ad mores et ad omnem vitae consuetudinem accommodatum; alterum, quod idem *pathetikon* nominant, quo perturbantur animi et concitantur, in quo uno regnat oratorio. Illud superius come iucundum, ad benevolentiam conciliandam paratum; hoc vehemens incensum incitatum, quo causae eripiuntur: quod cum rapide fertur, sustineri nullo pacto potest.

22. In the *Ecclesiastes* (1535), after repeating the distinction, Erasmus writes, "Yet neither *ethos* in Greek nor *mores* in Latin strictly speaking denotes what we mean here, inasmuch as *ethe* in Greek are the character on the basis of which we are said to be, and are, good or bad; but that word has been distorted both by them and by us for didactic purposes, so that it signifies the common and more moderate emotions by which everyone is affected because they are natural and that are recognized by everyone and cause delight rather than disturbance" (CWE 68:792).

23. See CWE 68:616; ASD V-4, 372.

24. ASD I 6, 277.

context. Valla, like Erasmus after him, acknowledged a concept from rhetoric out of the *Institutio oratoria* that "becomes formative of the entire person—less a discrete competence to be exercised at will, than a *habitus*, a culture, an ethos," a more rounded and deeply affective-discursive practice.[25] Erasmus thus continues the tradition inaugurated by Valla of Christianizing Quintilian and, to quote Cox again, understands rhetoric (and we might add literature) as "a branch of moral philosophy, but emotionally charged and exhortative rather than analytic."[26] Of course, it isn't only the rhetoricians who are relevant to the story here, but the literary figures mentioned in the taxonomy itself. While such categorization is perhaps to be expected in a work on rhetoric (like the *De copia*), the literary dimension of emotional explanation infuses Erasmus's theological works as well. Moreover, it should be noted that while one might expect that the more vehement or violent emotions always have a negative force in Erasmus's works, this is often not the case when it comes to religious life or instruction. In his treatise on prayer, for example, he argues that Jesus encourages *ardens ac vehemens affectus* (ardent and vehement emotion) and *affectus pii vehementia* (vehement pious affection) while praying, and he contrasts the stammering and repetitive "*battologia*" of the Gentiles from Matthew 6 with an affective but efficient approach. Paul's letters, too, as we will see in the fourth chapter, are commended for their vehement style.[27]

In the *De ratione studii*, a handbook and syllabus for students and teachers interested in studying the classics, Erasmus advises his readers to approach tragedy and comedy from the perspective of teaching about the emotions (*affectus*), but differently in each case: "In tragedy, he will point out that particular attention should be paid to the emotions aroused, and especially, indeed, to the more violent ones.... In comedy, he should show in particular that decorum and the portrayal of our common life must be observed, and that the emotions are milder and pleasing rather than violent."[28] He provides examples from Terence's *Andria*: "In the *Andria* Terence introduces two old men of widely different temperament [*ingenio*]: Simo is forthright, rather irritable, yet not stupid or dishonest. On the other hand, Chremes is polite and always calm, self-controlled on every occasion, resolving all differences as far as he can, gentle, but hardly simple-minded." Ctesiphus

---

25. See V. Cox, "Quintilian in the Italian Renaissance," in *The Oxford Handbook to Quintilian*, ed. Marc Van Der Poel et al. (Oxford, 2022).

26. Ibid. Erasmus also uses Quintilian's comments on emotion in *De conscribendis epistolis* (1522) and the *Ecclesiastes* (1535), in terms both of taxonomy and of rousing the emotions, to be discussed further later. From a rhetorical perspective, but also in some ways from a psychological perspective, Quintilian may be the most important classical pagan source for Erasmus's understanding of feeling.

27. *Modus orandi deum* (ASD V-1, 140).

28. CWE 24:687 (modified); ASD I-2, 142–3: In tragoedia praecipue spectandos affectus, et quidem fere acriores illo... In comoedia cum primis observandum esse decorum et vitae communis imitationem, affectus esse mitiores et iucundos magis quam acres.

from the *Adelphi* is "boorish and timid," Syrus is "wily and daring," and so on.[29] This brings Erasmus's conception of the milder emotional dispositions (*affectus mitiores*) in line with *ethos* as a form of *habitus*, its more conventional meaning, thus indicating the broader semantic range of *affectus* as Erasmus understands it. Erasmus also points to comedy's distinctive flexibility in creating characters constituted in large part by their affective dispositions.[30] For violent emotions might be found in comedy, too, and not only in tragedy. In the adage *Maritimi mores* ("As temperamental as the sea"), Erasmus cites Plautus's *Casket Comedy* as a source, and glosses it as "meaning a volatile and inconstant temperament . . . generally true of lovers, who are carried along by intemperate passion but whose feelings are not consistent."[31] *Amor*, as everyone knows, is rarely a calm emotion.

Erasmus does not give specific literary examples of the tragic *affectus* in the *De copia*, but he does so much later, in the *Ecclesiastes* (1535). "The principal emotions of this kind," he writes, "are pity, indignation, love, and hate."[32] Glossing the more violent emotions there, he tells us that while Homer is also apt at treating the milder emotions, especially in the *Odyssey*, "the sort of violent passion that tortures us and deprives us of judgment and peace of mind" is found also in Phaedra's love for Hippolytus, Medea's toward Jason, and Dido's toward Aeneas. In *De copia*, though, he does expand upon the ways in which the milder emotions please the audience, "because they help to make the description vivid and everyone is familiar with them."[33] But again, he reiterates that there are no hard-and-fast rules around generic conventions and the emotions depicted therein. One finds both the milder and the more violent passions illustrated narratively in epic, and especially in Homer, according to Erasmus. Even the *Iliad*, the tragic epic par excellence, contains scenes to be interpreted as illustrative of the milder and more pleasing feelings. Erasmus offers the example of the parting of Hector and Andromache in *De copia* as immensely pleasurable: "Is there anyone who does not get pleasure from reading the passage in Homer where Andromache runs to meet Hector at the gate of the city by which he was departing fully armed for battle?"[34] The vividness that arouses the emotions is due especially to the series of epithets (which Erasmus provides in Greek) attributed to both Hector and Andromache, and he also cites Horace to the effect that detail without too

---

29. CWE 24, 689–90.

30. Erasmus writes that the "essence of comedy is portrayal of character" in the *De pueris instituendis* (see CWE 26:336).

31. *Adag.* IV vi 29; CWE 36:232.

32. *Ecclesiastes*; CWE 68:794; ASD V-5, 72: amorem inter *pathe*, qua voce putat declarari vehementem affectum, qui nos discruciat ac iudicium mentisque tranquillitatem eripiat, qualem fingunt Phaedrae in Hippolytum, Medeae in Iasonem, Didonis in Aeneam . . . Huius generis affectus praecipui sunt misericordia, indignatio, amor, et odium.

33. CWE 24:654.

34. CWE 24, 654. Erasmus also refers to this scene in his gloss on the adage *Risus sardonius* ("Sardonic laughter") (III v 1).

much artifice lends both credibility and emotion. He had put the Andromache scene to a somewhat different use in the *Panegyricus*, a work composed for Archduke Philip in 1504 as an attempt at gaining patronage. There the focus is on the indescribability of emotions, and especially of mixed emotion, and he sets that scene alongside Eurycleia's recognition of Odysseus:

> Tell me, are there any greater signs of joy than those which are shown in action but left unspoken? Or any surer happiness than what declares itself in tears and is far removed from suspicion or artifice? For just as in the opposite situation grief has its own special laughter, which the Greeks call sardonic, and Homer's phrase is well known describing Andromache as *dakruoen gelasasa*, that is, "laughing through her tears," so joy too has its own tears, as the same poet says of Ulysses and Telemachus when father and son recognize each other, "and so both felt a longing for weeping" ... Homer describes this mixed emotion and the tears accompanying it in the case of Eurycleia: "Joy and grief seized her heart, and her eyes filled with tears."[35]

Again, the virtue of Homer's minimalism is highlighted—he shows but does not tell—but we also get a sense of the ways in which classical literature engages with a range of emotions simultaneously. Classical authors provide for Erasmus numerous literary examples for explaining the way emotions work, both through deployed rhetorical devices and also for providing more general psychological insight, but they also offer models for writers and speakers to effectively move the emotions of their audience.

Mythopoeia and Mythopatheia

Examples from classical literature are also ripe for tropological application to emotional contexts, and Erasmus instructs his readers in the method: "If [the speaker] is arguing that the function of the wise man is to control his emotions by reason and judgment," he writes in *De copia*, "he can bring in Homer's story in Book 1 of the *Iliad* where Achilles is already laying his hand on the hilt of his sword and Pallas Athene calls him back from behind."[36] In the *Adages*, Erasmus uses this example to more or less sum up all of the ancient philosophy of emotion.[37] If, moreover, he continues, "one is putting forward the idea that a genuine reputation for courage can only be won by the man who has been tossed by misfortune and tested by all sorts of danger, he can bring in Ulysses as Homer depicts him."[38] In

---

35. *Panegyricus*, CWE 27:72.
36. CWE 24:610.
37. See *Adag.* II i 1, "Make haste slowly", and discussion in the following chapter.
38. *De Copia*, CWE 24:610. It was long recognized that *exempla* bore emotional force and could be used effectively in teaching. Erasmus himself points out the importance of

the *De pueris instituendis*, Erasmus advocates use of the "fables of ancient authors" similarly:

> When a child hears how Ulysses' comrades were changed by Circe's magic into swine he will find the story amusing, but he also learns one of the basic principles of moral philosophy, that persons who refuse to be guided by the dictates of right reason, but are freely seized by the emotions, are not truly human but are only brutes. Could a Stoic sage proclaim this truth more seriously?[39]

Erasmus is here annotating the fables so that they teach a lesson about emotion that was not necessarily obvious in the original version, allegorizing Homer into a teacher of Stoic thought along the way. It is a lesson in hermeneutics, in rhetoric, and in moral philosophy.

This sort of allegorizing had been earlier expanded upon substantially in *De copia*, where Erasmus, again, exposits the various stopping places of Odysseus as a vast psychological journey:

> Ulysses, who was the only one not changed after drinking the cup and being touched with the magic wand, demonstrated that firm and constant purpose characteristic of the wise man, which cannot be weakened by fear or deflected from that which is honourable by any blandishments of the emotions. The lotus, which prevented his companions from leaving after they had once tasted it, teaches that the sweet, insidious poison of base pleasures, from which it is not all that difficult to give up once one has tasted it. The songs of the Sirens teach that flattery is the most seductive thing there is, and the most pernicious. Scylla and Charybdis, separated by such a narrow space, teach that the path of virtue is a narrow one, with related vices threatening on either side, for example, the path of frugality between extravagance and meanness.[40]

---

narrative forms and examples in stirring the emotions of a Christian congregation in his *Ecclesiastes* (CWE 68:871, for example). On the use of *exempla* for teaching through emotion in the medieval period, see Anne Scott, "The Role of *Exempla* in Educating Through Emotion: The Deadly Sin of "lecherye" in Robert Mannyng's *Handlyng Synne* (1303–1317)," in *Authority, Gender and Emotions in Late Medieval and Early Modern England*, ed. Susan Broomhall (Palgrave Macmillan, 2015).

39. CWE 26:336; ASD I-2, 66: Audit puer socios Ulyssis arte Circes versos in sues aliasque formas animantium. Ridetur narratio, et tamen interim discit puer, quod in morali philosophia praecipuum est, eos qui non gubernantur recta ratione, sed affectuum arbitrio rapiuntur, non homines esse, sed belvas.

40. CWE 24:612. On other sixteenth-century readings of Homer, especially Erasmus's frequent correspondent Bude who has a similar gloss on Ulysses at the end of his *De asse*, see Filippomaria Pontani, "From Bude to Zenodotus: Homeric Readings in the European Renaissance," *International Journal of the Classical Tradition* 14, no. 3/4 (2007): 375–430.

This rather commonplace tactic for interpreting the Odyssey has a long history, and Erasmus is keen in particular to associate Ulysses's avoidance of a slew of temptations allegorically with his ability to govern the emotions, and to insist that regulating them properly is the "path to virtue."[41] We get a sense, too, of the fine line between certain emotions and certain sins that will come into play more overtly in his writings on religious emotion.

Erasmus takes his own advice for applying myths to explicate emotional significance in his *Hyperaspistes 2*, the second installment of his response to Luther in their debate over free will in the mid-1520s. There, Erasmus defends reason the *hegemonikon* from Luther's charge that it is utterly corrupted by sin and should also be considered "flesh" (to borrow the Apostle Paul's language). All the examples Erasmus offers in his response are taken not from biblical texts (the source base that is ostensibly the focus of the dispute), but from classical literature:

> If reason struggles against emotions that are prone to immorality, then it must needs be that to some degree it discerns and approves of what is moral. The scholastics call this faculty synderesis, though I hardly know where they got the name. It remains even in the most wicked. . . . In the comedy Phaedria is upset with himself as his reason struggles against his vicious inclinations. He speaks as follows: "Living, I knowingly and deliberately am dying. I must drive this softness from my mind. I am too self-indulgent." You are listening to the spark of reason. So too in tragedies, when Medea or Procne are preparing to kill their children, natural affection tells them one thing, anger another. How fiercely does the language of Myrrha and Byblis inveigh against the flames of incest in their heart? We see the same thing in Dido, whose reason says: "But I would rather that the earth swallow me up, etc." and "before I would violate you, O chastity, and loosen your claims." A good many passages like this are found in the poets, for they know human emotions [*affectus hominis*] most deeply and depict them most skilfully.[42]

In this case, Erasmus invokes a series of ancient literary examples in order to hammer home a theological point, which is effectively that either reason or the neutral affections serve as an innate moral guide, as a check against sin (and a check against other emotions, like anger), and that counterexamples to Luther's condemnation of the entire person as irredeemably depraved can be found even in the worst sort of (literary) character. Even in his overtly religious works, seemingly unbothered by the notion that these are fictional characters, Erasmus invokes the ancient literary world for anecdotal wisdom in order to provide insight for his

---

41. On Cicero's appropriation of Ulysses as a masculine *sapiens*, as well as Cicero's use of Greek and Roman drama as a way of undergirding his philosophy of emotion, see Ruth Rothaus Caston, "Pacuvius hoc melius quam Sophocles: Cicero's Use of Drama in the Treatment of the Emotions," *Bulletin of the Institute of Classics Studies* 125 (2015): 129–48.

42. CWE 77:592.

readers into the human affective psyche, as well as to offer moral advice regarding emotional regulation. This only works well, of course, if the myths are established and recognizable, or if the proper explanatory framework is put into place. As Carlos Ginzburg puts it, commenting on the name "Oedipus" conjuring familiarity with the details of his fate: "Names, in truth, were micro-tales. They were the epitomes of myth, offering a powerful mechanism of identification for members of the group who shared in their meaning and excluding all outsiders. . . . Myth is, by definition, a story already told, a story that we already know."[43] The force of this familiarity, recognized in antiquity as much as it is today, is what makes myths powerful tools, not only of political power and rationalization (in the form of myths *qua* religious traditions, say, which is one of Ginzburg's ultimate points), but also of explanations of ordinary human experience. They become ingrained modes of discourse, pulled from and modified and transformed, that constitute a certain kind of shared understanding.

The *Adages*, too, are replete with many instances of emotionally laden proverbs, some less obvious than others, as in, for example, "the sorrows of Ino," shorthand for a psychological pain that "absolutely stupefies and deprives a man of consciousness," or "the rock of Tantalus," which expresses a kind of constant fear and anxiety.[44] *Odium agreste*, or "rustic hatred," is another bespoke feeling, which Erasmus derives from Lucian and explains thus: "The Ancients applied this name to any passionate dislike, because rustics are misanthropic as a rule, and their hatreds are bitter and irreconcilable. . . . In fact, when you want to convey anything that is barbarous, brutal, or cruel, you call it in Greek 'rustic.'"[45] Some instances are rather closer to home, as when Erasmus invokes a common myth and twists it into a thinly veiled (and eventually unveiled) scholarly autobiography. He thus glosses the Lernaean Hydra from the labours of Hercules at expansive length as emblematic of envy, lapsing into a lengthy digression on the jealousy of his contemporaries that arises when they judge the labors of those who "devote their efforts to restoring the monuments of ancient and true literature," which latter receive in return "a little reputation and a great deal of ill-will."[46] Erasmus explains the hydra-as-envy allegory along humoral lines as well: The hydra was, "for one thing, a plague that lived in a marsh; for, as we learn from those who research into natural causes, men are more liable to suffer from this disease who have a low and grovelling spirit, and these are people of a more cold-blooded type." He then quotes Ovid, however, rather than Galen, who says that Envy's home "Is in the valley-bottoms sunless hid/ Where no wind blows, but gloom and sluggish chill/ Fill all the place; no fire is ever kindled/ And darkness reigns." This is the sort of envious ill-will that springs from the dim corners of the psyche and is

---

43. Carlo Ginzburg, *Threads and Traces* (New York: Columbia University Press, 2001), 61.
44. *Adagia* II ix 78 and II ix 7 respectively (see CWE 34).
45. CWE 34; adage II i 78. Cf. Adage II ii 92, *Odium Vatinianum*.
46. *Adag.* III i 1; CWE 34: 167–82. Cf. the colloquy *The Lover of Glory* (CWE 40: 965–6; ASD I-3, 668), where the Lernaean hydra (*excetra*) is also associated with envy.

directed toward someone who has undertaken the thankless task of collecting ancient proverbs and sayings from "the whole range of the written word," which requires not only reading the best of Latin and Greek works but also the worst, and sometimes to restore the works from their extensive textual corruption as well (not to mention reading all the commentaries on those works "in hopes of one day picking some gold off the dunghill").[47]

Once Erasmus has established that his labors are indeed herculean (even greater, in fact, since the revised *Adages* hit the press at the same time as the complete works of Jerome and just after the groundbreaking *Novum Instrumentum*), he points out that they also resemble the mundane tedium of that other underappreciated figure from myth: Sisyphus. Erasmus is acutely aware of the copious ways in which a tale can be manipulated to serve his rhetorical purposes, and he is also using literature, in the words of Brian Cummings, as a "medium of subjectivity."[48] Erasmus is Hercules, his cold-blooded critics a many-headed monster, but the monotony of composing rejoinders to their attacks would have felt more akin to the toils of Sisyphus than to the ultimate glory of Hercules.[49] It is no surprise, perhaps, that Hans Holbein the Younger's 1523 painting *Erasmus of Rotterdam* depicts the scholar sitting at his desk with two hands resting on a book that reads ἩΡΑΚΛΕΙΟΙ ΠΟΝΟΙ. Many other examples of this sort of affective-subjective mythologizing can be produced from his letters, of course, as Wolfe has amply demonstrated with respect to discourses of strife. As one example of the tumults of mixed emotion Erasmus experienced late in life, complaining to Anton Fugger, he writes, "Evidently this is how the life of man is governed by Jupiter, who, as Homer testifies, mixes joys with sorrows and sorrows with joys from the two jars that stand on his threshold."[50]

Allegory of feeling coupled with *exempla* is provided also in an extended early section of the *Praise of Folly*, Erasmus's masterful satire, where Folly compares her ability to transform old people into happy senility to the mythological gods of Ovid's *Metamorphoses*, who themselves often transform the dead into trees, or locusts, or snakes: "Off you go, you foolish mortals, find a Medea, a Circe, Venus, and Aurora, and some sort of a spring you can use to give you back your youth! But I alone can provide this power and do so."[51] This can similarly be applied to

---

47. *Adag.* III i 1; CWE 34:167–82.

48. Brian Cummings, "Erasmus and the Invention of Literature," *Erasmus of Rotterdam Society Yearbook* 33 (2013): 29.

49. See CWE 40:972. He uses the hydra as a metaphor for envy elsewhere also: In the colloquy "The Lover of Glory," the Lernaean Hydra is also rendered as an allegory for envy, an unfortunate concomitant of all forms of glory. In his advice to Philodoxus, who seeks glory without envy, the Erasmian voice of Symbulus says that only preemptive kindness ("Greek fire") and not revenge (Hercules's use of the sword to cut off the heads) can ameliorate envy.

50. Ep 2192 to Fugger; CWE 15:341.

51. CWE 27:93.

the gods themselves and their various affective dispositions, for Bacchus, the most indulgent of the gods in folly ("never has any dealings with Pallas," that is, with wisdom), is clearly the most youthful and beautiful, and has the best time because of his affective disposition:

> [W]ho wouldn't choose to be this light-hearted fool who is always young and merry and brings pleasure and gaiety to all, rather than crooked-counselled Jupiter who is universally feared, or old Pan who confounds everything with his sudden alarms, ash-grimed Vulcan, always filthy from his work in the smithy, or even Pallas herself who strikes terror with her Gorgon and spear and fixed grim stare?[52]

Conversely, Folly is well aware of the foolishness of even the most sober-minded seeming gods: "I don't think I need to go into the behaviour of the others, as you're well aware of the love-affairs and goings-on of Jupiter the thunderer himself, and how even that chaste Diana who ignored her sex and devoted herself to hunting could still lose her heart to Endymion."[53] Finally, with no little irony, Folly celebrates Homer for repeatedly ascribing unhappiness to Ulysses on account of his wisdom (the implication being that idiots experience more joy). Erasmus here rewrites plain interpretations of classical myths for the purpose of sharpening the focus on their absurdities, which results in amplifying the ridiculousness of Folly's own case. Per Erasmus's Quintilianesque bifurcation of emotional types, Folly clearly operates in the comic realm of the gentler *affectus*.

A different approach is taken in Erasmus's preaching manual, the *Ecclesiastes*, where he short-changes the affective capacities of the Greek pantheon, contrasting the feebleness of pagan fables with the narratives of scripture for their power to elicit an emotional response. The same examples above are read differently here:

> Compare their incredible lies with our miracles. Daphne changed into a laurel tree, Io changed into a cow, Cadmus into a snake, the rustics into frogs, Arachne into a spider—what are they but childish jests if compared to the many that were raised from the dead, to the many ailments and wicked demons that were put to flight at a word?[54]

The Christian God is better able to provide peace of mind and true hope than Zeus and his cohort:

> What do they promise the worshippers of the gods? Saturn grants victory with the dice on certain days . . . Ceres an abundance of grain . . . but what are these compared to what God promises his people through his Son? . . . so great a thing

---

52. CWE 27:93–4.
53. Ibid.
54. *Ecclesiastes* CWE 68:796.

is a mind at peace with itself and ever eager and secure through hope of eternal happiness.⁵⁵

And Erasmus's God is also able to instill more intense fear: "Diana unleashed the Calydonian boar in anger, Juno a storm in her hostility to the Trojans; even if these things are true, what are they in comparison with hell?" Homer and Ovid are no match for Moses when it comes to stirring the emotions that lead to piety or fear of divine wrath. Biblical parables thus also function as forms mythographic shorthand useful for explaining emotion. Like a Proteus, Erasmus moves seamlessly between authors and genres in repeated acts of affective *accommodatio*.

In the *Ratio* of 1520, Erasmus likewise explains the usefulness of biblical myths for moving the emotions, but also for explaining them:

> Suppose you explain that a person's desire entices to sin when the opportunity arises; that unless reason rules, obeying the divine will rather than human affection, a brief pleasure is purchased with death; that often, moreover, affection steals in under the cloak of necessity or some other honourable reason and deceives. This statement will delight or affect the hearer less than if you introduce the story of Genesis: God commands, the serpent sets the trap, Eve entices her husband to share her sin, soon punishment becomes the companion of the pleasure tasted.⁵⁶

The *Ratio* was a methodological work outlining the tasks of the biblical theologian, and so examples of scriptural stories allegorized come as no surprise. Nevertheless, for all their theological shortcomings, pagan myths, Erasmus knows, are abundantly useful in other theological contexts. One last example will suffice: in the *De taedio Iesu*, Erasmus's debate with John Colet about Christ's emotional suffering in Gethsemane, he invokes epic heroes from classical literature in order to demonstrate that emotions ought not to be equated with cowardice or any other shortcoming in virtue:

> Virgil, in depicting the extraordinary bravery of his character Aeneas, is not afraid to give him all the outward signs of alarm, shuddering, trembling, groaning, and so on. For example, when a storm suddenly breaks at sea, he writes, "At once, Aeneas' limbs give way in a chill of terror / And he groans." Again,

---

55. Ibid.

56. *Ratio*, CWE 41:635; LB V 117E: Itidem, si narres, cupiditatem hominis objecta occasione sollicitare ad peccandum, cui ni ratio imperet magis obtemperans voluntati divinae, quam humano affectui, voluptatem brevem emi exigito: praeterea saepe fieri, ut affectus sub praetextu necessitatis, aut alicuius honestae rationis, obrepat atque imponat: minus delectabit, aut adficiet auditoem, quam si admoveas Geneseos historia: Deum praecipientem, serpente insidiante: Eva, maritum ad peccati consortiu sollicitantem, mox gustatae voluptatis comitem poenam.

hearing Polydorus' voice, the hero says, "I was struck dumb; my hair stood on end and my voice stuck in my throat." He often ascribes similar reactions to the Trojans, who were renowned for their bravery, for example, when they heard the Harpies: "At this my comrades' blood was chilled and froze / In sudden dread." . . . Scholars observe the same device in Homer's poetry; he will depict terror in cowards and heroes alike, but not in the same way. Although these writers will allow a brave character to groan, turn pale, or shiver, they draw the line at unseemly wailing, girlish lamentations, or cries of unbridled rage.[57]

Virgil and Homer here play the role of poetic philosophers of feeling, offering examples of the ways in which one might emote without violating normative (and gendered) expectations around affective conduct. The fact that these examples arise in a dispute about the ethics of emotion is also testimony to the uncertain and contested nature of emotional expression in the context of humanist theology in the late medieval and early modern period. Moreover, it highlights a distinctly Erasmian form of affective discourse, one that blends together a diverse cluster of modes of description and prescription from a variegated group of authors and genres from the ancient world.

Tragicomic Emotions in (Ps.-)Ovid's Nux

In 1523, Erasmus dedicated a commentary on Ovid's *Nux* to Thomas More's son John (the *Nux*'s Ovidian authenticity is now contested, although not by Erasmus, who wrote that Ovid was "no less Ovid" in the *Nux* than in the *Medea*). The poem itself is written from the perspective of a walnut tree grown weary of having its fruit knocked off by passers-by, especially children, who would use the nuts for their games. The Latin *nux*, *nuces*, as Erasmus points out, means not only nuts or a nut-tree, but also refers, both literally and figuratively, to children's games. By extension, the term becomes a metaphor for something incidental or of no value, a trifle (embodied in the Latin maxim *nuces relinquere*—"put away your toys"[58]). Erasmus's commentary is a lengthy exhibition of scholarly play, and one which Erasmus defends as a legitimate endeavor by comparing the *Nux* to the Homeric *Battle of Frogs and Mice* in his prefatory letter where he also defends the *Praise of Folly* as an ostensibly trifling work that in fact deals with serious moral topics.[59] It is also replete with comments on emotion from a range of perspectives, thus offering us an example of Erasmus's treatment of emotion in the specific context of

---

57. CWE 70:28.
58. *Adag.* I v 35.
59. For more on this text and its background, see Matthew McGowan, "The *Nux* Attributed to Ovid and Its Renaissance Readers: The Case of Erasmus," in *Constructing Authors and Readers in the Appendices Vergiliana, Tibulliana, and Ovidiana*, ed. Tristan E. Franklinos and Laurel Fulkerson (Oxford, 2020), 262–75.

a scholarly commentary on a classical literary source, a different genre from what we have considered to this point.

Recent scholarship on emotion and Ovidianism in the early modern period helps us to understand the wider significance of Ovid as a figure whose works shaped understandings of affectivity. As Cora Fox points out, classical literary texts served as "central loci for redefinitions of emotional life" in Elizabethan England, and that "in order to understand an individual or a society, and particularly such subtle but foundational aspects of everyday life as emotion, we need to turn to texts, and particularly to intertexts."[60] We have seen that Erasmus employs a striking array of intertextual references—including Ovidian ones—in his attempts to articulate truths about the emotional subject, and his works no doubt contributed to laying the groundwork for similar approaches throughout the sixteenth and seventeenth centuries. Moreover, while his references to the *Metamorphoses* perhaps served as more common and recognizable literary examples for shaping medieval and early modern subjectivities, in his commentary on the *Nux* we find Erasmus in a more overtly pedagogical mode, interpreting the text precisely and straightforwardly for a remote pupil.

Importantly for our purposes, Erasmus points out that "a great part of the poem deals with the emotions" (*magna pars carminis habet affectus*), both tragic and comic, and thus it serves as another site for Erasmus to explore Quintilian's two-pronged heuristic of assessing the emotions in a literary and rhetorical context. Erasmus's commentary likewise provides readers with a rather on-the-nose example of how he thinks about the relationship between myth and teaching the emotions, even if the myth at hand is not the most well known. The *Nux* itself is full of tragicomic pathos, along with a host of moral lessons, so long as the readers, per Erasmus's advice to the young More, permit themselves to "become Pythagoreans for a while" and imagine that trees have souls.[61] Erasmus repeatedly points out the ways in which poetic or literary devices are employed *ad affectum*, or *ad movendos affectus*, but none of it makes sense unless we are willing to indulge in a bit of Ovidian metamorphic fantasy. Matthew McGowan has suggested that Erasmus had more personal reasons in mind for composing his commentary during this period of his life, where he—like the *nux*—was being pelted from all sides by critics both Catholic and Protestant, a point worth keeping in mind.[62] A brief overview of the ways in which Erasmus teases out the emotional significance of the *Nux* allows us further to see how the tragic and comic emotions at times blend together.

To open the commentary, Erasmus begins immediately toying with the genre of the poem, suggesting he has found an alternative title that includes the prefix "An Elegy," which—because it "comprises a complaint about past injuries and an entreaty against injuries that still threaten it"—links the work to a long

---

60. Fox, *Ovid and the Politics of Emotion*, 3.
61. CWE 29:127.
62. McGowan, "The Nux Attributed to Ovid and Its Renaissance Readers," 267.

tradition of judicial or forensic oratory. "Consequently," Erasmus writes, "a good part of the treatment of the subject rests in the emotions, especially pity."[63] Pity, *misericordia*, Erasmus tells us, is aroused through notice of another's misfortune, and is especially aggravated when that person is undeserving of suffering. The walnut tree, accosted as it is by children with stones despite its pure innocence is, then, an appropriate subject for exploration of the theme. Moreover, as Erasmus writes, "the sequence of the argument is constantly enlivened by witty allusions to human emotions [*affectus humanos*], as in fables; the more wild the emotions, the greater the humour when they are applied to a trivial and absurd topic."[64] It is the more violent or savage emotions (*atrociores affectus*) that, because of their absurdity in an Ovidian fable, are especially conducive to comedic effect, an inversion of the genre-specific taxonomy mentioned by Erasmus earlier, but in keeping with his contention that emotional types have flexibility to transcend genres. Indeed, the tragicomic nature of the poem allows Erasmus his own flexibility in interpreting its affective valences, and the categories of *ethos* and *pathos* in Erasmus's analysis are applied with fluidity as both rhetorical and as taxonomic emotional categories.

The opening lines of the poem, composed in the voice of the tree, set the stage for an interpretation involving pity and pathos:

A nut-tree standing by the road, not charged with any crime,
Yet passers-by assail me with their stones.[65]

Erasmus comments that, according to the rhetoricians, opening with a *narratio*—"putting the events before the very eyes of the listeners"—both lays the groundwork for the argument and adds emotional effect (*additit affectibus*), a common rhetorical ploy.[66] The tree is *sine crimine* in the Latin—not only innocent, but not even *charged* with a crime—a circumstance which Erasmus says magnifies the harshness (*atrociorem*) of the injury.[67] That the tree is stoned for merely being *iuncta viae* (by the road—not even on it) is a "most cruel punishment," only made worse by the fact that it is done not as a result of a trial, but *a populo*—by the people. Erasmus increases the Ovidian pathos, pointing out that stoning was no ordinary

---

63. CWE 29:129; ASD I-1, 146: Proinde bona pars tractionis in affectibus sita est, praesertim misericordiae.

64. CWE 29:129, modified; ASD I-I, 147: Iucunditatem addit argumento faceta ubique allusio ad affectus humanos, quod idem fit in apologis. Qui quo sunt atrociores, hoc in re levi ludicraque plus habent voluptatis, veluti in Batrachomuomachia quam inscrubunt Homero.

65. CWE 29:129.

66. Nam narratio fusius rem explicat, additit etiam affectibus, et argumentorum veluti seminibus inspersis (ASD I-1, 147).

67. Rursus quum sim sine crimine vitae circumstantia est, reddens iniuriam atrociorem (ASD I-1, 150).

punishment, but was reserved for blasphemy among the Hebrews, and wasn't even legal in Rome, although for the most vicious of crimes was occasionally permitted to appease the mob.[68]

I've done no wrong—unless we grant that wrong consists in this,
To render to our farmer each year's growth.
But once, in the olden days, when better times prevailed, the trees
Competed for the crown of bearing fruit.[69]

Erasmus points out that Ovid humorously ascribes human *affectus* to trees, specifically invoking the Greek category of *ethos* as descriptive of trees of former times competing at fertility (*certamen fertilitatis erat*). As for *pathos*, Erasmus compares the lot of "sterile" trees to barren wives, the former who are "cultivated for empty pleasure rather than for utility," the latter whose beauty is valued more than their fecundity.

There follow several parallel allusions to women suffering in childbirth, the risks of which, Erasmus writes, draw special pity and thus allow for extensive emotional exegesis:

The mother would have suffered from the fruits, had not a fork
Been placed beneath to aid the branch in toil.[70]

On the phrase *Pomaque laesissent matrem* ("the mothers would have suffered from their fruit"), Erasmus suggests that it is employed to increase pathos: "The risk suffered by a pregnant woman in giving birth is to be pitied; and 'since, according to common understanding, particular favor is shown to the fecundity of women who produce many offspring at once, even more pity is felt for women who die from a multiple birth."[71] After drawing out a comparison between similarities in language describing the ailments of humans and trees, following Pliny, Erasmus takes advantage of the couplet for denouncing the contemporary prevalence of vanity in society, which has resulted, he says, in eschewing the Golden Age virtue of fertility, and perpetuates an abuse of abortifacients. That the Hebrews and other ancients shamed infertility and encouraged the *eupaidos* (i.e., "well-childed") woman—compared with Erasmus's own time when women with multiple children are called "sows"—only increases the shame felt by the tree. The climax of this section arrives with the walnut tree comparing herself to Clytemnestra, who wouldn't have been slain by her son Orestes had she never given birth to him in the first place: *'Assuredly I'd safer be, if child I'd never born': Thus justly Clytemnestra*

---

68. See CWE 29:134.
69. CWE 29:135–6.
70. CWE 29:137.
71. CWE 29:138.

*could complain.*⁷² Erasmus reminds us that Clytemnestra wasn't exactly innocent, but that this fact ought *a fortiori* to induce pity for the perfectly innocent walnut tree. Paraphrasing the tree, Erasmus writes:

> I am stoned for no other reason than that I am fertile; therefore, I would be safer if I were sterile. Clytemnestra and I have this complaint, at least, in common, as she was harmed by giving birth in that she was killed by her own son Orestes. The complaint was less justified in her case, however, as she herself had first killed her husband and thus provoked one crime by another; I, on the other hand, have done nothing except give birth. Yet Clytemnestra is thought worthy of pity for having given birth—how much more pitiable, then, am I!⁷³

The tree herself then warns that if her appeal fails, other trees, perhaps those with more desirable fruit like apples and pears, will *choose* spinsterdom.

We eventually receive from the tree a contrasting and envious portrait, where another tree, far from the road and passers-by, can live a life of happy tranquility:

> *Ah, lucky is the tree that grows in some secluded field / And pays its tribute to its lord alone! / It hears no din from humankind, it hears no screech of wheels / It's not begrimed with dust from a nearby road. / Its produce it can give as gifts to its own husbandman, / Its harvest it can reckon out in full.*⁷⁴

The tree returns to what Erasmus calls "pathos by comparison," that is, to lamentation over the most senseless sort of punishment: here *unripe* nuts are pelted from the tree (complete with an allusion to still-born children); the *foetus*, called a *munus inane* (empty prize), is struck down with projectiles, simultaneously injuring the tree while *not* benefiting the *viator* because the nuts are still inedible: *But I don't ever get the chance to bring forth ripened births: / My treasures get knocked down before their day.*⁷⁵ Erasmus continues, "The walnut's misery is emphasized by the fact that, far from being consoled for all its injuries, it is even cursed by its owner because his field has been made stony by the rocks that have been thrown."⁷⁶ The pinnacle of absurdity for the tree, however, isn't reached until the moment where the farmer comes, gathers up all the stones from beneath the tree, and tosses them back to the road again, thus creating a "constant store of missiles" for future passers-by. "It is a sad remedy," Erasmus writes, "that doesn't cure the disease, but fosters it."⁷⁷

---

72. CWE 29:143.
73. Ibid.
74. CWE 29:154.
75. Ibid.
76. CWE 29:155.
77. CWE 29:160.

Thus, the tree herself descends into despair: *But oh, how many weary hours of long, long life I've had / And often longed to wither up and die!* In response to which, Erasmus writes, "The remainder of the poem is taken up with emotional outbursts, though emotion is present in most of the poem." He mixes affective-literary analysis somewhat jarringly with practical information from Pliny: "Ovid's phrase 'weary hours of long, long life' alludes to [the longevity of trees]. To desire death is a tragic motif, a wish produced in utter desolation. Trees sometimes wither up from old age, but usually from disease or blight."[78] The motif of self-harm continues. If the walnut tree could, she would shed her fruit voluntarily, either through abortion or in the same way that the beaver chews off its own testicles to foil hunters seeking the "castor oil" from them: *Or would that sudden blasts might blow and snatch away my fruit, Or I myself might shake off all my nuts / Just as the beaver amputates the part that hunters seek / And thus preserves the residue in tact.*[79] Erasmus's gloss here is typical and indicative of the kind of playful scholarly indulgence that runs through the commentary, whose purpose is purportedly to teach the young John More both how the rhetoric of the poem functions to move the emotions, but also to indicate a syllabus for learning more about the natural world, derived from antiquity:

> Many writers testify that the beaver, or castor—an amphibious animal that lives both on land and in the water—bites off its testicles when it is endangered by the hunt. It knows that this is the main reason for its being hunted, as its testicles have medicinal properties—hence, "castor oil" (Pliny, book 8, chapter 30). Sestus, however, says that this is not true, as the beaver's testicles are tiny and withdrawn within its loins, and can only be removed by killing it. Ovid also described all this in his book entitled *Halieutica* on the nature and intelligence of fish, cited by Pliny, book 32, ch. 2 – I wish I had a copy of this work instead of Oppian.[80]

Regardless of anatomical accuracy, the way in which emotions are gendered is complex in both the poem and in Erasmus's commentary on it, even apart from the comparison of the female walnut tree to the self-emasculating beaver. Erasmus, on the one hand, acknowledges that women are uniquely the subject of strong pity insofar as they might miscarry, which gives the tree a special capacity to induce *pathos* (an undisputed virtue in the context of forensic rhetoric) as well as the power to threaten abstention from future procreation on the part of all fruit trees; but this assessment is based on the judgment that a fecund woman is the best kind, that it is the essential or at least the most virtuous aspect of a woman that she might bear children (and lots of them).[81] Erasmus is not only revealing his own

---

78. CWE 29:164–5.
79. CWE 29: 166.
80. Ibid.
81. There are other ways in which the emotions are specifically gendered in Erasmus, of course: in the *De pueris instituendis*, he advocates against picking just any woman to

feelings in such an exposition but is also attempting to educate John More (and his other readers) *into* an emotional community, staging emotional norms and values attendant to cultural attitudes around women, gender, and childbirth.[82]

However, Erasmus's assessment of the emotional ethics related to women's fertility is not only dependent upon an Ovidian-Pythagorean absurdity. He also takes a more literal tack by way of Pliny: "Writers have noticed," he writes,

> gender, marriage, and copulation in trees, to the extent that the female trees remain sterile unless there is a male tree close by; in fact, closer observers of natural history assert that the earth produces nothing that lacks in sex (see more fully Pliny, book 13, chapter 4). Just as women are rendered infertile sometimes through physical defect and invariably by old age, so are fruit-bearing trees. Almost every defect of the human body is also found in trees.[83]

What seemed like a somewhat far-fetched allegory, an Ovidian moment of transmogrification, has become an apt comparison through Erasmus's invocation of Pliny: trees are just like people.

At the same time, one must preserve the vividness of the presentation of the tree as a tree for full emotional effect. The tree is in such despair that, at the end of the poem, she longs for a lightning bolt, or at least a strong wind to come and knock off all her nuts. You may think that such a wind is causing her leaves to shake now, but she's actually trembling from fear. "Great fear induces pallor and trembling," Erasmus writes, explaining the anthropomorphism. "The poet could not attribute pallor to the tree, so he ascribes trembling to it."[84] The effects of emotional movement are accomplished further by imagery that mixes anthropomorphic metaphor with the realities of the tree's existence: *What spirit do I have, when passers-by take up their arms / And with their eyes mark out the target-spot? / I cannot move my trunk to dodge the threatened savage wounds - / Its root and grasping rootlets hold fast.* "Nothing," Erasmus writes, "arouses the emotions

---

instruct a child because of a particular kind of emotional propensity: "Nothing is more cruel than the opposite sex once its anger has been aroused; its passions are easily kindled and quietened only when the lust for revenge has been satisfied" (CWE 26:325). Generally, Erasmus's works embody a mix of traditionally misogynistic and relatively progressive views on women, and this holds true for his writings about gendered emotion also; see the introduction and compilation by Erika Rummel, *Erasmus on Women* (Toronto: University of Toronto Press, 2000).

82. The literature on emotion and gender in the early modern period is now considerable; see, for example, Susan Broomhall (ed.), *Gender and Emotions in Medieval and Early Modern Europe: Destroying Order, Structuring Disorder* (London: Routledge, 2015); and Broomhall (ed.), *Authority, Gender and Emotions in Late Medieval and Early Modern England* (Springer, 2015).

83. CWE 29:139.

84. CWE 29:167.

more effectively than presenting the scene before the listener's eyes."[85] While the poem (over 180 lines long) and Erasmus's commentary contain much that could not be considered here, it should be clear that Erasmus's exposition of the Ovidian *Nux* allows us to see, however briefly, how he brings a range of resources to bear on the emotional significance of the poem, and how the tragicomic structure of the emotions themselves provides a framework for his interpretation.

Attending to the ways in which storehouses of classical commonplaces, proverbial wisdom, and traditions of myth were employed in emotions discourse, or indeed constitutive of it in cases where Erasmus prescribes certain myths for certain emotional contexts, is a necessary task in writing the history of emotions for the intellectual and cultural setting of renaissance humanism. Recent scholarship has recognized the emotional force of literature in the early modern period in ways that pertain to our reading of Erasmus as well. Brian Cummings has argued eloquently that Erasmus's "literary" approach to philosophical and theological problems is bound up with his understanding of language as a kind of affective mimesis.[86] "Literature in Erasmus' mould is an engagement with the human," he writes, which "forces us to respond to how we represent the world in words; and simultaneously represent ourselves, emotionally as well as cognitively, such as we can communicate with others within a recognizable world."[87] Benedict Robinson has likewise sought recently to extricate reductive accounts of the emotions in the early modern period from medical discourse in order to more fully appreciate their rhetorical and literary significance. He attempts to show "how literature constitutes an irreducible method for analyzing emotion, one that needs to take place alongside other discourses—philosophy, neuroscience, sociology, cultural studies—that are part of our larger conversation about emotion."[88] In the sixteenth century, too (Robinson's work focuses on the seventeenth), classical literature was mined for characters, figures, and tropes in order to aid the art of persuasion, an irreducibly affective enterprise according to the classical definitions of rhetoric that Erasmus and his humanist contemporaries preferred.

Moving and describing the emotions is done more effectively through literature for Erasmus. This chapter has thus offered examples from a diverse set of Erasmian texts in order to illuminate the wide scope of his literary imagination when it comes to the reception of classical literature and its force on Erasmus's understanding of the emotions, both in descriptive and in prescriptive contexts. Aspects of these stories *become* idiom, and they do form a sort of mythographic shorthand for Erasmus, and not only for Erasmus as an allegorizing critic of ancient literature but also for Erasmus the satirist, Erasmus the theologian, Erasmus the autobiographer. His protean approach to the relationship between myth and emotion is only one of several ways

---

85. CWE 29:166.
86. See Cummings, "Erasmus and the Invention of Literature," 23–54.
87. Ibid., 29.
88. Benedict Robinson, "Disgust, *c.* 1600," *ELH* 81, no. 2 (2014): 556.

in which he contributed to a distinctively humanist mode of describing affectivity. Erasmus had not only thought about the precise ways in which certain ancient myths represented emotions, but repeatedly deployed allusions and references that he knew would have emotional impact. Classical literature (pagan and biblical, rhetorical and poetic) provides a key lens through which Erasmus perceives the world. Ancient philosophy provides another, which is the subject of the following chapter.

Chapter 3

BIND THIS PROTEUS

TRANSFORMING THE ANCIENT PHILOSOPHY OF FEELING

"The only road to happiness is first to know oneself and then to act, not according to the emotions, but in all things according to the judgment of reason."¹ This dichotomy, a Platonist and Stoic truism, appears in Erasmus's works in varying formulations—this time in the *Enchiridion* of 1503—but he also expresses the precise inverse of the formulation when writing about theology, an enterprise which he says rests in the emotions instead of in reason and scholastic disputation.² Elsewhere in the *Enchiridion*, in fact, he argues that the neophyte Christian must approach sacred scripture with the "greatest purity of mind" (*summa animi puritate*) so that the medicine may pass directly and immediately into the *viscera affectus*, the bowels or depths of the emotions: "You will feel," he continues, "that you are inspired, moved, swept away, transfigured in an ineffable manner by the divine power if you approach [the scriptures] with respect, veneration, and humility."³ In the *Antibarbari*, meanwhile, a work whose first version was written a few years before the *Enchiridion*, Erasmus had offered a third option: emotions are pedagogues that help us toward virtue (an Aristotelian idea), not the pernicious disruptors imagined by the Stoics.⁴ Erasmus therefore provides his readers with three different models for negotiating the ethics of emotion, and disentangling them is often not easy. If reforming feeling is one of Erasmus's primary goals for outlining a Christian philosophy, and if he identifies the root of many of the world's problems as disoriented *affectus*, he also elevates *affectus*—in the wider,

---

1. *Enchiridion*, Holborn, 46 (modified): Haec igitur est unica ad beatitudinem via, primum, ut te noris. Deinde, ut ne quid pro affectionibus, sed omnia pro iudicio rationis agas.

2. See, for example, the *Paraclesis*, where he writes, "Hoc philosophiae genus in affectibus situm verius quam in syllogismis vita magis est quam disputatio, afflatus potius quam eruditio, transformatio magis quam ratio" (ASD V-7, 293).

3. CWE 66:34; LB V 8B.

4. ASD I-1, 88: Neque in hac re plane cum Stoicis sentio, qui universos affectus non supervacaneos modo, sed et perniciosos arbitrantur. Mihi ad virtutem tendentibus animis, tanquam pedagogi quidam videntur adhibiti.

singular, sense—to a privileged position in a Christian's transformation in faith. This is a tension that pervades especially Erasmus's earlier works, and its genesis can be located in Erasmus's wide reading of ancient philosophy and his attempts to use it to undergird his *philosophia Christiana*.

It is the primary goal of this chapter to provide an exposition Erasmus's engagement with ancient philosophy in this regard, to outline the competing impulses in Erasmus's works when it comes to emotion, with a focus on three texts: the *Enchiridion* (first published in 1503), the *De taedio Iesu* (1503), and the *Praise of Folly* (first published in 1511). The last chapter illustrated how Erasmus used classical literature to frame his understanding of emotion, and this one will allow us to see how philosophical sources played a role in the same task, explicating emotions with respect to their relationship to body and soul, and clarifying their role in Christian ethics. While Erasmus's debts to ancient philosophical schools have hardly been ignored, it is necessary to revisit the matter here in order to elucidate the early phases of his approach to translating philosophical ideas into a Christian humanist milieu from the perspective of affectivity. For the aforementioned tension is a hallmark characteristic of the renaissance of feeling, and an indication of a wider struggle to adjudicate intellectual authority in the early sixteenth century.

Erasmus was no systematic philosopher, and he used texts and precepts about the emotions from ancient philosophers in a generally opportunistic manner. That does not mean he lacked a solid grasp of philosophical ideas or principles, however, nor does it mean he was generally inconsistent. Erasmus read ancient philosophical and rhetorical works on emotion directly (editing many, such as Seneca, and translating some, such as Plutarch's dialogue on anger, the *De cohibenda iracundia*, from the *Moralia*, in 1525). As Ross Dealy has argued, Erasmus was a better philosopher than he's usually given credit for, and the older scholarly penchant for reducing his *philosophia Christi* to broadly humanistic ethical considerations does an injustice to his philosophical acumen. By contrast, other Erasmus scholars have attempted to pin Erasmus down to one particular school and this chapter will show how, from the perspective of emotion at least, this is a misguided endeavor. Dealy, for example, seeks to demonstrate Erasmus's commitments to Stoicism, and suggests that Erasmus studies has failed by ascribing to the humanist too much of an interest in rhetoric (as opposed to philosophy).[5] John Monfasani, who has illuminated much of the ancient philosophical engagement in Erasmus's corpus, has made a similar argument, but with respect to Epicureanism: namely,

---

5. Positing a rigid distinction between philosophy and rhetoric to explain Erasmus seems unhelpful to me, although Dealy's clarifications about Erasmus's development of specific Stoic ideas are important, especially when reading the *Enchiridion* and *De taedio Iesu*. And his suggestion that Erasmus's identification of emotion as *indifferentia* (a "late Stoic" idea), as lying between the spirit and the flesh, is compelling (see, for example, Ross Dealy, *Stoic Origins of Erasmus's Philosophy of Christ* [Toronto: University of Toronto Press, 2017], 183).

that Erasmus understood it more accurately than, for example, Lorenzo Valla, and that he adhered to its principles (Christianized) throughout his life (but not particularly explicitly).[6] Others, of course, have emphasized Erasmus's debts to the Platonist tradition, and the work of Dealy and Monfasani do help us to move past reading Erasmus through an overdetermined Platonizing framework.[7]

Parsing influence is, moreover, complicated by the simple fact that many teachings from ancient philosophical schools had already been blended together in late antiquity (in the writings of the Neoplatonists, for example), and were not necessarily delineated clearly in the early modern era.[8] Reducing Erasmus's philosophical preoccupations to a single school from the ancient world requires not only ignoring a common renaissance philosophical eclecticism, but also ignoring a whole lot of Erasmus's writings. Monfasani showed, in particular, that scouring the *Adagia* reveals Erasmus to have read widely in the ancient philosophical corpus, for he utilizes nearly all of Plato's dialogues and nearly all of Aristotle's works.[9] In fact, we find, in Erasmus's gloss of the adage *Festina lente* ("Make haste slowly") a typical description of the three main ancient philosophical schools' positions on emotion, all in one passage:

> There will be another way of using [the adage], when we wish to point out that the emotions must be reined in, as it were, by reason. Plato, having divided the soul of man into three parts, reason, impulse, and desire, thinks philosophy can be summed up in this, that the emotions should obey the reason as their king, and considers that for this very purpose the seat of the reason is located in a kind of citadel in the brain. The Peripatetics, with Aristotle as their standard-bearer, consider that nature has endowed us with emotions, which are a kind of moving force in the mind, to be a kind of stimulus to rouse us to the practise of virtue; although this is rejected by the Stoics, and in particular by Seneca in the books *On Anger* which he addressed to Nero. Their view is that emotions of this kind make no contribution to virtue, and in fact are an obstacle; though they do not deny, any more than anyone else, that in the heart of their theoretical wise man

---

    6. John Monfasani, "Erasmus and the Philosophers," *ERSY* 32 (2012): 51. See also the helpful essay by Anita Traninger, "Erasmus and the Philosophers," in *A Companion to Erasmus*, ed. Eric MacPhail (Leiden: Brill, 2022), 45–67 (this volume came out as my book was in press, so I was unable to take full advantage of the several excellent essays in it here).
    7. See, e.g., J. B. Payne, "Towards a Hermeneutics of Erasmus," in *Scrinium Erasmianum* II, ed. J. Coppens (Brill, 1969), 13–30; M. A. Screech, *Ecstasy and the Praise of Folly* (Duckworth, 1980).
    8. For a nice overview of how this relates to renaissance Stoicism, see Ada Palmer, "The Recovery of Stoicism in the Renaissance," in *The Routledge Handbook of the Stoic Tradition*, ed. John Sellars (Routledge, 2016).
    9. Monfasani, "Erasmus and the Philosophers," 51. See also Dominic Baker-Smith, "Uses of Plato by Erasmus and More," in *Platonism and the English Imagination*, ed. Anna Baldwin and Sarah Hutton (Cambridge, 1994), 86–101.

there remain original impulses which normally forestall the reason and which you would find it impossible to root out altogether. But to prevent their proving acceptable, they are promptly rejected by the reason.[10]

As illustrated in the previous chapter, here, too, Erasmus goes on to give several examples from literature and history of characters who exhibit philosophical restraint when it comes to emotion, including Athena restraining Achilles as a metaphor for Stoic *apatheia*. More generally, Erasmus's engagement with ancient philosophy was heterogeneous and discriminating, but he is ultimately mostly concerned with using teachings from ancient philosophy to shore up his theological positions in order to articulate a new kind of philosophy, the *philosophia Christiana*.[11] He has no true, and certainly no exclusive, allegiances here, and a look at how he mined a variety of ancient philosophical ideas in his discussions of emotion (a foundational philosophical topic for Erasmus), allows us to see this more clearly, while also revealing a certain flexibility in the use of anthropological categories that remains a feature of his thought across his corpus.[12]

Unbridled Emotions in the Enchiridion

Erasmus leverages ancient philosophical denigrations of emotion at length and repeatedly in the *Enchiridion*, one of his most widely published and influential works.[13] This work most clearly channels a Platonist/Stoic encouragement to subordinate the emotions to reason. Erasmus viewed the *Enchiridion* as a handbook to help guide the Christian (who couldn't, he jokes, manage to lug the *Secunda secundae* of Aquinas around with them[14]) to correct not only their beliefs but also their feelings. In the 1518 dedicatory letter to Paul Volz, famous on its own for outlining Erasmus's Christian philosophy, and which marked the new-and-improved Froben edition of the text, Erasmus recalls that when composing the original version, he "could see that the common body of Christians was corrupt not

---

10. *Adages* II i 1; CWE 33.

11. Monfasani, "Erasmus and the Philosophers"; Maria Cytowska, "Erasme et la philosophie antique," *Ziva antika. Antiquité vivante* 26 (1976): 451–62. For Erasmus's Christian philosophy, see Kirk Essary, *Erasmus and Calvin on the Foolishness of God: Reason and Emotion in the Christian Philosophy* (Toronto, 2017), and bibliography.

12. Space does not permit a full bibliography of works that refer to Erasmus and ancient philosophy, so I refer the reader to the bibliography of Monfasani's article, idem.

13. The *Enchiridion* is also one of the most oft-cited Erasmus works in scholarship on the humanist's theology, in many ways unfortunately so on account of it having continued to shape perceptions of Erasmus that aren't fully appreciative of the complexities of his biblical theology, as Manfred Hoffmann pointed out some time ago (see *Rhetoric and Theology* [Toronto, 1994], 31).

14. See the introductory letter to Paul Volz, in CWE 66:9.

only in its affections but in its ideas."[15] What Erasmus calls *affectus* are, throughout the *Enchiridion* and elsewhere, often identified with specific vices or sins or as phenomena that lead to such, and here he was participating in a long theological tradition.[16] Some *affectus* are what we today would call emotions, such as anger, hatred, and envy; others would stretch the term a bit too far, such as avarice and ambition, even if they have affective force.

While the *Enchiridion* at first glance reads as distinctly anti-emotional (and this is how it has often been interpreted), with its relentless attack on a gamut of deleterious affective sins, upon closer examination we find that it is not the presence of the emotions in general that is the problem, but either the presence of the wrong sort of emotions, or the absence of the right sort. When, early on, Erasmus digresses on the "sickness or death of the soul," which everyone pays less attention to—unfortunately—than the death of the body, a true symptom of such a disorder is a lack of feeling: when "nothing moves the soul" (*nihil commovetur animus*).[17] The focus on the soul over and against the body is typical of this text, which, again, is probably Erasmus's most "dualistic."[18] It is full of boilerplate platonisms, including a reference to the *soma/sēma* metaphor, and an explicit endorsement of the Platonists as the philosophers closest to "the spirit of the prophets and the gospel."[19] But it also eschews precision and indulges in paradoxical flights and metaphor, as when Erasmus writes that one should also not imagine that a person is *even alive* if they rage angrily against their neighbor with effusive abuse and obscene words, for "a stinking corpse lies in the sepulchre of his heart and the foul smells given off from it affect all those who come near."[20] In other words, even in those moments where Erasmus is ostensibly laying out a stereotypically rationalist position we find a rather complex understanding of the relationship between affectivity and virtue.

---

15. CWE 66:12. In the same paragraph, however, it is possible for Erasmus to ask the question, "When did charity wax colder?" and throughout the letter to Volz a rhetoric of fiery and impassioned Christianity is a desirable trait, something lacking from contemporary Christian mores, and not a kind of affectivity that is to be condemned. In such formulations we find the difficulty and ambiguity of Erasmus's approach to affectivity.

16. Ultimately biblical, of course, but increasing in complexity, first among the desert fathers, then throughout the Middle Ages, as Naama Cohen-Hanegbi has shown for contexts where medicine and pastoral theology overlap; see Naama Cohen-Hanegbi, *Caring for the Living Soul: Emotions, Medicine, and Penance in the Late Medieval Mediterranean* (Brill, 2017), ch. 1.

17. CWE 66:28.

18. On the dualism of body and soul in Erasmus's thought more generally, see David Marsh, "Erasmus on the Antithesis of Body and Soul," in *Journal the History of Ideas* 37:4 (1976), 673–88.

19. CWE 66:33.

20. Ibid.

In a memorable section of the text where Erasmus dwells on the unfortunate separation of body and soul, he attempts to establish reason as king over the unruly emotions, echoing Plato's *Republic* and eventually citing the *Timaeus*. It is prima facie Erasmus's most stringent defense of reason against emotion, and thus deserves a close exposition.[21] Erasmus writes, first, that it is the *affectus corporis* (the bodily emotions) that attempt to overthrow reason. One would assume a distinction, then, between emotions of the body and emotions (of a higher order, perhaps) of the soul, but while we find something like that distinction in other works of Erasmus, later in the same passage, after assigning reason as king of the human person in the metaphor of a republic, he writes, "Corresponding to the nobles are certain bodily emotions [*affectus corporeos*], but not brutish ones [*non brutos*]."[22] The nobler emotions, too, are corporeal. By describing the emotions as corporeal Erasmus is, in fact, simply following Plato in separating out the lower functions of the soul from truly incorporeal reason. Among the non-brutish emotions he lists what he would in later works categorize, following Quintilian, as *ethē*, or milder emotions: love for one's parents, kindness towards friends, fear of disgrace, compassion for the downtrodden, and so on. These are to be contrasted with more base feelings, which he calls *motus animorum* and *morbi animi* (movements and diseases of the soul), and which are farthest removed from reason—they consist of lust, excess, and envy, for example.[23]

Similarly, paraphrasing Plato's *Timaeus*, Erasmus adds on various perturbations (*variis perturbationibus*) to the lower order of the soul: *voluptas* (pleasure, desire), *dolor* (sadness, pain), *metus et audacia* (fear and bravery, or recklessness), *implacabilis iracundia* (unbridled anger), *blanda spes* (seductive hope), *irrationabili sensu* (irrational feelings), and *amor* (love).[24] Erasmus writes, "such are Plato's views almost word for word," and he's only slightly exaggerating: each of these emotion terms (including *perturbationes*, a favorite of Cicero's but not of Erasmus's) is taken verbatim from Marsilio Ficino's Latin translation of the *Timaeus*, although Erasmus has modified the order.[25] The one who subdues these,

---

21. Even if, strictly speaking, as Dealy has pointed out, "Erasmus never in the *Enchiridion* sees emotion as a vice" (*Stoic Origins*, 311).

22. CWE 66:42; LB V 13D

23. As a later example of Erasmus using *affectus* to refer to a bodily passion, see Erasmus's *Paraphrase on Matthew* (vv. 19:11–12), where strong sexual desire is described as an *affectus corporis*, none of which is more vehement or unconquerable (*violentior* and *invincibilior*). Erasmus in some ways precedes Spinoza in employing *affectus* broadly and in various modes, although Spinoza would seem to be most interested in categorizing *affectus* via orders of activity and passivity; see Russ Leo, "Affective Physics: *Affectus* in Spinoza's *Ethica*," in *Passions and Subjectivity in the Early Modern Era*, ed. Brian Cummings and Freya Sierhuis (Ashgate, 2013), 33–49.

24. LB V 14A.

25. I have consulted the Vincent edition of Ficino, London, 1563, p. 489, second column. ASD V-8 also contains Plato's original (*Tim* . 69C-D) and Ficino's translation

he continues, is just and happy, and the one who is conquered by them is unjust and unhappy. The *affectus* are thus cordoned off from the divine part of the soul, per Plato, and in offering such an extensive list of emotions Erasmus provides his readers with the broad contours of a Platonist taxonomy of feeling. By reproducing Ficino's terminology, he is also invoking a specific emotional lexicon, and likewise situating himself within a particular linguistic emotional community—albeit one that will shift over the course of his career.[26]

Erasmus moves on, effectively, to join Plato with the Stoics and Peripatetics, for all agree that reason should rule over the emotions, even if they differ on the extent to which the latter should be suppressed.[27] One must be cognizant, he argues, of all the *motus animi* in order that they might be guided *ad virtutem*—to virtue. Erasmus is here clearly endorsing the Aristotelian view, which he had just described as having taught that the emotions should be used as "inducements to virtue" (*incitabula ad virtutem*), in contrast with the Stoics for whom the *affectus* are "pernicious" insofar as they inhibit attaining wisdom.[28] On account of that they can be rectified and put to use on the Peripatetic model, we must understand how all the movements of the soul (*motus animi*) work, Erasmus says, but generalization is impossible because everyone has a different temperament as a result of "the influence of heavenly bodies, or one's ancestors, or education, or physical makeup [*corporis habitu*]."[29] The neutral reference to astrology is rare in Erasmus, as is the explanation of certain emotions according to humoral theory that follows: "Some vices are associated with one's physical constitution [*corporis habitum*], such as passion for women and love of sensual pleasures in the sanguine; anger, ferocity, and abusiveness in the choleric; inertia and sluggishness in the phlegmatic; envy,

---

(p. 137). Erasmus was possibly using the 1491 Venice (Torresani) edition (see van Gulik, *Erasmus and His Books*, 344). He had two different editions of Ficino's Latin version, as well as the Greek *editio princeps* (but the latter wasn't published until 1513) in his library when he died. See further on Erasmus and Ficino, Maria Cytowska, "Érasme de Rotterdame et Marsile Ficin son maître," *Eos* 63 (1975), 165–79.

26. It is intriguing to ponder how an increasing familiarity with Greek and increasing access to Greek texts affected the emotional lexicons of humanists like Erasmus, not only by offering alternative terms, but also by forcing the translator to consider a wider array of Latin synonyms. Erasmus was studying Greek assiduously during this time of his life but would have had to wait until 1513 (barring access to a manuscript, which is possible) for the Greek *editio princeps* of the *Timaeus* (see further previous note).

27. The Stoics want to do away with them while the Peripatetics do not want them extirpated but reigned in (*non extirpandos affectos, sed coercendos*). Socrates, Erasmus says, agrees with the Stoics.

28. LB V 13E-14F. See Aristotle *Nic Eth*. 2.2.7. Erasmus may be getting the outline from Cicero's *Tusculan Disputations*; see ASD V-8, 141, notes. He also seems to quote from Cicero when he gives Aristotle's account of the emotions in the *Ecclesiastes* (CWE 68:791).

29. CWE 66:44.

sadness, and bitterness in the melancholic."[30] Other potentially influential factors include nationality, gender, and age. Some affective vices seem to cancel others out: one might have propensities to sensual pleasure and not be angry, for example, or a more chaste mind might be more irascible.[31] None of these, it should be emphasized, is *determinative* of a given person's affective disposition, but they might attend or accompany it (*comitantur*). The point of citing the Peripatetic position is to emphasize that spiritual training is possible (that problematic emotions can be rendered into virtuous ones), not that the choleric is irredeemably angry. This is important at the discursive level also: so close is *affectus* (here better understood as a general affective disposition) to virtue or vice that Erasmus offers a warning lest we confuse one for another by, for example, calling "sadness gravity, harshness severity, envy zeal, stinginess frugality, adulation friendliness, or scurrility wit."[32] The upshot of all this emotional parsing comes down to that old dictum: "know thyself" (here *primum, ut te noris*) and live according reason, not emotion.[33]

This level of introspection is not easy, of course, and Erasmus goes on to argue that even many Christians cannot distinguish between reason and the disturbances of the soul.[34] He then maps the reason/emotion distinction made by the philosophers directly onto the spirit/flesh distinction offered by Paul: "What the philosophers call reason Paul calls either spirit or the inner man or the law of the mind. What they call emotions he calls the flesh, the body, the outer man, or the law of the members."[35] Finally, after a series of allusions to biblical passages demonstrating the conflicting inclinations of the bi-partite person, he invokes Proteus in order to indicate the psychological mess we're in: "As the soul is inflamed by violent perturbations, press on using every means, push on, fall upon and bind this Proteus as 'in wondrous transformation he becomes / Fire and hideous beast and flowing stream' until he returns to his original form. What is so protean as the emotions and desires of the foolish?"[36] The philosophical thus becomes the

---

30. CWE 66:45; LB 15C: Quaedam corporis habitum comitantur, sicut sanguineos mulierositas, et voluptatum amor: Cholericum ira, ferocitas, maledicentia: Phlegmaticum inertia, somnolentia: Melancholicum invidia, tristitia, amaritudo.

31. Ibid.

32. CWE 66:44, modified; LB V 16A: tristitiam gravitatem, asperitatem severitatem, invidiam zelum, sordes frigalitatem, adsentationem comitatem, scurrilitatem urbanitatem.

33. See Dealy, *Stoic Origins*, 276–9, for an elaboration on the Stoic underpinnings of this section of the text, and for an argument that Erasmus scholars have overemphasized his debts to Platonism here.

34. LB V 15E: Ut ne norint quidem rationis atque perturbationum discrimen.

35. LB V 15F: Quod Philosophi *rationem*, id Paulus modo *spiritum*, modo *interiorem hominem*, modo *legem mentis* vocat. Quod illi *adfectum*, hic interdum *carnem*, interdum *corpus*, interdum *exteriorem hominem*, interdum *legem membrorum* appellat.

36. CWE 66:49–50, modified; LB V 18C: Interim dum vehementibus perturbationibus aestuat animus, tu modis omnibus preme, urge, immine, ac Proteum istum tuum vinclis stringe tenacibus, dum *Omnia transformat sese in miracular rerum, Ignemque, horribilemque*

biblical which then becomes the literary. By invoking Proteus and Virgil's *Georgics*, Erasmus can double down on the extraordinary nature of some emotions *qua* vices: "bestial lust, wild anger, and venomous envy."[37] Such disruptive emotions are the real worry. Only once the Christian soldier has crucified sins and desires (*vitiis et concupiscentiis*) can she experience peace (*tranquillitas et otium*), quasi-Stoic/Epicurean ends that Erasmus here identifies with spiritual consolation and, ultimately, Christian salvation.[38]

It has been suggested that Erasmus embodies a Christian Epicureanism above all other ancient philosophies, and though it may be that Erasmus sought a life of pleasurable *ataraxia*, detached as much as possible from worldly concerns, he does at times contrast Christian joy with the ideal pleasures of that ancient philosophical school.[39] The Epicureans do not feature heavily in Erasmus's discussions of emotion, probably because they did not offer the same sort of ready-made framework to apply to the topic when compared with their rivals of the Stoa or Academy. But it may be worth mentioning, *en passant*, a passage in the *Enarratio Triplex* on Psalm 22/23, where Erasmus contrasts spiritual happiness, or ecstasy, with the madness of the pagans, specifically the Epicureans:

> The inexpressible happiness of the church is signified by the word "oil" in the text of the prophet: "You have anointed my head with oil." . . . The oil is the hidden "oil of gladness" with which God has anointed above all his fellows him who is "fairer in form than the children of men." The followers of Epicurus also had their perfumes, with which they anoint themselves before they drink their fill to the point of madness. But the other is the oil of the Spirit, which alone makes the minds of men truly joyful.[40]

The contrast between Epicurean *insania* with Christian *laetitia* is expanded upon later, where Erasmus argues that the perfumes of the Epicureans are much less potent than those of the Christian, for the latter "has banquets a hundred times more magnificent [than those of Epicurus]. He has perfumes, not of the kind that flatter our noses with a trivial and fleeting pleasure, but those which buoy up the soul with continual joy; he has the cup of wine that truly cheers the heart of man,

---

feram, fluviumque liquentem; donec in nativam speciem redeat. Quit autem tam Proteus, quam adfectus et cupiditates stultorum?

37. LB V 18C: belluinam libidinem, iram ferinam, venenatam invidiam.

38. See CWE 66:50–1.

39. See Monfasani, "Erasmus and the Philosophers". Also, Reinier Leushuis, "The Paradox of Christian Epicureanism in Dialogue," *Erasmus Studies* 35, no. 2 (2015): 113–36.

40. CWE 64:164. Hanc ineffabilem ecclesiae laetitiam sermo propheticus olei nomine designavit. *Impinguasti oleo caput meum.* Hoc videlicet est illud oleum arcanae laetitiae, quo Deus ultra sodales omnes unxerat speciosum forma prae filiis hominum. Habent et Epicurei sua unguenta, quibus delibuti potant usque ad craterem insaniae. Hoc autem est oleum Spiritus, quod solum vere laetificat mentes hominum (ASD V-2, 357).

that causes a holy and sober drunkenness."[41] The purpose of the argument is to establish that the pinnacle of Christian feeling transcends that offered by rival philosophies.[42] This might also be kept in mind as relevant to the discussion of Platonist ecstasy from the *Praise of Folly* at the end of this chapter.

Returning to the *Enchiridion*, the dualistic schema gives way in the next section to an elaboration on the Pauline and Origenian tripartite division of the human person between body, soul, and spirit.[43] There is thus both a terminological and conceptual fluidity to Erasmus's presentation of affectivity in this text. The introduction to the third aspect, the neutral and indifferent soul, adds to this flexible approach: the neutral soul (*anima neutros*) is caught between the pious spirit and the impious flesh (*spiritus pios, caro impios*); its nature is impartial and neither good nor bad (*medium et indifferens*).[44] While the overt discussion of *affectus* is here put to the background, the implications are clear enough, namely, that the emotions are constitutive, in part, of this *tertium quid*. To love your family members is merely a natural disposition, not a virtue, although it's a vice if you don't. A certain emotion may seem honorable, but this could be a deception, and the virtue of any given action can only be found in interior intent, as Erasmus makes clear with a few examples.[45] The goal is not to extirpate, or even suppress, the emotions but to ensure that they are of the spirit and not the flesh. Not all *affectus*, though, are redeemable, and a typical list of those which are always or almost always turned to vices is given later in the text: "anger, ambition, greed,

---

41. CWE 64:197. [H]abet epulas illis centuplo lautiores, habet unquentum non mox peritura voluptatula delectans nares, sed intus iugi gaudio exhilarans animum, habet calicem vini vere exhilarantis cor hominis, quod sanctam ac sobriam adfert temulentiam (ASD V-2, 380). See also the *Explanation of Psalm 85* for a lengthy discussion of Christ's emotions as ethical models, including a digression on true "spiritual joy" (CWE 64:52–4).

42. Erasmus continues to argue, indeed, that undesirable emotions are felt by Jews and pagans who see the banquet prepared by the Lord in verse 22/23:5, the Jews who are "torn apart by envy" and the pagans who starve to death, but also shout "Woe unto us", and the devils who "hear and tremble." Pagan banquets, in other words, not only bring insufficient joy, but breed negative emotions as well.

43. See 1 Thess. 5:23; Godin and Screech have pointed out the probable debts to Origen's own tripartite emphasis, although of course the ultimate origin is Pauline. In his *Commentary on Romans*, Origen invokes the *anima* (the text survives only in Latin) as the relevant part of the soul for certain emotions multiple times. See, e.g., J. P. Migne, *Patrologiae cursus completus graeca* (Paris, 1857–66), 14, 850, 866, 1057, and Godin's introduction to the *De taedio Iesu* in ASD V-7, 202. See further Screech, *Ecstasy and the Praise of Folly*, 96–112.

44. LB V 18E. See further the *Hyperaspistes 2* for a nuanced discussion where Erasmus elaborates on the Pauline tripartite nature of the human individual, responding to Luther's criticism that Erasmus argued that the *hegemonikon* remained above fleshly sin (especially CWE 77:584–90).

45. See CWE 66:53 and LB V 20B.

pleasure, and envy."⁴⁶ These are the *affectus* that chain the souls in Plato's cave to gaze at empty shadows.⁴⁷ Even the neutral, human emotions (*humanos affectus*) need to be mortified, although such mortification is not painful but even ardently pleasurable.⁴⁸ The "epilogue" to the *Enchirdion* consists of specific advice given with respect to resisting a slightly different list of affective vices: lust, avarice, ambition, pride, and anger. It is worth emphasizing that Erasmus does not have a consistent list of "basic emotions," but a series of emotions and affective vices that constantly changes.

The notion that the true philosopher is the good Platonist whose judgment is undisturbed by emotion is not confined to the *Enchiridion* or the early works of Erasmus. It is, for example, reiterated explicitly in Erasmus's commentary on Psalm 2 (1522), as John Monfasani points out. In a passage where Erasmus is glossing verse 10 ("And now, you kings, understand . . ."), he writes,

> The first part of the verse refers to judgment, which is that part of our understanding which enables us to decide what it is best to do; the second part of the verse refers to control of the emotions. . . . The fool who lacks judgment always chooses the worst instead of the best, and similarly, if a man is distracted by anger, hatred, love, ambition, lust, pride, or spite, his mental perceptions are disturbed and he cannot discern the best course. It is the mark of a philosopher to be free from such distractions. Plato recognized this when he declared that the well-being of the state depended upon its rulers being philosophers as well. How can a man properly rule others, if he himself is subject to blind emotion? How can a man properly take care of his own people, if his council consists of foolish desires?⁴⁹

---

46. CWE 66:71; LB 31 V B: ira, ambitio, cupiditas, voluptas, invidia. Of these *ira* is the most ambivalent; it is typically condemned in Erasmus, but can be "spiritual" when it involves self-discrimination and hatred of sin (see the chapter on the Psalms below).

47. Vulgus sunt, quicumque in specu illo Platonico vincti suis affectibus inanes rerum imagines pro verissimis rebus admirantur (LB V 40B).

48. Id quod nobis non solum amarum esse non debet, verum etiam vehementer optabile ac iucundum, si modo spiritus Christi vivit in nobis (LB V 54C).

49. CWE 63:138; ASD V-2, 151: Prior huius versiculi pars pertinet ad iudicium, hoc est ad eam prudentiae partem qua diiudicamus quid sit optimum factu, altera pars ad sedatos affectus . . . Qui stultus est et iudicio carens pessima pro optimis eligit. Itidem qui perturbatur ira, odio, amore, ambitione, libidine, superbia, livore, quoniam mentis oculum habet perturbatum, non potest dispicere quid expediat. His igitur perturbationibus vacare est philosophum esse. Nam hoc sensit Plato qui prounnuciavit reipublicae felicitatem in hoc esse sitam si qui reges essent iidem essent philosophi. Nam quomodo recte imperabit aliis qui ipse servit caecis affectibus? Quomodo recte consulet populo qui stultas cupiditates habet in consilio?

Here we find a mostly straightforward endorsement of subordinating the unruly emotions to *iudicio*, but it is important to note that Erasmus is not offering an unqualified criticism of emotions in general, echoing the *Enchiridion*. Rather, it is the disruptive emotions, the blind emotions (*caecis affectibus*), the problematic or foolish desires (*stultas cupiditates*), and, later in the same section, the foolish and untamed emotions (*stultis et indomitis affectibus*) and the evil and earthly desires (*malis et terrenis cupiditatibus*), which are condemned. These examples indicate the importance of paying close attention to the original languages of feeling as well, for the English translations of "emotions" or "passions" are not always adequate: *cupiditates* is almost always negative for Erasmus, even without a pejorative adjective, in a way that neither "emotions" or "passions" or even "desires" is in English, while *affectus* is generally neutral but also usually ascribed a positive or negative force (either overtly or contextually). At any rate, Erasmus's comparison of the ruler with unbridled emotions to Phaethon losing control of the sun's chariot and threatening universal chaos gets his ultimate point across.[50] In the *Enchiridion*, then, we find a repeated theme wherein emotions are to be heavily regulated, if not suppressed, but that theme is only one aspect of a complex view, and one that taps into many different modes of his thinking about feeling. The wrong sort of emotion presents one of the great dangers to Christian virtue for Erasmus, but affectivity is not inherently blameworthy—it is also irreducibly human and potentially virtuous. This becomes clearer in a work published in the same year as the *Enchiridion*, the *De taedio Iesu*.

Fearing Death in the De taedio Iesu

Erasmus's *De taedio Iesu*, or "On the Sadness/Distress of Jesus," is a rather different kind of work than the *Enchiridion*, though it was composed around the same time.[51] While from an emotions perspective, the *Enchiridion* treats the

---

50. See CWE 63:138.

51. For scholarship on this text, see James D. Tracy, "Humanists among the Scholastics: Erasmus, More, and Lefevre d'Etaples on the Humanity of Christ," *Erasmus of Rotterdam Society Yearbook* 5 (1985): 30–51; Daniel T. Lochman, "Colet and Erasmus: The *Disputatiuncula* and the Controversy of Letter and Spirit," *Sixteenth-Century Journal* 20, no. 1 (1989): 77–88; G. J. Fokke, "An Aspect of the Christology of Erasmus of Rotterdam," *Ephemerides theologicae Lovanienses* 54 (1978): 161–87; Giovanni Santinello, "Tre meditazioni umanistiche sulla passione," in *Studi sull'umanesimo europea: Cusano e Petrarca, Lefevre, Erasmo, Colet, Moro* (Padua: Editrice Antenore, 1969), 77–128; Mara Maria Grazia, "Colet et Erasme au sujet de l'exegese de Mt. 26, 39," in *Theorie et pratique de l'exegese*, ed. Irena Backus and Francis Higman (Geneva: Droz, 1990), 259–72; Dealy, *Stoic Origins*; Essary, *Erasmus and Calvin on the Foolishness of God*, ch. 5; idem, "The Mind's Bloody Sweat: (Dis)embodied Emotions in Erasmus, More, and Calvin," *Parergon* 38, no. 1 (2021): 41–64; and Michael J. Heath's introduction to the *De taedio* in the *Collected Works*

subject with significant breadth, and especially from the perspective of emotions as vices antithetical to reason, the *De taedio* is an *apologia* of Christ's genuine human emotional suffering in the hours leading up to his death as reported in the Gethsemane/Mount of Olives scenes of the synoptic gospels.[52] The text recreates a debate over this topic between Erasmus (who defends the fact of Christ's emotional suffering) and his friend, the Englishman John Colet (who rejects the possibility that Jesus actually feared dying). The work's purpose, then, is not to denounce but to explicitly defend a specific form of feeling. While the text constitutes an involved theological investigation of the psychological and somatic aspects of Christ's suffering with reference to the longer history of biblical interpretation on the relevant passages, our purpose here—in keeping with the theme of this chapter—is only to highlight some key ways in which it indicates Erasmus's philosophical sources for his thoughts about emotion more generally.

Fear of death, the central subject of the text, is, like most *affectus*, neutral and natural for Erasmus.[53] He goes out of his way to argue that it is not sinful: "it is only human nature to dread death, and . . . such is the human condition, there would have been a place for it even in the state of innocence."[54] Even the irrational beasts and, perhaps, plants recoil from dying, he suggests, so integral is it to natural life. The Stoics themselves, Erasmus writes, quoting Aulus Gellius, "not only allow [humans] this dread of death, but even give it the leading place among the 'first principles of nature.'"[55] It would be, Erasmus continues, unnatural and defective for one not to fear death under imminent threat, and Erasmus plays (here and later) on the relationship between *apatheia*—a lack of mental feeling—and *analgesia*—a lack of physical feeling: "the effect of feeling pain in the present or fearing it in the future is the same, though in the one case the pain begins in the body and spreads to the mind, while in the other suffering starts in the mind and overflows into the body."[56] This is, strictly speaking, not true, as Erasmus will later acknowledge, but it serves his point that anyone who doesn't fear impending death has a malfunction similar to one who is insensible to pain.

The ultimate purpose of Erasmus's discussion is, in fact, to divorce the virtue of bravery (which all martyrs perfected) from the affects of fear—affects in the sense of bodily affective responses: brave philosophers of the past, Socratics and

---

of Erasmus (CWE) (Toronto: Toronto University Press, 1998), 70:2–8; and the introduction by Godin in ASD V-7 (Leiden: Brill, 2014), 192–206.

52. The text is a reconstructed debate that Erasmus and John Colet had over Christ's emotions in Gethsemane at Oxford in 1499.

53. For an analysis of emotion in the *De preparatione ad mortem*, see Gordon Raeburn, "Erasmus and the Emotions of Death," *Erasmus Studies* 40, no. 2 (2020): 157–73.

54. CWE 70:25.

55. Ibid.

56. CWE 70:27–8; ASD V-7, 227: Nam eadem est ratio vel sentiendi praesens incommodum vel instans exhorrescendi, quanquam in altero a corpore profectus dolor ad animum pervenit, in altero cruciatus in animo exortus redundat in corpus.

Stoics, both turned pale and shuddered in thunderstorms while at sail, but both are, to Erasmus's mind, braver than the "rich Asiatic" and the "libertine" who were unmoved in similar situations.[57] Courage is not a lack of fear, but an endurance of it. Lurching hearts, the draining of blood, hastened pulses, turning pale, hair standing on end, groaning—these are the affects of fear listed by Erasmus, natural responses to imminent death, no different from those which Christ felt sinlessly as a human in the moments leading up to his arrest. And while Erasmus at one point collapses the distinction between mental and physical suffering, elsewhere in the text he maintains a firm distinction between the two, complicating any easy anthropological schema for the locus of feeling.

In the *De taedio* he makes the point in a few ways, first by distinguishing between mental pain (*dolor mentis*—whose privatives are *analgesia* and *apatheia*) and physical pain (*dolor corporis*—whose privative is *anaisthesia*).[58] Erasmus cites the "most learned" of the Stoics as Panaetius of Rhodes, and recalls that he does not require the sage to abide by such a strict norm as withholding of all feeling, suggesting by implication that the Stoics who are not *doctissimus* might. Erasmus is following Aulus Gellius closely, including by invoking *analgesia* and *apatheia*, as well as the example of Panaetius, who is only mentioned in passing—making the *Attic Nights* a somewhat outsized source for Erasmus's earliest extensive treatment of Stoicism and emotion.[59] In terms of Latin usage, Erasmus is keen to point out that *dolor* can be used of both mind and body, and that it is actually used more often to refer to mental pain.[60] At any rate, both the philosophers and theologians agree, Erasmus tells us, that when it comes to *affectus*, the wise person practices moderation (μετριότητα in Greek) and not privation (στέρησιν in Greek), the former term which appears, for example, in Plato's *Republic*.[61] In the margins of the Froben 1518 edition (which also contained the letter to Volz prefacing the *Enchiridion* referenced earlier in this chapter), we find the following printed gloss on this passage: *non carentiam sed mediocratem affectuum requirunt*—that is, (the philosophers) require not freedom from the emotions, but moderation in them.[62]

When Erasmus paraphrases Colet's response, he marshals (for Colet's position) extensive evidence in favor of the strong Stoic position that the wise man in fact should not fear death, and that ascribing extreme emotion to Christ in Gethsemane is unbecoming. Erasmus asks, in return, if one might perhaps depart from the teachings of the Stoics (*a Stoicorum decretis desciscere*), and specifically from the notion that nothing should be feared except for "moral turpitude," on account of that the Bible says explicitly otherwise: death itself is evil, and therefore fearing it

---

57. CWE 70:29.

58. See CWE 70:31; ASD V-7, 230: Quanquam duo illa, *analgesia kai apatheia*, magis videntur ad animi dolorem pertinere, *anaisthesia* corporis.

59. See *Attic Nights* XII.5.

60. ASD V-7, 231: dolor autem saepius ad animum quam ad corpus.

61. See *Rep.* 560D.

62. See *De taedio Iesu* (Basel: Froben, 1518), 171.

is natural. Colet's argument is that one must avoid a slippery slope, while Erasmus continually makes the distinction between human emotions that might lead to sin in us and the same emotions which would never lead to sin in Christ.[63] Because of original sin, *most* emotions not only cloud our judgment, but they stir up disorder and are rendered into the very material for sin. But Christ was innocent. And in one of the few instances, in this text or in any of his other works, of Erasmus using the term *passio* for "emotion," he writes:

> Since Christ took nothing from fallen nature except the handicaps imposed on us as chastisement, and there was in him no capacity for sin, I shall boldly ascribe to him the natural passions (*passiones naturales*) appropriate to mind (*animi*) and body (*corporis*) respectively: grief, joy, hatred, fear, and anger in the mind; in the body, hunger, thirst, drowsiness, weariness, suffering, death.[64]

Erasmus thus attempts to neutralize Colet's hard-line Stoic arguments, first by suggesting that it is "natural" to fear death, and, second, by arguing that Christ's becoming fully human entails that he takes on the *affectus naturae* of an ordinary human being.

Early modern rejections of the Stoic doctrine of *apatheia* gained intellectual currency with the increased circulation of certain Stoic texts in the fifteenth and sixteenth centuries, ensuring that a Christian humanist "emotional community" had an antagonist against which to formulate this aspect of its own identity.[65] Richard Strier puts it most succinctly when he writes that "the Renaissance revived anti-Stoicism as well as Stoicism," and Barbara Pitkin has noted that the early modern reception of Stoicism was "extremely complex, highly eclectic, and dependent on the topic in question."[66] Regarding the emotions, the tendency in the late medieval and early modern period was typically to reject the Stoic doctrine

---

63. See, e.g., CWE 70:38.

64. CWE 70:39; ASD V-7, 237: animi, ut dolere, gaudere, odisse, sperare, metuere, irasci; corporis, ut esurire, sitire, dormiturire, lassari, affligi, more.

65. The bibliography would be quite large; for an overview see Jill Kraye, "Stoicism in the Renaissance from Petrarch to Lipsius," *Grotiana* 22, no. 1 (2001): 21–45. During the Reformation, Swiss Protestants even came to identify Anabaptists as neo-Stoics—one of many "heretical" positions that resulted in their occasionally violent suppression across Europe. According to the Strasbourg Protestant humanist Martin Bucer, for example, they did not permit mourning, and Wolfgang Musculus accused the Anabaptists of attempting to reintroduce *apatheia* back into the Church. See further Craig Farmer, *The Gospel of John in the Sixteenth Century* (Oxford: Oxford University Press, 1997), 164–8.

66. Richard Strier, "Against the Rule of Reason: Praise of Passion from Petrarch to Luther to Shakespeare to Herbert," in *Reading the Early Modern Passions*, ed. Gail Kern Paster (University of Pennsylvania Press, 2004), 23; Barbara Pitkin, "Erasmus, Calvin, and the Faces of Stoicism in Renaissance and Reformation Thought," in *The Routledge Handbook of the Stoic Tradition*, ed. John Sellars (Routledge, 2016).

of *apatheia* in favor of an appreciative position on the emotions, and so in this way Erasmus is not doing anything novel in the *De taedio*. Like the scholastic theologian as inscrutable sophist, the Stoic sage became a convenient strawman as a figure devoid of feeling and, therefore, inhuman. In a trajectory running from Lorenzo Valla through Erasmus to Swiss Protestant reformers such as Calvin and Bucer, Stoics were described as "marble statues," "tree trunks," "stones," "men of iron," and "monsters," all because of their rejection of emotion. The doctrine of *apatheia* became anathema in fifteenth- and sixteenth-century humanist circles, not least because of a conviction that Christ himself (the model for all Christian life) had felt emotions, and felt them even in extreme fashion in the Garden of Gethsemane and at the death of Lazarus. Erasmus later suggested that supporting *apatheia* was borderline heresy in his dispute with Francis Titelmans, but he presents a more balanced view of Stoicism generally in the *De taedio* by invoking later developments in the tradition that do not require such austerity.

There is a notable difference of emphasis in the *De taedio* when compared with the *Enchiridion*. Regarding ancient philosophy, Erasmus engages more closely with Stoic texts in the *De taedio*, no doubt because his rhetorical opponent is, ostensibly, arguing from a Stoic point of view. There is also more of a nuanced discussion of the anthropological locus of feeling in the *De taedio*, to the extent that the generally oversimplified distinctions proffered in the *Enchiridion* between *ratio* and *affectus* (the former of the immaterial soul and the latter of the lower orders of the soul most closely aligned with the body) are downplayed in favor of discussions of emotion as situated across body and soul in different ways. That said, Erasmus does include a passage in the *De taedio* quite similar to one we quoted earlier in the *Enchiridion* on the dualism of body and soul, which, as in the *Enchiridion*, gives way to a brief discussion of the Pauline tripartite person. Elaborating on the theological problem of multiple wills in Christ, Erasmus notes that humans, too, have conflicting impulses:

> These impulses reflect the two parts of our soul. The one, dwelling down amid the grosser bodily organs and anchored in the flesh, is brutish and inclined towards evil; the other shines like a beacon amid the smoke of emotion, and always strives towards good. It is pure and simple, and is called "reason" by the philosophers. The other, since it deviates from the supreme good, which is one and pure, is called by many different names after the various false objectives it sets itself. However, they come under the general heading of *pathē*, that is, emotions, or perturbations, or appetites. Paul calls the one "the law of the mind," and the other, variously, "the law of sin," "the law of the members," "the flesh," and "the body."[67]

---

67. CWE 70:59; ASD V-7, 254: Hae sunt velut duae partes animae, quarum altera crassioribus corporis organis immersa carnique concreta brutior est et ad turpia fertur, altera tanquam flammae fastigium ex affectuum fumis aemicat nititurque semper ad honesta. Illa simplex et a philosophis ratio vocatur; altera, quoniam a summo bono deflectit, quod unum

We have, then, another translation of pagan philosophical terms into Pauline ones, and an eloquent explanation of the ways in which reason shines through affective fog. But tying the emotions to the gross flesh also complicates what Erasmus says elsewhere about bodily and mental feeling.

Thus, regarding the relationship of the emotions to the mind and body, it is somewhat difficult to pin Erasmus down, for more than once he invokes a separation between bodily affect and emotion:

> Eagerness goes with love only in the same way that pallor goes with anger, blushing with shame, laughter with joy, tears with sorrow. These things are outward signs, not causes, and are extrinsic to the emotions they betoken . . . if you take away the pallor the underlying anger remains unchanged. You may take it for granted that the same is true for all other signs and emotions.[68]

Erasmus is trying to make the point, *pace* Colet, that Christ could love without eagerly rushing into death—that his fear of death could coincide with his love for humanity. In doing so he makes a quite radical suggestion, namely that stripping the physiological component out of emotional expression is not to strip anything out of the account (*ratio*) of the emotion itself, and that cuts against the notion cited above of emotions being anchored in the gross flesh. Moreover, it has often been suggested in scholarship on the *De taedio* that Erasmus follows a prominent medieval philosophical thread in his position against Colet, justifying Christ's emotions as a function of his two wills in the Garden of Gethsemane, but it is important to note that, while true in outline, he often uses different conceptual language.[69]

It is not our purpose, at any rate, to "rescue" Erasmus and make sense of the multiple frameworks of feeling he is operating under but, rather, to indicate what his sources are, and how he is utilizing philosophers of antiquity when it comes to writing about the emotions. For now, the salient points to take away from a quick look at the *De taedio Iesu* are that emotions, and especially the fear of death, are

---

ac simplex est, pro varietate falsorum bonorum in quae nititur, aliis atquae aliis nominibus appellatur; quanquam communi nomine dicuntur *pathē* id est affectus seu perturbationes sive appetitus. Paulus *legem mentis* appelat alteram, alteram nunc *legem peccati*, nunc *legem membrorum*, nunc *carnem* et *corpus* nominat.

68. CWE 70:48; ASD V-7, 244: Sic alacritas comitatur amorem ut iram pallor, pudorem rubor, gaudium risus, tristitiam lachrymae. At isthaec indicia sunt, non causae, extra naturam earum rerum quas arguunt, ut neque omnis qui palleat iratus sit neque iratus omnis statim palleat neque qui pallidior sit idem sit commotior neque ideo quis irascatur quod palleat, siquidem extra naturam irae pallor est ut, si pallorem irato detrahas, nihil tamen ex irae ratione demutaris. De reliquis item eadem iam me dixisse puta.

69. Peter Lombard, for example, distinguishes between the *affectus rationis* and the *affectus sensualitatis* to accommodate Christ's conflicted emotions. See further Simo Knuuttila, *Emotions in Ancient and Medieval Philosophy* (Oxford, 2004), 194–5.

natural, even if affected by sin in everyone but Christ; that Erasmus appreciated a complex milieu of Stoicism that embodied different approaches to affectivity; that *dolor*, *affectus*, and *passio* of the mind are as abundant and distinctive as the same phenomena when found in the body; and that external, physiological affects should not be imagined as definitive of either a virtue or an emotion. While we have only glimpsed the tip of the iceberg in terms of Erasmus's fully wrought discourse of feeling, it should already be clear that his approach is both complex in terms of intellectual sources, and also constitutive of a concerted effort to delineate the importance and definition of the emotions. They are a subject, for Erasmus, of considerable philosophical interest.

Emotion between Body and Soul

Given the references to physiological components of feeling, a brief note on humoral theory in the thought of Erasmus is necessary, linked as it is to the legacy of ancient philosophy and medicine. I have argued elsewhere that Erasmus's thought defies some recent scholarly generalizations about an early modern propensity for "psychological materialism" when it comes to describing the emotions, and that it is key to pay close attention to emotions discourse in religious writings from the period lest such generalizations be maintained across an intellectual and cultural landscape as complex as that of late medieval and early modern Europe.[70] Put simply, it is insufficient to explain early modern understandings of emotion in strong Galenic or humoralist terms, as reducible to or even always linked to humoral movement. We can add, too, that Erasmus himself is also not enticed by more nuanced natural-philosophical understandings of emotion that prevailed in renaissance medical texts.[71] He rarely cites medical authorities in discussions of emotion, and he largely avoids the language, for example, of humoral theory, of *accidentia animae*, of "animate spirits." He did show a fairly consistent interest in

---

70. Such materialist views have also been complicated and nuanced by historians of late medieval and early modern medicine in recent years, as well as by cultural and literary historians. See Brian Cummings and Freya Sierhuis, *Passions and Subjectivity in Early Modern Culture* (Routledge, 2013), introduction; Elena Carrera, "Anger and the Mind-Body Connection in Medieval and Early Modern Medicine," in *Emotions and Health, 1200–1700*, ed. Elena Carrera (Leiden: Brill, 2013), 95–146; and Cohen-Hanegbi, *Caring for the Living Soul*. Also See Kirk Essary, "Clear as Mud: Metaphor, Emotion, and Meaning in Early Modern England," *English Studies* 98, no. 7 (2017): 689–703, and Essary, "The Mind's Bloody Sweat," 41–64. For overviews of humoral theory in the context of medical and broader cultural contexts, see Nancy Siraisi, *Medieval and Early Renaissance Medicine: An Introduction to Knowledge and Practice* (Chicago, 1990); and for the classic study, see Raymond Klibansky, Erwin Panofski, and Fritz Saxl, *Saturn and Melancholy* (London, 1964).

71. For an investigation of anger in this intellectual context, see Carrera, previous note.

then-current and ancient medical knowledge, which in itself—given the lack of invocation of medical authorities in his discussion of emotion—is further evidence that for Erasmus the emotions were more the province of a kind of spiritual psychology than of anatomical medicine.[72] This should not be too surprising, for physicians themselves disagreed over the question of whether physiological or psychological treatments of emotions were more pertinent, as Naama Cohen-Hanegbi's excellent work on the subject has shown.[73]

Erasmus does, however, occasionally refer to humoral theory and other physiological components to feeling. It is worth briefly looking at a few such instances to see how he imagines these explanatory mechanisms to be useful, but also to assess this additional feature of Erasmus's affective archive. We quoted one passage from the *Enchiridion* above: "Some vices are associated with one's physical constitution [*corporis habitum*], such as passion for women and love of sensual pleasures in the sanguine; anger, ferocity, and abusiveness in the choleric; inertia and sluggishness in the phlegmatic; envy, sadness, and bitterness in the melancholic."[74] Erasmus does not offer much else by way of explaining the relevance of the humoral reference, other than listing these as important for general self-knowledge, so that one might be able to take advantage of the emotions as goads to virtue. In the *De taedio*, examples of humoral connections to emotion are invoked almost exclusively to demonstrate that they are neither determinative nor necessarily ethically significant, as when Erasmus asks, rhetorically: "If nature has endowed me with more hot blood or thicker spirits than others, does that make me braver? Conversely, if she has given me colder blood, and less of it, together with

---

72. Perhaps the most detailed discussion, although with scant reference to emotion, comes in the colloquy "Puerpera" or "New Mother", where the interlocutors go into some detail about the ways in which the soul is attached to the body, concluding mainly along Aristotelian lines; see CWE 40:598–600. Erasmus would eventually own works by Hippocrates, Galen, Dioscorides, and others, and he translated a few general treatises from Galen. He also owned copies of contemporary medical works, such as Joannes Manardus's *Medicinales epistolae*. The relevant references to his library are in van Gulik, *Erasmus and His Books*. Of course, one wouldn't need specialized medical knowledge to make the sorts of generalizations that Erasmus does about the humors. For an overview, see Simone Mammola, "Erasmus and Medicine," *Journal of Interdisciplinary History of Ideas* 3, no. 6 (2014); and further Yasmin Haskell, "The Well-Tempered Career: Erasmus on the Emotional Health of Scholars," *Erasmus Studies* 42, no. 2 (2022): 101–21.

73. See esp. Cohen-Hanegbi, *Caring for the Living Soul*, ch. 3, where some physicians are discussed who prescribe material treatment aimed at alleviating the symptoms of humoral disorders (although others prescribed models similar to "behavioral therapy" to resolve emotional problems, where the treatment was aimed at the mind rather than the body).

74. CWE 66:45; LB 15C: Quaedam corporis habitum comitantur, sicut sanguineos mulierositas, et voluptatum amor: Cholericum ira, ferocitas, maledicentia: Phlegmaticum inertia, somnolentia: Melancholicum invidia, tristitia, amaritudo.

thinner spirits, does that necessarily make me less bold?"[75] The answer to both questions is no. The lengthiest passage appears in his sermon on Psalm 4 (1525), where there is a substantive discussion, with reference to anonymous "doctors," of what the Psalmist could have meant by "enlarge" (*dilatasti*) in Psalm 4:1 ("when I was in distress, thou hast enlarged me"). There Erasmus writes about the impact emotions might have on the body and vice versa and, after quoting Prov 17:22 ("A joyful mind makes for a healthy life, but a gloomy spirit dries up the bones"):

> If we believe the doctors, the spirits are of great importance in the health or decay of the body; if they are constricted and confined, they weaken the body; if they are sufficiently lively and well dispersed they keep it healthy, but if they boil up too quickly they bring sudden death. There are a number of historical examples of people expiring as a result of sudden and unexpected joy, while it is not unusual for people to fade away gradually as a result of grief. The doctors explain that joy opens up the channels through which the spirits pass, and grief shuts them down. Thus it happens that when excessive joy expands the channels more than usual, the spirits fly out all at once and bring sudden death; on the other hand, when the spirits are constricted they slowly squeeze out life from the body. The conditions which cause lethargy in the human body are like those which cause greed in the human heart, when love has grown cold. On the other hand, it is excessive heat which brings on raving madness, for example in a mind which, burning with the fire of hell, plans the death of a brother, or in a tongue which, as James said, is inflamed by the same fire to speak evil of a fellow man without cause.[76]

This represents an attempt to gloss a tricky term from the Vulgate, and while it contains scattered references to medical nomenclature, it does not represent a straightforward humoral account whereby one's emotions can be explained according to a hydraulic model. It is an emotion, joy, or grief, which has effects on the body's "channels," dilating or constricting them, but it is not clear whether those emotions precede or follow another bodily movement. And in the subsequent examples, Erasmus resorts to metaphor to explain the ambiguity of heat, comparing a physiological ailment (lethargy) with the analogy of love growing cold, and (conversely) invoking the fire of hell which might pervade the mind of a murderer.

Other examples are scattered throughout Erasmus's corpus. In the *Lingua* of 1525, Erasmus writes, in the vein of the *Enchiridion*, that "it seems that no one can control his tongue until he has accustomed his emotions (*motus animi*) to obey his reason." This is a special problem, apparently, for the choleric person: "We see that

---

75. CWE 70:34. Si mihi plus calidi sanguinis, si spiritus crassiores indidit natura, num ideo fortior ero? Rursus, si sanguinem frigidiorem, parciorem, si spiritus tenues addidit, num illico minus ego gnavus? (LB 1274E).

76. CWE 63:228–9.

men of excessive bile often have the experience that when they have resolved either to keep silence or reply most moderately, anger arises like a hurricane and breaks away the helm, sweeping their tongue into every kind of abuse. Uncontrollable joy does the same thing, or uncontrollable grief, fear, or hope."[77] The person who has achieved moderation of the emotions, Erasmus continues, will also be able to moderate the tongue. But Erasmus immediately, again, divorces the embodied humoral problem from the emotional one: "Just as it is futile to advise a lunatic to 'Walk like this, straighten your clothes, and control your features like this,' until you have first driven out his bile by drugs and brought about a different physical condition, so you will warn to no effect a man dominated by ambition, anger, pride, greed, lust, jealousy, love, and hatred, a man tormented by hope or fear, the special tyrants of human life," unless you convince him to bridle his emotions with reason.[78] *Corporis habitus* is contrasted here, in terms of the subject of treatment, with *motus animi*. Thus, the remedy for emotions that are out of balance— even if on account of some complexional complications—is psychological, not physiological. As in the *Enchiridion*, Erasmus frames the regulation of *affectus* in the *Lingua* under the order of reason as a form of self-knowledge, but here he cites the Pythian oracle, and then adduces the example of Socrates as one who has so universally subdued all his emotions and bodily affections that he might properly be referred to as ἀπαθής.[79] (This is a term, it might be noted, that Erasmus uses pejoratively to describe the Stoic sage in his colloquy "Lover of Glory," as well as to describe the frigid style of Thomas Aquinas—actually Thomas *Aristotelicus*—in the *Ciceronianus*.[80]) With Socrates himself, Erasmus is most impressed, it seems, by his ability to reign in his bodily appetites (hunger and thirst, for example), but he goes on to describe anger, pleasure, and love (*ira, voluptas et amor*) as particularly

---

77. CWE 27:387; ASD IV-1, 350: ubi videtur illud in genere praecipiendum, neminem posse temperare linguam, nisi qui motus animi consueferit obtemperare rationi. Videmus enim hoc usu venire his qui bilem habent immoderatam, ut quum certo statuerint aut obticescere, aut moderatissime respondere, tamen ira ceu turbo quidam insurgens excusso clavo rapiat linguam in omne conviciorum genus. Idem efficit impotens gaudium, aut dolor, aut metus, aut spes.

78. CWE 27:388; ASD IV-1, 351: Quemadmodum enim frustra moneas phreneticum, sic incede, sic compone vestem, sic moderare vultum, ni prius pharmacis expurgaris bilem, et alium corporis habitum induxeris: sic in vanum moneas cui dominature ambitio, ira, superbia, avarita, libido, zelotypia, amor, odium, quem excruciat spes, aut metus praecipui humanae vitae tyranni. Sic loquere, sic moderare linguam, nisi prius persuaseris, ut rebelles animi motus rationis freno coherceat.

79. ASD IV-1, 351: Non sine causa laudatur a multis Socratis patientia, qui praeter naturam omnes affectus, multa vi multaque consuetudine sic domuerat ac cicuraverat, ut prosus ἀπαθής videri posset.

80. Thomas Aristotelicus prorsus est, ἀπαθής in dicendo, tantum hoc agens, ut doceat lectorem. (ASD I-2, 660). For the colloquy, see CWE 40:966.

potent emotions in need of restraint, invoking Homer, Plautus, Plutarch, and Jesus along the way.[81]

What do we take away from the fact that Erasmus was clearly aware, at least to some extent, of ancient and contemporary medical and other natural-philosophical ideas about the emotions and the body, but that he usually eschewed them in favor of literary, philosophical, and theological explanations and advice? One easy answer is that Erasmus was a literary scholar and theologian, not a physician, and that literary, moral-philosophical, and theological forms of discourse about emotion were more attractive or ready at hand. The fact that such competing discourses exist is itself noteworthy, of course, and is another feature of humanist approaches to emotion. Relatedly, Brian Cummings and Freya Sierhuis have suggested that the "bodily turn" in cultural history and the related, and at least partially simultaneous, tendency to pathologize emotional states in modern scientific, literary, and historical discourse, at times results in an overly simple account of conceptions of emotion and subjectivity in early modern thought.[82] In other words, our own presuppositions about affectivity may lead us, if we are not careful, to misread texts from the past by assuming that medical explanations would have been obviously authoritative. Likewise, Erin Sullivan has sought to recover a spiritually oriented hermeneutic from seventeenth-century autobiographers describing melancholy, who, "even when they did acknowledge physiological influences they rarely if ever emphasized them above theological concerns."[83] Indeed, Sullivan reveals the emphases on the "disembodied" emotions of grief, despair, and sadness in seventeenth-century religious writings, which lie in contrast to the medical emphases on physiological movements. These accounts go some way toward explaining Erasmus's approach as well: he seemed to think that medical and/or humoral explanations were at times relevant, but generally not as useful as other ways of thinking about affectivity.

Foolish Feeling

Erasmus's *Moriae Encomium*, or *Praise of Folly*, first published in Paris in 1511, is yet again a rather different sort of work from either the *Enchiridion* or the *De taedio Iesu*. It is an ironic encomium, subversive and erudite, written in the voice of personified Folly herself. It is often impossible to know when Erasmus means what Folly says. And yet it contains multiple references to ancient philosophies of feeling that reveal another dimension of an Erasmian emotional style. The text has many rhetorical postures and tones of voice, but two important ones are the satirical, where Folly lays claim to all the reprehensible things in the world but attempts

---

81. See ASD IV-1, 351.
82. *Passions and Subjectivity in Early Modern Culture*, introduction.
83. Erin Sullivan, *Beyond Melancholy: Sadness and Selfhood in Early Modern England* (Oxford: Oxford University Press, 2016), 136.

to redeem them ironically (idiots have more fun), and the closing of the text where Folly identifies herself (somewhat more seriously) with a kind of affective Christian-Platonist mysticism. In both parts the emotions play a fundamental, if quite different, role.

The first substantive digression on emotion occurs when Folly embraces the emotions, eschewing reason, and provides a Ciceronian definition of the Stoic sage, whose doctrine of *apatheia* is pitted against the foolish feelings of the majority of humanity, ruled as it is by anger and sexual desire:

> By Stoic definition wisdom means nothing else but being ruled by reason; and folly, by contrast, is being swayed by the dictates of the emotions. So Jupiter, not wanting man's life to be wholly gloomy and grim, has bestowed far more passion than reason—you could reckon the ratio as twenty-four to one. Moreover, he confined reason to a cramped corner of the head and left all the rest of the body to the passions. Then he set up two raging tyrants in opposition to reason's solitary power: anger, which holds sway in the breast and so controls the heart, the very source of life, and lust, whose empire spreads far and wide, right down to the genitals.[84]

Erasmus's resources for understanding emotion came from a wide reading of ancient sources, and while we've seen that Erasmus used Ficino's Latin Plato directly, Cicero provided another conduit for Stoic-Academic ideas. In Cicero's *Tusculan Disputations*, for example, we find the following passage that contains ideas echoed here and in the *Enchiridion* by Erasmus:

> Now, what the Greeks call the πάθη, I prefer to translate as "emotions," rather than "sicknesses." In treating of these emotions, I shall preserve the familiar distinction made long ago by Pythagoras and later by Plato. They make a division of the mind into two parts, one of which has a share in reason, while the other does not. In the part which has a share in reason they put tranquillity (that is, a calm and quiet consistency); in the other, the turbulent motions of anger and desire, which are opposed to reason and inimical to it.[85]

---

84. CWE 27:95; ASD IV-3, 90: Etenim cum Stoicis definitoribus nihil aliud sit sapientia quam duci ratione, contra stulticia affectuum arbitrio moveri, ne plane tristis ac tetrica esset hominum vita, Iupiter quanto plus indidit affectuum quam rationis? Quasi semiunciam compares ad assem. Praeterea rationem in angustum capitis angulum relegavit, reliquum omne corpus perturbationibus reliquit. Deinde duos quasi tyrannos violentissimos uni opposuit: iram quae praecordiorum arcem obtinet atque adeo ipsum vitae fontem, cor, et concupiscentiam, quae ad imam usque pubem latissime imperium occupat.

85. *Tusc. Disp.* IV.10; qtd. in Margaret Graver, *Cicero on the Emotions: Tusculan Disputations 3 and 4* (University of Chicago Press, 2009), 43. See also the doctoral thesis, Javier Gomez Gil, *La Retorica del Vir Bonus: El Ethos del Orador y Los Lenes Adfectus en el De Oratore de Ciceron* (Universidad Zaragosa, 2015).

The Greek term *pathē* is used by both philosophers and rhetoricians to describe the more violent types of feeling for Cicero, and this is typical of Erasmus's usage as well. In the *Ciceronianus*, too (Erasmus's dialogue composed against the hardline Ciceronian rhetoricians of his day), Erasmus has Bulephorus make reference to the tragic emotions, which "the rhetoricians call *pathē*," a reference that could just as easily be ascribed to Quintilian as to Cicero. The division of the soul into two parts, governed respectively by anger and desire, is likewise adopted by Folly for her definition of Stoic psychology, and it is extrapolated into a judgment on humankind more generally.

The delineation of affective psychology in the *Moria* serves, of course, the opposite purpose when compared with invocations of ancient philosophy in the *Enchiridion*, and it is not the only instance where Folly disparages the Stoics as buzzkills. Later in the text, Folly again claims the *affectus* for herself, in this case with a seemingly more direct criticism of Stoicism; it's worth quoting the passage at length:

> First of all, it's admitted that all the emotions belong to Folly, and this is what marks the wise man off from the fool; he is ruled by reason, the fool by his emotions. That is why the Stoics segregate all emotions from the wise man, as if they were diseases. But in fact these emotions not only act as guides to those hastening towards the haven of wisdom, but also wherever virtue is put into practice they are always present to act like spurs and goads as incentives towards good deeds. Yet this is hotly denied by that double-dyed Stoic Seneca who strips his wise man of every emotion. In doing so he leaves nothing at all of the man, and has to fabricate in his place a new sort of god who never was and never will be in existence anywhere. Indeed, if I may be frank, what he created was a kind of marble statue of a man, devoid of sense and any sort of human feeling.[86]

Erasmus provides a more caricatured portrait of the Stoic sage—modeled after Seneca who in his *Epistulae morales* in fact distinguishes *morbi animi* from *affectus*[87]—here than he does in either the *Enchiridion* or *De taedio*, and so we know that the embellishment serves a rhetorical purpose. It's also comedic: the

---

86. CWE 27:104; ASD IV-3, 106: Iam primum illud in confesso est, affectus omnes ad stulticiam pertinere, quandoquidem hac nota a stulto sapientem discernunt, quod illum affectus, hunc ratio temperat; eoque Stoici perturbationes omnes ceu morbos a sapiente semovent. Verum affectus isti non solum paedagogorum vice funguntur ad sapientiae portum properantibus, verumetiam in omni virtutis functione cei calcaria stimulique quidam adesse solent, velut ad bene agendum exhortatores. Quanquam hic fortiter reclamat bis Stoicus Seneca, qui prorsum omnem affectum adimit sapienti. Verum cum id facit, iam ne hominem quidem relinquit, sed novum potius deum quendam *demiourgei*, qui nusquam nec extitit unquam, nec extabit; imo, ut apertius dicam, marmoreum hominis simulacrum constituit, stupidum et ab omni prorsus humano sensu alienum.

87. See *Ep. mor.* 75.11–12.

wise person as a *simulacrum hominis*, totally devoid of feeling, is only a dream. At the same time, the parodied Stoic sage is not an ideal model, and Erasmus has thus sandwiched in an Aristotelian ethical gloss on emotions as pedagogues and spurs to do good deeds (*ad bene agendum exhortatores*), a line which has no comedic value but is in line with the rejection of Stoic rigidity we have seen elsewhere. Folly continues her riff on the Stoic sage:

> Well, if that's what they like, they can enjoy their wise man, love him without a rival, live with him in Plato's Republic or in the kingdom of Ideas, if they prefer, or else in the gardens of Tantalus. Who wouldn't flee in terror from a man like that as a monstrous apparition, deaf as he is to all natural feelings, and no more moved by love or pity or any emotions "than if hard flint or Parian rock stands fixed"?[88]

Like the consistent practitioner of *apatheia*, the philosopher devoid of all emotion, the ideal republic and the gardens of Tantalus are also non-existent.

There are numerous references to Plato and the Platonists in the *Moria*, too, but the most relevant for our purposes comes in the final act, as it were, when Folly compares the Christian philosophy to Platonism because they share a desire for the soul to escape the body and ascend to enraptured contemplation of God. After making a distinction between the five bodily senses, which are "more crass" than the memory, intellect, and will—because the latter are farther removed from the body (*magis a corpore semoti*)—Erasmus describes the emotions:

> Again, take the affections of the soul (*affectibus animi*). Some have more traffic with the grossness of the body, such as lust, desire for food and sleep, anger, pride, and envy, and on these the pious wage unceasing war, while the crowd thinks life is impossible without them. Then there are what we could call intermediate affections (*affectus medii*), which are quasi-natural to all, like love for one's country, and affection for children, parents, and friends. The crowd sets great store by these, yet the pious strive to root them too from their soul, or at least to sublimate them to the highest region of the soul. They wish to love their father not as a father, for he begot nothing but the body, and this too is owed to God the Father, but as a good man and one in whom is reflected the image of the supreme mind, which alone they call the *summum bonum* and beyond which they declare nothing is to be loved or sought.[89]

---

88. CWE 27:104, modified. Proinde si libet ipsi sup sapiente fruantur citraque rivalem ament licet cumque eo vel in civitate Platonis vel, si malint, in idearum regione vel in Tantaliis inhabitent hortis. Quis enim non istiusmodi hominem ceu portentum ac spectrum fugitet horreatque, qui ad omnes naturae sensus obsurduerit, qui nullis sit affectibus, nec amore nec misericordia magis commoveatur, *quam si dura silex, aut stet Marpesia cautes.*

89. CWE 27:152; ASD IV-3, 200: Rursum in affectibus animi quidam plus habent cum pingui corpore commercii, veluti libido, cibi somnique appetentia, iracundia, superbia,

The division found here is akin to what we saw in the *Enchiridion*, as is the reference to the *affectus naturales* as a middle way, neither sinful per se but also not virtuous in the highest order. Love of God as the *summum bonum* is then implied to be the sort of *affectus* that is striven for by the pious, but only truly achieved once the soul has left the body. Erasmus then returns to the topic of madness as a form of affective departure from the body, with references to the ordinarily insane who—on account of their half-way status between earth and heaven—wax between joy and dejection, between tears and laughter. They are happiest (*felicissimos*) when they are truly foolish (*desiperent*).[90] The digression on insane joy at the end of the *Moria*, which simultaneously reiterates the Platonic division of reason and emotion as well as the tripartite Pauline anthropology of the *Enchiridion,* while elevating a kind of ecstatic affectivity above reason, effectively concludes the encomium.

The purpose of this chapter has been to chart the ancient philosophical resources that underpin Erasmus's discussions of emotion in three major works, in order to demonstrate further the diversity of his source base as well as the malleability of his approach. The definitive, if not final, version of the *Praise of Folly* was published in 1515, just before Erasmus's career turned definitively toward biblical scholarship. Brian Cummings has suggested that Erasmus's "affective turn" came during the late-teens, that is, in the years coming directly behind the *Moria*. How hard the turn is, especially given the variegated nature of the approach to affectivity in Erasmus's works from the first decade and a half of the sixteenth century, is a question worth keeping in mind. Certainly the more rote expressions of anti-affective rationalism evinced at times above are, generally speaking, left behind, as Erasmus begins his work in earnest on the New Testament. Indeed, by 1530, Erasmus could write to Pieter Gillis about emotion in a way that feels rather distant from the *Enchiridion*:

> Nowadays anyone who chose to stand stubbornly by the Stoic doctrine of *apatheia* would even be considered a heretic. For joy, grief, hope, fear, love, hate, benevolence, pity are unquestionably emotions [*affectus*], and yet throughout the sacred writings they are used of men living not just according to the flesh but according to the spirit, they are also used of Christ, indeed they are even used of the divine nature. . . . Do we not read in the Gospel that the Lord exulted in spirit, shouted in anger, wept, was indignant and moved to pity? And the word

---

invidia; cum his irreconciliabile bellum piis, contra vulgus sine his vitam esse non putat. Deinde sunt quidam affectus medii quasique naturales, ut amor patriae, charitas in liberos, in parentes, in amicos. His vulgus nonnihil tribuit. At illi hos quoque student ex animo revellere, nisi quatenus ad summam illam animi partem assurgunt, ut iam parentem ament non tanquam parentem (quid enim ille genuit, nisi corpus? quanquam hoc ipsum deo parenti debetur) sed tanquam virum bonum et in quo luceat imago summae illius mentis, quam unam summum bonum vocant et extra quam nihil nec amandum nec expectendum esse praedicant.

90. ASD IV-3, 194.

affectus encompasses all these movements of the soul. . . . And are not joy and love attributed to the angels, even though they are incorporeal?[91]

While the ancient philosophical underpinnings described in this chapter are never fully forsaken by Erasmus, and while he had never been consistently negative in his assessment of affectivity, the next phase of his career is preoccupied with religious and biblical emotion. In the following chapter, we will pursue the significance of Erasmus's New Testament scholarship, and specifically Paul's writings, to elucidate his understanding of religious emotion.

91. Ep 2260.

Chapter 4

BIBLICAL EMOTIONS I

AFFECTIVE THEOLOGY AND THE NEW TESTAMENT

In a series of proclamations around the publication of his revolutionary *Novum instrumentum* of 1516, the first critical edition of a Greek New Testament, accompanied by Erasmus's new Latin translation, Erasmus argues that the very discipline of theology ought to be fundamentally emotional. In his *Methodus*, one of several paratexts Erasmus wrote to accompany the first edition, he writes, "the profession of theology abides in the emotions rather than in clever arguments," a signal to the importance of affectivity over dry and tedious intellectualism.[1] Likewise in the *Paraclesis*, another of Erasmus's prologues to the New Testament, he writes, "This kind of philosophy [i.e., the Christian kind] sits more truly in the emotions than in syllogisms, more in life than in disputation, more properly in inspiration than in erudition, and more in transformation than in reason."[2] The biblical text, the word of God, is the fundamental conduit for such transformation, of course, and God himself in condescending into *Logos*, or *Sermo*, in John 1:1, did so "so that he might wind his way into our emotions" (*in affectus nostros insinuaret*).[3] Similar examples could be reproduced from across Erasmus's works, especially given his assiduous anti-scholastic rhetoric which hinges on depicting school theology as frigid, but these should suffice to show that it will be worth exploring how exactly Erasmus imagined theology, and biblical theology in particular, to subsist in engaging and shaping Christians' emotions. While we have glanced at the centrality of affectivity to Erasmus's religious thought, our discussion thus far has focused primarily on the pagan resources of his understanding of emotion. The purpose of this chapter is to show how his New Testament scholarship and exegesis allow for different ways

---

1. "[P]rofessio Theologica magis constat affectibus quam argutiis" (*Desiderius Erasmus Roterdamus: Ausgewählte Werke*, ed. Annemarie Holborn and Hajo Holborn (Munich: Beck, 1964), 187.
2. My translation. "Hoc philosophiae genus in affectibus situm verius quam in syllogismis vita magis est quam disputatio, afflatus potius quam eruditio, transformatio magis quam ratio" (ASD V-7, 293).
3. LB VII 499E.

(largely more positive) of describing affectivity, given the nature of the sources themselves. The first part of the chapter on the "Paratextual Passions" considers primarily the *Ratio*, Erasmus's most detailed treatise on theological method, with reference, where appropriate, to the *Annotations* and *Paraphrases* on New Testament texts; in the second part, the "Pauline Passions," I will show how—in his letters, his exegetical works on the New Testament, and in his dispute with Martin Luther over free will—Erasmus's understanding of affectivity was shaped by Paul's letters but also shaped his interpretation of them.

Paratextual Passions

In the second edition of the *Methodus*, revamped and vastly expanded into a standalone treatise called the *Ratio seu methodus*, which was published independently in 1518 and then appended to the second (1519) edition of the *Novum Testamentum*, Erasmus writes, "The chief goal of theologians is to explain prudently divine literature, to give an account of the faith and not of frivolous questions, to discourse seriously and effectually on godliness, to elicit tears, to set our souls aflame for heavenly things."[4] Eliciting tears and setting souls aflame is contrasted in the text here with "practising exercises in dialectic and philosophy," a familiar Erasmian dig at scholastic theological method which, to his mind, was ineffective precisely because of its lack of emotional engagement. Erasmus is attempting to carve out a new approach to theology altogether, or at least to argue for an alternative method that rivals the theology of the schools, and one that fundamentally engages the emotions. Moreover, Erasmus here uses the terms *enarrare* and *disserere*: the method lies in language, in a discourse that arises from appropriately attuned affectivity in the writer or speaker, but also one that successfully moves its readers and hearers. The close connection between theological discourse (including preaching) and a certain brand of affective piety is also a fundamental aspect of what Erasmus called the *philosophia Christiana*, and not unlike what Charles Trinkaus first designated *theologia rhetorica*, a heuristic he found useful for describing the approach of some of Erasmus's Italian humanist predecessors.[5] I have argued elsewhere that history of emotions

---

4. Mark Vessey (ed.), *Erasmus on Literature: His* Ratio *or "System" of 1518/1519* (Toronto: University of Toronto Press, 2021), 130. "At praecipuus Theologorum scopus est, sapienter enarrare divinas litteras: de fide, non de frivolis quaestionibus rationem reddere: de pietate graviter atque efficaciter disserere: lacrymas excutere, ad coelestia inflammare animos" (LB V 83-4). For the history of the text, see the introduction in CWE 41, and the essay by Mark Vessey in *Erasmus on Literature* (ibid.). The February 1520 Froben (Basel) edition was itself almost 220 pages long.

5. See Charles Trinkaus, *In Our Image and Likeness: Humanity and Divinity in Italian Humanist Thought*, 2 vols. (University of Notre Dame Press, 1995), 126-8, and 306-7, e.g. We are perhaps better served, at this point, in speaking instead of "rhetorical theologies," as

research has shown how we might extend the concept of rhetorical theology to meaningfully describe various theological trends over the course of the Middle Ages as well—that Erasmus is indebted to a long and complex series of affective-theological traditions, the main thrust of which is an insistence upon a movement of the heart in order for Christian teaching to truly take place.[6] Erasmus articulates the importance of such an approach in a variety of ways and places, some more subtle than others. But the denunciations of the frigidity of scholastic dialectic, as seen earlier, and its consequent impropriety for theological discourse, persist as the broad contours of his approach to developing an affective theology.

We have seen, for example, that Erasmus refers to Thomas Aquinas, the scholastic theologian par excellence, as ἀπαθής, as one who teaches (*docere*) but does not move (*movere*). Erasmus traces the "apathetic" nature of scholastic method back to its ancient origins as well. In a 1530 letter to Balthasar Merklin, itself an introduction to Erasmus's edition of Alger of Liege's treatise on the eucharistic doctrine of "real presence," Erasmus digresses on questions of style and emotional substance in theological method. The recent scholastics, he writes, are arid in proportion to how much they take pride in Aristotle: "It is true that Aristotle dispensed with emotional effects [*affectus*] and stylistic ornaments, but he did so to produce a high degree of elegance, an accomplishment that is beyond the powers of these people." Nevertheless, Erasmus continues, it would be better to involve the affections in theology: "But it seems to me only fitting that, in explaining the mysteries of faith, we should seek by one means or another to achieve a certain dignity of language and that one's feelings (*affectus*) should not be hidden. For in this way not only will the reader understand what he is being taught by his teacher, but come to love what his teacher loves."[7] Erasmus doesn't elaborate on this point any further, but it's clear enough that the idea is

---

it is evident that humanist approaches to theology as a fundamentally rhetorical enterprise are not in every way uniform. The relationship between rhetoric and theology has been the focus of extensive scholarship in Erasmus studies, and a full bibliography is not possible here, but see, for example, Marjorie O'Rourke Boyle, *Erasmus on Language and Method in Theology* (Toronto: University of Toronto Press, 1977); idem, *Rhetoric and Reform: Erasmus's Civil Dispute with Luther* (Cambridge, MA: Harvard University Press, 1983); Manfred Hoffmann, *Rhetoric and Theology: The Hermeneutics of Erasmus* (Toronto: University of Toronto Press, 1994); Jacques Chomarat, *Grammaire et Rhetorique chez Erasme* (Paris, 1981); Brian Cummings, *Grammar and Grace: The Literary Culture of the Reformation* (Oxford: Oxford University Press, 2002).

6. Kirk Essary, "Rhetorical Theology and the History of Emotions," in *The Routledge History of Emotions in Europe, 1100–1700*, ed. Susan Broomhall and Andrew Lynch (Routledge, 2020), 86–101.

7. CWE 16:222. Allen Ep 2284: At nescio quo pacto mihi decere videtus, ut in mysteriis explicandis adsit quaedam orationis dignitas nec absit affectus. Ita demum fit ut lector non solum intelligat quod a docto docetur, verumetiam amet quod ab amante traditur.

that the fullest pedagogical experience for the Christian involves feeling. "Mere" knowledge is insufficient.

The purpose of the *Ratio* is to provide a theological method grounded in biblical hermeneutics, in the appropriate way of reading and teaching the Bible, which for Erasmus always also includes first transforming how one lives. As mentioned, Brian Cummings has thus argued that we find an "affective turn" in the development of Erasmus's biblical hermeneutics in this period of his career, and one "which he identifies in the Epistles of Paul almost as much as he does in the Gospels." We will examine Erasmus's development of specifically Pauline ideas about the emotions later; for now it is crucial to recognize that, as Cummings puts it, "Reading Scripture is like an education of the emotions, teaching us everything from trust in ourselves, to shame and remorse."[8] The biblical text not only teaches us how to indulge in or regulate certain emotions, but also, in virtue of its own discursive idiosyncrasies, it shows theologians how to practice their discipline with a specific emotional style.

This training occurs at general and specific levels. At the general level, Erasmus encourages the prospective theologian thus: "Let this be your first and only goal, this your prayer, attend to this alone, that you be changed, be swept away, be inspired, be transformed into what you are learning. The food of the soul is useful not if it remains in the memory as in the stomach, but only if it penetrates into the affections themselves and into the very viscera of the mind."[9] Anticipating a series of affective metaphors of digestion that will appear in his Psalms commentaries (treated in the next chapter), Erasmus writes that the *affectus* and the *viscera mentis* are the organs of digestion (of teaching), which must fully absorb Christian doctrine so that the reader herself becomes a different person altogether. Reinier Leushuis has shown how Erasmus utilizes this way of thinking in his *Paraphrases* of the New Testament; for example, regarding the paraphrase of James 1:19-21, "we learn that for Erasmus the believer's inner affective domain is independent from, but can be negatively influenced by worldly emotions, or passions."[10] Glossing James, Erasmus contrasts *cupiditates* (anger and lust, for example) with the gospel itself which subsides in the very center of the heart (*subsidat in cordis*

---

8. Brian Cummings, "Erasmus, Sacred Literature, and Literary Theory," in *Erasmus on Literature*, ed. Mark Vessey (Toronto, 2021), 61–2.

9. CWE 41:494–5. Hic primus et unicus tibi sit scopus, hoc votum, hoc unum age, ut muteris, ut rapiaris, ut affleris, ut transformeris in ea quae discis: animi cibus est, ita demum utilis, non si in memoria ceu stomacho subsidat, sed si in ipsos affectus, et in ipsa mentis viscera traiiciatur.

10. Reinier Leushuis, "Poetics or Homiletics? Hearing and Feeling the New Testament in Erasmus's *Paraphrases*," *Erasmus Studies* 40, no. 2 (2020): 113. This article has several excellent examples of the ways in which Erasmus blends the imagery of feeling, hearing, and touching in his NT paraphrases.

penetralia).[11] True gospel teaching has the capacity to displace sinful emotions, transforming a depraved heart into a spiritual one.

The wider context of the partial quote from the *Ratio* with which we opened this chapter is also germane, but more specific. It comes in a longer discussion where Erasmus recommends to the teacher the use of classical literary figures (the student of theology must be familiar with these, not least because of the usefulness of allegorical interpretation) as well as the familiar distinction between *ethos* and *pathos*, in this instance credited to Aristotle:

> You might, for example, apply the story of Tantalus to the rich man brooding over and gaping at his wealth, and yet not enjoying it, or the story of Phaethon to the dangerous temerity of one who assumes a magistracy though he is unsuited to bearing office.[12] There should also be practice in fables, in comparisons . . . further, and with respect to rhetoric, [one should treat] those parts especially that treat "essential questions," propositions, proofs, amplifications . . . and that discuss the twin emotions, one of which the gentler, is called *ethē*, the other, more severe, is called *pathē*—about these no one wrote more carefully than Aristotle.[13] For practical knowledge of these things especially determines judgment, something that is of particular importance in every kind of study. And since the theological profession rests rather on emotions than on clever arguments, which even in pagan philosophers the pagans themselves ridicule, and Paul denounces in a Christian—and in more than one place—it will be well to be vigorously practised in this field throughout youth.[14]

---

11. See ibid. 113n31; LB VII 1123C-D.

12. NB: Erasmus himself uses the example of Phaethon as a parallel to a ruler losing control of their emotions in his commentary on Psalm 2 (see CWE 63:138).

13. The Quintilianesque gloss and the reference to Aristotle were not present in the *Methodus*, but added in the 1518 version of the *Ratio*.

14. CWE 41:505–6. Veluti si Tantali fabulam accomodes ad divitem, incubantem et inhiantem opibus suis, nec tamen fruentem. Si Phaetontis, ad periculosam termeritatem suscipientis magistratum, qui magistratui gerendo non sit idoneus. Idem fiat in Apologis, in Similibus, de quibus a nobis nonnihil est proditum. Tum in his praecipue partibus rhetorices, quae tractant de statibus, de propositionibus, de probationibus, de amplificationibus, de quibus accuratissime tractat Fabius: denique geminis affectibus, alteris quos *ethē* vocant, mitioribus: alteribus acrioribus, quos *pathē* dicunt, de quibus nemo diligentius scriptist Aristotele: quod harum rerum peritia maiorem in modum faciat ad iudicium, quae res in omni studiorum genere valet plurimum. Et quoniam professio Theologica magis constat affectibus quam argutiis, quas in ethnicis quoque philosophis ipsi rident ethnici, Paulus in Christiano detestatus, idemque non uno in loco: convenient non segniter per aetatem in hoc geneer exerceri, quo postea dexterius in theologicis allegoriis, locique communibus tractandis versari possit (*Ratio* [Basel: Froben, 1520], 30).

Not only does Erasmus offer examples of emotion in mythographic shorthand, but he refers to the "twin emotions" (*geminis affectibus*), which, together with other matters of pedagogical import, are to be used in constructing a new kind of theological discourse to replace the old one (dialectic), which Erasmus goes on to refer to as flat, frigid, and lifeless.[15]

The linguistic style of the biblical text is itself inherently emotionally powerful: "A parable is effectual," Erasmus writes, "not only for teaching and persuading but also for stirring the emotions, for alluring with its charm, for bringing clarity, for implanting one central idea deep within the mind, beyond the possibility of escape."[16] The parable of the prodigal son moves the mind vehemently (*vehementius afficit animum*), and strikes it more sharply (*acrius feriunt animum*) than if the lesson had been conveyed without the story.[17] Allegories are more effective in accommodating to the hearer, Erasmus writes, which in turn moves them more effectively, even if (somewhat paradoxically) they are often a difficult feature for the reader to comprehend without training.[18] Later, in the *Ecclesiastes*, Erasmus will argue that biblical allegory may even be tailored, by the Holy Spirit, to particular readers' feelings: "It is not absurd that the Holy Spirit also intended for Scripture sometimes to give rise to a variety of meanings according to each person's emotional disposition [*pro cuiusque affectu*], in the same way that manna had for each person the flavour that he desired; and this is not the uncertainty of Scripture but its fertility."[19] The affective malleability of scripture strengthens its power, while literary figures also teach how to regulate unwanted desires, as Erasmus suggests in the *Ratio*:

> If you state in a straightforward way that nothing is more peaceful, nothing more pleasant than a good conscience that evil desires no longer molest, the auditor will be sleepier than if you add the wrapping of allegory: Isaac was born to Abraham and Sarah only when Abraham's body was dead and it had ceased to be with Sarah after the manner of women.[20]

---

15. See CWE 41:507.

16. CWE 41:633; LB V 117B: Neque vero tantum ad docendum ac persuadendum efficax est parabola, verum etiam ad commovendos affectus, ad delectandum, ad perspicuitatem, ad eamdem sententiam, ne possit elabi, pernitus infigendam animo.

17. Ibid.

18. LB V 118A: vehementius commoverit auditores si accommodet allegoriam.

19. CWE 68:962; ASD V-5, 250: Nec absurdum est hoc quoque voluisse Spiritum sanctum, ut scriptura nonnumquam varios gignat sensus, pro cuiusque affectu: sicuti manna cuique sapiebat quod volebat. Nec haec est scripturarum incertitudo, sed fecunditas.

20. CWE 41:636; LB V 118A: Ad haec si simpliciter pronuncies, nihil esse tranquillius, nihil jucundius animo sibi bene conscio, cui non iam obstrepant malae cupiditates: magis dormitabit auditor, quam si addas allegoriae involucrum. Ex Abraham et Sara non nasci Isaac, nisi cum huic corpus esset emortuum, et illi desissent muliebria.

A litany of examples is provided in the text of the ways in which the merely didactic falls flat because of its lack of feeling, which may be remedied by literary devices.

In a discussion of Jesus's own emotions, judged as key evidence of his truly human nature but also as soteriologically significant, Erasmus writes: "What of the fact that not even his example would be sufficiently effective if what was done in Christ was not done with true feelings, but was a sort of stage play, merely fictional, presented to the eyes?"[21] The point, somewhat obliquely expressed here, I take to mean that if he hadn't actually felt, Christ's life as an ethical model and sacrifice in death would not be efficacious—an argument Erasmus had presented more forthrightly a decade and a half earlier in the *De taedio Iesu*. He continues, listing the emotions that Christ felt:

> We read that he often pities the crowd, as in the twentieth chapter of Matthew. In Mark, the third chapter, he is angry and grieves; in the eighth chapter of the same Gospel he groans in spirit. Again, in the twelfth chapter of John, long before the passion, he is troubled in mind; in the garden he suffers anguish of mind to the point of sweating bloody drops. On the cross he thirsts, the usual result of that kind of punishment. He weeps after looking upon the city of Jerusalem, and at the tomb of Lazarus he both weeps and is troubled in mind.[22]

In demonstrating his own susceptibility to emotion, Christ has rebuked generalized denunciations of emotion, as well as offered himself as an example of appropriate forms of feeling.

It is worth briefly considering how Erasmus interprets a few of these biblical episodes in other works, for he especially expands upon their emotional significance in his *Paraphrases*. Regarding pity in Matthew 20, the biblical scene is quite a compact one where two blind beggars ask Jesus three times to have mercy on and heal them, which he does. Erasmus, in his *Paraphrase of Matthew*, retains the Latin *misertus* ("pitied") from the Vulgate (the same word used in the *Ratio*) to describe Christ's feelings, which in Greek are described as σπλαχνίσθεις, a word whose root is used relatively often in the New Testament for having "compassion" and "mercy," and which literally means "bowels" or "viscera."[23] Erasmus also lengthens the scene

---

21. CWE 41:559; LB V 94F: Quid quod ne exemplum quidem sat efficax futurum erat, si quod in Christo gestum est, non veris affectibus gestum, sed ficta modo quaedam fabula obiecta sit oculis?

22. CWE 41:559-60; LB V 95A: Saepenumero legitur misertus turbae, veluti Matthaei capite vigesimo; apud Marcum capite tertio, irascitur et indolescit; apud eumdem capite octavo, ingemiscit spiritu; rursum Joannis capite duodecimo, multo ante passionem turbatur animo, in hortulo usque ad sanguineum sudorem angitur animo; in cruce sitit, quod ex more solet in eo supplicii genere accidere; flet, conspecta civitate Hierosolyma; flet et apud Lazari monumentum, et turbatur animo.

23. The term *viscera* is often used metaphorically for pity or compassion in the Christian tradition—no doubt in part because it translates versions of the Greek σπλάγχνον, whose

significantly in his *Paraphrase*. There, first, Jesus deliberately ignores the cries of the beggars for mercy so that "their faith and ardor [*fides et ardor*] would be more obvious to all." After the third time (of four in the *Paraphrase*) that the beggars yell at Jesus, he is satisfied that they've demonstrated their faith to the masses, as well as "taught us by their example that we must bombard the ears of God with fervent zeal and unwavering determination [*ferventer et constanter pulsandas aures dei*] if we want to obtain something."[24] After asking Jesus one more time, with great feeling—*magno dicunt affectu*—Jesus touches their eyes. And here Erasmus gives a full gloss of the Greek term: "showing by his very countenance and eyes the feeling of pity [*affectum misericordiae*], a feeling that befits every gospel person in grieving for others' misfortunes."[25] In all, Erasmus expands the original passage in his paraphrased version to heighten the emotional tone significantly. What Reinier Leushuis writes about Erasmus's hermeneutics of feeling for several other passages of his New Testament *Paraphrases* is applicable here as well: Faith in Christ as presented in the *Paraphrases* "is predicated on emotional experience guided by a sensorial perception that focuses on the role of touch and hearing."[26] In this case, the touching and hearing are for the benefit of the crowd as much as they are for the blind men—the crowd must hear the blind men yelling before Jesus acts—with the further lesson for the reader that they must often yell at God for mercy, all the result of a literary process Leushuis refers to as reader-oriented mimesis.

Erasmus does not comment in his *Annotations* on Jesus's anger in Mark 3:5, and his *Paraphrase* is not especially remarkable, although he does emphasize Jesus's feelings: He has Jesus look around at the Pharisees not simply with anger and

---

deponent verb form σπλαγχνίζομαι typically means "to have compassion." Erasmus often has it stand in for the emotions in general, which is also consonant with classical usage. On Phil. 1:8 (whose Greek reads σπλάγχνοις Χριστοῦ Ἰησοῦ) Erasmus retains the Vulgate's *in visceribus Iesu Christi*, but offers the gloss that "*viscera* signifies *affectum animi*" (ASD V-9, 276). This example again reinforces Erasmus's contention that *affectus* itself—and emotion more generally—has no inherent moral valence. At Ephesians 4:32, where the Greek reads εὔσπλαγχνοι, Erasmus writes, "This pertains not only to mercy but to every feeling of devotion (*pietatis affectum*), as though one were to say "good bowels" (*bonum viscerum*). For Sacred Scripture uses the bowels to mean feelings (*affectibus*)" (CWE 58:191). Likewise, at 2 Cor. 6:12, where *viscera* again translates σπλάγχνοις, Erasmus notes that this is what Paul calls his *affectibus* (*Ann. 2 Cor.* 6:12, on the lemma *Non angustiamini in nobis*).

24. CWE 45:289–90. Dissimulavit clamorem illorum Iesus, quo magis esset omnibus perspicua fides et ardor illorum . . . Iesus igitur ubi satis spectatam reddidisset omnibus illorum fidem, nos que illorum exemplo docuisset, ferventer et constanter pulsandas aures dei, si quid velimus impetrare, constitit (Basel: Froben [1524], 134).

25. CWE 45:289–90. Tum Iesus vultu quoque ipso et oculis prae se ferens affectum misericordiae, quo decet unum quenque virum Evangelicum indolescere malis alienis, tetigit oculos eorum (Basel: Froben [1524], 135).

26. Leushuis, "Poetics or Homiletics?" 120.

grief, but *cum ira quantoque dolore*—with great anger and sorrow.[27] Similarly, on the scene in John 12, where Jesus is contemplating his imminent arrest, Erasmus makes no comment in the *Annotations*, but after a lengthy digression about how Jesus's followers must push through the fear of punishment and death toward the bliss of everlasting life, Erasmus emphasizes Jesus's troubled mind with a series of rhetorical questions:

> In fact, I feel my own soul troubled at the approaching day of death. I see that a very severe storm threatens. What am I to say, or where shall I turn? Shall I heed the weakness of my body, which shudders at death? Shall I flee to the protection of the world? Shall I disregard the life of the world out of love for my own life? By no means. I shall fit myself to the Father's will. The weakness of my nature, troubled by the dread of death, will say to him, "Father, if it can be done, save me from this pressing danger of death."[28]

There are echoes here of the *De taedio*, a rendering of John's Jesus—the least "human" of all the gospels from the perspective of fearing death—in a "synoptic" mode, shuddering at death and recognizing his own psychological agony. Later in the *Ratio* Erasmus also seems to comment on this passage, rendering the scene into a classic instance of Christian *caritas*: "Now, in John, that whole scene in the presence of his disciples—what he says, what he does as the time of his death is approaching—what else does it signify, what else does it manifest except a fiery love intensely burning [*igneam ac flagrantissimam caritatem*]? Who is so unfeeling that he reads those words without tears?"[29] It might be noted that Erasmus typically uses *caritas* for love in a theological context, but as Robert Sider reminds us, the *Paraphrase* on John is preoccupied with the theme of love in particular, and in it Erasmus uses a variety of terms (*caritas, amor, dilectio*), and at one point Erasmus writes that God will render human affection (*affectus humanus*) into

---

27. Erasmus does offer a translation different from the Vulgate, ascribing to Jesus *iracundia* as opposed to *ira*, a somewhat surprising choice given that elsewhere Erasmus writes that *iracundia* is a *habitus* while *ira* is the *affectus*, a distinction drawn from Cicero and Quintilian. See, e.g., Erasmus ASD I-V, 219; and Cicero, *Tusc. Disp.* IV.XII.27; Quintilian, *Institutio oratoria* V, 10, 29: "temporarium animi motum, sicut iram, pavorem." The sense in the Gospel text is rather that Jesus was temporarily angry, at a particular situation.

28. CWE 46:154. Quin et mihi ob instantem mortis diem sentio turbatam animam. Video gravissimam tepestatem imminere. Quid dicam, aut quo me vertam? An obtemperabo corporis imbecillitati mortem horrentis? An ad mundi praesidia confugiam? An amore vitae meae, mundi vitam negligam? Nequamque. Ad patris voluntatem me accomodabo. Dicet illi naturae infirmitas, mortis horrore conturbata: Pater, si fieri potest, saluum me fac ex hoc instanti periculo mortis. Sed mox addet humanae salutis avida charitas (Basel: Froben [1524], 134).

29. CWE 41:598; LB V 106D: Quis tam saxeus est, ut illa legat absque lacrymis?

celestial love (*amor caelestis*).³⁰ Erasmus also developed the notion of Christ's human emotions while extensively paraphrasing the shortest verse in the Bible from the previous chapter, John 11:35, "Jesus wept." I have written on that segment of the paraphrase elsewhere (and on Jesus sweating blood in Gethsemane), but it is worth remarking here that Erasmus suggests that Jesus wept not over Lazarus's dead body, but because of anger at all the souls who were perishing through sin, and also (explicitly) in order to teach us how to regulate our own emotions with Christ as an ethical example.³¹

Returning to the *Ratio*, Erasmus also runs through a litany of the "earthly desires" (*cupiditates terrenas*) that Christ prepares his followers to eschew, not unlike the list offered in the epilogue to the *Enchiridion*, but in this case with extensive examples taken from biblical texts. It is the most direct example of how reading scripture for Erasmus can be, as Cummings puts it, an education in the emotions. While the examples are numerous, a few here will suffice. Christ stripped away, first of all, the *affectus* of luxury and sensual desire with the parable of the rich man and Lazarus: in Luke 16 the former begged for mercy from Hell while Lazarus, a poor leper, was carried by the angels to Abraham's bosom.³² Erasmus makes this explicit also in his paraphrase of the parable, adding to the original that the rich man was a slave to "ambition, luxury, and sensual pleasure."³³ Likewise, by teaching that the rich cannot enter the kingdom of heaven, Jesus wards off inevitable sorrow (*moerens*) for those who follow his teachings, unlike the man in Mark 10 who refused to sell everything he had and give it to the poor. Jesus also chastens the neutral emotions, such as love for parents and children (*parentum et cognationis affectum*), which might distract from zealous piety (*studio pietatis*).³⁴ He does so not only with prohibitions but by the example, primarily, of not being very nice to his own mother (!), proof that the natural human affections are not virtuous in themselves.

At times a particular affective vice needs to be inhabited before it can be expunged, as is the case with love of honor or ambition, and Erasmus runs through several Gospel stories that offer examples of how this might work. The Sons of Zebedee, he writes, suffered this feeling (*hoc affectu passus est*) in Matthew 20 when they asked to be seated on either side of Jesus in heaven, only to be told it wasn't up to him, which led to further strife among the disciples. In exhibiting extraordinary humility by washing his disciples' feet, Jesus shows that his life is a more effective doctrine (*doctrina efficacior*) even than his preaching against the love of honor, an emotion Erasmus describes as tumultuous, vengeful, and pugnacious.³⁵ To

---

30. CWE 41:245; Cf. CWE 46:171.

31. See Kirk Essary, *Erasmus and Calvin on the Foolishness of God: Reason and Emotion in the Christian Philosophy* (Toronto: University of Toronto Press, 2017), ch. 5, and idem. "'The Mind's Bloody Sweat,'" *Parergon* 38, no. 1 (2021): 41–64.

32. See CWE 41:580; Luke 16:19–31.

33. CWE 48:99; ASD VII-2, 404: ambitioni serviens et luxui, et voluptati.

34. CWE 41:518; LB V 101B.

35. LB V 102A.

extinguish violent rage (*saevitiae*), Erasmus writes that Christ gives many parables of moderation or forbearance (*clementia*), and calls his followers back to a disposition of gentleness (*revocat ad affectum mansuetudinis*).[36] He proceeds to give several examples of how Christ and Paul teach against the *affectus* of *fiducia nostri*, or trust in ourselves, which he says is an especially destructive disposition (*affectum noxium et pestilentem*). The biblical authors also reject the "strange power" of shame (*pudor*) through various examples (Jesus himself says he will be ashamed of those who are ashamed of him). Erasmus writes, moreover, that Christ offers reprieve from the seemingly ineradicable emotion of fear through a catalogue of instances (*metus, formido, terrere*).[37] And, contrasting emotions that ought to be avoided with those which should be cultivated, Erasmus finishes this section with a brief list of virtuous dispositions: love (*caritas*), gentleness (*animi lenitas*), simple prudence (*simplex prudentia*), and certain faith (*certissima fides*). After providing examples of faith and love as the central dispositions of Christ's teaching in the New Testament, Erasmus moves on in the *Ratio* to discuss the ways in which his disciples, and especially Paul, followed his example:

> What now is the point of bringing forward some passages concerning love, when all of Paul everywhere breathes, resounds, thunders with nothing but the most ardent love? His words are pure fire, and yet you might think when you read him that you feel something still more ardent that the stammering of human speech is not able to express. Paul's tongue is fiery, but it suggests rather than exhibits the burning in his breast.[38]

The deepest religious affections are ineffable. Let us turn, then, to look more closely at the ways in which Erasmus's Paul is an affective-rhetorical and theological model.

Pauline Passions

Paul is, unsurprisingly, second only to Christ as the ideal instructor of the Christian philosophy according to Erasmus. Like Christ he accommodates himself to his

---

36. LB V 102B.
37. CWE 41:592–3; LB V 104E-F.
38. CWE 41:605; LB V 108E: Iam de caritate quid attinet locos aliquot adducere, cum totus ubique Paulus nihil spiret, nihil crepet, nihil tonet, nisi flagrantissimam caritatem? Meras flammas loquitur, et tamen ardentius quiddam tibi sentire videare, cum legis quod humani sermonis balbuties non queat effari. Ignea Pauli lingua, sed pectoris incendium subindicat magis, quam explicit. Cf. CWE 64:56 (*Explanation of Psalm 85*): "Do the letters of Peter or of Paul contain anything base, anything earthly? Their speech is pure flame, it flashes with lightning and its thunder resounds through the heavens. Roused by their example, we should entreat the Lord to draw our souls to him, so that with this assistance we may lift out souls to him and obtain true joy from him who is the source of all joy."

interlocutors, shape-shifting as a Proteus, and like Christ (Erasmus uses identical phrasing), he ignites the most flagrant love (*flagrantissimam caritatem*). Paul engages the emotions extensively in ways that mirror Christ's teaching. In his letter addressed to the reader introducing the *Paraphrase of Matthew*, Erasmus writes of Christ that "he teaches, he terrifies, he threatens, he coaxes, he consoles."[39] Likewise of Paul, according to Erasmus in his commentary on Psalm 2: "At times he coaxes, pleads, and consoles with the tenderness of a mother; at others he threatens the disobedient with all the authority of the Apostle . . . Paul always prefers to use pleasant and soothing words, but sometimes he is obliged to grieve the hearts [*contristat animos*] of his audience."[40] Paul's rhetorical theology even abides, implicitly, the two-fold distinction of gentleness and vehemence derived from the classical tradition.

In the *Ratio*, after providing several examples of Paul's coaxing and pleading and consoling his various interlocutors in various ways, Erasmus writes, "But notice, reader, what a large admixture of gentleness is found even in the severity of Paul."[41] While a few examples of severity are given, Paul is primarily described here as gentle (the language is *lenitas, mansuetudine, melior, materculam*), and he is successful because of his calm approach.[42] Remember, Erasmus tells us, that he referred to Onesimus as a brother, even though he was in fact a fugitive slave:

> Now this affability is particularly effective in making one's way into human hearts. Thus those whose business it is to tame wild beasts first adapt themselves in every way to the nature and emotions [*ingenium et affectus*] of the beasts. So wine slips soothingly into a person's body, and spreading at once through all the veins, it unleashes its force and places the whole person under its power. Accordingly, Paul entices with praise those he wishes to amend.[43]

Again, the whole person is transformed via the *affectus*, represented metaphorically here by wine coursing through the veins, one of many digestive metaphors Erasmus deploys when describing the religious affections.

It is not the only time that Erasmus analyzes Paul according to this schema, although he does not always depict Paul as operating on the milder side of the

---

39. CWE 45:16.
40. CWE 63:115–16.
41. Sed adverte, lector, quantum ipsa etiam Pauli severitas lenitatis habet admixtum? (LB V 100A).
42. Erasmus modifies the Vulgate translation of the Greek *makrothumia* at Gal. 5:22 from *patientia* to *lenitas*.
43. CWE 41:575. LB V 99B: Est autem haec comitas in primis efficax, ad illabendum animis hominum. Sic qui feris cicurandis student, primum ad illarum ingenium et affectus per omnia sese accommodant: sic vinum blande illabitur in corpus hominis, ac mox diffusum per omnes venas, vim suam explicat, et totum hominem in suum ius rapit. Proinde laude illectat, quibus vult mederi.

affective-rhetorical spectrum. In 1529 Erasmus published a revised edition of the works of Seneca with Froben in Basel. And even though Erasmus knew that the ancient epistolary exchange between Seneca and the Apostle Paul was a forgery ("The claim to authorship is mistaken, but sometimes in human affairs some silly and worthless fiction assumes a surprising importance"[44]), he nevertheless included it in his edition, with a letter to the readers that contains comparisons between the styles of Seneca and Paul. One of the ways in which Erasmus adjudicates the forged nature of the correspondence is by noticing a lack of a certain kind of affectivity in the Pauline forgeries:

> Think of how much eloquence and emotion [*quanta copia, quanta affectus*] with which Paul writes to a certain Philemon on a commonplace matter. Are we to believe, then, that in writing to a famous man like Seneca on what is the most important subject of all—the acceptance of the Christian faith—he would have employed such a feeble and anaemic style?

The forger, Erasmus continues, "should at least have made some effort to copy Seneca's style and to borrow from Paul's epistles something of the intensity and sublimity [*vehementia et sublimitate*] of their language."[45] Here Paul does not convince with gentleness (*lenitas*) but with vehemence (*vehementia*). An example of Erasmian-Pauline vehemence is found in Erasmus's *Paraphrase of Ephesians*, where he indulges in a series of affective metaphors in Paul's voice:

> Finally, let your right hand always be armed with that spiritual sword which both lops off the soul's deformed desires as it penetrates to the inner recesses of the heart and repels those who resist evangelical truth as it slaughters falsehood so that truth may flourish. This is the word of God penetrating with the constant vigour of faith, not grazing with human twaddle, but rather smiting. For the human word is watered down, seeing that it discourses on matters that are without substance and in flux; but the word of God is efficacious, savouring only of what is heavenly, penetrating even to the joints of the soul and making its way through the inmost parts of bone and marrow.[46]

The word of God is a vehicle of affective transformation that penetrates the person to destroy sinful feelings while simultaneously enhancing pious ones.

In another letter from 1529, this one to Alonso de Fonseca, Erasmus provides more detail on Paul's emotional style, but also argues that Paul himself was deeply emotional, which should serve to console his readers (and, in this case, to justify Erasmus's own melancholy):

---

44. CWE 15:47; Ep 2091.
45. Allen Ep 2092; CWE 15:66–7.
46. *Para. Eph.* 6:17f.; CWE 43:355.

Paul, that great champion of the church and divinely chosen instrument of the philosophy of the gospel, a man of more than human powers who was accustomed to converse with heaven, confesses often to a deep sorrow in his heart [*ingentem cordis dolorem*] and a sadness that makes him weary of life [*tristitiam ad vitae taedium*]; sometimes his letters are stained with tears, he tries to find comfort in the conversation of the pious, and prays to be spared the buffeting of Satan's minister. So is it surprising if I, who am no more a match for Paul's strong spirit than a worm crawling on the ground can match an eagle, feel in a human way [*aliquid humanum sentio*] when I am harassed by so many ills that I am disinclined to burden the ears of so great a prelate by recounting them?[47]

Not only, then, do Christ's emotions serve as an example for Christian feeling, but Paul's should as well. Moreover, there is no one less boring, Erasmus had written to his Seneca readers, than Paul. And this has to do not only with his ability to move the emotions in multiple affective styles, but also because his own strong emotions are on display, something which perhaps transcends rhetoric.[48] There is a balance to be struck, ultimately, between the calm and violent emotions, which is often determined by occasion and interlocutor. Thus, in his dedication of the *opera omnia* of Augustine—also to de Fonseca—Erasmus invokes Peter and Paul to praise the bishop of Hippo's emotive style, which itself is apostolic: Augustine advises gentleness in persuasion, he is not *plēktēs* ("a brawler," from 1 Tim. 3:3—a term Erasmus will later ascribe to Martin Luther), but he also possesses *makrothumia* ("moderation," from Eph. 4:2) and "an unruffled gentleness" which Peter calls *prautēs* (1 Pet. 3:15).[49]

Erasmus also discusses Paul's abilities in engaging the emotions in the *Ecclesiastes*. He notes, explaining the importance of voice, that Paul desired to be with the Galatians *in person* so that he could change his tone, "now frightening them, now beseeching, now coaxing."[50] Erasmus refers here to 2 Tim. 3:16, which he also invokes in his *Paraphrase* of Galatians 4:19-20. If we turn to his paraphrase of the former, we find "Paul" digressing on the importance of the living voice (*viva vox*) for affective movement, contrasting it with the less effective/affective written word:

> Would that you could turn your eyes into my heart. You would certainly see with how great a sadness of spirit I write these things. . . . But a letter does not

---

47. CWE 15:168.
48. In a letter to Johan Koler in 1529 Erasmus writes (somewhat rhetorically) that a letter Koler had written to him "breathes a spirit of deep affection, which you could not have achieved by rhetoric alone. This is convincing proof to me that everything you write springs from a true and genuine heart" (Ep 2195; CWE 15:349).
49. CWE 15:224–5.
50. CWE 68:743.

adequately express the feeling of my heart. Would that I might now be among you so that what I express inadequately in a letter I might be able to communicate to you with the living word (*viva voce*). My face, my tears, the ardour of my voice itself would add something. I would change myself in every way so that I could recall you to Christ, now coaxing, now entreating, now reprimanding. I would better accommodate my speech to the varieties of your moods and to the matter at hand.[51]

Conflating organs of knowing and feeling, Erasmus's Pauline voice would allow the Galatians, if they could *hear* it, to *see* into his heart. Epistolography comes up short, in terms of expressivity, when compared with talking face to face, for fully affective communication and the possibility of conversion only happens in conversation.[52]

Paul also features heavily, naturally, in Erasmus's dispute with Luther over free will, even if most of the overtly emotional content in that context is about Luther's lack of moderation, as we will see in the final chapter. But Erasmus does, in the *Hyperaspistes 2*, offer a brief discussion of *synderesis* in the wider setting of the Pauline distinction between spirit, soul, and flesh, whose relevance to emotion we saw earlier in Erasmus's *Enchiridion*. "If reason struggles against emotions that are prone to immorality," he writes to Luther, "then it must needs be that to some degree it discerns and approves of what is moral. The scholastics call this faculty 'synderesis', though I hardly know where they got the name."[53] Remarkably, most of the examples Erasmus gives of reason's struggle against emotion are in fact emotional responses themselves:[54] the shame of adolescents caught red-handed, the pleasure felt by someone who helped out another, the tears of a person who witnesses extraordinary virtue, and so on. In other words, the way in which

---

51. CWE 42:118, modified. Utinam liceret vobis oculos vestros in pectus meum inferere, cerneretis nimirum, quanto cum animi dolore scribam haec. Sed affectum animi mei non satis exprimit epistola. Utinam nunc liceat apud vos esse, ut quod literis utcunque significo, possim viva voce vobis aperire. Nonnihil adderet vultus, nonnihil lachrymae, nonnihil ipse vocis ardor. In Omnia me mutarem, quo vos revocarem ad Christum, nunc blandiens, nunc obtestans, nunc obiurgans. Orationem melius ad varietates animorum et ad rem praesentem accommodarem.

52. For a nice treatment of this idea in Erasmus's colloquies, see Brian Cummings, "Erasmus and the Colloquial Emotions," *Erasmus Studies* 40, no. 2 (2020): 127–50. And for a different sort of affective convincing in Erasmus, see Leushuis, "Poetics of Homiletics?," 101–26.

53. CWE 77:592. LB X 1463B: Si ratio pugnat cum affectibus, ad inhonesta proclivibus, necesse est ut aliquousque prospiciat, probetque quod sit honestum. Hanc partem Scholastici haud scio under hausto vocabulo *synderesim* appellant, quae manet etiam in sceleratissimis.

54. We briefly looked at the same section of the *Hyperaspistes 2* from a different angle in the chapter on classical literature.

the rational soul navigates adverse emotional situations is through remedial feelings. There is, then, an extraordinarily close connection between synderesis as conceived in these examples and the affective responses that accompany the process.

The feedback loop of the "spark of reason" and affective movement is described further in the *Hyperaspistes 2* with reference to Plato, the Stoics, and Aristotle:

> Don't such instances make it clear that the seeds of virtue are deeply seated in mankind and that they reveal themselves when they are stirred up by some incident? This is the point of Plato's myth about souls having fallen from heaven into their bodies, so that, when the souls perceive sensible pictures of something beautiful, they are moved to remember that supreme beauty. And if we believe the Peripatetics, the emotions, which to the Stoics are diseases, were given to us by nature as goads to virtue for those in whom reason is not yet perfect, as when anger acts as a spur to fortitude and justice, envy leads to the emulation of good deeds, mercy to relieving the oppressed, the love of children to providing a liberal education. What is it, then, that flashes forth so brightly when it is aroused by the highest faculties of reason deeply seated in all mankind?[55]

While Erasmus's point is, *contra* Luther, that "even in the most depraved" we find at least something (a *scintilla*) of a healthy moral inclination (Judas hanged himself, after all![56]), the discussion also helps us to see a bit more clearly the way in which emotions function in Erasmus's favored Peripatetic framework: namely that by harnessing them properly one might use them for virtuous ends. Erasmus is responding to Luther's association of the will (which is fully sinful) and its affections (which are also fully and irredeemably sinful) by arguing the opposite position. As Simeon Zahl has put it, describing Luther, "to a significant degree the bondage of the will is itself understood, in Luther, as the bondage of the affections."[57] To the extent that that is true of Erasmus, the emotions also offer

---

55. CWE 77:593, modified. LB X 1463E: An non ista declarant homini penitus insita virtutum femina, quae per occasionem mota vim suam exserunt? Huc spectat illud Platonis aenigma, de animabus e coelo in corpora delapsis, quae per sensibiles pulcri imagines, ad illius summae pulcritudinis recordationem expergiscuntur. Et si Peripateticis credimus, affectus, quos Stoici morbos appelant, in hoc dati sunt a natura, ut in his, in quibus nondum absoluta est ratio, stimuli sint ad virtutem: velut ira calcar addit ad fortitudinem ac justitiam, invidia ad aemulationem recte factorum, misericordia ad subveniendum oppressis, caritas erga liberos ad liberalem educationem. Quid igitur est illud quod excitatum adeo gliscit, nisi summa rationis pars penitus insita cunctis hominibus? Haec scintilla manet etiam in depravatissimis.

56. CWE 77:593.

57. Simeon Zahl, "The Bondage of the Affections: Willing, Feeling, and Desiring in Luther's Theology, 1513–1525," in *The Spirit, the Affections, and the Christian Tradition*, ed. Dale Coulter and Amos Yong (Notre Dame, 2016), 181.

the way out. Both Erasmus and Luther conceive of *affectus* as fundamental to Christian virtue and justification, but they understand the relationship between emotion and sin differently.

Erasmus gives a Pauline justification for his position:

> When *Discussion* [i.e., Erasmus's first treatise on free will] first deals with philosophers, that is, pagans, she teaches that reason, that is, the principal part of the soul, has certain inclinations towards mortality. But what the philosophers call reason or *to hēgemonikon* Paul calls the spirit, and what they call *pathē* or disordered emotions Paul calls the flesh. Feelings in between the two, that is, purely natural feelings, he calls the soul, as in 1 Thessalonians 5: "that your spirit may be sound and your soul and body without complaints, etc."[58]

This outline differs little from what we have seen before when Erasmus invokes this line of reasoning, except, perhaps, for the explicit identification of the *anima* with the *medios affectus*, the natural emotions; in the *Enchiridion*, the neutral part of the soul only encompassed such affections. The soul *qua* affective disposition can, again, bend in either direction:

> The spirit loves what it knows is pleasing to God; the flesh pursues vengeance, pleasure, the honours of this world; placed between, the soul bends towards either side and it turns towards the one it is devoted to. To love our wives, to care for our children are acts we have in common not only with pagans but even with brute beasts. If we guide such feelings according to the will of God, they belong to the Spirit. If we neglect God's commandments out of love for wife or children, that love belongs to the flesh.[59]

This, again, echoes a long-standing formulation for Erasmus of ordering the emotions toward the higher faculties so that they become spiritual as opposed to carnal.[60]

---

58. CWE 77:594; LB X 1464A: Diatriba primum agens de Philosophis, hoc est, Ethnicis, docet rationi, hoc est, animae parti principali, inesse nixus quosdam ad honesta. Caeterum quod Philosophi vocant rationem sive *to hegemonikon*, Paulus appelat *spiritum*, et quod illi vocant *pathe* sive *morbos*, Paulus appelat *carnem*, medios affectus, hoc est, mere naturalest appelat animam 1. Thessal. V *ut integer spiritus vester, et anima et corpus sine querela, etc.*

59. CWE 77:594; LB X 1464A-B: Spiritus amat quae Deo grata novit, Caro quaerit vindictam, voluptates et honores huius undi, Anima in medio posita utrocunque se flectit, in hoc vertitur, cui semet applicuit. Diligere uxorem, curare liberos, est nobis cum brutis quoque commune, non modo cum Ethnicis. Si hunc affectum temperamus ex voluntate Dei, sit spiritus. Si caritate uxoris aut liberorum negligimus praecepta Dei, sit caro.

60. Neither the *Annotationes* on nor the *Paraphrase* of the pertinent verse in 1 Thessalonians provides much more, other than that it substantiates Paul's anthropology (*In has enim partes hominem dividit Paulus* [*Ann.* 1 Thess 5:23, ad loc. in ASD VI-9, 428]).

A somewhat more elaborate explanation of the way in which emotions are seated in relation to reason and the will comes later in the treatise, where Erasmus responds to Luther (referred to as "Achilles" throughout this section, for his propensity to violent rhetoric), who had contended that Erasmus had not dealt properly with Romans 7 and Galatians 5, "concerning the fight between the spirit and the flesh." Luther's argument is that nothing is untouched by sin, that "flesh" covers all the human faculties; Erasmus interprets him, in part, to mean that not only the "grosser emotions" are sinful but also that "in the reason and the will there are also impious emotions and perverse judgments."[61] Erasmus doesn't disagree, but responds that even those impulses "have their origin in those grosser emotions, which cause us to love what is seen more than what is unseen." He then suggests an upward movement of the ugliest emotions to the more intellective, but still depraved, ones: "Greed is a gross matter; often enough it gives rise to envy. Lust is a gross affair; it frequently gives rise to deadly anger. Debauchery is a gross business; not infrequently it leads to slander. And so it is true that in the reason and will of wicked persons these detestable vices reign."[62] Erasmus has thus, to some extent, conceded the point to Luther (although he says he had already acknowledged as much in the first sortie of their battle). Proof, however, that the soul is not totally corrupted is to be found in the fact that the virtuous *affectus* of "charity, joy, peace, and patience" also reside in the higher order of the soul.[63] Paul is not addressing all of humanity (*non . . . ad naturam hominis*) when he refers to the litany of sins associated with the flesh in Galatians 5:19-21, but those who are still weak (*ad animum vitiis depravatum*).[64] The ones who easily overcome the pernicious emotions have free will which is collaborating with the Holy Spirit.[65] Emotions are the problem, but they're also the solution.

---

61. CWE 77:699, modified. LB X 1513A-B: Etiam in ratione et voluntate esse affectus impios et perversa iudicia. An non hoc ingenue fassa est Diatriba? Quanquam hi quoque affectus originem habent ex illis crassioribus, quibus magis amamus ea quae videntur, quam quae non videntur . . . Avaritia crassa res est, hinc plerunque nascitur invidia. Crassa res est libido, hinc frequenter capitales irae. Crassa res luxus, ex hoc non raro nascitur blasphemia. Verum est igitur, quod in impionum ratione ac voluntate regnent ista detestanda crimina, sed in quibus hominis partibus regnant fruitus, caritas, gaudium, pax, patientia, etc.

62. CWE 77:699–700. Latin in note above.

63. Ibid.

64. Ibid.

65. "It qui Spiritu ducuntur, multo facilius superant tales affectus, libero arbitrio simul Spiritui qodammodo collaborante" (LB X 1514A). A note on the semantics of what are clearly the more sinful emotions in Paul's letters may be apt here: Erasmus quotes Galatians 5:24 in this section as well, in the Vulgate version, which suggests that Christ's followers have crucified their *vitiis et concupiscentiis* (vices and desires). Elsewhere, however, his own translation of the Greek *pathēmata* and *epithumia* differs, for in the *Novum Testamentum*, he has *affectibus et concupiscentiis* (emotions and desires). He points out, after citing various patristic translations, that per Jerome *pathēmata* can be used exclusively for bodily

Arguing about Affectus

As we have noted, an important task for establishing Erasmus's emotional style, and for further assessing the contours of a biblical-humanist emotional community, is to more closely examine his "emotional lexicon." Erasmus's New Testament scholarship provides an invaluable resource for considering the usage and translation of emotion terms with these goals in mind. As noted, Erasmus's preferred term for emotion(s) is *affectus*, but he is happy to use a variety of terms if the context demands something more specific. Erasmus's philological work on Romans allows us to see more clearly his thinking on the matter. In his annotation on Romans 1:26, which contains the Greek phrase πάθη ἀτιμιάς ("shameful emotions"), Erasmus writes:

> The Greek πάθη sometimes means *perturbationes animi* or *motus* or *morbos* or (a word that Fabius [i.e. Quintilian] strongly prefers) *affectus*. In such a great abundance of acceptable terms, where was the need for the strange and artificial word *passio*? *Morbos* would have been especially fitting in this place, since Horace, too, calls effeminate lust a "disease." Further, the addition of *ignominiae* [of shame] appears to have been derived from Hebrew idiom, to mean "disgraceful" or "reproachful" or "shameful" *affectus*.[66]

Despite Erasmus's list of several other appropriate alternatives to *passiones*, he himself opts for *cupiditates* in this case, although one could say that *affectus* greatly pleases (*maxime placet*) Erasmus as much as it did Quintilian. As Andrew Brown notes in his critical edition of the *Annotationes*, Erasmus may have been influenced here not only by Quintilian but by Cicero and Lorenzo Valla.[67] We may add Rudolph Agricola, too.[68] Echoing his criticism of the strange and artificial *passio*, in his annotation on 2 Corinthians 1:6, Erasmus says that the word is "harsh on Latin

affections, but that *epithumia* is added by Paul in order to make clear that the desires of the soul are also meant (See CWE 56:95–6; ASD VI-9, 148–50). In his annotation on Romans 7:5, where Paul also uses the term *pathēmata*, Erasmus writes, "id est morbos, cupiditates sive affectus sive perturbationes"—that is, diseases or desires or emotions or perturbations. The Vulgate reads *passiones peccatorum*, but Erasmus had changed it in his edition to *affectus peccatorum*. Thus, while *affectus* captures both positive and negative valences of feeling, Erasmus makes clear that Paul's use of *pathēmata* indicates primarily sinful feelings and desires, for he offers the glosses of *morbos* (diseases), *cupiditates* (strong desires), and *perturbationes* (disturbances).

66. CWE 56:56, modified.
67. See ASD VI-7, 77, note on ll. 842–52.
68. See Kirk Essary, "The Renaissance of *affectus*? Biblical Humanism and Latin Style," in *Before Emotion: The Language of Feeling, 400–1800*, ed. Juanita Feros Ruys et al. (Routledge, 2019), 156–69. For a recent treatment of the distinction between these terms in Spinoza and others (including Augustine and Erasmus's contemporary Vives), see Russ Leo,

ears."⁶⁹ The choice of largely negative *cupiditates* in Romans no doubt reflects its accompanying adjective, which Erasmus translates as *ignominiosas*, disgraceful or shameful. In other words, while *affectus* is fine as a translation of the Greek *pathē* in many circumstances, in this case something with clear negative connotations (*morbos, cupiditates*) is more accurate. The wider context of this section of Paul's letter to the Romans is Paul's claim that God had "given up" humankind to their dishonorable desires, specifically, it seems, varieties of sexual and homosexual licentiousness. In his *Paraphrase*, Erasmus retains *cupiditates*, but modifies the adjective(s) to *foedus* and *probrosas* (filthy and shameful) and concludes the list of sins Paul offers in verses 29–31 by describing those at fault as also "devoid of every pious emotion" (*vacantes omni pietatis affectu*).⁷⁰ The Romans are not only cultivating sinful desires, but they're lacking in the virtuous feelings too.

The translation of these terms exacerbates a minor controversy, illuminating the importance of translating emotional language in humanist theology. In a few instances of his translation of Romans 8 that led to a rebuttal by the Flemish Franciscan Francis Titelmans—a staunch defender of the Vulgate version— Erasmus chose the term *affectus*. Titelmans was a student of Jacobus Latomus at Louvain and eventually came to serve as a lecturer on scripture and theology. In 1529 he entered the complex of controversies which Erasmus's New Testament had occasioned, with the publication of his his *Collationes super Romanos*. The work begins with a lengthy defense of the Vulgate Latin version of the New Testament, and proceeds to a point-by-point refutation of the scholarship on Romans that had been carried out by three biblical-humanist luminaries: Lorenzo Valla, Lefèvre d'Etaples, and Erasmus. It was an ambitious project, and one which led to Erasmus addressing his rejoinder (in the title) to "a certain youth who would teach his elders."⁷¹ Titelmans strenuously rejects Erasmus's translation of the Greek φρόνημα (in Romans 8:6, 8:7, and 8:27) as *affectus*, as well as Erasmus's further gloss in the *Annotationes* of the same word as *sensus* (the Vulgate reads *prudentia*). Titelmans offers multiple objections to Erasmus's choice of *affectus*. Apart from a criticism of Erasmus's *inutilem copiam* (useless variety—a dig Erasmus himself had made against the Vulgate translator⁷²), Titelmans objects specifically to applying *affectus* to what to his mind is an *intellective* Greek word, not one that refers to the emotions or other lower movements of the soul. The Greek φρονεῖν, Titelmans writes, refers

---

"Affective Physics: *Affectus* in Spinoza's *Ethica*," in *Passions and Subjectivity in Early Modern Culture*, ed. Brian Cummings and Freya Sierhuis [Ashgate, 2013], 33–49).

69. "'passio' vox est dura Latinis auribus" (ASD VI-8, 330).

70. *Tomus secundus continens Paraphrasim D. Erasmi Roterodami* (Basel: Froben, 1532), fol. b2r-v.

71. See also CWE 73:xxix-xxxviii. Also, Paolo Sartori, "La controversia neotestamentaria tra Frans Titelmans ed Erasmo da Rotterdam (1527–1530 ca): linee di siviluppo e contenuti," *Humanistica Lovaniensia* 52 (2003): 77–135.

72. See Erika Rummel, *Erasmus as a Translator of the Classics* (Toronto: University of Toronto Press, 1985), 95n36.

"more to the mind and intellect . . . than to the emotions."[73] For Titelmans, *affectus* is an emotion term but not one appropriate to operations of the rational faculty, which latter, by implication, is what Paul is writing about in Romans. Titelmans cites Quintilian and Cicero (via Valla[74])—somewhat surprisingly, given that Valla rejects *passio* in his own *Annotationes* on this verse[75]—in order to make his case that *affectus* refers not to reason, or *ratio*, but to movements of the baser orders of the soul. Erasmus has thus erred, he thinks, in rendering a mental category into an emotional one.

Titelmans's criticisms, despite his novice status, troubled Erasmus enough that he wrote a proper rejoinder, but also complained about this specific point of criticism at length in his correspondence. In addition to the *Responsio ad Collationes* of 1530, Erasmus also wrote a lengthy letter to Pieter Gilles the same year (Ep 2260). He later, additionally, expanded the 1535 edition of the *Annotationes* in order to counter some of the points raised by Titelmans. Erasmus's comments reveal the complexities involved in translating emotion terms from Greek into Latin. Erasmus does not entirely disagree with Titelmans's point that *affectus* is not appropriate as a translation for strictly intellective dispositions. But he disagrees with the contention that the Greek word φρόνημα is to be used only *ad intellectum*, as he reiterates several times in his responses. And if that is the case, then *affectus* is perfectly acceptable.

Responding to Titelmans's claim that the Latin *affectus* is equivalent to the Greek πάθη (the latter quite obviously descriptive of emotional or bodily and not rational movements), Erasmus offers a nuanced criticism of his interlocutor's anthropological rigidity: "There is nothing to stop me saying in Latin *pius affectus* for God, for the fatherland, for children, since this *affectus* is not in the lower

---

73. "ad intellectum magis quam ad affectum sive curare"; also: "Quae licet intellectum diffialia sint, tamen clare satis testantur, graeca vocabula potius illum ad mentem et intelligentiam, vimque sive cognoscendi sive sentiendi retulisse, quam ad affectum" (*Collationes quinque super Epistolam ad Romanos beati pauli Apostoli* [Antwerp: Vorsterman, 1529], 204).

74. Citing Valla's *Elegantiae*, Book 4, Titelmans writes: "Affectus est pars animae qualitatis, illa quae e regione rationis est. Quicquid enim in anima, practer partem illam memoriae, ratio non est, affectus est. Et rursus, quicquid non est affectus, ratio. Aut si affectum pro affectione sumas, definitur a Cicerone, affectio esse animae et corporis, ex tempore, aliqua de causa, mutatio. Quintilianus, quod graece dicitur pathos, id est passio, affectum nominat . . . Quod graeci *pathos* vocans, nos vertentes recte ac proprie affectum dicimus" (ibid.). For Erasmus's own summary of Valla's position on *affectus* and *affectio*, see the *Paraphrasis in Elegantias Laurentius Vallae* in ASD I-V, 218–19.

75. "Passiones non probe dici Latine *pathē* Hieronymus quoque testatur, nec morbos Cicero, sed perturbationes. Quintilianus autem proprie dici affectus ait, et ita fere autores usurpant; quare ego transtulisem, affectus contumliae, *atimias*, quod congruit cum illo superiori, ut contumeliis afficiant corpora sua, *atimazesthai*" (qtd. in ASD VI-7, 77; Valla, *Annot.*, Garin vol. 1, p. 856).

part of the soul, but in the higher. Accordingly, I liked the word because it was applicable to both parts of the soul, spirit and flesh."[76] This is a renovated *affectus* when compared with Erasmus's tendencies in the *Enchiridion* and *De taedio*, but echoes similar later developments that we have seen, for example, in the dispute with Luther. *Affectus*, as a function of the will, occupies a middle space in the psychological hierarchy: "For when the will inclines to reason, it loves things eternal; when it lets itself descend to the flesh and bodily things, it loves that which should not be loved. Both *affectus*, however, are in the part of the soul called the will."[77] Erasmus thus rejects Titelmans's claim, where he channeled the ancient rhetoricians, that *affectus* lies outside of that part of the soul which contains *ratio* by again blending psychological categories, and invoking the biblical language of eternity and flesh in order to establish the close connection between *affectus* and *ratio*: there are, Erasmus writes, two kinds of emotions (*duplices affectus*), the good and bad, of the spirit and of the flesh.[78]

Erasmus employs these examples to demonstrate a fluidity of both the *verba* and the *res*. Affective and intellective terms can be stretched to overlap with respect to their common referents. They are often equivocal. Classical hard-and-fast categories are eschewed. Human experience, comprised of reason, volition, and feeling, is messy, and distinguishing discrete movements is difficult, often impossible. Erasmus makes this explicit: "It is no surprise that commentators include both [*affectus* and *intelligentia*] in the words they use since the realities are interrelated; for a corrupt *affectus* is born for the most part from a corrupt *intellectus* and vice versa."[79] The interrelation between *affectus* and *intellectus*, a blurry hybrid of feeling and knowing, is a striking feature of Erasmus's mature thought and not only a matter of semantic slippage.[80] It is noteworthy in this instance as well, for it seems to bear quite heavily on Erasmus's Latin usage, or at least as a retroactive justification of his rendering of Paul.

76. CWE 73:217, modified; LB 997C: Hic scilicet ex *Laurentio Valla* docet nos quid intersit inter *affectionem* & *affectum: affectus* enim dici, quae Graeci vocant *pathe*. Ita prorsus distinguunt Latini, quoties tractant Graecam philosophiam. Nihil tamen obstant nobis quo minus Latine dicamus *pium affectum erga Deum, erga patriam, erga liberos*, cum hic affectus non sit in infima animi parte, sed in summa. Proinde mihi placuit verbum, quod ad utramque animi partem pertinebat, spiritum et carnem.

77. CWE 73:217; LB 997C-D: Nam voluntas rationi obtemperans amat aeterna, ad carnem ac res corporeas sese demittens, amat non amanda. Uterque tamen affectus est in ea parte animi, quae dicitur voluntas.

78. CWE 16:154.

79. CWE 73:219; LB 997D: Nec mirum si interpretes utrumque attingunt verbis, cum res inter se cognatae sint: nam depravatus affectus fere nascitur ex depravato intellectu, et contra.

80. For more on anthropological imprecision in renaissance theology, see, e.g., Debora Shuger, *Sacred Rhetoric: The Christian Grand Style in the English Renaissance* (Princeton: Princeton University Press, 1989).

Erasmus's *Responsio* was not, apparently, self-satisfying, for Erasmus recounts the dispute to Pieter Gillis (as mentioned) in a 1530 letter. In it, Erasmus expands some of his earlier arguments.[81] For example, Erasmus situates Titelmans's attacks in the wider context of sixteenth-century Christian anti-Stoicism:

> He had heard perhaps that the stricter Stoics condemned the πάθη "passions," which some translate as *affectus* "feelings" or *perturbationes* "perturbations." But it does not immediately follow that "perturbations of the mind" is the only meaning of *affectus*, since Latin writers, in trying as best they can to convey the thought of the Stoics, have translated πάθη "passions" by *affectus, motus, perturbationes, cupiditates*, and *morbi*. Moreover, this paradox of the Stoics was rejected long ago not just by Christians, but also by other philosophers and even by the later Stoics themselves. Nowadays anyone who chose to stand stubbornly by the Stoic doctrine of *apatheia* would even be considered a heretic. For joy, grief, hope, fear, love, hate, benevolence, pity are unquestionably *affectus* and yet throughout the sacred writings they are used of men living not just according to the flesh but according to the spirit, they are used also of Christ, indeed they are even used of the divine nature.[82]

This is the clearest explanation of *affectus* in Erasmus's scholarship on the New Testament (if we can include a letter in that scholarship), as well as the strongest endorsement for emotion as a crucial component of Christian virtue. We might even attribute *affectus* to the divine nature of Christ! Paul, too, was "tortured by grief, filled with joy, and torn apart by fear," while Mary and Jesus experienced familial affections toward each other, and Jesus himself was angry, wept, felt pity, and so on—"the word *affectus* encompasses all these emotions."[83] Erasmus here implies that Titelmans is both misguided in his understanding of the semantics of these emotion terms, and also—with a slight twisting of Titelmans's argument—that he is toeing the line between heresy and orthodoxy in roundly rejecting all *affectus*. Erasmus goes on to note that multiple virtuous emotions or emotive actions, such as "exulting in the spirit" and "penitence" (*poenitens*), are also kinds

---

81. For further consideration of this episode, see Essary, "The Renaissance of *Affectus*?"
82. CWE 16:152; Allen Ep 2260: Audivit fortassis a Stoicis rigidioribus damnari *pathe*, quae nonnulli vertunt *affectus*, alii *perturbationes*. Atqui non ideo protinus affectus nihil aliud sonat quam animi perturbationes, si Latini, dum quomodocunque student explicare Stoicorum mentem, *pathe* verterunt *affectus, motus, perturbationes, cupiditates* ac *morbos*. Deinde hoc Stoicorum *paradoxon* non solum a Christianis verum etiam a caeteris philosophis., imo ab ipsis Stoicis recentioribus, iam olim explosum est. Nunc etiam haereticus sit habendus qui Stoicorum *apatheian* velit tueri pertinaciet. Nam gaudium, dolor, spes, metus, amor, odium, ira, benevolentia, misericordia citra controversiam affectus sunt; et tamen haec passim in mysticis literis tribuuntur hominibus non iuxta carnem sed iuxta spiritum viventibus, tribuuntur et Christo, denique tribuuntur Divinae naturae.
83. CWE 16:153.

of *affectus* which are "produced in us by the Spirit of God."[84] Taken all together, Erasmus's broad usage of *affectus* across his corpus cannot be confined to any specific trajectory of usage among the variety of his predecessors.

That said, it may be helpful to point out that Erasmus is in the company of Bernard of Clairvaux and other medieval theologians (despite their absence from his discussions here) in particular by utilizing *affectus* to describe the emotions specific to the human-divine relationship, but he also uses the term to describe the whole spectrum of human feeling (religious and not).[85] In this way, he sits between one aspect of the medieval monastic tradition and the "lay" scholarly tradition as represented by someone like Juan Luis Vives, Erasmus's contemporary and friend. As Elena Carrera has written in an astute analysis of the renaissance usage of *affectus*,

> Whereas Bernard of Clairvaux and his monastic contemporaries had focused on the narrower meaning of the singular term *affectus* as the capacity to love God and to desire union with him, which could be cultivated through acts of the will in response to experiential knowledge of God's love, Vives was writing for husbands [in the *De officio mariti*] and thus focused on ordinary people's experiences of *affectus* in a wider range of situations.[86]

Carrera traces multiple traditions of *affectus* in the period, including the Platonist and Augustinian tradition regarding the need to control *affectus*, and thus the multiple ways in which these various traditions shaped Erasmus's usage becomes even clearer. Erasmus enriches classical *affectus* with biblical, patristic, medieval monastic, and humanist valences.

The Pauline Psalms and Intertextual Emotion

We may gain further insight into Erasmus's understanding of the theological significance of the Pauline emotions by examining pertinent intertextual references between the Old and New Testaments. Erasmus often glosses a Psalm in one way in his commentaries, but employs the same text in a different manner when interpreting the New Testament. The biblical text itself is, moreover, polyphonic. In the commentary on Psalm 2, for example, Erasmus interprets God's alternating wrath and mercy as one of "a thousand similar passages in the Old Testament,

---

84. CWE 16:157.

85. For several helpful essays on patristic and medieval uses of *affectus* and *affectio*, see Ruys et al., *Before Emotion*. On Bernard, see also Simo Knuuttila, *Emotions in Ancient and Medieval Philosophy* (Oxford: Oxford University Press, 2004), 198ff.

86. Elena Carrera, "Augustinian, Aristotelian, and Humanist Shaping of Medieval and Early Modern Emotion: *Affectus, affectio,* and 'affection' as Traveling Concepts," in Ruys et al., *Before Emotion*, 174.

in which the Lord constantly changes the tone of his voice."[87] Changes in tone of voice always correspond, of course, to changes in a desire to modify an affective response.[88] Even the New Testament, Erasmus acknowledges, has God "speaking in both tones of voice," and as an example he invokes the blinding of Paul on the road to Damascus as "an illustration of the words from Psalm 2, 'And in his fury he will confound them.'" "In this case," Erasmus writes, "his anger brought healing, and Paul, cured at once by the treatment, replied: 'Lord, what do you want me to do?'"[89] Divine wrath is medicinal, but its side effects may vary. Paul's own use of the Psalter in his writings about emotion provides a fruitful locus for analyzing intertextual references to emotion in Erasmus's interpretation of the Bible.

Erasmus's heuristic of accommodation allows him maximum interpretative flexibility in such instances, and the analogy of the figure of Paul sheds light, for Erasmus, on the shifting tones of voice God himself uses. For Paul uses similar rhetorical techniques (Erasmus was rebuked by the Sorbonne for calling Paul a chameleon), and Erasmus, as noted, interprets Paul's penchant for "grieving" his correspondents as a similar affective technique to displays of divine wrath in his commentary on Psalm 2: "At times he coaxes, pleads, and consoles with the tenderness of a mother; at others he threatens the disobedient with all the authority of the Apostle . . . Paul always prefers to use pleasant and soothing words, but sometimes he is obliged to grieve the hearts [*contristat animos*] of his audience."[90] Paul himself felt similar emotions in this dialogic relationship: it pained [*dolebat*] him to bring grief [*moerore*] to his followers, but he rejoiced [*gaudet*] in their being healed. Old Testament fury is thus turned into New Testament grief. In the same text, Erasmus also cites Paul's opening apology in 2 Corinthians, noting that even though his previous letter may have grieved his readers, nevertheless "grief [*tristitia*] which is inspired by God brings that earnest repentance which leads to salvation, whereas worldly grief [*tristitia*] brings death."[91] Both the God of the Old Testament and his New Testament apostles engage the *affectus* in various but similar ways according to need and personality as a part of the redemptive process. It is worth emphasizing the variety of emotion terms invoked here, all of which more or less point to the same thing, and most of which are taken from the

---

87. CWE 63:115.

88. In the *Ecclesiastes*, Erasmus advocates for occasional use of censorious or monitory forms of discourse (in Greek the *epitimetikos* and *nouthetikos*), writing, "for it suits the gentleness of the gospel that the preacher should admonish rather than rebuke, though sometimes the enormity of the crimes demands that a preacher do what Isaiah commands him to do, 'Shout, do not cease; like a trumpet raise your voice and announce their crimes to the people and their sins to the house of Jacob.' St Paul gives Timothy the same instruction to accuse and rebuke, but he is mindful of evangelical gentleness and adds oil to his wine, saying, 'Beseech' and 'With every gentleness'" (CWE 68:574).

89. CWE 63:115.

90. CWE 63:115–16.

91. CWE 63:116.

Vulgate passages cited. While Erasmus elsewhere delineates with some precision the valences of emotion terms, just as often he deploys them in a copious barrage, as here, where *ira, furor, tristitia, moeror* are all collapsed into a sort of affective punishment that serves as redemptive medicine.

Not all emotions, though, and especially not all angers, are spiritually useful. Another intertextual opportunity is provided by Paul's quotation of the Septuagint version of Psalm 4:4 ("Be angry and do not sin") in his letter to the Ephesians (verse 4:26). By comparing Erasmus's sermon (*concio*) on Psalm 4 with his *Paraphrase* of and annotation on Ephesians 4, we can see further how he approaches the Psalms and Ephesians versions of the same emotional advice in different ways. His paraphrase of Eph. 4:26 runs thus:

> To be perfect is to be untouched by anger, but if on account of the frailty of human nature some outburst of anger seizes your soul, be mindful of what the holy Psalmist advises: so restrain your anger when it longs to burst out, that it does not result in wrangling or injury or hatred. Let your anger not only do no harm, but let it also be short lived, the sort that leaves your hearts sooner than the sun the earth. When the earth, at the coming of night, has ceased to be torrid, you should not continue meanwhile to burn with wrath.[92]

As in Paul's letter, the thrust of Erasmus's paraphrase then focuses on a wider array of emotive dispositions that run unchecked if anger is left to burn, and are disruptive to the community, such as hatred, bitterness, insolence, ferocity, and wrathfulness.[93] But Erasmus is more explicit than Paul that anger itself will give rise to hatred (*odium*), for example, if (following v. 27) the devil is allowed space or, in a common refrain, if the tongue is not blameless. Anger becomes, as elsewhere in Erasmus's corpus, a sign of, or a spur to, divisive discourse: speech is the image of the mind—*mentis imago est oratio*—and thus noxious discourse (*turpiloquio*) proceeds only from an impure mind via a *mala lingua*. The *Annotation* on the same verse is, unsurprisingly, more technical, and it provides a bit more insight into the semantics of anger terms:

> As this is taken from a Psalm, so it is expressed in Hebrew fashion. For the meaning is, "if you happen to get angry, do not sin," that is, "check your anger." Paul is not telling us not to get angry, but he does not want anger to be continuous

---

92. CWE 43:336. Perfectum est ira non tangi, sed si ob imbecillitatem humanae naturae nonnullus irae impetus perstringat animum, memores quid admoneat sacer ille psalmographus, sic iram erumpere gestientem cohibite, ut non exeat in convitium, aut iniuriam, aut odium. Sit autem non solum innoxia, vetumetiam brevis ira vestra, quae citius animos vestros relinquat, quam sol terram, Ne cum illa servere desierit noctis adventu, vos nihilo secius interim aestuetis iracundia (*Paraphrasim . . . in omneis epistolas apostolicas* [Basel: Froben, 1532], 201–2).

93. He refers, for example, to *amarulentia, tumor,* and *ferocitas*.

nor to progress to the point of injury. In Greek it is not *iracundia*, a word which in Latin signifies not so much anger [*ira*], but a natural vice or at least the habit of a mind that easily gets angry. The Greek word is *parorgismo*, that is, "anger" or "emotional disturbance" or "irritation" so that we understand that for the person who is wounded by some injury, even if he is pained to some extent, nevertheless the pain ought to last briefly and between Christians it should end without retaliation for the injury.[94]

The here gloss is more or less the same as it was in the *Paraphrase*: don't let your anger get out of hand and develop into something more dangerous. Regarding *iracundia* as a "natural vice," Andrew Brown notes that—despite this gloss—Erasmus attributes *iracundia* to Jesus at Mark 3:5, and to God at Rev. 15:7 in his translation of the New Testament.[95] The Greek term, though, refers rather to a more violent emotional disturbance (*iram sive commotionem aut irritationem*) but one that is, ideally, temporary.[96]

In his sermon on Psalm 4, Erasmus's tone is rather different from his direct interpretations of Paul, not least because according to one level of interpretation the original audience of the *psalmographus* is not Paul's community at Ephesus, but the Jews: "The Lord rebukes the Jews for envy of this kind when he says: 'Be angry; do not sin; say these words in your hearts and examine your conscience in your private chambers.'" Erasmus continues in the form of a paraphrase of the voice of Christ:

> What? he says, "Are you angry, envious Jew? Has some promise made to you not been kept, simply because God has extended his mercy to the whole world? This anger of yours is a sin almost more grievous than that of nailing me to the cross; you destroy yourself inasmuch as you envy your neighbor; you deny the Father inasmuch as you do not believe his Son. If you must be angry, let your anger be without sin. Be angry with your sins and you will receive mercy."

---

94. CWE 58:187. Id quemadmodum e Psalmo sumptum est, ita iuxta formam Hebraei sermonis extulit. Nam sensus est, Si continget irasci, tamen ne peccetis: hos est, compescite iram. Neque enim Paulus iubet nos irasci, sed iram non vult esse diuturnam, nec ad iniuriam usque progredi. Nec est Iracundia Graece, quae vox Latinis, non tam iram quam naturae vitium, aut certe habitum significat animi facile irascentis, sed *parorgismo*, id est, Iram, sive commotionem, aut irritationem: ut intelligamus ei qui lacessitus sit iniuria, etiamsi quid doleat, tamen eum dolorem brevem esse oportere, et citra retaliationem iniuriae debere consistere inter Christianos (Erasmus, *In novum testamentum annotationes* [Basel: Froben, 1540], 609).

95. ASD VI-3, 528 on Eph. 4:26.

96. For more on Erasmus's annotation on this verse, see Kirk Essary, "Annotating the Affections: The Philology of Feeling in Erasmus' New Testament and Its Reception in Early Modern Dictionaries," *Erasmus Studies* 37, no. 2 (2017): 207–9.

And Erasmus's Christological paraphrase increasingly takes on a Pauline resonance: "Why do you vainly flatter yourself that you are righteous, and shun the uncircumcised as unclean? . . . Salvation comes from faith, not from works. If you would be angry to some purpose, emulate the gentiles' anger; God became more gracious towards them after they became angry with themselves and showed remorse for their former lives."[97] Here is a completely different interpretation of the Psalm than that given in the context of explicating Paul's use of it, albeit one with a Pauline gloss: anger is not necessarily meant to be curbed but redirected toward sinful selves in search of forgiveness and redemption.

This, however, is only the first part of Erasmus's sermon—or, in fact, the first sermon—where he has interpreted the psalm in Christ's voice. He also offers what is, in effect, a second sermon in the same text, elucidating the moral sense as more germane to everyone. Feigning a preacher in the pulpit, he thus begins Part Two: "I would ask that those of you who have nodded off should rouse yourselves, and that those who have been wide awake should now pay even closer attention."[98] In the section of the mock sermon on verse 4:4, he continues by offering the example of a holy figure as an object of anger and hatred by non-Christians because they are different. This sort of anger is contrasted with Christian anger (*irascitur christianus animus*), which "is full of good will towards its object; such anger is no sin, for Christian love does no wrong, even when it starts a quarrel. When the world is angry, it kills, and when it loves, it corrupts. When *caritas* loves, it rejoices in doing good; when it grows angry, it heals."[99] It is not exactly clear what Erasmus has in mind in suggesting a virtuous but angry type of *caritas*, other than contrasting worldly anger at Christian virtue with Christian anger at the sinful self, which latter is elaborated on in the sermonic commentary. There, Erasmus offers two more glosses on Psalm 4:4:

> The first is: "If anything angers you, be angry in such a way that your anger does not erupt into wrongdoing"; in this reading, we are not ordered to be angry, but to moderate our anger once it has started. The alternative is: "Grow angry, indeed, but with yourselves, not with me." Such anger involves no sin . . . [O]ne might call "blessedly angry" [*feliciter iracundi*] people who, observing someone else's virtues, are annoyed with themselves, are angry with themselves, quarrel and fight with themselves.[100]

---

97. CWE 63:187. Ex fide salus est, non ex operibus. Si vis gentibus salubriter irasci, imitare gentium iram, his Deus coepit esse propicius posteaquam ipsi sibi coeperunt irasci per vitae prioris poentitentiam (ASD V-2, 204).

98. CWE 63:212.

99. CWE 63:251, modified. Sic irascitur christianus animus, ut bene velit iis quibus irascitur. Qui sic irascitur non peccat. Nec enim peccat charitas, etiam quum litigat. At mundus quum irascitur occidit, quum amat corrumpit. Charitas quum amat, beneficio iuvat, quum irasicitur, sanat (ASD V-2, 256).

100. CWE 63:252. Atque huius versiculi duplex potest accipi sensus. Alter hic erit: si quid irascimini, sic irascimini, ut ne prorumpat in maleficium ira vestra, atque hoc

The struggle between the spirit and the flesh is one which permits anger to be manifest in ways that are, rather than deleterious to the community, in fact conducive to Christian virtue. When *caritas* and *ira* condition each other, especially when internally directed, they offer potent healing properties.

As an aside, Erasmus notes—seemingly aware of his lack of engagement with the extensive ancient literature on anger—that earlier commentators, including Augustine, had written on emotional moderation (*de motibus animi coercendis*), and had also taken the opportunity of commenting on this passage to consider the question of the proto-passions (*primos impetus*, in this case), the initial affective reactions that are not technically sinful if they do not give way to full-blown emotional vices (on the Stoic model). Erasmus, however, while not rejecting the interpretation,[101] does not pursue that line of inquiry, but concludes this section with a consideration of the different possible translations of the Hebrew emotion term (not given by Erasmus, but *rig-zu*—רִגְזוּ), pointing out, rather liberally, that "be angry" (*irascimini*) and "tremble" (*contremiscite*) are both possibilities:

> It does not make much difference to the meaning whether we read "be angry" or "tremble," which some commentators suggest for the Hebrew word, perhaps because violent anger results in trembling. Unbridled anger (*impotens ira*) produces two effects in man, pallor and trembling; pallor because the blood becomes concentrated round the heart, and trembling because of the violent movement of the spirits; the same effects are produced in us by extreme fear (*vehemens metus*). But no anger is more violent (*vehementior*) than a sinner's when he acknowledges his worthlessness and boils with rage (*effervescit*) against himself, to the point that he may rush off to find a noose or the edge of a cliff. Again, no fear is greater than a sinner's when he considers the magnitude of his crimes and shudders (*horret*) at the thought of God's justice and the punishment he deserves.[102]

Taking the less difficult rendering of the Hebrew would have gotten Erasmus out of various interpretative difficulties, given the awkwardness of the Vulgate's rendering of *irascimini*.[103] But Erasmus suggests that it doesn't matter, not only because

---

modo non iubentur irasci, sed iram obortam moderari. Alter hic: irascimini quidem, at non mihi, sed vobis ipsis. Sic irascentes nihil peccabitis . . . Sed feliciter iracundi sunt, qui conspecta alterius integritate, sibi displicent, sibi irascuntur, secum rixantur ac pugnant, sibi conviciantur dicentes (ASD V-2, 256).

101. He does, a bit later, paraphrase the Psalmist via Augustine: "Do not follow the impulses of the first flush of anger (*primus impetus irae*), but the course suggested by reason, after you have carefully weighed the matter in your own mind" (CWE 63:253).

102. CWE 63:253, modified.

103. Technically, the Hebrew term can have both valences, and the fact that a single Latin term cannot bear both fear and anger as referents is itself interesting to note as one of the many difficulties of translating emotion terms.

anger occasionally results in trembling, but also because in specific theological contexts, even anger and fear have the same outcome when they result from the recognition of human incapacity in the face of divine wrath. Overall, we see Erasmus's hermeneutical flexibility in considering this verse in different contexts, and according to different senses of scripture, as offering multiple valences on the Psalmist's emotional prescription, or proscription, as it pertains primarily to what Erasmus would call *ira*. Anger, or anger-like emotions, are multivalent, here spiritually conducive and there spiritually destructive, depending on their object (and subject).

In considering the biblical and intertextual significance of emotion, with a focus on Erasmus's New Testament scholarship, we are better able to appreciate the dynamic range of affective activity in the Christian individual, given, for example, the vast difference between the spiritually affective fervor of *affectus* as the subjective center in the *Ratio* and New Testament paraphrases, and the suicidal despair resulting from too much rage upon the realization of one's sinfulness in the Psalms commentary. Christian life itself operates in and through the emotions for Erasmus in a complicated array of possible movements. In this chapter, I have tried to demonstrate the fundamental role of emotional activity in Erasmus's very conception of theology and biblical hermeneutics, first by examining paratextual writings associated with his New Testament, and then by considering how he interpreted the Pauline emotions in his exegetical works on Paul's letters. The following chapter extends the conclusion of this one by considering further the extraordinary affectivity of Erasmus's commentaries on the Psalms, which were composed after the bulk of his work on the New Testament, and which were the only Old Testament texts Erasmus exposited formally. We will thereby have a fuller portrait of the manner in which Erasmus understood the biblical emotions, and the ways in which his affective theology rests on the reading of scripture.

Chapter 5

BIBLICAL EMOTIONS II

STOMACHS, STRINGS, AND SYNECDOCHE IN THE PSALMS

In 1522, Erasmus published a *Paraphrase* of the Gospel according to Matthew, dedicated to none other than Emperor Charles V. The preface to the reader is largely devoted to overturning the notion that uneducated layfolk shouldn't read the Bible: "They cry," he writes, "that it is an unseemly act if a woman or a tanner speaks about Holy Scripture. But I would rather hear some girls speaking about Christ than I would certain teachers who are commonly regarded as exalted." And then, in one version of a famous Erasmian refrain, "Indeed, if I have my way, the farmer, the smith, the stone-cutter will read [Christ's words], prostitutes and pimps will read him, even the Turks will read him." Erasmus's hope is that everyone will have access to the Bible, not only those who are trained in academic theology. However, he does have a tiny qualification: "Among the books of the Old Testament perhaps there are some you would with good reason keep out of the hands of the uneducated. Ezekiel is one, also The Song of the Betrothed, *and nearly all the books of the Old Testament*, because in them one stumbles often over either an apparently absurd story or the obscurity of the riddles."[1] The Old Testament is, quite simply, harder than the New.

A decade later, and just a few years before his death, in 1533, Erasmus composed a work in the genre of *ars moriendi*, called the *De preparatione ad mortem*, partly in response to a request from Anne Boleyn's father, Thomas. Variously throughout the work, Erasmus draws together the religious affections of fear of God on the one hand, and hope and faith on the other, at times blurring the boundaries between them. For example, he writes, "Faith of the devout is always joined with religious fear" (*religioso tremore*) and "those who tremble at God's justice have a more certain hope of his mercy" (albeit, he emphasizes, not a *totally* certain hope, with Martin Luther ever in the back of his mind).[2] Nevertheless, Erasmus goes on to make a rhetorical distinction between the need to arouse fear and the need to arouse hope, depending on the type of person who is dying. He lays out a distinction useful for

---

1. CWE 45:11, my emphasis.
2. CWE 70:428.

our project: "The words of the New Testament are better suited than those of the Old to drive away despair and to raise our hopes." Erasmus elaborates:

> Moses terrified the Jews with the Commandments, Christ gave consolation to all peoples through faith and grace. The sacred books have an abundance of examples and words that can cause terror or console the terrified. All that the prophets say unfolds generally in this way: they exaggerate how God punishes those who have turned away from him, but also emphasize the mercy of God to those who have turned to penitence. Each is a remedy bringing salvation if applied judiciously and in the appropriate circumstances. Words that evoke terror should be applied to those who are physically healthy but who are weak in resolve, and to those who are recklessly intoxicated by the prosperity of this life or who are drugged by the pleasures of the world as if they have consumed mandrake. In this way . . . they will rouse themselves by being more vehemently reviled and railed at. Words offering hope of forgiveness should be spoken to those who are agitated and fearful, especially if they are at the critical moment of death. Yet we should not inject terror in the former without instilling at the same time the hope of forgiveness, and we should not speak soothing words to the latter in such a way that they are misled.[3]

Unfortunately, Erasmus does not here provide specific examples (beyond the prophets) of which biblical texts are best for which circumstances, but he lays out a program of selective Bible reading geared toward the movement of specific types of emotions in dying persons depending on the person and context. The general framework of privileging the New Testament for affections conducive to the virtuous Christian emotions and the Old for invoking terror, in some ways a cliché, is repeated by Erasmus elsewhere (although, as we will see, it does not determine his course in expositing the Psalms).

---

3. CWE 70, 446; ASD V-I, 388: Ad excludendam desperationem et erigendam spem aptiores sunt literae Novi Testamenti quam Veteris. Nec mirum: Moses Iudaeos terrebat praeceptis, Christus universos consolatus est per fidem et gratiam. Habent autem sacra volumina non exempla tantum, sed et dicta quamplurima, partim, quae terrorem incutiant, partim, quae territos consolentur. Per haec enim fere voluitur omnis prophetarum sermo, Dei vindictam exaggerans aversis a Deo, ac rursus Dei misericordiam amplificans ad poenitentiam conversis. Utrunque pharmacum salutiferum est, si scite et in loco adhibeatur. Quae territant admovenda sunt corpore sanis, sed animo laborantibus, ferocibus et huius vitae prosperitate temulentis aut mundi deliciis quasi mandragorae indormientibus, quo velut elleboro ingesto resipiscant, aut brassica sumpta redeant ad sobrietatem aut vehementius inclamanti vellicatique expergiscantur. Quae veniae spem faciunt, adhibenda trepidis ac meticulosis praesertim in mortis discriminae. Quanquam nec illis sic ingerendus est terror, ut pharmaco non admisceatur veniae spes, nec his ita sunt adhibenda lenimenta, ut fallantur.

This is one of the many ways, at any rate, in which the Bible serves, for Erasmus, as a kind of affective literature, and one that can and should be analyzed in literary terms. In the *Ratio* of 1518–19, considered at length in the previous chapter, Erasmus links the Old and New Testaments together for their dramatic possibilities: "[W]e will enjoy an important advantage if we diligently read through the books of both Testaments and consider closely that wonderful circle and harmony of the entire drama of Christ (if I may use the expression), a drama acted out for our sake by the one who was made man."[4] As he puts it elsewhere, regarding the "divine letters" (*litteris divinis*), in his commentary on Psalm 1, "Let [the Christian] drink deeply of them, let him learn them by heart—and not merely learn them, but 'meditate' on them, that is, apply them to his mental attitudes [*habitum animi*], his emotions [*affectus*], his morals, and his life."[5] In the *Ecclesiastes*, he repeats what we saw earlier with respect to the Old Testament, namely, that it provides instruction in specifically affective terms: "What does the Scripture of the Old Testament present to us, as it tempers its speech to the emotions of an unlearned people, now threatening external discomforts, now promising the comfort of this world, if not an example of the thoughtful steward?"[6] It is this twofold rhetorical posture that Erasmus ascribes to scriptural speech of *accommodatio* and *movere*, of teaching through moving the emotions, that constitutes a framework wherein Bible reading becomes the site for emotional transformation.

Erasmus was, of course, primarily a New Testament scholar, or even *the* New Testament scholar *par excellence* of his era. His output on the New Testament spans about twenty volumes (or roughly 6,000 pages) of modern editions, and it includes Greek editions, Latin translations, philological and theological annotations, paraphrases, treatises, apologiae, and various other writings dedicated to explicating the base text of what he calls the "Christian philosophy." On the Old Testament, by contrast, the only formal works Erasmus produced were commentaries on eleven of the Psalms, and these were not written and published in any systematic fashion. In fact, they are, technically, composed according to multiple generic conventions: an *ennarratio*, a *concio*, a *commentarius*, even a *paraphrasis* (though structurally they are mostly similar, especially for our purposes[7])—and the commentary on Psalm 28 is in actuality a treatise on the question of a pre-emptive war against the Turks, which Erasmus wrote just after the Ottoman Sultan Suleiman's failed attempt to lay siege to Vienna in 1529.[8] Taken together, his exegetical works on

---

4. Mark Vessey (ed.), *Erasmus on Literature: His* Ratio *or "System" of 1518/19* (Toronto: University of Toronto Press, 2021), 146.

5. CWE 63:44, modified.

6. CWE 67:280.

7. See the introduction in CWE 63, and of each individual work on the Psalms in CWE 63, 64, and 65, for more information about structure, style, and context of composition.

8. On the titles, see further CWE 63, xvi; also, Carolinne White, "Allegory and Rhetoric in Erasmus' Expositions of the Psalms," in *Meditations of the Heart: The Psalms in Early*

the Psalms are nothing like Erasmus's rather more systematic and near-exhaustive attempts at producing scholarship on and editions of the New Testament.

Nevertheless, they are still substantial (occupying three volumes in the CWE series) and could vie for the status of the most emotionally rich texts that Erasmus produced. Crucial insights for understanding Erasmus's affective theology therefore lie in his expositions of the Psalms, partly because of the inherently emotional nature of the Psalms themselves. As Carolinne White has written, "the Psalms are particularly suited to the human spiritual and moral condition because of the wide range of universal situations and feelings they deal with."[9] Erasmus also allows himself more liberty in explicating them, partly because of generic conventions, which allow him the freedom of lengthy digressions, and partly because his lack of Hebrew meant he would not have been as tempted to get bogged down in the philological and text-critical issues that occupied much of his scholarly attention on the New Testament. The results are some of the most affectively laden and mystical writings in all of his works. Examining the Psalms commentaries for their affective depth in comparison with his New Testament exegesis (in the previous chapter) allows us to see how he mobilizes the emotional possibilities of biblical literature from a different angle. This chapter is divided into three parts: first, a consideration of Erasmus's discussion of *affectus* as an organ of piety in various Psalms; second, an exposition of Erasmus's commentary of Psalm 38(9), where he develops the metaphor of a harmonious musical instrument for explaining emotion; and, third, a look at Erasmus's treatment of God's emotions as synecdoche and the problem of anthropomorphism.

Our Stomach Is Our Affectus: *Organ and Emotion in the Psalms*

We have examined the significance of the term *affectus* for Erasmus's understanding of emotion, as well as its wide semantic range, but Erasmus develops the term's theological significance even more in his writings on the Psalms. In the exposition of Psalm 22/23 ("The Lord is my shepherd, I shall not want, etc."), which was first published in 1529, Erasmus demonstrates the centrality of *affectus* for the Christian person as well as the necessity of reforming it. Erasmus elevates the emotions to a privileged place in Christian anthropology not only by recognizing the affective benefits of religious knowledge but also by recognizing the potentially disordered nature of the earthly feelings and dispositions. This is illustrated nicely in an extended metaphor where he links *affectus* to *stomachus* in a striking image that blurs the boundaries between reason, emotion, memory, and the body:

Christian Thought and Practice: Essays in Honour of Andrew Louth, ed. A. Casiday et al. (Turnhout: Brepols, 2011), 258.

9. White, "Allegory and Rhetoric in Erasmus' Expositions of the Psalms," 261.

Christ's sheep have for a palate their understanding [*intellectus*], which they use in simplicity to take in health-giving doctrine; they mash it for a while with serious consideration, turning it over in their minds; then they commit it to their upper stomach, that is, their memory. Then refreshed by drinking from the spirit, they withdraw from the tumult of worldly cares, and lying down in the pastures of the Lord they recall to the understanding those things which they have stored in their memory and chew them over again with more careful consideration. Then finally they send it down to the stomach, so that from there it may be absorbed into the whole body and become the substance of the mind. Our stomach is our *affectus*; if we love what we have learned and believe it, we have sent food to our stomachs. And if we have begun to practise through acts of charity what we have received, then by vigour and activity we show that the food has become the substance of the spirit.[10]

Affectus here is the organ of Christian understanding, even a *telos* of sorts of Christian education, where the mind is supplemented with (or perhaps supplanted by) moral and emotional force. Synonymous with the heart elsewhere in Erasmus's works and in the longer Christian tradition, in this case the stomach qua *affectus* is thus also the organ of transformation.[11] As Reinier Leushuis argues in his work on affectivity in the *Paraphrases* on the New Testament, such a transformation goes beyond "mere exegetical understanding or oratorical persuasion."[12] Indeed, as Emily Kearns puts it, glossing the passage just cited, "Erasmus indicates that the necessary end of the [gustative] process is an emotional, not an intellectual, apprehension of the truths of religion, a central point in his whole approach."[13] Faith is perfected not in intellective comprehension, but only when it is fully digested and inhabited in affective movement. Erasmus even extends this idea to cover the line between orthodoxy and heresy, inverting it, as it were, in his commentary on Psalm 33, where he writes that "those whose error is a merely intellectual one

---

10. CWE 63:185. Sed oves Christi palatum habent intellectus, quo simpliciter excipiunt salutarem doctrinam, eamque sobria consideratione nonnihil atterunt in animo versantes, mox demittunt in superiorem ventriculum, hoc est, in memoriam. Deinde recreatae haustu spiritus secedunt a tumultibus curarum temporalium, et in Domini pascuis acquiescentes quod in memoria reposuerant, ad intellectum revocant, ac diligentiore consideratione remandunt. Ita demum demittunt in stomachum, ut a stomacho per universum corpus digeratur et transeat in animi substantiam. Stomachus noster affectus est, qui amat quod didicit et credit, in stomachum demisit pabulum (LB V 339 C).

11. See further Baker-Smith's discussion of this and other points related to rhetorical affectivity in Erasmus's Psalms exegesis in his introduction, CWE 63:xxxi–xxxiv, and idem, "Erasmus as Reader of the Psalms," *Erasmus Studies* 20, no. (2000): 12.

12. Reinier Leushuis, "Poetics or Homiletics? Hearing and Feeling the New Testament in Erasmus's *Paraphrases*," *Erasmus Studies* 40, no. 2 (2020): 20.

13. CWE 64:185n398.

and whose emotions have not been seduced are easily brought back to the path."[14] Kearns suggests, I think rightly, that this is evidence that *affectus* is more central to religious subjectivity than *intellectus* in Erasmus's works.

Affectus (here a singular organ or faculty of piety) is also contrasted, in a section connected to the passage earlier, with *morbi animi*, diseases of the soul such as avarice, ambition, and the sensual pleasures of love, and Erasmus writes that those inflicted with such sicknesses are unable to "chew over the food of the gospel."[15] But those who can ruminate properly and efficiently, Erasmus says—invoking a series of affective virtues—have grown "more courageous in bearing injuries, stronger in faith, more ardent in love."[16] The one who is not *flagrantior caritate*—inflamed passionately with Christian love—is also unable to effectively teach or preach the gospel: "one who is cold himself [*friget ipse*] will scarcely kindle enthusiasm in others."[17] This is a common refrain in Erasmus's works that touch on Christian pedagogy, derived ultimately from Quintilian but influenced as well by the medieval mystical tradition.[18] "The first concern of the true shepherd," he continues, "which he must always be aware of, is that the sheep should lack nothing. He should not offer them food from lips that are cold and unmoved but from a heart burning with love: fire kindles fire . . . the living voice [*viva vox*] of the shepherd, giving instruction, bestowing rebukes, imploring, spurring on, affording consolation, inflicting terror."[19] These descriptions foreshadow those that Erasmus ascribes to the ideal preacher in the *Ecclesiastes*. Erasmus renders these thoughts into another repeated theme, suggesting that female religious (women in monasteries) are especially deprived of spiritual ardor because they are deprived of the preacher's *viva vox* on account of being cloistered, and that parents should thus not recommend them for the convent (this text, too, it should be mentioned, was dedicated to Thomas Boleyn, father of Anne).

---

14. CWE 64:368.
15. CWE 63:184.
16. CWE 63:185.
17. Ibid.
18. See, e.g., Hildegard of Bingen writing to a Premonstratensian abbot: "Charity without affection [*sine affectu*] seems like a frigid fire. For just as fire without heat cannot weld iron to iron, so charity without affection can by no means cause believers to be of one heart and one soul in God" (qtd. in Barbara Newman, "*Affectus* from Hildegard to Helfta," in *Before Emotion: The Language of Feeling, 400–1800*, ed. Juanita Feros Ruys, Michael Champion and Kirk Essary (Routledge, 2019)); See further Elizabeth Dreyer, "The Transformative Role of Emotion in the Middle Ages," in *The Spirit, the Affections, and the Christian Tradition*, ed. Dale Coulter and Amos Yong (Notre Dame, 2016).
19. Hic igitur cumprimis vigilat veri pastoris cura, ne quid desit ovibus. Nec ex ore frigido porrigat illis cibum, sed ex caritate flagrante corde . . . sed viva vox pastoris melius afficit, erudiens, increpans, obsecrans, exstimulans, consolans, territans. (LB V 339F – 340C).

The extended use of such affective imagery aligns with Dominic Baker-Smith's reminder that Erasmus's treatment of the Psalms is more pastoral than strictly exegetical or philological, more akin to his *Paraphrases* of the New Testament than to the *Annotations*.[20] For this reason, these texts are also rhetorical in a different way: Erasmus is able to move between analyzing rhetorical and literary forms as an exegete, and producing them as a pastor. The Psalms are also emotionally significant as they relate to prayer (as Baker-Smith also reminds us, it is sometimes easy to forget that Erasmus was an Augustinian canon regular, for whom prayer would have been an act essential to the ordering of his religious practice). Erasmus's gloss on this relationship in his sermon on Psalm 85 is also typical of his distrust of ceremony and his criticism of monks for practicing a religion gone cold: "A cry is an expression of a strong emotion, not just a projection of the voice like the shouts of the priests of Baal . . . the physical voice is ineffectual unless the emotions cry out; nor should the shouting be done with the voice but with the feelings which, even in silence, strike God's ears."[21] In contrast to the portrait of the physical *viva vox* as efficacious above, here communication with God happens only fully via the inner *affectus*, which Erasmus sets up as more authentic than outward proclamations. As Baker-Smith explains, the Latin *affectus* is in this passage used both to criticize "token gestures" and as a stand-in for subjectivity itself.[22]

Affectus as definitive of subjectivity itself is a striking notion, if one difficult to nail down in Erasmus's thought. It is not unrelated to the renaissance reappropriation of Augustine and the ancient rhetoricians, but it is also akin to the medieval Cistercian tradition that saw a conceptual emphasis on emotions as neutral or natural, and therefore as more conducive to Christian virtue (recently treated by Constant Mews)—a stronger appreciation of affectivity than that found in Augustine's writings.[23] As mentioned in the introduction, Augustine's view

---

20. CWE 63, intro.

21. CWE 64:47. Cf. Erasmus's *Paraphrase* of Col. 3:16: "You are not to fight to the death with one another over the pre-eminence of a worldly philosophy. May the word of Christ, which teaches what pertains to authentic piety, abide and continue in you abundantly so that you may have such a feel for it that you yourselves not only can know what is pleasing to Christ but you can also teach one another in turn if anyone should err, offer an admonition if anyone is remiss, all the while being cheerful in the hope of future bliss, with psalms and hymns and spiritual canticles, singing to the Lord his praises and his kindnesses, singing, however, not only with your physical voice, but especially in your heart. For God is delighted by songs precisely of this kind, so no one should think it a great thing to raise a din with his mouth to the powers above" (CWE 43:423).

22. Baker-Smith, "Nineteenth Annual Birthday Lecture: Erasmus as Reader of the Psalms," *Erasmus of Rotterdam Society Yearbook* 20, no. 1 (2000): 3.

23. See C. Mews, "*Affectus* in the *De spiritu et anima* of Alcher of Clairvaux and Cistercian Writings of the Twelfth Century," in *Before Emotion*, ed. Juanita Feros Ruys et al. (Routledge, 2020); But cf. Michael Barbezat, "Desire to Enjoy Something Thoroughly: The Use of the Latin *affectus* in Hugh of Saint Victor's *De archa Noe*," in ibid., 76–85, for a look

of *affectus* would seem to have been, ultimately, too pessimistic for Erasmus, as was Luther's after him. But *affectus* is, nevertheless, multivalent. Reaching and transforming the *affectus* (singular), pedagogically and spiritually, is conceptually different from properly ordering the *affectus* (plural). That is, ingesting "health-giving doctrine" is not exhausted by moderating one's anger or grief, or maximizing one's hope. While Erasmus is no mystic, properly speaking, he comes closest in his exegesis on the Psalms.[24] His *affectus* as a descriptor for interiority may be partly understood as arising out of a literary-rhetorical tradition, but it is also shaped by biblical imagery and language in an irreducible way, resulting in a conceptualization that pits itself against a scholastic dialectical mode in the context of religious discourse. Both valences of *affectus* are inextricably linked in Erasmus's theological imagination, indeed absolutely central to his vision, even if they are analytically different. To borrow Erasmus's metaphor, the food has not become the substance of the spirit if one's emotions are not channeled properly.

There are also ways in which God may aid in sheep's digestion, using, for example, the "waters of refreshment" from Psalm 22/23 to "make ready the stomach of their mind, so that they may be empty and eager to take what they are given."[25] Commenting on the passage, Erasmus continues the pastoral metaphor of a sheep who, in less than good health, prefers sweet grass to bitter willow leaves, resulting in a complex blend of humoral and mystical discourse:

> So those who are not yet purged of fleshly desires and who feel nausea in the face of those that are heavenly should ask their shepherd that he may deign to lead them to the waters of refreshment where they may drink more copious draughts of the spirit, the fiery force of which dries up the phlegm in the stomach, and that he may make them turn completely to God, when in their previous lukewarm state they divided themselves between the world and Christ, limping with both legs, as it were, since no one can serve two masters. In Revelation, too, Christ threatens the lukewarm and declares he will spew them out unless they grow hot.[26]

---

at Hugh of St Victor's more pessimistic assessment of the natural affections. On Augustine's own thoughts, Jonathan Teubner has recently argued that the mature Augustine sought for *affectus* or *affectiones* to be molded by the Holy Spirit into *constantiae*, which would be a more negative understanding of *affectus* than Erasmus maintains (see "The Failure of *affectus*: *Affectiones* and *constantiae* in Augustine of Hippo," in Ruys et al., *Before Emotion*, 9–25).

24. Dominic Baker-Smith's introduction to the English translation of this volume of CWE helpfully teases out the connections between Platonist mysticism (his "loosely Platonic orientation") in Erasmus's early works, like the *Enchiridion*, and his Psalms exegesis.

25. CWE 64:186.

26. ASD V-2, 374: Ergo qui nondum defecati a carnalibus desideriis, nauseant ad ea quae sunt coelestia, rogent pastorem, ut dignetur ipsos ad aquas refectionis deducere, ubi copiosus hauriant de Spiritu, qui vi sua ignea excoquit stomachi pituitam, totusque convertat ad Deum, qui prius tepidi mundo et Christo semet partiebantur, velut utroque

Language from humoral theory is deployed here, as elsewhere, as a metaphor: the phlegm of the *affectus* (or, again, the *stomachus*) stands in for spiritual frigidity that needs to be fired, counterintuitively, by refreshing water.[27] It is not, though, an *absurda metaphora* if one appreciates that it is the *concupiscentiae* (carnal, or earthly, desires) that need cooling so that the *mens* might burn with properly heated *affectus*:

> This lukewarm state arises from the phlegm of the emotions becoming infected, which causes fever in the mind, so that we find no pleasure and no means of growth in spiritual learning. Let us then hurry to the waters of refreshment, so that we may grow warm with love. It may be objected that this is ridiculous, since cold water as a rule refreshes those who are too hot; it does not fire the lukewarm. Beloved, the figure is not ridiculous if we interpret it appropriately. This is water which heats by cooling. How is this? It cools the heat of desires, which "rebel in tumult against the spirit," and when these are cooled the human mind grows warm towards those things that are of the spirit.[28]

One must avoid fever by inducing fervor, by finding the appropriate balance of warmth by heating the correct elements of the soul. While other late medieval and early modern thinkers might dwell on the hydraulic or humoral models of emotion that were relatively popular in Galenic medicine, Erasmus is more interested in literary-theological figuration. Virtually every aspect of this Psalm commentary's extensive imagery—of the body, of digestion, of hot and cold, of phlegmatic stomachs—is a metaphor for the soul.

The tripartite division of emotions is, once again, mapped onto Paul's division of the individual between flesh, soul, and spirit, with a further elaboration on the *affectus naturae*, in Erasmus's exposition of the next verse (which is very similar to a passage from *Hyperaspistes 2* cited in the previous chapter):

genu claudicantes, quum nemo possit servire duobus dominis. Et in Apocalypsi Christus minatur tepidis, evomiturus illos nisi incalescant.

27. For an argument that Erasmus and others did not participate in the "new humoralism" or a "psychological materialism" which has been argued to be a dominant approach in early modern thought, see Kirk Essary, "'The Mind's Bloody Sweat': (Dis)embodied Emotions in Erasmus, More, and Calvin," *Parergon* 38, no. 1 (2021): 41–64 and idem "Clear as Mud: Metaphor, Emotion, and Meaning in Early Modern England," *English Studies* 98, no. 7 (2017): 689–703.

28. ASD V-2, 374: Tepor quidem ille nascitur ex supputri pituita affectuum, quae febriculam gignit in animo, ut non delectemur neque vegetemur doctrina spirituali. Ad aquas igitur refectionis properemus, ut incalescamus charitate. Quod dico forsitan alicui videbitur absurdum, eo quod aqua frigida soleat reficere aestuantem, non inflammare tepentem. Non absurda metaphora dilectissimi, si commode interpretemur. Haec aqua refrigerando calfacit. Quonam pacto? Refrigerat aestum concupiscentiarum quae tumultuantur adversus spiritum, his refrigeratis incalescit mens hominis ad ea quae sunt spiritus.

This is made clear by the prophet when he says: "He has turned my soul." For Paul divides the human soul into three parts: the flesh, which tends towards earthly things, the spirit, which strives towards heavenly things, and the soul in the middle, which moves this way and that. Our natural emotions belong to this last part: concern for personal safety, tenderness towards one's wife, dutiful affection towards our parents and children, and regard for neighbours and friends. . . . If these feelings are attached to the spirit, so that those whom we love we love only in Christ and if the need were to arise we would prefer to abandon them rather than depart from the love of Christ, they turn the soul towards the spirit. But if in order to gratify such feelings we depart from God's commandments, the soul is turning to the flesh. So in order that the whole man's spirit be aglow, our shepherd must turn the soul to himself.[29]

The *affectus* themselves turn the soul toward the spirit (*animam vertunt in spiritum*). Erasmus has again translated the Quintilianesque schema of *ethē kai pathē* (and its *via media*) into a Pauline taxonomy of affectivity, all in the service of clarifying the Psalmist's affective theology.

Feeling Harmony in Psalm 38

The inherent neutrality of the emotions, and their importance to Erasmus's mind for the Christian's spiritual achievements, plays an important role in other expositions of the Psalms as well. With respect to individual feelings, we find in Erasmus's *Enarratio* on Psalm 38 (first published in 1532) an even lengthier metaphor explaining their scale from virtuous to vicious and how they might be made harmonious. Erasmus plays on the recipient of Psalm 38's name, "Idythun" (Jeduthun in modern English versions), rendering its force overtly affective:

When you hear the phrase "to Idythun" (a name which means "leaping over them" in Hebrew), you are made to think of a devout soul, worn down by the hard grind of human existence which contains far more aloe than honey, and exhausted, so to speak, by the false accusations, reproaches, and insults of the

---

29. CWE 64:188; ASD V-2, 374: Id explanat Propheta, dicens: *Animam meam convertit*. Nam Paulus animam hominis partitur in tres partes, in carnem quae vergit ad terrena, spiritum qui nititur ad coelestia, et animam mediam, quae nunc huc, nunc illuc voluitur. Hoc genus sunt affectus naturae, cura propriae incolumitatis, charitas erga uxorem, pietas erga parentes ac liberos, affectus erga propinquos et amicos. Nam haec nobis cum ethnicis, partim etiam cum brutis communia sunt. Hi affectus si se applicent ad spiritum, ut illos non amemus nisi in Christo et si incidat necessitas, malimus illos deserere, quam a Christi charitate recedere, animam vertunt in spiritum. Sin in horum gratiam divaricamur a mandatis Dei, iam anima vertitur in carnem. Ut ergo totus homo ferveat spiritu, necesse est ut pastor noster animam ad se convertat.

wicked. It is a soul sighing in its desire to fly from the refuge provided by this wretched dwelling place and to find that perfect rest of blessed minds from whose eyes God has wiped away every tear, who now have no grief, lamentation, or suffering to fear. When you hear the word song, you must understand that these things are not uttered in a loud voice but with a prodigious emotion of the heart [*ingenti cordis affectu*].[30]

Thus, again, in reading the Psalms Erasmus finds a place to play on the contrast between the physical voice and the internal heart, but also to promise existential relief, respite from the more troubling emotions and the tears of human suffering. (One also senses, no doubt, a bit of personal reflection of an old Erasmus grown tired.) The feelings are not mild, either, but *ingenti* and, a bit later, *impotenti* (unbridled or violent)—language Erasmus more typically reserves for criticism of someone who is emotionally intemperate in a negative way[31]—when he writes, "he who is transported by a violent emotion leaps forward."[32] Unbridled affectivity is appropriate, even beneficial, when the soul's strings are tuned to the divine will.

The song, moreover, silent like the Psalmic prayer mentioned above, is also played on a lyre, and in his exposition of the verse Erasmus maps the emotions onto its strings. Extending the metaphor of leaping to the instrument itself, and emphasizing music's power to not only move the soul but even to heal the body (as in those classical anecdotes of a flute's melody alleviating the pain of sciatica), Erasmus equates a dissonant note to disordered human desires (*cupiditates humanas*) such as a desire for glory, anger, hatred, or fear of humans (as opposed, presumably, of God).[33] He then writes:

> If you have raised your mind's eye to the hills, then you have leaped up onto the mountains, for these leaps are accomplished not physically but spiritually, and faith undoubtedly has eyes while our emotions are the feet of the soul [*fides habet oculos, affectus sunt pedes*]. Anyone who takes a leap first fixes his eyes on the place which his feet are aiming for, and in the same way believing precedes loving, not so much in a temporal sense as by nature. A man has as many spiritual feet and as many strings to his lyre as he has emotions.[34]

---

30. CWE 65:11–12, modified.
31. See the final chapter on Luther.
32. Saltu fertur, qui impotenti fertur affectu (ASD V-3, 178).
33. ASD V-3, 177: Sed bonus citharoedus esse non potest, qui non sit Idythun, omnesque cupiditates humanas spiritu transilierit. Etenim si inter canendum obstrepat, emolumenti studium, aut gloriae sitis, aut ira odiumve, aut metus hominum, aut haereticus error, una chorda dissonans vitiat totam harmoniam.
34. CWE 65:26–7; ASD V-3, 180: Sustulisse mentis oculos in montes, est subsiliisse in montes. Neque enim hi saltus corpore peraguntur, sed animo: In eo nimirum, fides habet oculos, affectus sunt pedes. Qui saliunt, prius destinant oculis locum, quem petunt pedibus.

The imagery of emotions as feet is, originally, Augustinian, but it has a rich medieval afterlife as well.[35] Erasmus, too, repeats it more than once, sometimes without much explanation. Here, though, the *affectus qua pedes* serves to ground the soul, as it were, again completing the spiritual movement that is begun with the eyes.

Erasmus then reiterates the Pauline-Origenian notion of the division of the soul into carnal, psychic, and spiritual parts.[36] One must leap from the wicked, or base [*turpibus*] emotions to transform from a monster into a human being, but to make the final leap to the spiritual emotions one must give everything over to Christ.

> But just as there are some emotions which are wicked [*improbi*], some natural ones [*naturales*], and some which are spiritual [*spirituales*], so there are also different strings which produce different sounds, and those strings which spoil the harmony one must either suppress or, if this is impossible as long as the mind inhabits the earthly body, then one must leap over them. If you have managed to leap up from the wicked emotions to those which are natural, then you have become a man instead of a monster. For if you love your wife or your parent or children with the kind of affection which a virtuous pagan feels for his family, you are merely a man who is living dangerously, should your love for your family on occasion lead you to do wrong. But if you have leaped over what is natural and flown up to what is spiritual, you are now something greater than man and you have begun to approach the heights where the angels dwell.[37]

The examples Erasmus gives are somewhat limiting, given that they only apply to a married man (loving your wife as a pagan is tantamount to natural emotion;

Ita prius est credere quam amare, prius, inqam, non tam tempore, quam natura. Quot sunt affectus in homine, tot sunt chordae in cithara, tot sunt pedes in anima.

35. See references in Juanita Feros Ruys, "Before the Affective Turn: *Affectus* in Heloise, Abelard, and the Woman Writer of the *Epistolae duorum amantium*," in *Before Emotions: The Language of Feeling, 400–1800*, ed. Juanita Feros Ruys, Michael Champion, and Kirk Essary (Routledge, 2019), 63 and notes.

36. On this division, see the discussion in M. A. Screech, *Ecstasy and the Praise of Folly* (Duckworth, 1980), and Debora Shuger, *The Renaissance Bible: Scholarship, Sacrific, and Subjectivity* (Waco: Baylor University Press, 1994).

37. CWE 65:26–7; ASD V-3, 180: Sed ut sunt affectus quidam improbi, quidam naturales, quidam spirituales, ita sunt variae chordae diversa sonantes. At chordae quae vitiant harmoniam, aut incidendae sunt, aut si hoc fieri non potest donec animus versatur in hoc terreno corpore, certe transiliendae sunt. Si ab affectibus turpibus subsilisti ad affectus naturae, e monstro factus es homo. Nam si diligius uxorem, aut parentem, aut liberos eo affectu, quo probus Ethnicus diligit suos, nihil aliud es quam homo, vicinus periculo, si per occasionem, necessariorum caritas te pertrahat ad injustitiam. Verum si naturam transilieris, ac subvolaris ad spiritum, iam homine major, coepisti ad Angelorum sublimitatem accedere . . .

willingness to desert her for Christ is tantamount to spiritual emotion), but love for one's family also features as a "neutral" emotion when Erasmus schematizes *affectus* elsewhere, as we have seen. And the general idea is fairly straightforward: the soul must be harmonious with respect to its affections in order to please God.

Less common is Erasmus listing specific emotions as serving a preeminent function in the organization of the soul, but he does so here, followed by an explanation of how specific neutral emotions might become spiritual ones (how the strings should be precisely tuned):

> There are four emotions in the human soul which tyrannize men's lives: hope, fear, joy, and sorrow. If you tune these strings to worldly matters the harmony is spoiled, but if you tune them to an attitude of devotion—in other words if you set your hope in God, if you refrain from wicked deeds through fear of God . . . then the strings produce the sweetest sounds.[38]

Erasmus moves to a consideration of examples from pagan antiquity, in particular Socrates, who sought via moral philosophy to regulate his desires with reason. Lest we think, however, that this is the path of the Psalmist or the Christian, he writes: "Human philosophy cannot, however, produce this melody which is suitable for the temple of the Lord as its strings are tuned to human reason; and human reason is often at variance with the spirit of God, for unless all the strings of our mind are tuned to his will they are unable to produce a tuneful melody."[39] The particular emotions or affective dispositions themselves need refinement or *tuning* so that they are in accord with spiritual things, but note that they do not need to be subsumed beneath reason. In earlier works like the *Enchiridion*, we found Erasmus aligning reason against the emotions with the support of ancient philosophy. Here he invokes Socrates only to undermine him.

When Erasmus finally turns to explain the Psalm itself (the first thirty-odd pages are devoted to unpacking "Idythun" according to the spiritual sense), he writes that it "not only starts in sorrow—and in the course of it the distress increases—but it also ends in lamentation."[40] It is a story of deep mental anguish and emotional turmoil. At the same time, Erasmus finds parallels in the Old Comedy, recalling several examples to illuminate the tortured soul of the subject:

---

38. CWE 65:27; ASD V-3, 180: Sunt quatuor affectiones humanae mentis, tyrannidem exercentes in vita humanam, spes ac metus, agudium et dolor. Has fides si intenderis ad res huius mundi, vitiant melos: sin ad pietatem, hoc est, si spem sigas in Deo, si metu Dei abstineas a turpibus, si nihil aeque doleat ac turpitudo, si nihil jucundius lucro bonae mentis, male tetendit chordam.

39. CWE 65:26–7; ASD V-3, 180: Verum humana philosophia non potest hanc melodiam reddere, quae digna sit templo Domini, quoniam illic ad rationem humanam tenduntur chordae. At humana ratio frequenter discrepat a Spiritu Dei, ad cuius voluntatem nisi tendantur omnes animi nostri chordae, non potest reddi bene modulata cantio.

40. CWE 65:37.

first, from Aristophanes, the recurring song "Oh Alas! Alas!" which represents the fact that "our happiness is contaminated by sorrow or fear" so long as we're here on earth;[41] second, the character Timon the Alexandrian, a misanthrope represented by both Aristophanes and Lucian (and, later, Shakespeare).[42] Those who experience significant sorrow (*ingens moeror*), Erasmus tells us, just want to be left alone, either to talk to themselves or to weep.[43] The recalling of exempla from classical literature, though not as frequent in the Psalms exegesis as elsewhere in his writings, is a recurring feature of Erasmus's humanist discourse about feeling. The identification of Idythun with a Timon-like character allows Erasmus to expand the emotional possibilities of expositing concise psalmic verse: "*In the same way* [as Timon the misanthrope], Idythun here is sick of talking to men in whom he finds no sense. The waves of suffering have upset him and he has perhaps not yet turned his thoughts to God."[44] But, like Terence's Phormio, he eventually finds resolve, represented by his proclamation that he has spoken (*dixi*).[45]

The solution is silence: "I shall guard my ways that I may not sin with my tongue." As part of a lengthy gloss on this verse, Psalm 38:2, Erasmus invokes specific emotions again as potentially sinful, and as in need of a corresponding silence: "And so whenever the heart is seething with envy, hatred, anger, desire for revenge, with lust or some such emotion [*affectu*], the safest course is to maintain silence."[46] Similarly, later, commenting ostensibly on the same verse, Erasmus describes the danger of hatred, for it destroys judgment by obscuring everything negatively: in the same way that the lover sees everything through rose-tinted glasses, the mind "when corrupted by emotion, makes errors of judgment," and "no one whose mind is corrupted by hatred and malice should trust himself or assume the task of judging."[47] Erasmus presents the story of this psalm as one of a man who, though full of indignation and a desire for revenge, not only refrains from violence but also maintains silence on account of his recognition that the tongue is the most difficult organ to restrain.

While this is not, as Erasmus points out, the story of a perfectly stoic hero or even of a good Christian one (Erasmus says it has a "Jewish tone" for its strung-out lamentation), this section of the *enarratio* comprises a short treatise on anger management, with a series of classical examples. For instance, Erasmus cites the story of Athenodorus recommending that Augustus recite the Greek alphabet

---

41. CWE 65:39.
42. CWE 65:40. See Aristophanes, *Lysistrata*, ll. 808–20.
43. CWE 65:40.
44. CWE 65:40. Sic et nostrum Idythun hominibus loqui taedet in quibus nihil sani reperit: Deus fortasse nondum venit in mentem afflictionum undis perturbatam (ASD V-3, 190).
45. CWE 65:41.
46. CWE 65:41. Quoties igitur cor aestuat invidia, odio, ira, vindictae cupiditate, amore, aliove simili affectu, tutissimum est silentium (ASD V-3, 191).
47. CWE 65:57.

when angry before reacting, but recommends the Christian recite scripture instead, and he collects a dozen-odd verses on anger that might be appropriate: "If one recites such incantations when the spirit is boiling over, it will be easy to restrain one's tongue and prevent it from blurting out insolent words."[48] He paraphrases Horace: *Ira vehemens brevis est furor*; violent anger is brief insanity. But he adds that if it morphs into hatred, there is no remedy for it.[49] Indeed, this comes close to happening to the subject of the psalm, and Erasmus is then forced to change tack, acknowledging that silence is good if it results in violent emotions subsiding, but suppression can also result in undesirable festering. "It is in vain," he writes, "that the man in this psalm has sought a remedy in stubborn silence: so far from allaying his mental agony, as long as it remained suppressed it grew increasingly violent and painful."[50] Here Erasmus invokes an Ovidian adage: a covered flame burns more fiercely.[51] The sprinkling in of classical literary examples enlivens the exposition and also provides for a more well-rounded conception of affectivity. To Erasmus's understanding, the emotional suffering of Idythun and the lessons to be derived from it are not confined to the context of the Old Testament, but are cross-cultural characteristics of feeling.

Moreover, in offering multiple glosses on the verses of Psalm 38, Erasmus provides multiple ways of coping with emotional distress, with the recognition that the result will depend on the individual. Sometimes repression works, sometimes you need talk therapy: "One can obtain some relief in distress by giving voice to one's anxieties and disturbances [*animi curas aestusque*]; and anger [*ira*] sometimes abates if one retaliates."[52] This isn't prescriptive advice, but an appreciation of the complexities of emotional suffering and the difficulties of alleviating it. *Aestus*, translated earlier as "disturbances," is a term that appears infrequently in Erasmus, and has the sense of the commotion, ardor, or fire of an emotion, a swelling tumult; it fits with the imagery of blazing and fiery feelings in this section of the exposition, leading to the next verse: "My heart grew hot within me and a fire burned in my thoughts." Erasmus explains of that verse that *meditatio* (translated in the verse as "in my thoughts") is not, in fact, a *cogitatio* (thought), but a "strong desire to do

---

48. CWE 65:63. The anecdote about anger and the alphabet also appears in the *Lingua* CWE 27:389.

49. ASD V-3, 205: Ira vehemens, brevis est furor: quae si transeat in odium, furor est immedicabilis.

50. CWE 65:72.

51. CWE 65:72; Cf. Ovid *Met.* 4.64: Tectus magis aestuat ignis.

52. CWE 65:72, modified. And, further, "But throwing water on to a burning pitch makes the fire blaze more strongly, and in the same way, if you try to resist the violent irritation you are feeling, your anguish only increases" (Tum enim fit furor, saepius laesa patientia. Hi sunt tumulus carnis, adversus spiritum identidem effervescentis [ASD V-3, 210]).

something" (*studium vehemens aliquid agendi*), providing the Septuagint reading of *meleté* (attention, care, anxiety) as an apt equivalent.[53]

The question, Erasmus then says, is about what the plan is, now that the man is *totus igneus* (consumed with fire). Such a man, "whose great anguish has got the better of him" might do a number of different things: seek vengeance, placate his enemies, elevate his status beyond the reach of lowly jealousies, seek refuge in the magical arts, commit suicide. The reference to the *artes magicas*, at first glance obscure, becomes clearer in the following pages where Erasmus gives multiple examples of people suffering mental anguish seeking clarity as to the end of their lives, from "magicians or fortune tellers, from mediums or chiromancers, from astrologers or soothsayers," and so on.[54] These practices are perhaps still understudied as early modern therapies (and this is not the only instance in the Psalms commentaries where Erasmus links violent emotions to suicidal tendencies[55]).[56] In any case, what Michael McCarthy has written about Augustine's use of the Psalms in the *Confessions* is applicable also to Erasmus's exegesis: "The Psalms offer a therapeutic program to heal a disordered fixation on the self and to help a person gradually cling to God."[57] That is, the affective portrait Erasmus develops here overall of the psalm's voice is of a person overwhelmed with a mixture of strong emotions—including anger, sorrow, incipient hatred—but mainly of a nonspecific form of psychological anguish, the only true remedy for which is to turn to the Lord: "fortunate is the disaster which drives us to God."[58]

Continuing with the emotional narrative of the man in the Psalm, and expositing verse 7 ("But yet man passes in a shadow"), Erasmus invokes Plato's allegory of the cave. Comparing Idythun to the individual who had emerged from the cave and who then tries to explain the false nature of the shadows, he paraphrases with added emotional content: "That wise man who saw reality in the light of day cries out to no effect: 'Why do you act like madmen, you wretched creatures?' These are illusory images of things which make you applaud, rejoice, feel sad, or frightened.

---

53. ASD V-3, 210.
54. CWE 65: 76
55. See further on Psalm 4:4 below.
56. Erasmus comments on the emotional damage of relying on fortune tellers in the *Ecclesiastes*: "Finally, even today atrologers, palm readers, 'belly talkers,' and wizards predict many future occurrences, but there is no particularly great profit in this foreknowledge; for if what they predict is going to come to pass, precognition of the inevitable is the height of misery: if it does not, the very fear of misfortune is a great part of misfortune" (CWE 67:389). It's worth mentioning, perhaps, that Erasmus does not criticize the validity of the practices (although he lambasts them elsewhere), but their negative emotional side effects.
57. McCarthy, "Augustine's Mixed Feelings: Vergil's 'Aeneid' and the Psalms of David in the 'Confessions,'" *Harvard Theological Review* 102, no. 4 (2009): 455.
58. CWE 65: 74–5.

There is nothing real there; they are illusions created by shadows which either terrify or delight you" (*vel territant, vel delectant*).⁵⁹ These *affectus humani* are of a lower order than truly pious feelings. Idythun leaps, Erasmus says, continuing the Platonic riff, over "human happiness" (*felicitatis humanae*) in order to contemplate the true Ideas with the eyes of faith.⁶⁰ Idythun, otherwise hopeless and dejected—Erasmus uses broad emotional vocabulary to describe his state of mind, including, here, *afflictum ac pene delassatum animum* (a despondent and worn-out spirit)—can only hope for things unseen.⁶¹

Erasmus then makes a notable distinction between hope (*spes*), that great biblical and apocalyptic emotion, and expectation (*expectatio*), with some litotes:

> There is very little difference between hope and expectation except that hope can exist in varying degrees of intensity—strong, moderate, or feeble [*vehemens, mediocris et languida*]; one can also hope for things which are far away. Expectation, however, is a powerful feeling [*vehemens*] and it is directed towards something which is already visible and close at hand. The Latin word derives from the fact that people who are seized by a strong desire for something usually keep a constant watch to see if it is coming.⁶²

Hope can be vague and can be felt in varying degrees, but *expectatio*—almost a false cognate with the English term, given Erasmus's gloss—is vehement, the result of a violent desire [*magno desiderio*] for something. Erasmus equates the sense with that other biblical virtue, endurance, using the Septuagint's rendering (which has the sense of "endurance" as opposed to expectation) as a jumping-off point to cite several New Testament verses that pertain "to someone who holds on in misfortune in expectation of a reward, and is sustained by hope, which prevents him from collapsing, crushed by the burden of his misfortunes."⁶³ Endurance is thus the theological virtue which corresponds to the related affections of hope and expectation.

The final overt affective exposition on this Psalm comes in Erasmus's gloss of verse 13, "Hear my words, O Lord, and heed my cries; do not be deaf to my tears." Erasmus moves between bodily affect and spiritual affection, ultimately locating the significance of both in the effectiveness of their communicative force, in their

---

59. CWE 65: 90.

60. ASD V-3, 222: Itaque qui cum Idythum transilierunt omnem sublimitatem felicitatis humanae, oculisque fidei contemplati sunt verorum bonorum ideas.

61. ASD V-3, 223-4.

62. CWE 65:94, modified. ASD V-3, 235: Minimum interest inter spem et expectationem, nisi quod spes potest esse qualiscunque vehemens, mediocris et languida. Rursus sperantur et quae procul absunt. Sed expectatio vehemens est ac rei iam e propiinquo apparentis. Vox enim inde Latinis dicta est, quod qui magno rei cuiuspiam desiderio tenentur, solent subinde prospicere si iam appareat.

63. CWE 65:94.

role as a medium of expression between created and Creator. The words and cries, Erasmus tells us—as he did earlier on Psalm 85—are not of the physical voice but by fiery emotion. They are an answer to the call to pray vehemently (*precandi vehemens*), required because of the distance between humanity and God: "and yet from those heights the Lord heeds the prayers of the lowly who call to him although their cry is not the sound produced in the body by a powerful breath, but an ardent emotion (*igneus affectus animi*)."[64] The ignited *affectus* is here, again, the organ through which the person is able to implore God. Tears are another unconventional mode of religious communication, with a voice different from that expressed with the tongue, but one with more affective purchase. Despite this explanation, the "unusual turn of phrase" *do not be deaf to my tears* forces the interpreter of the psalm to consider the mystical sense (*mysterio dictum*). It is worth quoting the passage at some length, for weeping is not something Erasmus endorses very often:

> It is often the case among men that people who cannot be moved by any entreaty are softened by silent tears and become merciful. So importunate a thing is a tear—indeed, there is no sound more effective than that of tears, when sobs interrupt one's speech. It does however make a difference to whom the flowing tears make their appeal. There is no help to be gained from men and that is why the blessed Job says: "My friends are talkative, my eye flows with tears to God." Anyone who prays is admitting his poverty; he who calls out is in the grip of great need, but he who weeps is making an assault. Moreover, Ecclesiasticus bears witness to the fact that his tears and sighs have a voice of their own when he says: "The Lord will not scorn the prayers of the people nor of the widow if she pours forth the speech of her groaning. Do not the widow's tears run right down her cheeks, and does she not cry out over the one who causes them? For they run down from the cheeks as far as heaven and when the Lord heeds them he will not be pleased by them." And so there is nothing more silent than tears but also nothing more clamorous; there is nothing weaker than tears but also nothing more violent.[65]

Clamorous tears is a wonderful image. Tears are, Erasmus tells us, the mechanism by which what one needs is extricated from an interlocutor, whether human or divine. There is no sound (*vox*) more efficacious. Tears are a sign of force (*vis*) that moves God to mercy, which is the final plea of the subject of the Psalm in seeking redemption and emotional solace.[66]

---

64. ASD V-3, 236: Quanquam hic clamor non est vox corporis spiritu vehementi producta, sed igneus affectus animi.

65. CWE 65: 112–13.

66. Ubi sunt lacrymae, ibi quodam modo vis admovetur divinae misericordiae (ASD V-3, 237).

"Anything Metaphorical is Ambiguous": Divine Feelings as Synecdoche in Psalm 2

Having established the deeply affective nature of Erasmus's exegetical theology as borne out in the Psalms commentaries, we can now examine what other aspects of Erasmus's thinking about feeling can be clarified from these texts. Perhaps the most obvious problem that arises in an examination of emotion in general in the Old Testament is the question of anthropomorphism: What does it mean to ascribe the tumult of affectivity to an unchanging deity?[67] In most ways, Erasmus does not attempt to chart any new territory here, but his commentary on Psalm 2 (1522), contains some noteworthy moments, and also gives us a good sense of where he stood on the issue. Glossing Psalm 2:4 ("He that dwells in heaven shall laugh them to scorn, etc."), he expands upon the patristic exegetical tradition on the topic:

> In the Holy Scriptures, human emotions [*affectus humani*] are very frequently attributed to God: fury, anger, regret, joy, grief, pity, although none of these is appropriate to the divine nature, which is utterly immutable; none the less, following the tradition of the mystical Scriptures, words expressing the emotions which result from changes in *our* fortunes are applied to God.[68]

This is a typical formulation, which in general, but not in all particulars, is indebted to Augustine and other patristic commentators.[69] Erasmus does not much contend with the well-developed medieval notion of divine impassability and simplicity, but reads divine emotions as primarily reflective of God's enactment of justice in creation. He writes,

> For example, He is said to be angry whenever our crimes are punished by the infliction of some misfortune, and when the affliction is still more grievous he is said to be furious. He is said to show compassion whenever we enjoy more good fortune than we deserve or whenever, by some lightening of our misfortunes, we are urged to return to our right senses. He is said to be regretful whenever we live in such a way that we seem quite undeserving of his kindness and he must deprive us of his gifts which we are wasting. Thus either the causes or the effects

---

67. For a recent treatment of this question from a variety of angles, see the collection of essays in Chrystel Bernat and Frédéric Gabriel (eds.), *Émotions de Dieu: Attributions et Appropriations Chrétiennes (XVIe-XVIIIe Siècle)* (Turnhout: Brepols, 2019).

68. CWE 63:102–3; ASD V-2, 122–3: Nunc de schemate sermonis quod polliciti sumus praestabimus. Frequenter in divinis literis affectus humani tribuuntur Deo: furor, ira, poenitentia, gaudium, dolor, misericordia, quum nihil horum cadat in naturam divinam quae prorsus est immutabilis. Sed ex rerum mutatione quae nobis accidit iuxta consuetudinem mysticae scripturae affectuum vocabula Deo tribuuntur,

69. See, e.g., Augustine, *Ennarationes in Psalmos*, on Psalm 2:4, *ad loc.*

of these emotions [*affectionum*] are within ourselves, while God remains serene and unmoved [*tranquillus et immotus*]; and since he is free from all emotions of the soul [*affectionibus animorum*], bodily emotions [*affectionibus corporis*] are still less applicable to him. God is Mind, and utterly undivided; in no way can he be called body, unless you call body anything that subsists in its own nature.[70]

The distinction between the *affectus* of the soul and those of the body is a potentially interesting one that Erasmus unfortunately does not go into here, but it may be similar to that offered in the *De taedio* between bodily affects and psychological emotions, as discussed in the third chapter.

Erasmus elaborates further on the embodied nature of some emotions in his gloss on the Psalmist's phrase, "laughs to scorn," offering a physiological assessment of laughter that, he says, is used in the biblical text for purposes of accommodation:

> Moreover, when someone laughs at us he stretches his mouth wide open, the physiologists think that laughter is produced by movement of the spirits around the pericardium, which separates the heart from the lower organs, and they say that its origin is the spleen. It is usually the result of joy, but sometimes of bitterness, as when it is called sardonic laughter. However, when someone "laughs to scorn", he wrinkles his nose in mockery; the ancients particularly associated the nose with scorn. These expressions [i.e., "laughs to scorn", e.g.] are all quite inappropriate to God, since they are even considered unbecoming in the better sort of men, but the Holy Scriptures have adopted the language of human emotions in order to be more intelligible.[71]

Thus, God's emotions are in some sense better understood as our emotions, or at least our experiences as wrought by God, but rendered in language accommodated

---

70. CWE 63:102–3, modified; ASD V-2, 123–4: ut irasci dicatur quoties afflicti malis scelerum nostrorum poenas damus; furere, quoties durius affligimur; misereri, quoties praeter meritum nostrum rebus laetioribus fruimur aut quoties mitioribus malis admonemur ut resipiscamus; poentiere, quum ita vivimus ut illius beneficio prorsus videamur indigni quotiesque sua munera quibus abutimur aufert a nobis. In nobis igitur sunt affectionum huiusmodi vel causae vel effectus, quum Deus semper sit tranquillus et immotus. Ergo quum ille sit immunis ab omnibus animorum affectionibus, multo minus in illum competunt affectiones corporis. Mens est Deus, sed simplicissima; corpus nullo modo dici potest nisi corpus dixeris rem quae suapte natura subsistat.

71. CWE 63:102–3; ASD V-2, 123: Sed nobis irridet qui rictum oris diducit. Id physici putant accidere motis spiritibus circa reticulum diaphragmatis, quod dirimit cor ab inferioribus, nasci dicunt e splene. Proficiscitur autem fere e gaudio nonnunquam ex amarulentia qui risus dicitur Sardonius. Subsannat autem qui corrugato naso deridet. Nam nasum irrisioni dicavit antiquitas. Haec adeo non conveniunt in Deum ut probis etiam viris habeantur indecora. Verum quo magis intelligatur scriptura sacra suum sermonem ad nostros affectus attemperat.

to human understanding. We can compare this passage to one from his sermon (*concio*) on Psalm 85:

> God's mind is of the most pure and simple kind, it contains nothing corporeal, nor any corporeal accident, nor any human emotions... Instead, Scripture, by lisping indistinctly with the words of men so that it may be understood in a less forbidding way, accommodates itself to men's weakness, like a nurse or a mother using baby language to her child to make herself understood.[72]

Feeling emotion is a fundamental way in which humans experience the world, and thus the phenomenon can helpfully be used as an interpretative analogy for comprehending the divine nature.

God's emotions, indeed, are a classic counterexample to a method of scriptural interpretation that insists on literality, or a "simple" sense, as Erasmus suggests in the *Ecclesiastes*:

> Why should I mention here the language with which the holy books, especially of the Old Testament, abound everywhere, through which things that appertain either physically or mentally to us are attributed to God, such as when he is said to grow angry, rage, regret, hate, forget, remember, take notice, avert his face, extend his arm, sit, rise, incline his ear, and countless other things of this sort, which have a false and impious meaning if you take them in their simple sense?[73]

God's emotions mean something else. Divine linguistic accommodation is necessary (and has long been recognized as a fundamental feature of Erasmus's hermeneutics). It becomes even more evident as the commentary on Psalm 2 progresses.

At the same time, Erasmus thought that emotion words employed to describe God in the biblical texts, even if accommodated to our understanding, still caused particular exegetical difficulties. In his 1534 *Purgatio* against Luther, a late work and part of the most vicious back and forth he had with the German Reformer, he accuses Luther of disingenuousness for inveighing against Erasmus for pointing out ambiguities in the language of the Bible. Erasmus responds that "anything metaphorical is ambiguous," and as examples mentions specifically "when hatred, love, anger, rage, regret, and mercy are attributed to [God]."[74] Thus understanding the role of metaphor in biblical language is crucial for appreciating biblical discourse on affectivity. But Erasmus gets more specific in terms of the application of literary figures to exegetical problems about divine feeling. Erasmus's gloss on the next verse, Psalm 2:5, runs thus:

---

72. CWE 64:21.
73. CWE 68:895.
74. CWE 78:438–9.

The next words are, "Then he will speak to them in his wrath, and in his fury he will confound them." First, we must recall here what I said earlier, that the divine nature cannot be disturbed by passions [*perturbationibus*], and that such expressions as these refer, by synecdoche, not to an actual stirring of the emotions [*animi motum*], but to the effects normally produced in us when our spirit is perturbed [*ex animi commotione nasci*] or otherwise moved. For example, whenever our blood boils up around the heart, we are roused to seek revenge, and thus it is quite usual for the divine eloquence to describe as wrath the just vengeance of God, by which he punishes the incorrigible, and as fury his more severe or final vengeance.[75]

Again, not a radical interpretation of the verse. Erasmus has followed, but expanded on, Augustine's argument that the wrath and fury of God are representative both of God's justice and vengeance in general (and has adopted some of Augustine's Ciceronianisms, viz. *perturbationes* and *motus animi*), but also as reflective of an emotion (or the effect of an emotion) produced *in us*.[76]

Erasmus's treatment is significantly longer in this case, however. He repeats the Aristotelian idea that anger is represented physiologically by blood boiling around the heart and, socially, by a desire for revenge. And then he notes that this sort of divine wrath is found in the New Testament as well: "It is not only in the Old Testament," he writes, "that punishment inflicted on sinners is called the wrath of God; in the New, these are the words of John the Baptist in the Gospel: 'Generation of vipers, who warned you to flee from the wrath that is to come?' And Paul, to the Romans: 'For the wrath of God is revealed from heaven.'"[77] Erasmus also offers a brief digression on the affective language of the Septuagint's Greek for "fury," allowing us a view of the historical semantics of emotion pertinent to multilayered biblical translation:

> Now the word which the Latin translator renders as *furor* is not the Greek μανία, which describes people who are ill and not in their right mind (although according to the principles of the philosophers wrath is nothing other than a brief madness), but θυμός, which in Greek sometimes means simply "the spirit" and sometimes "a disturbance of the spirit" when it has been violently upset. Latin tends to use the plural *animi*, rather than the singular *animus*, when describing this sort of disturbance: hence the satirist's words: *Animos a*

---

75. CWE 63:111; ASD V-2, 130: Hic primum oportet meminisse, quod superius dictum est nobis, divinam naturam nullis perturbationibus esse mutabilem, sed per synecdochen huiusmodi vocabulis significari non ipsum animi motum sed quod ex animi commotione nasci solet in nobis aut contra. Nobis enim quoties effervescit sanguis circa praecordia commovemur ad vindictam. Proinde solenne est divinis eloquiis iustam Dei ultionem qua punit incorrigibiles iram appelare, severiorem aut extremam vindictam furorem.
76. See Aug. *Ennar. in Ps.* 2:4, *ad loc.*
77. CWE 63:112.

crimine sumunt "they take mad courage from their crime." Apparently there is little difference in Hebrew between the words translated "wrath" (*ira*) and "fury" (*furor*), and it is thus clear that the same idea is repeated, as it was earlier with "laugh" and "laugh to scorn."[78]

Erasmus's point is perhaps not remarkable from a theological perspective but is noteworthy for his comment on the lexical equivalence of the Hebrew terms (not provided) that have been rendered by the Vulgate translator as two rather different emotions. The use of *ira* and *furor* is not meant to indicate any sort of transition from anger to divine madness (as the Latin might suggest), but is simply a dexterous way of handling two Hebrew terms that mean substantially the same thing.

Returning to the problem of metaphor, even though Augustine himself does not use the term, he seems to have inspired Erasmus to draw out the notion of God's emotions *as synecdoche* of ours (or vice versa?), and it is not the only case where he refers to this particular rhetorical device to explain this verse. In his manual for preachers, written a decade later, he again refers to Augustine's gloss on this Psalm in a series of examples of synecdoche, writing that for Augustine "it is the custom of Scripture to attribute to God himself what he does within us."[79] Other examples of biblical synecdoche adduced here are Matt 10:20, ("For it is not you who are speaking but the spirit of your father that speaks in you"), and Romans 8, ("The Spirit itself entreats for us with indescribable groans"). Without reading too much into these passages, they would seem to have significant theological implications for Erasmus's use of synecdoche in an affective context, as in the case where our own feelings are enactments of God's "wrath." Affectivity is not only a conduit for true transformation of the godly, an idea we traced in the first sections of this chapter, but it is a means of divine punishment as well.

God's emotion as "synecdoche" does not, for Augustine, need to reflect the same emotion felt in humans. For Erasmus reports Augustine's comment that the "wrath of God" could be understood not as human anger, but as a "mental darkness" (*obscuratio mentis* in Augustine; *caecitatem mentis* in Erasmus) that descends upon those who have not come to repentance—a hardening of the heart, as it were. The important point is that emotional suffering is represented in synecdoche but also actually felt by humanity. It is also a mechanism by which Erasmus

---

78. CWE 63:112; ASD V-2, 130: Porro quod Latinus interpres vertit furorem non est Graecis *mania* qua correpti, mente capti dicuntur (etiam si iuxta philosophorum placita ira nihil aliud est quam brevis insania), sed *thumos*, quae vox Graecis aliquando simpliciter significat animum aliquando impetum animi vehementer concitati. Latini malunt animos dicere quam animum quoties hunc impetum intelligi volunt. Unde Satyricus: *Animos a crimine sumunt*. In Hebraeis vocibus aiunt esse minimum discriminis, ut appareat et hic esse repetitam eandem sententiam *in ira et in furore*, quemadmodum superius in *irridebit et subsannabit*.

79. CWE 68:892. See 893f. for other examples of synecdoche related to emotion.

eschews crude anthropomorphisms, as Jacques Chomarat has noted.[80] But while Erasmus acknowledges that Augustine's reading "contains nothing which clashes with orthodox interpretation," he himself prefers to understand wrath and fury as "both a punishment and a reproof, by which God seeks to bring us back to our senses." He then offers the analogy of these two kinds of retribution, namely of a doctor sometimes cauterizing a wound but other times applying soothing ointments.[81] Examples of cauterization include scourges of God, naturally, which Erasmus describes in his commentary on Psalm 28 as "healing terrors." God might reform us through mercy or destroy us through vengeance, both of which are, to Erasmus's mind, understandable as forms of his "wrath." Thus the ineradicable ambiguity of emotive metaphor.

We find a different, but still relevant, reference to synecdoche in his *Enarratio* of Psalm 38, where Erasmus explains the figure in a seemingly anodyne way: "The grammarians recognize a type of synecdoche when one thing is understood from another, as when someone seized by fear is said to have turned pale or when someone who is embarrassed is said to blush."[82] These examples of psychosomatic correlations between an emotion and its bodily manifestation are important, I would suggest, for further fleshing out Erasmus's understanding of the intersubjective relationship between God's "emotions" and those of his creatures.[83] As Brian Cummings has written of Erasmus's theological discourse, "Literary categories become interchangeable with psychological and even epistemological terms."[84] In other words, to say that the locus of a nebulous sort of divine justice lies in human feeling is not *only* to say something about human experience. Especially if we read these passages together with those delineating *affectus* as the primary location for individual religious transformation, we find in Erasmus a robust if still somewhat elusive expression of a thoroughly emotional form of theological, or religious, activity that is fulfilled by God in a person properly affectively tuned. To borrow a phrase from Simeon Zahl, herein lies the "affective salience" of Erasmus's biblical theology as it pertains to the Old Testament.[85]

80. *Grammaire et Rhetorique*, 677.
81. CWE 63:114.
82. CWE 65:113.
83. In his manual for preachers, though, Erasmus offers a slightly different reading: In a warning against being duped by homonyms, he says, "And I am not certain whether all the things that are predicated of God and of creation are not of a *different genus*, such as when God is said to repent, hate, love, be angry, pity" (CWE 68:684).
84. Brian Cummings, "Erasmus and the Invention of Literature," *Erasmus of Rotterdam Society Yearbook* 33 (2013): 33.
85. "On the Affective Salience of Doctrines," *Modern Theology* 31, no. 3 (2015): 428–44, and see further Zahl, *The Holy Spirit and Christian Experience* (Oxford: Oxford University Press, 2020), for a more extensive treatment of the importance of affectivity in (primarily) the history of Protestant theology.

Dominic Baker-Smith has suggested that the biblical-humanist interpretations of the Psalter are similar to monastic *lectio divina* in their reliance on patristic commentary, "and, most importantly, by the fact that both see the biblical text as a means to personal transformation rather than to intellectual demonstration," a claim for which we have seen extensive evidence in this chapter.[86] Baker-Smith calls this biblical-humanist hermeneutics a "combination of textual scholarship with an affective mode of exegesis," citing Jacques Lefèvre d'Etaples's comment that those who read the Psalms according to the letter find them depressing,[87] and then quoting Erasmus himself (from the *Enchiridion*): "I think the principal reason why we see that monastic piety is everywhere so cold, languid, and almost extinct is that [monks] are growing old in the letter and never take pains to learn the spiritual sense of Scripture."[88] In an extensive display of allegorization, Erasmus demonstrates repeatedly the affective meaningfulness of the Psalms, and shows how important figurative language is for teasing out the most emotionally moving aspects of the text. He also uses the homiletic opportunity of exposition of the Psalms to digress on multiple issues attendant to the understanding and description of affectivity in ways consonant with his New Testament exegesis, but in a heighted mystical-emotional mode. The Psalms commentaries show, moreover, how Erasmus had developed his earlier understanding of Christian affectivity, from works like the *Enchiridion* and *De taedio Iesu*, into more intricate elaborations of the indispensible role of emotion in Christian life and spiritual experience.

86. CWE 63:xxx.
87. Ibid.
88. Ibid. Cf. CWE 66:35.

Chapter 6

Passionate Preaching

Affective Rhetoric in the Pulpit

In a letter from the year 1521 to Justus Jonas, Erasmus provides brief biographies of two of his friends, Jean Vitrier and John Colet. Erasmus especially admired the preaching method of Vitrier, and he describes the virtues of his approach in some detail:

> Vitrier used as it were a continuous flow of language to connect the Epistle with the Gospel, so that his hearers went home not only better informed, but kindled with a new desire for a pious life. There was no purposeless gesticulation, no noisy ranting; he was entirely concentrated, and brought his words out in such a way that you felt they came from a passionate and simple yet sober heart, nor did he ever dwell on any point till he was tedious or make a parade of citing various authorities, like those who cobble up an insipid [*frigidos*] patchwork at one moment from Scotus or Thomas or Durandus, at another from the civil and canon law, or from philosophy or the poets, that the public may think there is nothing they do not know. Every sentence he produced was full of Scripture, nor could he utter anything else. His heart was in what he said.[1]

Amabat quod loquebatur. Vitrier *loved* what he was saying, and this love resulted not only in sound teaching, but in an audience that was inflamed with a new zeal for piety. Although Erasmus's manual for preachers, the *Ecclesiastes*, wouldn't see the light of day for another decade and a half, this description of Vitrier's preaching

---

1. CWE 8:227–8; Ep 1202: At hic perpetuo quodam sermonis fluxu connectebat sacram Epistolam cum Evangelica lectione, ut auditor domum rediret et eruditior et inflammatior ad studium pietatis. Neque gesticulationibus ineptiebat, nec vociferationibus tumultuabatur, sed totus apud se sic promebat verba ut sentires ex ardenti ac simplici sed sobrio pectore proficisci: nec usquam immorabatur ad taedium usque, neque iactabat sese variis citationibus nominum; quemadmodum nunc e Scoto, Thomas, Durando, nunc ex iuris utriusque libris, nunc e philosophis, nunc e poetis centones frigidos consarcinant, quo populo nihil nescire videantur. Totus sermo quem promebat, erat sacrae Scripturae plenus, nec aliud ructare poterat. Amabat quod loquebatur.

could have served as a book-jacket abstract for the work: each of Vitrier's rhetorical and pedagogical attributes receives extensive treatment in the *Ecclesiastes*, which finally came off the press in 1535, still unfinished.

In the letter Erasmus also recalls an anecdote about Vitrier's preparation for passionate pedagogy: "I asked Vitrier once in familiar conversation how he prepared his mind when setting out to preach, and he replied that he usually opened Paul, and went on reading him until he felt his mind take fire. At that point he paused, praying to God with passion, until told that it was time to start."[2] Vitrier's explanation is transformed into a piece of practical advice for the preacher in the *Ecclesiastes*: "If the speaker," Erasmus writes in the later work, "when he is about to speak, feels rather listless, he should read a passage of Scripture especially suitable for setting the mind on fire, dwell upon it until he feels his mind warming, and climb up into the pulpit before that warmth cools."[3] The Latin is important here, as elsewhere, for determining with more precision Erasmus's understanding of affectivity in the context of faculty psychology. *Incalescere* is the verb in both instances for "setting the mind on fire," although in the letter it is the *pectus* (chest, or heart) that is set ablaze while in the *Ecclesiastes* it is the *animus*, a term that can be synonymous with *pectus*, but is also used to describe the rational soul. We might suggest that Erasmus is keen to emphasize the importance of both the cognitive and affective aspects of Christian preaching, or to blur the boundaries between them.

While the relationship between Christian pedagogy and Christian feeling do not differ radically here from Erasmus's treatment of the biblical emotions, we will see that the sermon setting provides for more specific emotional possibilities to do with space, body, gesture, and voice, as well as content, which latter also depends upon the congregation. In her recent book on emotions and rhetoric in the Middle Ages, Rita Copeland points out that the classical tradition bequeathed to subsequent rhetorical schools two important notions of the ways in which emotion "is a value shared between speaker and audience."[4] The first, which Copeland suggests is not widely adopted in the Middle Ages, is Quintilian's advice and judgment regarding the ways in which an audience will be more receptive to an orator's persuasive techniques if the orator is feeling the emotion they are trying to inculcate in their auditors; and the second, an idea adopted widely in medieval rhetorical handbooks, is that

---

2. Ep 1202: Rogatus a me in familiari colloquio quibus modis praepararet animum suum iturus ad concionandum, respondit se solitum in manus sumere Paulum, et in eius lectione tam diu commorari donec sentiret incalescere pectus. Illic haerebat, addens igneas ad Deum preces, donec admoneretur esse tempus incipiendi.

3. CWE 68:810; ASD V-5, 92: Tertius est, ut concionaturus si senserit animum languidiorem, locum aliquem Scripturae legat quam maxime appositum ad inflammandum, ei immoretur donec sentiat animum incalescere et, priusquam calor ille refrigescat, conscendat suggestum.

4. Rita Copeland, *Emotion and the History of Rhetoric in the Middle Ages* (Oxford: Oxford University Press, 2022), 11.

emotion can and should be conveyed through style. Medieval rhetoricians taught "style, especially the figures and the tropes, as something that could be charged with emotional impact."[5] Both ideas are crucial for Erasmus's understanding of the role of emotion in rhetoric, and in this way he is indebted to both the classical and medieval traditions for his approach to preaching.

Erasmus, as noted earlier, derives his theory of affective teaching partly from Quintilian's *Institutio oratoria*—whose reception, as Peter Mack has recently pointed out, reached a high-water mark in northern Europe when Erasmus was writing[6]—as well as a variety of other affective-rhetorical models from the patristic period to his own day.[7] In sketching out a *via media* between scholastic dialectic and Ciceronian eloquence, Erasmus learned something from the example of Vitrier, in whom he found a living voice, as he says, expressive of an ideal model of Christian teaching praxis. One could trace the relationship between teaching and moving from a variety of angles in his rhetorical manuals, but two of Erasmus's adages illuminate especially well the ways in which the preacher most effectively moves and teaches his parishioners. *Tanquam in speculo*, "as in a mirror," and *viva vox*, "the living voice," crop up several times in Erasmus's corpus in the context of rhetorical effectiveness—in the *Colloquies*, the *Ciceronianus*, and the letters, for example. The purpose of this chapter is to trace in more depth Erasmus's ideas about emotion in the context of preaching, focusing first on the recurrence of these two adages scattered across his works, and moving from there to an exposition of the advice Erasmus gives regarding the solicitation of the emotions in a sermonic setting in his preaching manual, the *Ecclesiastes*. In doing so, we will get a better handle on the interplay between the emotions, teaching, and subjectivity in Erasmus's understanding of the dynamics of in-person communication as well as in a live sermon.

Affective Adages and Emotional Expression

Speech, Erasmus writes in the *Ecclesiastes*, paraphrasing himself from a number of places in his corpus, "is the truthful image of the preacher's mind, and is reflected in his words *as in a mirror*." In expositing the adage *tanquam in speculo*, Erasmus

---

5. Ibid., 12.
6. Peter Mack, "Quintilian in Northern Europe during the Renaissance, 1479–1620," in *The Oxford Handbook to Quintilian*, ed. Marc Van Der Poel et al. (Oxford: Oxford University Press, 2022), 380–1.
7. On the connection to Augustine, see Marc Fumaroli, *L'Age de l'éloquence* (Geneva: Droz, 1980) esp. 70 and 106ff.; Charles Bene, *Erasme et Saint Augustin* (Geneva: Droz, 1969), 400ff.; and Kathy Eden, *Hermeneutics and the Rhetorical Tradition* (New Haven: Yale, 1997), 41–78. Debora Shuger points out that the *Ecclesiastes* attempts to work out the specifics of Christian eloquence in far more detail than Augustine had (*Sacred Rhetoric: The Christian Grand Style in the English Renaissance* [Princeton: Princeton University Press, 1988], 63).

wonders at the "truly marvellous" nature of the mirror, especially at "the way in which it reflects so very clearly not only the shapes of all the things placed in front of it, but the distances between them, their colours and their motions, in a word the things themselves—one could almost say—more vivid than they really are."[8] Only speech is truly representative of the thoughts and feelings of the individual. This twofold cognitive-affective luminescence of the mirror of speech means that the preached sermon is the ideal means of conveying the Christian philosophy for Erasmus, which has been inhabited, ideally, by the Christian preacher. But speech is also more efficacious for moving and teaching, and he expresses this efficacy by employing another adage, *viva vox*. While Robert Kilpatrick, in an illuminating study of the "mirror" *topos* in Erasmus's *Adagia*, assumes an equivalence between speaking and writing (speech as mirror functioning similarly in both media), Erasmus at times insists on the superiority of the spoken over the written word for truly passionate pedagogy.[9]

In the colloquy "The Whole Duty of Youth" the character named Erasmus asks his interlocutor Gaspar how he feels about sermons. "Fine," Gaspar responds,

> I attend them no less reverently than holy communion. Yet I choose which preachers to hear, because there are some it is profitable not to have heard. If such a one turns up, or if none turns up at all, I pass the time with Sacred Scripture; I read the Gospel and Epistles with commentary by Chrysostom or Jerome or any other holy and learned interpreter I happen to meet.[10]

"Erasmus" responds, "Yet the living voice (*viva vox*) is more effectual."[11] In glossing *viva vox* in the *Adages*, Erasmus writes that "the living word" was "the term used in old times for anything not written, but taken straight from the mouth of the speaker, lifelike, as it were, and effectual." The written word, by contrast, Erasmus continues, "is indeed a kind of voice, but as it were an artificial one, somehow mimicking the real voice. Gesture and movement are lacking; in a word, life."[12] This may seem striking, or perhaps a bit disingenuous, coming from a man who did not preach, but instead dedicated all of his energy to writing and editing an extraordinary number of books filled with *dead* words—who, as Mark Vessey has put it, made the printing press his pulpit.[13] The preacher's words, Erasmus writes in the *Ecclesiastes*, must be couched in an appropriate emotional disposition. "The

---

8. Adage II iii 50, CWE 33, ad loc.

9. "'Clouds on a Wall': The Mirror of Speech in the *Adagiorum Chiliades* and the *Moriae encomium*," *Erasmus of Rotterdam Society Yearbook* 33, no. 1 (2013): 66.

10. CWE 39:96.

11. For a recent treatment of emotion in Erasmus's *Colloquies*, see Brian Cummings, "Erasmus and the Colloquial Emotions," *Erasmus Studies* 40, no. 2 (2020): 127–50.

12. Adagia I ii 17; CWE 31:162.

13. Vessey, in Pabel and Vessey, *Holy Scripture Speaks* (Toronto: University of Toronto Press, 2002), 8.

voice that produces [genuine] emotion in the audience's minds is that which comes from a mind that is itself deeply moved, especially when assisted by appropriate expression and gesture."[14] The notion that the preacher or orator must emote in order to move the audience is common in rhetorical handbooks from antiquity on, and Erasmus repeats the injunction often.[15] "A fiery mind makes a fiery tongue," he writes, "nor can fire do anything except burn if you approach too near."[16] Erasmus has quite a lot to say about the role of good oratory for the purposes of teaching, as well as how the pedagogical efficacy of the living voice is bound up with emotions of both preacher and congregation.

He continues expositing the adage *viva vox* with a line from Pliny the Younger: "The living voice, as they say, has more power to move us. For even if the things you read are more acute, yet those which are impressed on the mind by pronunciation, expression, appearance, and gesture of the speaker penetrate more deeply."[17] This is an insightful bit of analysis: the written word might teach more precisely, but pedagogical communication in person, because it engages with the emotions more extensively, is more effective. In the very next adage, *muti magistri* ("silent teachers," that is, books) Erasmus brings the living voice and his specular notion of speech together. "Just as the voice," he writes,

> according to Aristotle, is a kind of image of the meaning in the mind, so the shapes of letters can properly be called reflections, as it were, of the sounds of speech. Nor is it to be wondered at if that direct image of the heart (*archetupon pectoris*) proves a better way of reproducing and communicating the heart's affections (*transfundit affectus animi*) than that other method, writing, which imitates the imitation rather than the thing itself.[18]

The extra mimetic step required for writing and reading serves as a filter which dampens the affective connection. Erasmus understands the spoken word not only as a more effective way of engaging the emotions of those listening, but also argues that speech is a more faithful representation of mind and emotions of the speaker—speech *is* the *imago mentis*.

Erasmus is keen to develop the connection between moving and teaching, but he is also keen to repudiate its converse, to establish that artificial emotions as well as pedantry—affectations of feeling and knowing—are deleterious to the enterprise of pastoral instruction. Passionate teaching consists of navigating between the Scylla of excessive affectation and the Charybdis of dry and ineffective discourse. This

---

14. CWE 68:762.
15. See Quintilian, *Institutio oratoria*, trans. Donald A. Russell. Loeb Classical Library. 5 vols (Cambridge, MA: Harvard University Press, 2002), 6.2.26; also the introduction to the *Ecclesiastes* in CWE 67, esp. 161.
16. CWE 68:804. See also, e.g., 68:807–9.
17. *Adages* I ii 17; CWE 31:162.
18. *Adages* I ii 18; CWE 31:163, modified.

is a tension Erasmus had tried to resolve in multiple works over the course of his career. While at work on the *Ecclesiastes* Erasmus published the *Ciceronianus*, and the Erasmian voice in that work, the character Bulephorus, presses his interlocutor to reject both the "artificiality and theatrical pleasure" of the ancient Cicero as well as the later scholastic approach, represented at one point in the dialogue with a reference to Thomas Aquinas's discourse as ἀπαθής—emotionlessness—which seeks only *docere*, to teach. Bulephorus there offers the prerequisites for effective teaching:

> An understanding [*pectus*] richly supplied with a thorough knowledge of all kinds of subjects, especially the ones you have decided to talk about, an understanding prepared by theory, by much practical experience in writing and speaking, and by long thinking on the subject; and, the fountain-head of the whole activity, a heart that genuinely loves what it proclaims and genuinely hates what it attacks . . . [Moreover] speech that holds the hearer's attention, that moves him, that sweeps him away on some tide of emotion, is born out of the depths of the speaker's person, not out of his skin.[19]

As with the example of Vitrier, Bulephorus maintains that emotional commitment of the speaker is a prerequisite for adequate engagement of the hearer's affections, and thus of proper instruction (of the heart).

Bulephorus later elaborates on the matter with extensive affective imagery demanding, as in the above, affective sincerity that is born out of one's interior life:

> Your speech will not be a patchwork or a mosaic, but a breathing out of the image of your soul, a river welling out from the spring of your heart. Above all, you must make sure you thoroughly understand the matter you undertake to treat. That will supply you with a flood of things to say, with genuine (i.e., unaffected) emotions. That will make your speech live, breathe, move, influence, carry away; it will make it express you wholly.[20]

---

19. CWE 28:401; ASD I-2, 651: Pectus opulenter instructum varia rerum omnium cognitione, praesertim earum, de quibus institueris dicere: pectus artis praeceptionibus, tum multo scribendi dicendique usu, diutina meditatione praeparatum: et, quod est totius negocii caput, pectus amans ea quae praedicat, odio prosequens ea quae vituperat . . . Ex intimis enim vaenis, non in cute nascitur oratio, quae moratur auditorem, quae movet et in quemvis habitum animi rapit.

20. CWE 28: 442; ASD I-2, 704: Nec oratio tua cento quispiam videature aut opus Musaicum, sed spirans imago tui pectoris, aut amnis e fonte cordis tui promanans. Sit autem prima praecipuaque cura penitus cognoscendae rei quam tractandam suscipis. Ea tibi suppeditabit orationis copiam, suppeditabit affectus veros ac nativos. Ita demum fiet, ut tua vivat, spiret, agat, moveat et rapiat oratio, teque totum exprimat.

Authenticity, too, is a necessary condition for truly affective and effective rhetoric. Eric MacPhail has traced the ambiguity of the metaphor of speech as a mosaic in the renaissance, and has connected the less ambiguous metaphor of the *imago* of the speaker's heart, soul, or mind (here it is *imago pectoris*) from the *Ciceronianus* to the *Ecclesiastes*, while Brian Cummings has helpfully fleshed out the affective and subjective import which this particular Erasmianism has for Erasmus's mimetic approach to language.[21] The clarity of the *imago*, reflected adequately in a mirror, supplants the obscurity of the mosaic in Erasmus's Christian rhetoric, for it is crucial that the depths of the person be revealed in such situations.[22] "There is a familiar story of Socrates," Erasmus writes in the *Ecclesiastes*, "when a youth approached him saying, 'My father told me to meet you so that you could see me,' he said, 'Speak then, so that I may see you,' believing that the true man (*verum hominem*) is the one within that is not seen with the eyes of the body but is reflected in speech as if in a mirror."[23]

The idea has special theological meaning, too, in the *Ecclesiastes*, or, perhaps, is itself grounded in a biblical example: "To have Christ's spirit inhabiting the heart," Erasmus writes, "is in fact common to all Christians, but it especially befits the preacher, who could set before himself no more perfect model than that of the highest orator, who was called 'the Word', that is, the image and voice of God."[24] The force of Erasmus's (in)famous decision to render *logos* as *sermo* rather than *verbum* at John 1:1 in his Latin New Testament likewise gives substantial theological force to the mirror metaphor. Therefore, we should not be surprised to find Erasmus earlier expressing his specular rhetorical theology in his paraphrase of the Johannine prologue:

> Speech is truly the mirror of the heart which cannot be seen with the body's eyes. . . . And for this reason chiefly God first delivered his word, so that through it he might become known to us in speaking, as it were, and so that through it, having become known by means of our wonder at the beauty of the workings of the universe, he might wind his way into our affections.[25]

It is possible, then, to knit together—from a variety of works across at least two decades—a fairly consistent image of the centrality of emotion for Erasmus's conception of ideal preaching and teaching. As we have seen, the living voice is transposed into various pedagogical settings as the conduit for affective teaching,

---

21. Brian Cummings, "Erasmus and the Invention of Literature," *Erasmus of Rotterdam Society Yearbook* 33 (2013): 22–54.

22. See Eric MacPhail, "The Mosaic of Speech: A Classical Topos in Renaissance Aesthetics," *Journal of the Warburg and Courtauld Institutes* 66 (2003): 249–64.

23. CWE 68:694.

24. CWE 67:258.

25. CWE 46:16.

and we will see again that Paul is second only to Christ as the paragon of this movement.

We might also mention the discussion in *De recta pronunciatione* about the affective aspects of writing a letter in one's own hand (versus dictating to an amanuensis): "Even if you dictate rigidly," Erasmus writes, "intimacy will still be missing."[26] A letter also does not allow for a thorough application of *accommodatio*, arguably the most important feature of Erasmus's affective rhetoric, which he models after Paul himself, whose abilities he refers to again, non-disparagingly, as chameleonic. In a lengthy description of Paul's malleability, Erasmus's concerns reflect what James Weiss almost a half-century ago called the mutual conditioning of affectivity and understanding in the *Ecclesiastes*:

> Consider how Paul, in whom we see that the greatest simplicity is joined with equal judgment, adapts himself to every circumstance, not always pondering what is allowed but what is expedient, how he at times abases himself, then how he exalts his sublimity in Christ. Sometimes he exercises his apostolic power and threatens the rod of severity, but more often he implores, cajoles, and shows himself more a mother and nurse than an apostle. . . . How cleverly he adapts the witness of Scripture to his present case; how wisely he opens the cloud of allegory when the letter has little significance for piety. Among the perfected he speaks of wisdom hidden in secret; among the weak he knows only Jesus and him crucified. He has milk with which to nourish children; he has solid food to offer adults.[27]

This goes on for some time, and we might wonder how this versatility relates to speech as the perfect image of the *true person* reflected as in a mirror; in other words, how the mirror image of the speaker—static, clear, and objective—becomes accessible to each listener in their own circumstances, or how Paul becomes, in his own words, "all things to all people." There is something of a paradox in Erasmus's metaphor of the mirror alongside that of a protean preacher revealing himself to each member of the congregation specially, imparting both knowledge and feeling *ad hoc*. Robert Kilpatrick recognizes this, arguing that Erasmus's use of the mirror *topos* when paired with his own rhetorical versatility renders the "*ingenium* at the origin of speech" elusive or even illusory, especially in the figure of Folly and the author of the *Adagia*. Perhaps in the *Ecclesiastes*—Erasmus's last major work, and also one of his most direct and serious—Erasmus hazards one final attempt at articulating the notion that the ideal Christian preacher can only truly reveal himself fully as a chameleon in a mirror. Maybe the *ingenium* is essentially chameleonic. "In the course of accommodating himself to everyone," Erasmus himself writes, "[Paul] is so variable that he sometimes appears to be

---

26. CWE 26:391.

27. James Weiss, "Ecclesiastes and Erasmus: The Mirror and the Image," *Archiv für Reformationsgeschichte* 65 (1974): 91.

self-contradictory and to speak inconsistencies, though he is everywhere quite consistent with himself. This is the good judgment of the faithful steward and manager, as it were, of heaven's rich store."[28] The intersubjective connection built into the rhetorical strategies revolving around *accommodatio* is grounded in the notion that Paul is better able to reveal himself affectively when he can give voice to what is inside his heart. In other words, it is only through accommodating himself emotionally to his audience by means of his living voice that Paul's speech, and the sermon of any preacher, may truly succeed at passionate pedagogy.[29] This is the conceit which lies at the heart of Erasmus's understanding of effective rhetoric in general, and it also undergirds his conception of ideal preaching as it is spelled out more fully in his most mature work, the *Ecclesiastes*.

Emotion in the Ecclesiastes

In 1535, just a year before he died, Erasmus of Rotterdam published his monumental and long-awaited treatise on preaching method, which he had begun work on over a decade earlier. The *Ecclesiastes sive de ratione concionandi* has been described by John O'Malley as "the great watershed in the history of sacred rhetoric" as well as a "monument to the continuation of the reception of the classical tradition."[30] The *Ecclesiastes* is also the culmination of Erasmus's endeavors to set forth a renewed approach to learned piety in the Christian tradition in the dual context of preaching and the renaissance revival of ancient texts, both Christian and pagan.[31] If it is a watershed, this is due to its breadth and ambition in laying out every conceivable aspect of preaching method—which seemingly had a substantial influence on sacred rhetorics well into the seventeenth century—and also of largely eschewing the medieval *ars praedicandi* as a model.[32] Its status as a monument to

---

28. CWE 67:179–80.

29. For more on emotion and rhetoric in Erasmus's New Testament *Paraphrases*, see Reinier Leushuis, "Poetics or Homiletics: Hearing and Feeling the New Testament in Erasmus's *Paraphrases*," *Erasmus Studies* 40, no. 2 (2020): 113; and, idem, "Emotion and Imitation: The Jesus Figure in Erasmus's Gospel Paraphrases," *Reformation* 22, no. 2 (2017): 82–101.

30. John O'Malley, "Erasmus and the History of Sacred Rhetoric: The *Ecclesiastes* of 1535," *ERSY* 5 (1985): 13.

31. As James Weiss puts it, in a work ostensibly on the Christian preacher Erasmus talks about everything ("*Ecclesiastes* and Erasmus: The Mirror and the Image"). For a brief overview of the contents of the work, see Jacques Chomarat, *Grammaire et Rhetorique chez Erasme* (Paris: Les Belles Lettres, 1981), 1061–71. For a longer overview, see James Butrica's thorough introduction to the work in *Collected Works of Erasmus* (hereafter "CWE"), vol. 67.

32. But cf. Francois Kilcoyne and Margaret Jennings, "Rethinking 'Continuity': Erasmus' *Ecclesiastes* and the *Artes Praedicandi*," *Renaissance and Reformation / Renaissance et Reforme* XXI, no. 4 (1997): 5–24.

the continuation of the reception of the classical tradition is evident in its most complicated conceit, namely, that the modes of oratory described by prominent Greco-Roman orators, which Erasmus painstakingly and near-exhaustively delineates, should be employed in the service of Christian preaching.[33] Additionally, the work contains Erasmus's typical bewildering array of references to ancient literature and philosophy, both pagan and biblical. Moreover, not least because of its sheer size, the work represents Erasmus's most comprehensive descriptions of emotion in the context of Christian teaching. And while the importance of emotion in the *Ecclesiastes* has been appreciated by Erasmus scholars, especially by Jacques Chomarat, Debora Shuger, and Manfred Hoffmann, a fresh look at the *Ecclesiastes* promises several benefits for current scholarly trends, including the history of emotions, the history of preaching, the study of sermons as literature, and recent developments in classical reception studies.[34]

Whether Erasmus was doing something new is not the primary question of this chapter. But, as Rita Copeland has pointed out, "the medieval *artes praedicandi*, which represent the main body of theoretical precept on how to preach [in the Middle Ages], contain very little discussion of emotion, little systematic advice about the passions and passionate appeals."[35] By contrast, in the *Ecclesiastes*, the emotions do not only feature heavily in Erasmus's attempts to adjudicate the manner in which it is incumbent upon the preacher to *move* the congregation, but a specifically Christian sort of affectivity governs the way Erasmus imagines the preacher to be learned, and thus also to teach. As Frederick McGinnis writes, "Stirring (*movere*) the emotions is the preacher's craft, which is what so many of *Ecclesiastes*' instructions intend to refine."[36] Even though Erasmus himself didn't preach any sermons, as far as we know, his preaching manual operates on the assumption that the preacher has the most significant role in Christian teaching, itself a thoroughly affective enterprise.

---

33. For general studies of Erasmus and rhetoric, see the monumental work by Chomarat, *Grammaire et Rhetorique* (for the *Ecclesiastes*, see 1053 ff.); also Peter Mack, *A History of Renaissance Rhetoric (1380–1620)* (Oxford: Oxford University Press, 2001), 98–103; idem, "Twenty-fourth Annual Margaret Mann Phillips Lecture: Erasmus' Contribution to Rhetoric and Rhetoric in Erasmus' Writing," *ERSY* 32 (2012): 27–45; idem, *The History of Renaissance Rhetoric 1380–1620* (Oxford, 2011); Manfred Hoffmann, *Rhetoric and Theology: The Hermeneutic of Erasmus* (Toronto, 1994); idem, "Erasmus: Rhetorical Theologian," in *Rhetorical Invention and Religious Inquiry*, ed. Walter Jost and Wendy Olmsted (New Haven: Yale University Press, 2000); see also Fumaroli, *L'Age de l'éloquence*, e.g. 70 and 106ff. on the *Ecclesiastes*.

34. See Shuger, *Sacred Rhetoric*, 60f., and Hoffmann, *Rhetoric and Theology*, 201–4. See also Peter Mack's brief comment about emotions in the *Ecclesiastes* in "Erasmus' Contribution to Rhetoric and Rhetoric in Erasmus' Writings," *ERSY* 32 (2012): 40–1.

35. Copeland, *Emotion and the History of Rhetoric in the Middle Ages*, 286.

36. CWE 67:162.

Language of a fiery heart, of an ardent spirit, of an inflamed tongue, of moved minds pervades Erasmus's last great work. A thoroughly affective approach to preaching method can be discerned in the *Ecclesiastes* via a consideration of Erasmus's repeated references to (and conflation of) the fiery heart and the learned tongue as requisite organs of *pietas* and *persuasio* in his exhortations for preachers to adopt an impassioned approach to learning and teaching. In this way, the work fits perfectly well into Erasmus's long-standing endorsement of affectivity in Christian life, and also with his understanding of the importance of emotion in Christian rhetoric more generally. In the *Ciceronianus*, for example, Bulephorus says, "The mysteries of Christ should be handled not only with learning but with religious feeling. It is not enough to regale the mind of the reader with some trivial, temporary delight [*delectatiuncula*]; one must arouse emotions worthy of God [*affectus deo digni*], and that can only happen if you have an intimate grasp of the subject you are treating."[37] Anticipating a persistent theme of the *Ecclesiastes*, Bulephorus continues, "You will set no one on fire if you are cold yourself, nor will you inflame your reader with love of things heavenly if you care for them little or not at all."[38] The *Ecclesiastes* thus brings together many fundamental aspects of Erasmus's lifelong investment in defending and defining a program of a deliberately affective sort of learned piety, which rests on the assumptions that true learning cannot be accomplished without impassioned investment, that the preacher must be moved in order to move, and that there is an inextricable link between learning and feeling.

Despite the considerable debts to classical tradition, Erasmus does distinguish the task of the Christian preacher overtly from the approaches of ancient philosophical and rhetorical traditions in his discussion of a "more prolix kind of peroration," which he identifies as "conclusion," and which "is comprised especially of emotions, which are more easily roused when the hearer has already been convinced and is inclined on his own either towards pity or towards indignation or towards penitence or towards any other emotional state." He continues:

> Furthermore, the doctrine of the Stoics, who approved of no emotions, has been rejected and dismissed not only by Christians but also by some more reasonable Stoics themselves; for an argument can be used to defend the fact that the Athenians excluded the emotions from the pleading of cases. In those days their speeches were timed by water clocks: they were unwilling for water to be used up on irrelevant matters and for the judge to be detained excessively long with hearing the case; in addition, since an honest sentence was required of a judge bound by religious sentiment, they preferred to abstain from rousing the emotions, since these often cloud the judgment and sometimes carry an arbiter

---

37. CWE 28:438; ASD I-2, 701.
38. CWE 28:438; ASD I-2, 701: Quod fieri non potest, ni penitus cognitum habeas argumentum quod versas: nec enim hic inflammabis, si frigeas ipse: nec ad amorem rerum coelestium accendes lectorem, si tibi talium vel levis admodum, vel nulla cura est.

away, so that he pronounces sentence not in accordance with the law but in accordance with his mental excitement.[39]

Stoics, then, and Athenians in the law courts, discouraged emotion for different reasons, some philosophical and some circumstantial. Erasmus then compares these to the rather different situation of a preacher and their congregation:

> But the man who speaks before a Christian congregation has a far different purpose, since his only reason for stirring the emotions is to make his hearers grow warm towards all that belongs to piety, such as when they are inspired through the praise of harmony towards love of concord and hatred of schism, when by praise of alms they are inflamed towards generosity to the needy and scorn for greed, and by praise of innocence they are kindled towards a zeal for piety and the love of a more reformed life.[40]

There are a number of reasons for the preacher to engage with the emotions of the audience, and to avoid Stoic proscriptions and recognize that they are not confined by Attic legal norms, or haunted by the specter of Gorgias's sophist who only moves emotion in order to sway the audience regardless of the truth of the matter. Erasmus prefers the Aristotelian approach, and quotes "that famous Peripatetic" (via Cicero, it seems): "the goads of the emotions have been given to us by nature as teachers towards virtue, for example, anger towards fortitude, love and mercy towards beneficence, shame and fear towards innocence."[41] Erasmus then proceeds to give a series of biblical examples of a Peripatetic approach to affective rhetoric: "By teaching we aim at making our listener understand, by emotion at making him love or hate."[42] In the remainder of this chapter, I will flesh out the details of Erasmus's portrait of the affective Christian preacher, examining two key aspects of Erasmus's approach to the emotions in the *Ecclesiastes*: first, the importance of the "fiery heart" and related concepts in Erasmus's understanding of the preacher's disposition; and, second, the manner in which Erasmus thought the emotions should (or should not) be stirred in the congregation.

Wise Hearts and Minds on Fire

Book 1 of the *Ecclesiastes* details the importance of the moral uprightness of the preacher. For Erasmus, any flaws of character threaten to undermine the preacher's authority. For our purposes, one of the most interesting aspects of the first book is the prominence of discourse surrounding the heart and the tongue. While Erasmus

---

39. CWE 68:721–2.
40. CWE 68:722.
41. CWE 68:791.
42. Ibid.

lists many things as necessary for preparation for the office of preacher—for example, knowledge of the Bible, varied reading of the Fathers, sound judgment, prudence, a method of teaching along with fluency of speech—the preacher must especially "take care first and with the greatest effort to render his heart the purest possible source of speech."[43] The heart as an organ of piety, prevalent as it is in the Bible, enjoys a place of prominence in the long history of Christian discourse.[44] Despite its near-ubiquity, however, more can be said about its significance in a humanist context. Indeed, its familiarity may very well give way to glossing over it as a sort of tenuous or banal metaphor for a vague and mysterious piety. Discourse about the heart is, however, often revealing of certain tendencies related to the way in which, for example, religious knowledge is bound up with the emotions, or how moving specific emotions is important for Christian life, but it is also polyvalent in Erasmus's works, a receptacle of multiple religious meanings.

Sixteenth-century Christian humanists are often, on principle, predisposed to elevating biblical language over philosophical and classical rhetorical language as typical, which all but guarantees a more widespread usage of the language of the heart.[45] In this way they fall onto a trajectory of theological discourse which ran from antiquity through the Middle Ages that Eric Jager refers to as a "pectoral psychology," prominent especially in Augustine.[46] The *Ecclesiastes* represents Erasmus's most fully developed use of language of the heart as normative for theological ethics and anthropology. To speak of the heart rather than the mind is itself representative of a certain emotional style. Erasmus, in using such language to describe psychological categories, is participating in a Pauline and Augustinian tradition which, as Jager puts it, "evokes the heart mainly in its biblical sense as

---

43. CWE 67:260.

44. For some recent studies, see Katie Barclay and Bronwyn Reddan (eds.), *The Feeling Heart in Medieval and Early Modern Europe* (Berlin: De Gruyter, 2019); Eric Jager, *The Book of the Heart* (Chicago: University of Chicago Press, 2000); and, idem, "The Book of the Heart: Reading and Writing the Medieval Subject," *Speculum* 71, no. 1 (1996): 1–26; Heather Webb, *The Medieval Heart* (New Haven: Yale University Press, 2010); idem, *Culture, Body, and Language: Conceptualizations of Heart and Other Internal Body Organs Across Languages and Cultures*, ed. F. Sharifian et al. (De Berlin: Gruyter, 2008); Jacques Le Goff, "Head or Heart? The Political Use of Body Metaphors in the Middle Ages," in *Fragments for a History of the Human Body*, ed. Feher et al. (New York, 1989), 12–27; for a recent theological attempt to overcome the divide between reason and emotion by examining Augustine's and Pascal's conceptions of faith and the heart, which contains some descriptive aspects of Augustine and Pascal on the heart, see James Peters, *The Logic of the Heart: Augustine, Pascal, and the Rationality of Faith* (Baker Academic, 2009).

45. An obvious example of this interest is found in Erasmus's *Ciceronianus*, but criticisms of abstruse scholastic dialectic and overly embellished rhetoric run throughout his corpus. In the context of Christian preaching, see, for example, the annotation on 1 Cor. 1:17, where Erasmus contrasts the *sermonis de cruce* with the *sermone philosophorum et rhetorum*.

46. Eric Jager, "The Book of the Heart," *Speculum* 71, no. 1 (1996): 2.

the center of moral and intellectual life, including conscience, understanding, the affections, volition, and memory."[47] The Latin *cor* is the standard term for "heart," but Erasmus readily uses synonyms such as *pectus* and *anima*, often with little clear semantic distinction. It is redolent of the *affectus* as *stomachus* in his Psalms commentaries considered above, where the key takeaway is that affectivity and religious cognition blend together in an inseparable manner. Erasmus employs a literary and poetic range of terms at the (deliberate) expense of terminological precision, using metaphorical organs to explicate affective and psychological movements, which itself is an affective strategy: the goal is not to carve out a precise philosophico-theological anthropology, but to induce the reader to piety. A lexicon of organs with sliding referents is, in itself, more flexible than technical anthropological terms. The heart, for example, has moral, anthropological, and even noetic valences that make it a convenient and malleable vessel for thinkers like Erasmus wishing to forego as much as possible scholastic vocabulary and reinvigorate Christian discourse with biblical language. This discursive tactic clears the way for a more prominent role of the heart, the stomach, the tongue, the *viscera*, in conceptualizations of man as *homo religiosus* without losing sight of the importance of learning for Christian piety.[48]

While at first glance, Erasmus's use of the heart in Book 1 in fact seems reducible to moral uprightness—he argues, for example, for the need of a "clean heart," a "new heart," an "upright heart," a "sincere heart"—it also plays a crucial role in situations where, as Erasmus writes, the fiery Spirit "bestows a fiery heart and fiery tongue" upon the preacher.[49] The language of fire and warmth employed in contradistinction to frigidness, as we have seen, pervades Erasmus's discussions of Christian learning and teaching. What was colder, Erasmus asks, than the tongues of the Apostles before they had drawn completely into their heart that "heavenly craftsman of new hearts?"[50] The contrast between *frigidus* and *igneus* governs not only Erasmus's conception of ideal speech but also the disposition of the auditor. In other words, it extends beyond the ethical prescriptions and inspired speech of the preacher into the realm of religious knowing for all Christians. Rendering a heart pure is necessary, according to Erasmus, not only "for teaching and inflaming the minds of the audience . . . but also for acquiring knowledge of the heavenly philosophy that you are going to hand on to others."[51]

Moreover, the partition between *frigidus* and *igneus* is mapped on to a distinction between knowledge and wisdom. "To know is one thing, to be wise another," Erasmus writes.[52] Even the demons have *scientia*, but the conditions

---

47. Jager, *The Book of the Heart*, 29.
48. See, e.g., in the *Ecclesiastes*, CWE 68:698.
49. CWE 67:261; ASD V-4, 46: Ille largitur cor igneum, ille linguas igneas.
50. CWE 67:261; ASD V-4, 46: Quid frigidius Apostolorum linguis, priusquam hausissent toto pectore coelestem illum novorum cordium opificem?
51. CWE 67:260.
52. Aliud est enim scire, aliud sapere.

for *sapientia* are that one be *moved and transformed* by what one has learned.[53] Transformation, as Chomarat notes, is the *forme extrême* of rhetoric's *movere*; it is the end of sacred rhetoric.[54] This is a critical distinction that has implications for how Erasmus construes the importance of religious emotion. Bare intellectual assent lacks virtue without transformation. And wisdom is not accomplished through *humana philosophia* (i.e., through ordinary processes of knowledge acquisition) but it must be sought with *assiduis et ardentibus precibus*—continual and impassioned prayer—and not sought *frigide*.[55] Those who seek wisdom coldly, Erasmus says, are *double-hearted*, which actually means that they "have no heart at all."[56] Finally, Erasmus is also able to refer to the heart as the organ of knowing, which rounds out his scheme of impassioned religious cognition: *corde sapimus, spiritu loquimur*—we know (or are wise) through the heart, and we speak through the spirit.[57] This is not only a pithy and poetic doublet, but it illustrates a fundamental intersection of a cluster of important aspects of the ideal preacher: of the heart and the tongue, of wisdom and piety, of knowing and speaking. "The end of man," after all, Erasmus writes, "is to know, fear, and love his creator."[58] Erasmus's preacher has achieved a balance of all these things, which culminates in an affective sort of wisdom, located in the heart, that ultimately results in a successful teaching and moving of the congregation. But the heart is not the only organ in need of cultivation.

In addition to a fiery and wise heart, Erasmus writes that the preacher has been uniquely given a "learned tongue" by God. Given the seemingly endless and meticulous treatment of figures of speech and the rules of rhetoric that follow Book 1 of the *Ecclesiastes*, one might understand this to be an invocation to imitate the paradigmatic Roman orator in attempting to convert the congregation. But the phrase "learned tongue" itself is not Erasmus's, nor is it taken from Quintilian, but from the book of Isaiah: "The Lord hath given me a learned tongue, that I should know how to uphold by word him that is weary."[59] Moses had a learned tongue and without it, Erasmus argues, none of the Hebrews would have reached the land of milk and honey. Erasmus makes a clear qualification early on, advocating not "a tongue trained in philosophers' syllogisms or adorned with the embellishments of

---

53. CWE 67:268; ASD V-4, 52. There are parallels here (and elsewhere) in the *Ratio*, e.g.: Hic primus et unicus tibi sit scopus, hoc votum, hoc unum age, ut muteris, ut rapiaris, ut affleris, ut transformeris in ea quae discis: animi cibus est, ita demum utilis, non si in memoria ceu stomacho subsidat, sed si in ipsos affectus, et in ipsa mentis viscera traiiciatur (Basel: Froben, 1520, fol. 18).

54. ASD V-4, 43 n. 172.

55. Elsewhere Erasmus also argues that God wants prayers "neither infrequent nor frigid" (*nec raris nec frigidis*); see ASD V-4, 108.

56. ASD V-4, 54. See CWE 67:257.

57. ASD V-4, 108.

58. CWE 68:635.

59. Is. 50:4. See also *Lingua*, CWE 29:411.

the rhetorician but learned in the speech of the Lord."[60] Here we find the language of Erasmus's Paul in his criticisms of the Greeks in the *Paraphrase* of 1 Corinthians and 2 Timothy.[61] In the *Paraphrase* of 2 Tim. 2:24-26, "Paul" explains that this form of disputation only ends in a "mad rage" because of youthful *cupiditates*, and, further, that Christ did not attempt to persuade in this way:

> He overcame by modesty and mildness, and his voice was not heard in the streets. It is appropriate, therefore, for the servant of the Lord to follow closely in his master's footsteps and not to be pugnacious but to be calm and gentle towards everyone, for persuasion is easier for one who is commanded by his love and his self-control; to be ready to teach rather than to scold, to be lenient and not at all irritable in his tolerance of evils, capable of correcting recalcitrant opponents with dignity rather than with harshness.[62]

The language of the calm emotions in rhetoric suffuses the paraphrase of these verses and it signals again Erasmus's preference for the gentle over the vehement emotions as rhetorical targets. Manfred Hoffman helpfully summarizes Erasmus's tendencies in this regard: "Erasmus generally mentioned vehemence and delight together. But when it came to the question of which of the two is to be preferred he seemed to opt for mediating delight because he associated it with both the harmony of nature and the healing function of medicine, an important image of Erasmus's reforming program."[63] While vehement speech and rousing the violent emotions are at times necessary, it is less preferable to engaging the calmer feelings, on the model of Jesus himself.

In 1525, Erasmus had published his treatise on the tongue, the *Lingua*, which extensively examined that organ's destructive power when used for

---

60. CWE 67:295; ASD V-4, 78: Nec dicit linguam instructam philosophorum syllogismis aut rhetorum flosculis ornatam, sed eruditam in sermonibus Domini.

61. See, e.g., CWE 43:44, 48. Also, see Kirk Essary, "Milk for Babes: Erasmus and Calvin on the Problem of Christian Eloquence," *Reformation and Renaissance Review* 16, no. 3 (2014): 246–65.

62. CWE 46:48; ASD VII-5: Christus non hac via persuasit mundo; modestia ac mansuetudine vicit nec audita est vox eius in plateis. Decet itaque servum Domini sui vestigiis inhaerere nec esse pugnacem, sed placidum ac mitem erga omnes (facilius enim persuadet qui charitate modestiaque commendatur, paratus ad docendum magis quam ad obiurgandum), in malis tolerandis lenem minimeque iritabilem, qui graviter magis quam aspere corripiat eos qui reluctantur, declarans sese nihil alid agere his rebus omnibus quam ut illis medeatur.

63. *Rhetoric and Theology*, 189. John O'Malley describes the concerns of the Italian papal court preachers in related terms: "The preachers meant to teach as well as to move and to please. They meant to move and to please by means of their teaching" (*Praise and Blame in Renaissance Rome: Rhetoric, Doctrine, and Reform in the Sacred Orators of the Papal Court, c. 1450-1521* [Durham, NC: Duke University Press, 1979], 124).

divisive discourse—the treatise was written in the midst of his involvement in bitter disputes both with Luther and with the Sorbonne—but it finishes with an extended metaphor on the healing power of the tongue when used appropriately and in a Christian manner, "sober, sparing, modest, decent, careful, truthful, mild, peaceable, kindly, honest."[64] He picks up where he left off in the *Ecclesiastes* as well: The one with a learned tongue plays the role of the physician of the soul, providing the antidote to spiritual lassitude, heading off oncoming disease, sustaining the weak in faith, and so on.[65] The tongue is the preacher's weapon in the same way that the sword is the soldier's, but it must be noted that it is much more difficult, according to Erasmus, to move people's minds through speech than to compel their bodies through physical force. In fact, Erasmus writes, bodies can *only* be compelled, while minds are bent or turned.[66]

Erasmus moves between emphasizing the importance of the tongue and then of the heart: "A voluble tongue, a melodious quill, strong lungs, faithful memory, knowledge of Scripture are only wine blended with hemlock if sincerity of heart is absent, for this mixture makes the poison more potent."[67] Here a sincere heart holds everything else together. But elsewhere, of all the other virtues the preacher must have—purity of heart, chastity of body, sanctity of character, wisdom, and so on, "eloquence worthy of the divine mysteries" holds primacy of place.[68] Ultimately, the division between the heart and the tongue is artificial. Late in Book 1 of the *Lingua*, for example, Erasmus gives definition to Paul's phrase διδακτικός εἶναι (being suited to teach), another reference to 2 Tim 2:24: "This undertaking requires a lofty soul and a heart trained in a philosophy like no other; this clearly is what the prophet calls 'a learned tongue.'"[69] The learned tongue *is* a heart trained in Christian philosophy. To cite Jager on Augustine again, Erasmus is preceded by the Bishop of Hippo in "treat[ing] the heart as not just the psychological but the distinctly

---

64. See CWE 29:403 and following.

65. ASD V-4, 80. For an earlier discussion of the use of the "learned tongue" in warding off evil, see the *Lingua* (esp. CWE 29:402f.). For an excellent recent study of the positive and negative valences of the tongue in Erasmus, specifically in the context of his reception and use of Homer, see Jessica Wolfe, *Homer and the Question of Strife from Erasmus to Hobbes* (Toronto: University of Toronto Press, 2015), chapter one.

66. See, e.g., CWE 27:339, 380; and ASD V-4, 172.

67. CWE 67:284; ASD V-4, 68: Nam linguae volubilitas, plectra vocalitas, laterum firmitas, memoriae fidelitas, Scripturarum cognition, si desit animi synceritas, nihil aliud sunt quam vinum cicuta temperatum. Hac enim mixture venenum fit praesentius.

68. CWE 67:302.

69. CWE 27:339; ASD V-4, 126: Nimirum haec provincia sublimem animum ac pectus eximia quadam philosophia instructum requirit. Hoc videlicet est illud quod propheta vocat linguam eruditam, beatus Paulus *didaktikon einae*, id est, ad docendum appositum esse. Ad docendum divina nemo idooneus est, nisi doctus divinitus. Cf. ASD V-4, 126 also for the heart being instructed with salvific teaching (*instruit pectus suum salutifera doctrina*).

verbal center of the self."[70] The "heart" and the "tongue" are more important than the heart and the tongue. As Manfred Hoffman puts it, "Language is the means by which humans placed in the middle between God and animals, can move either up or down as they respond to the drawing power of divine love or fall into the pull of brutish passions."[71] And Erasmus, recalling the adage discussed earlier, writes that speech is the "truthful image of his mind, [which is] reflected in his words as in a mirror; 'for thoughts proceed from the heart.'"[72] Speech is to such an extent the *imago mentis* for Erasmus, and the heart likewise the source of discourse (*fons orationis*), that he writes, "if it differs from the heart from which it proceeds, it does not deserve even the name of speech any more than a mask deserves to be called a face."[73] The organs of affective piety, like the musical strings in the Psalm discussed earlier, must function harmoniously.

In the *Ecclesiastes* the heart, the tongue, and the mind must all operate together for adequate instruction (both active and passive) in the Christian philosophy. The metaphorical organs may fail at a certain point to have distinctive referents, but the affective end-goal is the same: "The most important thing for persuasion," Erasmus writes, "is to love what you are urging; the heart itself supplies ardour of speech to the lover, and it brings the greatest force to effective teaching if you display within yourself whatever you are teaching to others . . . teaching is weak and ineffective unless it proceeds from a burning spirit."[74] Erasmus finds corresponding testimony for this prescription, complete with emotional language, in the Gospels as well. Glossing John 5:35—where John the Baptist is described as a "burning and shining lamp" for his abilities as a preacher—Erasmus emphasizes that the burning precedes the shining, and suggests that burning refers to the mind, while shining light refers to learning. *Lux doctrinae* must emanate from *ardor mentis*.[75] Erasmus is attempting to drive home, repeatedly, the necessity of an affective and impassioned approach to what he often refers to as the heavenly philosophy. At a general level, then, cultivating a warmly affective disposition is of vital importance for Erasmus's notion of the ideal Christian teacher. As Debora Shuger has pointed out, the novelty of Erasmus's approach in the early modern period lies in reconnecting a rhetorical style to moving and teaching in the context of the sermon: she writes that "the integration of theology, psychology, and

---

70. Jager, "The Book of the Heart," 6.
71. Hoffmann, *Rhetoric and Theology*, 77.
72. CWE 67:255; ASD V-4, 38. This is reminiscent of Augustine *De Trinitate* XV.18.
73. CWE 67:257. ASD V-4, 40: si dissideat ab animo unde proficiscitur, ne orationis quidem meretur vocabulum. For *fons orationis*, see ASD V-4, 42.
74. CWE 67:299; ASD V-4, 84: Praecipuum igitur ad persuadendum est amare quod suades: amanti pectus ipsum suggerit orationis ardorem; et ad doctrinae efficaciam plurimum adfert momenti si, quae doces alios, in teipso praestes . . . doctrina diluta est et inefficax, nisi ab ardenti spiritu proficiscatur.
75. ASD V-4, 84.

language" constitutes Erasmus's most important contribution to the subsequent history of sacred rhetoric.[76]

Erasmus's goal is twofold with respect to what the preacher's ardent disposition accomplishes in the congregation, and he invokes the long Platonist tradition to explain it: first, so that they "grow warm towards all things that belong to piety" (e.g., to love concord and hate schism); and, second, so that they love to learn:

> What Augustine said in imitation of Plato is true, that nothing is loved except in so far as it is known and that nothing is known unless it is in some degree loved. Thus the instructor's love makes the pupil open to teaching, and our admiration for a discipline makes us learn it more willingly and more quickly. Someone will be more ready to learn theology if he is convinced that the Holy Spirit is the author of the divine books and if he is convinced that theology alone renders a man truly learned, wise, and even blessed. Cicero in the *Hortensius* fires his readers towards love of philosophy by praising it before he teaches it, and those who teach a discipline first inflame the audience, showing through amplification the greatness of its worth.[77]

What I have been calling Erasmus's affective approach to Christian learning does not only consist in metaphoric appeals to hearts and tongues, and exhortations to embrace a fiery spirit. An ardent zeal must attend and motivate the preacher's duty to learn and teach,[78] but it is also true that learning (in the humanities) itself creates a fruitful space for God to operate through the hearts of the preacher and his congregants. "The Holy Spirit," Erasmus writes, "works more fully if it finds a heart readied by the liberal disciplines."[79]

The requisite zeal for learning on the part of the preacher is also occasionally provided by the congregation, thus creating a space for what has recently if in

---

76. *Sacred Rhetoric*, 64. See also Hoffmann, *Rhetoric and Theology*, esp. 39–54.

77. CWE 68:722–3; ASD V-4, 470: Postremo verum est quod Platonem imitates dixit Augustinus, nihil amari nisi quadantenus cognitum, rursus nihil cognosci nisi aliqua ex parte amatum. Sic praeceptoris amor docilem reddit discipulum et admiration disciplinae facit ut lubentius ac celeries eam percipiamus. Ad theologiam docilior erit, cui persuasum fuerit divinorum voluminum autorem esse Spiritum Sanctum, cuique persuasum fuerit solam esse theologiam, quae hominem vere doctum, sapientem atque etiam beatum reddat. M. Tullius, prius in Hortensio laudata philosophia accendit ad illius amorem, quam eam docuit. Et qui disciplinam aliquam profitentur, prius inflammant auditorem, per amplificationem ostendentes quanta sit illius dignitas, a quibus viris exculta, quid magni promittat, quantam adferat utilitatem. Haec cui persuasa sunt, non prorsus expers est eius disciplinae et tamen docilis est potius illius quam doctus.

78. See, e.g., ASD V-4, 238 for a section on *studium discendi*.

79. CWE 68:471; ASD V-4, 250: plenius operatur Spiritus Sanctus, si reperiat pectus liberalibus disciplinis praeparatum.

a slightly later context been referred to as emotional "intersubjectivity":[80] in the same way that it is the preacher's duty to instill passion for learning among his flock, the preacher "will be stimulated to become more vigilant in his study of Holy Writ, more ardent in his teaching, more frank in his admonition," if his audience "listens cheerfully to his teaching, patiently to his criticism, if they retain what he has taught, etc."[81] There is a complicated interplay of affective learning in the emotional community (to borrow a term from Barbara Rosenwein) of Erasmus's church.[82] Moreover, the gospel itself—always the implied subject matter of the preacher—is inherently affective, or given over to affectivity (recall the advice Erasmus learned from Vitrier about reading the Bible before preaching in order to cultivate the proper affective mood). Erasmus argues that for the preacher it is both easier and more necessary to rouse the emotions than for the lawyer in a courtroom. This is because of the nature of the subject at hand:

> [M]any things of which he must speak are, first of all of undoubted truth and are more sure than what we have perceived with the eyes and all the senses; then they are so great that in comparison to them everything that either happens in human affairs or has been devised by eloquent men to stir the emotions is received coldly and seems trifling.[83]

And even though everything the preacher teaches is "so ardent that the simple narration, even without amplifying, wrings tears from the hardest persons," Erasmus is consistent insofar as the ultimate aim of moving the emotions of the congregation is not to make them weep temporarily, but to instill in them a "zeal for emulation" of Christ and the saints.[84] The preacher inflames the minds of the audience while their engagement induces the preacher to study; the affective disposition required to preach effectively is acquired by studying Holy Writ; divine wisdom must come from without, and the liberal arts are grist for the Holy Spirit's mill.

---

80. Christopher Tilmouth, "Passion and Intersubjectivity in Early Modern Literature," in *Passions and Subjectivity in Early Modern Culture,* ed. Brian Cummings and Freya Sierhuis (Ashgate, 2014), 13–32.

81. CWE 67:441.

82. On emotional communities, see Barbara Rosenwein, *Emotional Communities in the Early Middle Ages* (Ithaca, NY: Cornell University Press, 2006).

83. CWE 68:795 (modified); ASD V-5, 72: Porro quemadmodum utilius est ecclesiastae solicitare affectus auditorum quam patronis, ita non paulo facilius est eo quod pleraeque res, de quibus illi dicendum est, primum sint indubitatae veritatis, his quoque certiores, quae oculis et omnibus sensibus percepta tenemus; deinde tam magnae, ut prae his omnia quae vel accidunt in rebus humanis vel a facundis hominibus in hoc ipsum conficta sunt, ut moveant affectus, frigeant meraeque nugae videantur.

84. CWE 68:798.

Affective vs. Affected Rhetoric

While Erasmus clearly endorses deeply affective movements in the preacher and his congregation, he does not advocate uninhibited expression of emotion. Erasmus had witnessed and heard tell of a wide variety of techniques for stirring the emotions of the congregation, some quite extravagant, but his own advice is rather conservative. While a "fiery heart" is a necessary condition of effective teaching, Erasmus repeatedly criticizes the use of "perverse affectations" on the part of the preacher: for these not only fail in orienting the congregation toward true piety, but they belie the insincerity of the preacher himself. Moreover, stirring the emotions should never be an end in itself; preaching without the aim of instilling long-lasting virtue may be deleterious to the hearer's spiritual growth. Training emotional dispositions via preaching is not the same thing as using emotions in the immediate context of pastoral persuasion, of course, even if both are crucial to the larger purposes of Christian homiletics. The latter might serve the former. What emotions, then, are appropriately drawn out by the preacher, and what are the best methods for moving the congregation according to Erasmus?

In Book 3, Erasmus expands the now-familiar account of the emotions from the end of the *De Copia* (largely taken from Quintilian's *Institutio oratoria*[85]), explaining that there are two kinds of emotions (*affectuum*), "one gentler and more like those of comedy, the other more powerful and tragic," although he reserves the right to posit a kind of emotion in between as well.[86] The principal kinds of *pathē*, or vehement emotion, listed in the *Ecclesiastes* are pity, indignation, love, and hate, while *ethē* more properly covers general ethical dispositions.[87] But, unsurprisingly,

---

85. Erasmus's indebtedness to Quintilian in the *Ecclesiastes*, which is substantial, is thoroughly documented both by Chomarat in the ASD edition and by the editors of CWE 67 and 68. Here cf. *Inst. Orat.* VI.2.8, 17; VI.3.93. A briefer citation of the same distinction comes in Erasmus's *Ratio* (Basel: Froben, 1520), 30, with the additional comment that Aristotle treats these things better (*diligentius*) than anyone.

86. CWE 68:792. ASD V-5, 68: Constat autem imprimis duplex esse affectuum genus, alterum mitius et quasi comicum, alterum vehementius ac tragicum. Nec quicquam vetat inter hos collocare medium, quod a Fabio factum video. Prius illud Graeci vocant *ethe*, Latini mores. Posterius hoc Graeci *pathe* vocant, Latini quoniam propriam vocem non inveniunt, alii generali nomine abutentes pro specie vocant "affectus", alii "perturbationes" aut "motus animorum", alii "cupiditates", alii "morbos".

87. Examples, in Erasmus's estimation, include "greater severity of uncles towards their nephews," or politeness in Italians and bellicosity in Germans; see CWE 68:792–3. Chomarat writes of Erasmus's definition of *ethe*: *non pas psychologique, mais morale* (ASD V-5, 69), a distinction that resembles one made earlier in the work by Erasmus between *natura animi* and *commotio*: the former describes a temperament, like fearfulness, while the latter describes an emotion, like fear (see CWE 68:616). But, of course, we have seen that Erasmus utilizes the distinction in a variety of ways, some of which are certainly psychological as well as moral.

Erasmus touches on a longer list of emotions in his lengthy discussions of the affective duties of the preacher in this work. And, again, the invocation of Quintilian's taxonomy inevitably comes up short, which results in Erasmus finding his way to Paul's tripartite framework for its more adequate explanatory power when it comes to feeling.[88]

Some emotions are always to be encouraged by the preacher. Christian affection, pity, compassion, and love are to always be stimulated, while emotions like anger, "are to be stirred not so much against persons as against the vices themselves and against Satan."[89] When it comes to the *manner* of moving the congregation, Erasmus's foremost concern is that this not be done artificially or without the ultimate aim of teaching. Moreover, the Bible is itself a deeply moving and fundamentally emotional text according to Erasmus, and so adhering to the biblical stories and examples in sermons does important affective work for the preacher.

> It is more useful for a preacher than for advocates to rouse the audience's emotions and rather easier as well, because many things of which he must speak are, first of all, of undoubted truth and are more sure than what we have perceived with the eyes and all the senses; they are so great that in comparison to them everything that either happens in human affairs or has been devised by eloquent men to stir the emotions falls flat (*frigeant*) and seems a mere trifle.[90]

Scripture is like a "fine painting," which, "when the preacher has surveyed the individual parts with careful reflection, he will both be moved more himself and will inflame others more powerfully."[91] Channeling the biblical text, therefore, is itself emotionally productive. Biblical authors and patristic writers, too, serve as

---

88. For discussion, see Hoffmann, *Rhetoric and Theology*, 204.
89. CWE 68:802.
90. CWE 68:794–5; ASD V-5: Porro quemadmodum utilius est ecclesiastae solicitare affectus auditorum quam patronis, ita non paulo facilius est o quod pleraeque res, de quibus illi dicendum est, primum sint indubitatae veritatis, his quoque certiores, quae oculis et omnibus sensibus percepta tenemus; deinde tam magnae, ut prae his omnia quae vel accidunt in rebus humanis vel a facundis hominibus in hoc ipsum conficta sunt, ut moveant affectus, frigeant meraeque nugae videantur.
91. CWE 68:808; ASD V-5, 88: Siquidem Scriptura similis est insigni picturae, quam quo diutius contempleris, hoc plus videas quod admireris. Ad hanc qui artifices et exercitatos admoverit oculos, longe alia videbit quam viderit imperitus aliquis parum attente contemplans. Proinde concionator ubi singulas partes attenta cogitatione lustrarit, et ipse magis commovebitur et alios vehementius inflammabit.

apt rhetorical exemplars: Paul and Chrysostom were especially skilled at "vivid preaching."[92]

The affective power of specific literary devices is also treated extensively in Book 3: certain rhetorical forms, like metaphor, *narratio*, and *exempla* are especially conducive for inculcating proper affections. Metaphor "holds primary place among all the powers of language," Erasmus writes: "Nothing persuades more effectively, nothing lays something more clearly before the eyes, nothing stirs emotions more powerfully."[93] *Exempla*, moreover, "have great power both for persuading and for inflaming minds with the emulation of virtue."[94] Accommodation to *circumstantia* is also vital: emotions (both *ethē* and *pathē*), Erasmus writes, "are generally drawn ... from all the circumstances both of fact and of person."[95] This requires the preacher to diagnose his audience as a physician would, for every malady is different and each person requires tailored treatment: "Applying the same sort of language to everyone when consoling or rebuking is nothing more than, as they say, putting the same shoe on each foot or applying the same cure to every body."[96] There is no rhetorical cure-all for a motley Christian congregation: accommodation occurs not only at the level of the divine word (where it is inherent), but the preacher must also be attuned to the varied needs of the audience.

Erasmus then provides a rather extended example of how to apply such techniques in a mock sermon on the healing of the paralytic (Matt. 9 and Luke 5). Such a sermon, he says, might be given with various *genera dicendi* through proper use of *accommodatio*, gesturing occasionally to which aspects have the most emotional force. He writes, "If the story is told appropriately, the language will contain much delight and clarity, and not a little emotion as well."[97] The use

---

92. CWE 68:808; ASD V-5, 88: *Ante quorum oculos Christus crucifixus est*, ait Paulus. Atqui Galatae nunquam viderant Christum in cruce, sed ex evidenti praedicatione Pauli, sic erat repraesentatus animis illorum, quasi vidissent quod audierunt. Sic Chrysostomus ex omnibus circunstantiis amplificat hospitalitatem Abrahae, mansuetudinem Davidis erga Saulem, aliaque fere omnia quae tractat. Atqui isthuc non est affingere nostra phantasmata Scripturae, sed ipsam Scripturam, velut insigne peristroma explicare et oculis subiicere.

93. CWE 68:871; ASD V-5, 154: Restat metaphora, quae principatum tenet inter omnes orationis virtutes. Nulla persuadet efficacius, nulla rem evidentius ponit ob oculos, nulla potentius movet affectus, nulla plus adfert dignitatis, venustatis aut iucunditatis aut etiam copiae.

94. CWE 68:871; ASD V-5, 154: de qua nunc dicendum est, si prius admonuerimus exempla magnam habere vim et ad persuadendum et ad inflammandos animos aemulatione virtutis.

95. CWE 68:794.

96. CWE 68:629 (and following).

97. CWE 68:881 (modified); ASD V-5, 164: "Primum si res gesta commode narretur, multum delectionis ac perspicuitatis habebit oratio, nonnihil etiam affectuum." See also CWE 68:889 where Erasmus concludes that he has shown how he has shown from "rhetorical theory" (*ex arte*) how narration is useful for eliciting emotion.

of *hypotyposis* is especially important for moving the congregation, and Erasmus elsewhere describes the way in which vivid description induces the affections: "There will be an opportunity here for *hypotyposis*, to lay before the eyes that pitiable spectacle of the paralytic lying on his cot. For the unhappy man could only lie there, no longer a man but a corpse half alive, sallow, filthy, covered with mould and decay and stinking almost in his very blankets."[98] The treatment of allegory, Erasmus continues, "will allow even greater emotions if you declare that a paralysis of the mind is far and away more pitiable than paralysis of the body."[99] Erasmus had earlier digressed similarly on the centrality of compassion and pity as emotions in need of special elicitation by the preacher:

> Certainly the preacher will often have to try the effect of the emotion of compassion [*misericordia*] when he exhorts his hearers to help the needy, or to encourage or console those afflicted with disease or human injustice or some other disaster.... But this emotion has a broader application than the common man thinks. When we see a man sallow with disease, full of sores, needy, shrieking in pain, we are distressed by the mere perception of his physical condition; but far more wretched than he is the one who has a mind leprous with heretical errors, devoid of all virtues, dead from lust, greed, envy, hatred, and other fatal diseases, ulcerous with disgrace, tormented by the pricks of conscience.... Therefore the preacher will display his δείνωσις [forcefulness] to make those who are so pitiably pitiable pity themselves, so that they flee for refuge to the mercy of the Lord, like fugitives from a cruel master.[100]

It is most virtuous for the preacher to learn to apply the appropriate rhetorical tools to biblical narratives to stir the emotions in the congregation. Physical maladies are more easily received and rendered into compassion, perhaps, but the

---

98. CWE 68:885; ASD V-5, 170: Rursus hic locus erat hypotyposi, quae ponat ob oculos miserandum illud paralytici in grabato iacentis spectaculum. Nihil enim aliud poeterat infelix quam iacere, iam non homo, sed semivivuum cadaver, luridus, squalidus, situ et carie obsitus atque in ipsis pene stragulis putrefactus.

99. CWE 68:889.

100. CWE 68:799–800 (the discussion of pity continues to p. 802); ASD V-5, 76–8: Misericordiae quidem affectus crebro tentandus erit ecclesiastae, sive quum exhortabitur ad subveniendum egenis, sive ad sublevandos aut consolandos vel morbo vel hominum iniuria vel alia quapiam calamitate afflictos, sive criminum conscientia de desperatione periclitantes... Caeterum hic affectus latius patet quam vulgus existimat. Quum videmus hominem morbo luridum, ulceribus plenum, egentem, eiulantem prae cruciatu, merito indolescimus ipso naturae sensu. Sed hoc longe miserabilior est qui mentem habet haereticis erroribus leprosam, virtutum omnium inopem, amore, avaritia, invidia, odio, caeterisque capitalibus morbis emortuam, infamia ulcerosam, conscientiae stimulis discruciatam... In hoc igitur ecclesiastes proferet *deinosin* suam ut, qui tam misere miseri sunt, sui misereantur et, a crudeli domino profugi, confugiant ad Domini misericordiam.

orator can describe psychological maladies to the same effect if one recognizes that they are in fact more dangerous, and here Erasmus endorses what he elsewhere denounces for its violent propensity: δείνωσις, or forcefulness of speech through vivid examples, is permissible if compassion can be aroused.[101]

Equally often Erasmus approaches the subject by discussing improper forms of rousing the emotions. He rejects all material props, along with most forms of bodily contortion and facial gesture, which he counts as insincere methods of exciting the crowd. "It is not good for the preacher to stir the emotions in just any way," Erasmus writes: he must do it "not with gross facial distortion, not with buffoonish physical gestures, but with words."[102] "Perverse affectation," or in the Greek which Erasmus retains, κακόζελος, neither leads to true teaching of the congregation nor does it fool the intelligent.[103] The use of the preacher's body for conjuring emotional responses particularly troubles Erasmus, but his tacit acknowledgment of its effectiveness attests to competing emotional communities and practices in the context of late medieval and early modern preaching. Though no Stoic, cultivating the highly wrought emotions, as might happen in practices associated with affective piety is rejected by Erasmus, as is what he perceives to be a specifically Italian penchant for physicality in the pulpit. Erasmus's recounts a series of anecdotes of such practices. As an instance of the manipulation of emotional space, Erasmus recalls Girolamo Savonarola, who would "grow so hot at the crimes of his congregation that he would suddenly dash off the pulpit and go home, with his sermon unfinished and the congregation left in suspense."[104] Presumably his departure was meant to instill shame and draw out contrition in the congregation, but for Erasmus this was a touch dramatic. The tactics of Roberto Caracciolo, meanwhile, Erasmus calls "more shameless": Caracciolo, in an attempt to rouse his congregation against the Turks, at the "most fervent" point of his sermon cast off his Franciscan habit in order to reveal a long military cloak and a gigantic sword, and proceeded to preach for half an hour decked out in military attire. Erasmus compares Caracciolo's use of clothes as a way of drawing pathos to Marc Antony's funeral oration for Caesar: Antony held up Caesar's cloak, which was "punctured by many wounds and stained with much blood," and a theretofore calm crowd arose in such an uproar that "the conspirators who were present had to flee to escape being torn to pieces."[105] This is *hypotyposis* unleashed.

Another preacher, in the middle of a sermon on Satan's wiles, called forth "a man disguised as the devil, with fiery eyes, hooked nose, boar's tusks, an eye on his

---

101. For recent scholarship on cultures of compassion in medieval and early modern Europe, see the special issue edited by Diana Barnes in *Parergon* 39:2 (2022), and Richard Meek, *Sympathy in Early Modern Literature and Culture* (Cambridge: Cambridge University Press, 2023).
102. CWE 68:811.
103. CWE 68:747.
104. CWE 68:812.
105. CWE 68:813.

chest, curving nails, a frightening hook, bellowing loudly"—many were terrified, Erasmus writes, but soon their fear turned to mockery. "It is not appropriate," he says, "for a preacher to use such methods to stir a crowd's emotions, because such a move often becomes ridiculous."[106] He continues, arguing that the cheap tricks of some preachers are objectionable specifically because they do not result in any actual education:

> People marvel at novelty and are moved more easily by outward appearance than by examples of true piety or by sound teaching ... some unduly exploit this flaw in human nature, more for their own glory than for the salvation of many, for whatever displays a foreign and affected novelty should be suspect, especially since no example of this sort was offered us by Christ and the apostles.[107]

Outrageous, especially, is the preacher who, in order to make a point about human pride, "smuggles two skulls under his robe taken from the cemetery, then produces them when the sermon reaches the emotional climax and smashes them together with such a great crack that the teeth are shaken out and scatter among the congregation."[108] These strikingly physical and visual methods of emotional arousal are, Erasmus admits, highly effective in their aim, but they are also disingenuous distractions. "The heart's emotions are not infrequently evident in a person's outer appearance," Erasmus writes, "just as hidden ailments of the blood and intestines betray themselves in the body's external state."[109] Another preacher, he tells us, had a particular penchant for disorienting a congregation through use of his body: he covered his head entirely with his hood; he only preached outside; he slept in the dirt, and because of his meager diet looked "more like a corpse than a living man"; he spoke only through a translator and terrified the multitude with shouts and strange gestures, "sometimes putting his neck in a noose and imitating a choking man with his bulging eyes."[110] Erasmus likewise denounces priests who "prostrate themselves on the pulpit in such a way that they produce a loud crack from the impact of their knees."[111] Susan Karant-Nunn, following Caroline Walker Bynum and others, has noted a deep connection between "physicality and fervor" in late medieval and early modern devotion, and has suggested that "sacred objects ... were the meditative points that facilitated the recollection of the devout and elicited their affective response."[112] Erasmus affirms the connection between physicality and fervor, but laments it: non-sacred material objects could also be

---

106. Ibid.
107. Ibid.
108. CWE 68:766.
109. CWE 68:466–7.
110. CWE 68:814.
111. CWE 68:492–3.
112. Susan Karant-Nunn, *The Reformation of Feeling: Shaping the Religious Emotions in Early Modern Germany* (Oxford: Oxford University Press, 2010), 64.

highly effective for eliciting emotions in a congregation, but such a tactic should be eschewed.

Erasmus also considers the emotional significance of facial expression. Each part of the face receives special consideration, both of a descriptive and prescriptive manner, for, as Erasmus puts it, "the mind is so clearly expressed [in the face] that it frequently serves in place of speech." Raising the head signifies confidence, lowering it bashfulness or hesitation; moving it often is unseemly for serious people, while "whirling the hair is downright fanatical."[113] A smooth brow signals cheer, a furrowed one sadness; raised eyebrows, meanwhile, reveal arrogance, lowered ones show modesty, and uneven eyebrows indicate "severity joined with gentleness." "There is no emotion—love, hate, joy, grief, annoyance, concern, fear, hope, innocence, deceit, suspicion—that is not expressed in the eyes."[114] It is precisely because of the intensely and irreducibly emotional nature of the body, of face and gesture, that Erasmus finds it necessary to delineate the many ways in which a preacher can err, and to encourage moderation in the pulpit.

At the same time, further acknowledging the emotional power of visual imagery, Erasmus argues that it can be produced (via the *phantasia*) with the words of the preacher, but less objectionably than by way of theatrical tactics. One can do this, first, he says,

> through mental pictures or impressions by which the preacher represents to himself, after careful thought, images of the subjects about which he proposes to speak. What we behold with our eyes moves us more powerfully than what we only hear; for who would not be disturbed more keenly, should he see a foe with burning eyes and drawn sword advance with a terrible roar and plunge his sword into the breast of a cringing suppliant, and saw the wounded man collapse and breathe out his soul with a great groan, than if he only heard that a man was cruelly slain?[115]

The notion that the sense of sight is more emotionally responsive is translated to the situation where the preacher is able to contemplate a scene in order to arouse his own emotions for the sake of moving the audience.[116] Erasmus does not explain why such use of the imagination is less troubling than seeing an emotive scene acted out, but rather suggests that the preacher conjure a "temporary mental

---

113. CWE 68:757.

114. But one must beware, for eyes can also be "droopy, lethargic, bewildered, lusty, shifty, and almost swimming as though some pleasure were welling up" (ibid.).

115. CWE 68:807. ASD V-5, 88: Primum imaginationem sive phantasiam, qua sibi rerum, de quibus verba facturus est, imagines attenta cogitatione repraesentat. Vehementius nos commovent quae spectamus oculis quam quae tantum audimus. Quis enim non acrius animo perturbetus . . .

116. For the history of the connection between vividness, imagination, and emotion from Aristotle moving forward, see Shuger, *Sacred Rhetoric*, 201ff.

ardour" so that he can preach more effectively, seemingly advocating the very emotional experience he condemns when the same sort of temporary emotions are elicited from the congregation.[117] The rule can apparently be sacrificed if the end result of the preacher, to teach affectively, is successful. Conversely, short-lived emotions in a congregation do not lead to lasting piety. Erasmus denounces *affectus temporarios qui mox refrigescunt*—temporary emotions which cool quickly—in favor of permanent and virtuous emotional dispositions like pity, anger at sin, hatred of schism, and love of God.[118] By seeking to elicit the violent *pathē*, the preacher also runs the risk of desensitizing the minds of the audience, for "just as the body is hardened by constant blows ... so the mind may be hardened from excessively frequent and bitter displays of emotionalism."[119] The preacher, again contrasted with an actor or lawyer for whom quick bursts of emotion are useful, must instead "leave in the minds of his listeners barbs that hold fast and to scatter upon them, as it were, good seed on good ground, so that it exercises its power gradually until it bursts forth into the fruit of piety."[120] A similar comparison may be made of written sermons as well, for Erasmus tells us that Origen of Alexandria virtuously stirs "only the emotions that the subject itself stirs," while Jean Gerson, on the contrary, *frequenter affectat affectus*—frequently affects affections.[121]

Erasmus's castigation of affectation becomes concretely related to his affective approach insofar as adept preacherly oratory, which includes appropriate emotional dispositions, must be habituated: "Worrying about applying the rules blunts creativity and chills the ardour of speech," he writes.[122] This does not mean that the rules are unimportant, but that the preacher must employ them in the same way that a good musician plays music: without thinking of the individual notes or the theory. They must be *in habitum quasi in naturam*, lest they appear cold and calculating.[123] *Habitus* converges here with *affectus*. The criteria for deciding which norms to habituate are ever-shifting, but Erasmus sets forth an ideal Christian eloquence that he considered Pauline, and which is governed foremost by the principle of accommodation.[124] "Consider how Paul," he writes,

---

117. Some are more susceptible than others at this sort of thing, and Erasmus gives the example of those who can bring about stigmata by contemplating Christ's crucifixion, or, more pedestrian, those who vomit at the sight of another's vomiting (he calls this an *affectus naturae*). Moreover, the best of preachers is able to keep his emotions *in potestate* and to control *immodicos animi motus*.

118. See, for example, CWE 68:806.

119. CWE 68:811.

120. CWE 68:806.

121. See CWE 68:492–3.

122. CWE 68:736; ASD V-5, 14: Primum enim hebetius reddit ingenium ac dicendi calorem refrigerat anxia cura.

123. ASD V-4, 250.

124. The clearest digression on accommodation comes at CWE 67:279–81. On accommodation in the *Ecclesiastes*, see Chomarat, *Grammaire et Rhetorique*, 1107–18,

"adapts himself to every circumstance, not always pondering what is allowed but what is expedient, how he at times abases himself, then how he exalts his sublimity in Christ."[125] Intellectually, the preacher must find the right pitch or risk half the congregation not comprehending; rhetorically, the preacher must employ language that is understandable to a lay audience,[126] in the same way that Paul spoke plainly to the Corinthians; in terms of the emotions, the preacher's feelings should serve as a model for the congregation's feelings. Paul's own discourse is modeled on (and representative of) God's "babbling to infants."[127] God in the Old Testament, too, "tempers his speech to the emotions of an unlearned people."[128] A diverse population demands that the preacher exercise *prudentia* in order that he likewise aptly accommodates his speech to the audience.[129] The classical rhetorical principle of accommodation takes on significant theological and affective import with great versatility in Erasmus's understanding of sacred rhetoric.

The relationship between teaching and moving is fluid in the *Ecclesiastes*. At times Erasmus writes explicitly that delighting and moving are not even possible if the hearer does not already know and believe what is being urged.[130] At other times, however, he writes that for the unlearned and ignorant multitude, it is sometimes more important to "inflame than teach" and "drag than lead"—for some laypeople "are not much different from livestock so far as the capacity to be taught is concerned."[131] Typically, however, Erasmus is careful to reiterate the ways in which edifying teaching as the ultimate goal of moving the emotions of

and Hoffmann, *Rhetoric and Theology*, 1106–12. For specific examples of how Paul (the "chameleon") accommodates himself to various audiences, and to their *affectus*, see also the *Ratio* (Basel: Froben, 1520), fol. 91f.

125. CWE 67:279; ASD V-4: Paulus, in quo videmus summam simplicitatem cum pari prudentia fuisse coniunctam, ut sese vertit in omnia, non semper expendens quid liceat, sed quid expediat, ut interdum abiicit sese! Rursus ut attollit suam in Christo sublimitatem!

126. CWE 68:486.

127. God babbles to infants in Erasmus's *Enchiridion* (CWE 66:35; LB I 501A), and Paul conquers the Mediterranean with "babbling eloquence" (*eloquenti balbutie*) in Erasmus's dedicatory letter to the *Paraphrase of First Corinthians* (see CWE 43:10).

128. ASD V-4, 66: Postremo dum Scriptura Veteris Instrumenti sermonem suum ad populi rudis affectus attemperat . . .

129. ASD V-4, 66: Nunc si reputemus, in eodem populo quanta sit varietas sexuum, aetatum, conditionis, ingeniorum, opinionum, vitae institutionis, consuetudinis, quanta oportet esse praeditum prudentia ecclesiasten, cui sic temperanda est oratio. . . . (see CWE 67:280).

130. ASD V-4, 274: In summa spectat qui dicit ut doceat, put delectet, ut flectat. Nullus enim delectatur aut movetur iis quae non intelligit aut non credit. (On good and bad delighting, see CWE 68:505ff.)

131. CWE 68:791–2; ASD V-5, 68: inter quos sunt qui quod ad docilitatem attinet, non ita multum absunt a pecudibus. Ad hos corrigendos aut erudiendos plurimum momenti adferent affectus.

the congregation. As we have seen in Erasmus's biblical scholarship and earlier theological writings, in the *Ecclesiastes*, too, the emotions are to be transformed by the preacher into goads to virtue, as well as the means by which the Christian may obtain true wisdom.

Chapter 7

Epistolary Emotions

Authenticity, Exile, and Consolation

A century ago, Johan Huizinga—biographer of Erasmus and great foil of modern history of emotions scholarship—suggested that there was a progression in Erasmus's letters (and, by extension, in his life) from an excessive emotional exuberance to a tempered moderation of feeling. In this way Erasmus was for Huizinga a microcosm of European society more generally, which during this period—according to Huizinga, in a since much-criticized formulation—matured from emotionally childlike and unrestrained to well mannered.[1] Huizinga argued that after some particularly affectionate outbursts to a fellow monk, Erasmus was shamed into moderating his emotions in print, transforming himself from overly passionate and effusive into something of a reserved stoic. Huizinga's psychological assessment comes off as rather speculative when read today: "A young and very tender heart, marked by many feminine traits, replete with all the sentiment and with all the imaginings of classic literature, who was debarred from love and found himself placed against his wish in a coarse and frigid environment, was likely to become somewhat excessive in his affections. . . . He was obliged to moderate them."[2] Certainly Erasmus does become known as an uncompromising champion of *moderatio*, but we might ask whether Huizinga's portrait is more misleading than helpful with respect to the emotions. After all, the letters from Erasmus's mature career are hardly devoid of emotionality; they are enriched by much affective language, of descriptions of his own emotions as well as those of others, and of extensive advice about emotional regulation and expression. Accounts such as Huizinga's did, however, force later scholars to ask whether Erasmus's correspondence should be evaluated as accurate self-reporting, as reflective of his actual emotional states (or, at least, of his emotional proclivities) at any given time.

---

1. For a discussion of the history of emotions, especially as carried out in medieval studies, as partly a reaction against narratives begun by Huizinga, see Barbara Rosenwein, "Worrying About Emotions in History," *The American Historical Review* 107, no. 3 (2002): 821–45.
2. Johan Huizinga, *Erasmus* (New York: C. Scribner's Sons, 1924), 12.

More recent scholarship on Erasmus's letters is somewhat less vivid and speculative about Erasmus's feelings, but the question of whether his letters reflect his actual emotions remains prominent. Erasmus himself can on some level be credited with this preoccupation, for he argued overtly that familiar letters are irreducibly emotional, or at least that they should be. Several commentators thus cite his claim—which itself was made in a letter from 1521—that "letters which are deficient in true feeling and do not reflect a man's actual life do not deserve to be called letters."[3] But not every reader of Erasmus has interpreted this claim equally. Charles Fantazzi, responding to a scholarly judgment that many early letters were closer to literary exercises than genuine expressions of feeling, takes Erasmus at his word: "Those charges [of letters not reflecting their writer's feelings] certainly cannot be levelled at Erasmus. Of all letter-writers he perhaps best illustrates the prescription in the treatise *On Style* attributed to Demetrius of Phaleron that a letter should be the image of the soul, *eikon psuches*."[4] Fantazzi thus more or less follows Huizinga in arguing that the affective flourishes of the earlier letters are more than literary exercises, although he acknowledges that a gap between affection and affectation is discernible. Regarding a series of highly affectionate letters Erasmus penned to a fellow monk, Servatius Rogerus (which Huizinga was also commenting on), Fantazzi writes: "It seems clear to me that Erasmus was under the influence of a passing emotion, a sincere and deeply felt admiration for his confrère. Underneath the rhetorical flourishes one can perceive a transparent honesty, a fear of rebuff."[5] On this reading, despite obvious exaggeration, genuine emotion is nonetheless discernible. Detecting sincerity, or genuinely felt emotion, in the epistles of an early modern humanist is fraught ground, but the questions related to claims of authentic or fabricated feelings are irresistible.

Lisa Jardine famously intervened in this long scholarly history of evaluating the emotions of Erasmus's letters by offering an elaborate assessment of the affective nature of Erasmus's epistolary theory while at the same time remaining rather more skeptical of the letters' (and thus of the feelings') authenticity. It is helpful to quote her at length:

> Nothing could, apparently, be less contrived emotionally than Erasmus's *Letters*. Erasmus studies, indeed, are premised on the "authenticity" and transparent truthfulness of those letters as *the* source of Erasmian biographical information. It will be argued here, however, that Erasmus's letters are crucially affective, and that they are major contributions to the Renaissance's construction of letter writing and reading as emotionally charged events. Moreover, they were centrally influential in the pedagogic construction of a certain kind of reading:

---

3. Ep 1206; CWE 8:219–20.
4. Charles Fantazzi, "The Evolution of Erasmus's Epistolary Style," *Renaissance and Reformation* 13, no. 3 (1989): 284.
5. Ibid., 270–1.

a version of emotionally compelling communication in the second half of the sixteenth century. . . . As discussed in Erasmian handbooks on letter writing, the familiar letter structures and organizes feeling so as to manipulate its intensity at a distance and, in the absence of the persons involved, enabling persuasion to a desired outcome.[6]

Jardine is arguing simultaneously that Erasmus's own letters are disingenuous in terms of their expressed affectivity *and* that they had deep emotional effects on both their readers and on other letter-writers throughout the early modern period. The emotional success of the letters seems to come at the expense of reflecting Erasmus's actual emotions. While Jardine qualifies this stark dichotomy in various places, including in her highly influential book on Erasmus's constructed charisma, the issues raised are important for any reconsideration of Erasmus's letters in light of history of emotions scholarship.

In this chapter, then, we will explore the Erasmian possibilities of emotional expression from necessarily limited swaths of his correspondence: which emotions and emotion terms he applies to himself, how he writes about his feelings toward other people (or toward fish), and how his correspondence can also serve the purpose of explicating a humanist approach to emotion. In the first part, we will rehash some of the key points of the scholarly discussion of Erasmus's emotional epistolography by linking them to more recent developments in history of emotions scholarship, with the hope that we might find our way out of some of the difficulties of descrying the spectre of sincerity. In the second part, we will turn to a cluster of Erasmus's letters from 1529 to 1531, the early years of Erasmus's exile from Basel, as a test case for exploring the ongoing scholarly conversation about early modern emotions in letter-writing, but also in order to assess a sample from an emotionally fraught period in Erasmus's own life. Finally, we will look at Erasmus's approach—both theoretical and practical—to writing letters of consolation.

Performative or Constitutive Emotions?

Erasmus defines a letter, following the church father Jerome, as "a kind of mutual exchange of speech [*mutuus sermo*] between absent friends."[7] Jardine in turn quotes the same Jerome letter at more length, including its most affective-oriented aspects: "If you love me, write, I beseech you. If you have been angered, you are entitled to write angrily. I will have great solace, and that which I long for, if I receive my friend's letters, even if my friend is displeased."[8] To communicate the

---

6. Jardine, *Reading Shakespeare Historically* (London: Routledge, 1999), 76. See, in addition to the above, Kathy Eden, *The Renaissance Rediscovery of Intimacy* (Chicago: Chicago University Press, 2012), 75.
7. Jardine, *Erasmus, Man of Letters* (Princeton: Princeton University Press, 1993), 150.
8. Ibid.

true self via epistolary exchange, for Jerome and Erasmus after him, is (at least ideally) to communicate one's emotions. *Mutuus sermo* is a discursive exchange of feeling, one that bonds its correspondents in thought and affection. As Jardine says, again quoting Jerome, it is the "passionate 'making present of absence,'" and, likewise, in Erasmus's Hieronymian epistolary philosophy, letters are "full of the vivid representation of emotion."[9] The familiar letter, unlike any other genre of writing, is inherently deeply affective—its very raison d'être is to convey and induce feeling—even while its emotional *sincerity* remains tantalizingly difficult to authenticate. A vivid representation of emotion is not necessarily a legitimate representation of any given subject's affective life: it could be a vivid fabrication.

In some cases, indeed, it is clear that Erasmus or his correspondent was being overly effusive or deliberately affective—he himself confesses, after all, to toning down the acrimony of some letters when editing them for publication[10]—while in other cases there is no especially good reason to doubt whether the reporting of emotion is disingenuous (as when he writes, for example, "I have always had negative feelings about Vienna"[11]). Erasmus and his correspondents often comment upon the sincerity or lack thereof regarding a letter or its contents, and they are keenly aware of the possibilities and pitfalls of affectation. Writing to Pietro Bembo in 1530, Erasmus praises Bembo's own letter, on account of its style, as "lovelier and more precious than pearls and emeralds," and after several more compliments, writes, "But better not to say anything more in case my carefully considered judgment is put down to affection, and words that come from the innermost recesses of the heart are thought to have been designed to please the ear, for this sort of thing happens often enough."[12] Erasmus's acknowledgment here hints at the slipperiness of the mechanics of sincerity in letter-writing, whereas elsewhere he points out that emotional expression is also a function of the topic being treated in writing.

In writing about his feelings, or in expressing himself emotionally, Erasmus had to make choices, some of which no doubt reflected his interior state more or less accurately and some of which were exaggerated. He was aware of this obligation,

---

9. Ibid., 151–2.

10. See CWE 15:379, Allen Ep 2203: the ones especially bitter ("haberent acrimoniae") he made more gentle ("lenirentur"). In this case, interestingly, he would be potentially subtracting some original emotion, to put it awkwardly, rather than adding emotion that wasn't there. Conversely, Erasmus also says he omitted all the "tiresome and superfluous baggage" of introductory titles, "most reverend lordship," "venerable," and so on. These titles could cause tension if the recipient found them too formulaic, thus indicating a lack of familiarity and "genuine" friendship, as was the case it seems with Juan Luis Vives; see Charles Fantazzi, "The Erasmus-Vives Correspondence," in *Erasmus and the Republic of Letters*, ed. Stephen Ryle and Lisa Jardine (Brepols, 2014), 149.

11. See Ep 2222, CWE 16:22.

12. CWE 16:239.

too, as we see in his advice to temper one's emotional tone to the subject at hand in the *De conscribendis epistolis*:

> A letter will work itself up into a tragic outburst and will make use of "bombast and sesquipedalian words" when the topic so requires. One will not adopt the same style when addressing learned and important persons on issues of war and peace as he would in giving instructions to a servant about sousing salt fish or cooking vegetables. In a letter on ordinary subjects (unless there is a good reason for special treatment) Atticism will be quite satisfactory. I shall not expect here the thunder and lightning of Pericles as long as the language flows along like the clear water of a spring with a pleasant, gentle murmur and does not seem dead and sluggish like fen water, devoid of all emotion.[13]

In this case, the requirement for emotion is one of style, not necessarily of subjective feeling. The purpose of a letter is, at least partially, to delight and to move the reader, while also giving the given topic its full affective due. There is a potential tension, then, between the affective force of a letter due to its rhetorical requirements and the genuine letter as one which makes present an absent writer.

Historians of emotion have recently attempted to take us beyond the polarization of sincerity and insincerity.[14] As William Reddy and Barbara Rosenwein have pointed out (in ways that Jardine had anticipated), sincerity itself is "culturally managed," meaning that it (or its opposite, insincerity) should not be invoked as an ahistorical heuristic, or sought out as a universal phenomenon.[15] Indeed, we can see how Erasmus himself attempts to manage it: the very grounds on which Erasmus adjudicates whether an alleged letter counts as a legitimate letter are specifically to do with whether they are, as Jardine puts it, "sufficiently emotional": "He is committed to the view that letters convey feeling with immediacy."[16] (She here quotes the Erasmus line mentioned above: "If letters lack real feelings and fail to represent the very life itself of a person, they do not deserve the name of letters."[17]) But while Jardine documents the extensive evidence of Erasmus's own thoughts about the affective significance of epistolary exchange, and about

---

13. CWE 22:15.

14. For an overview of Renaissance notions of sincerity, albeit with a focus on Protestants as inaugurating the connection between sincere expression and interior emotion, see John Martin, "Inventing Sincerity, Refashioning Prudence," *American Historical Review* 102, no. 5 (1997): 1309–42.

15. Barbara Rosenwein, "Worrying About Emotions in History," *The American Historical Review* 107, no. 3 (2002): 839. And Reddy, "Sentimentalism and Its Erasure," *The Journal of Modern History* 72, no. 1 (2000): 109–52.

16. Jardine, *Erasmus, Man of Letters*, 152.

17. Ibid., 152. On the other hand—and no doubt because Erasmus felt the heavy burden of frequent correspondence—he writes to Francisco de Vergara in 1529: "From now on, my dear Francisco, let us not compete by reckoning the number or the bulk of our letters, but

the illegitimacy of dispassionate letters, she was also skeptical of the sincerity of Erasmus's correspondence. For Jardine, Erasmus's epistles *in particular* constitute a calculated "construction of charisma in print," and a "remarkably poised presentation of himself" (the implication being he wasn't so poised on the inside).[18]

Jardine is suggesting, then, that we should never assume we are getting the *real* Erasmus in his letters, both for reasons of style and for reasons of manipulative intention. "Where," Jardine asks, "are we to ascribe authenticity as we scrutinize the mass of 'data' which Erasmus's voluminous correspondence provides? What would count as sincerity in an oeuvre which conscientiously emulates classical letter-writing, both in form and content?"[19] Jardine demonstrates how Erasmus's writing, editing, and publication of letters—composed at particular times, for specific correspondents, with reference to intellectual centers of learning—was part of a conscious effort to build an ideal scholarly community that transcended national borders. And she goes further:

> I suggest that we have missed the point if we treat Erasmus's *epistolae* and his many published *declamationes* as attempts at sincerity or authenticity in our own post-Romantic sense. The issue for Erasmus is one of affective *presence*: what are the modes of discourse which will make the absent *praeceptor* a vividly present force, an influential source of learning, wherever his texts are read?[20]

There is not, from this perspective, a one-to-one correspondence between Erasmus's actual feelings and his emotions as depicted in his correspondence.

Jardine is not arguing, of course, that the letters were altogether lacking in actual feeling, but rather that they were deliberately affective in ways that take us beyond "data" into the realm of intention and style—their goal was to move the emotions of their recipients and not (necessarily or always) to accurately reflect the emotions of their author. Erasmus and his correspondents "regarded the familiar letter as a highly crafted form of communication which could act as intermediary between separated individuals linked by bonds of shared feeling and an emerging trans-European intellectual ideal of *humanitas*."[21] In assessing Erasmus's correspondence as "confected" and "highly crafted," Jardine was attempting to upend a long scholarly tradition of taking it at face value, and was arguing for a more critical assessment of the possible underlying motivations that Erasmus and his interlocutors may have had when writing and publishing their correspondence. By pointing to the emotional power of Erasmus's rhetoric in his letters, while also showing that Erasmus was keenly aware of and used such power,

---

only in the warmth of our feelings. If these are strong and lasting, it will not matter how brief and infrequent our letters are" (CWE 15:140).
18. Jardine, *Erasmus, Man of Letters*, 148.
19. Ibid., 149.
20. Ibid., 174.
21. Jardine, *Reading Shakespeare Historically*, 87.

Jardine's analysis has forced us to read Erasmus's letters differently, to always be cautious before assuming something he writes is sincere.[22]

We are the inheritors, in some ways, of early modern notions of feigned feeling, of the contrast between inward, and thus genuine, emotion and outward, and thus possibly fabricated, expressions of emotion. But this itself can and should be historicized further. As Monique Scheer has pointed out,

> notions of interiority and sincerity are so deeply embedded in the modern Western habitus that they creep into scientific and scholarly definitions of emotion and inform research questions and interpretations as well. . . . Rather than seeking to reconstruct emotional "truth", the question becomes how and why historical actors mobilized their bodies in certain ways, cultivated specific skilled performances, and debated emotional practices among themselves.[23]

Scheer's suggestion that emotions "do not have an existence prior to or completely separate from social scripts," alongside the notion that sincerity is culturally managed, can contribute as well to Jardine's attempts to liberate us from thinking of Erasmus's letters as data, but with more direct respect to his descriptions of feeling. In other words, asking when Erasmus is sincerely effusing as opposed to when he is affecting affection is to start off on the wrong foot.

This is also true when Erasmus is operating at his most literary, for lack of a better way of putting it. We cannot dismiss Erasmus's expressed feelings as disingenuous simply on the grounds that they are composed according to literary conventions or rhetorical tropes: this, after all, is how emotions are often expressed in any culture.[24] Certainly by the late 1520s Erasmus was no longer merely "emulating classical letter-writing in both form and content," as Jardine puts it, but had come fully to inhabit such a world of discourse, adapting his own discursive style according to classical and biblical conventions, and molding them to his tastes so that they might become truly habituated. This is what a Christian humanist emotional community would be expected to look like on paper. And it was a matter of both theory and practice, as we can see in the *Ciceronianus*:

> I approve of imitation, but not imitation enslaved to one set of rules, from the guidelines of which it dare not depart, but imitation which gathers from

---

22. See also Kathy Eden, *The Renaissance Rediscovery of Intimacy*, 85–90, for a discussion of the relationship between intimacy and *affectus*.

23. Monique Scheer, "Are Emotions a Kind of Practice (and Is That What Makes Them Have A History)? A Bourdieuian Approach to Understanding Emotion," *History and Theory* 51, no. 2 (2012): 215.

24. Ep 2169 and 2170, relatedly, deal with questions of the sincerity of love and of speech, as well as with *parrhesia* in the context of academic discourse—further evidence that the members of the *respublica litterarum* themselves were well aware of the possibilities of feigned affections in epistolary correspondence.

all authors, or at least from the most outstanding, the thing which is the chief virtue of each and which suits your own cast of mind; imitation which does not immediately incorporate into its own speech any nice little feature it comes across, but transmits it to the mind for inward digestion, so that becoming part of your own system, it gives the impression ... of something that springs from your own mental processes, something that exudes the characteristics and force of your own mind and personality.[25]

Questions of authenticity are not exactly rendered moot here—because Erasmus continues on to argue that "your speech will not be a patchwork or a mosaic, but a lifelike portrait of the person you really are, a river welling out from your inmost being"—but they are to be understood in the context of training in a particular style. If we are thinking of the deployment of *imitatio* or *mimesis* as the makings of affective rhetoric, of language that exhibits and moves the emotions, Monique Scheer's concept of emotion as a kind of practice is likewise helpful. On that model, affective rhetoric, for Erasmus, has been habituated in a Bourdieuian sense, so that—in Erasmus's words—it has become "a part of [his] own system." And one of the ways in which such an emotional practice was carried out, especially for Erasmus, was via correspondence.

Working from the *Ciceronianus*, Kathy Eden has, relatedly, demonstrated the importance of intimacy in the *respublica litterarum*, noting that "Erasmus expects from his reading nothing less than an understanding of the writer's thoughts and feelings, an understanding modelled on the long years of living together characteristic of the most intimate friends."[26] Erasmus puts it thus: "The very thing which the reader enjoys is getting to know the writer's feelings, character, disposition, and type of mind."[27] There is no doubt in Erasmus's mind of the possibility of conveying one's feelings with pen and paper (part and parcel of what Eden refers to as Erasmus's "rhetoric of intimacy"), and in some sense he seems to suggest that by closely studying someone's style, one gets to know their mind and concomitant affections regardless of whether they're writing about their feelings or not. Erasmus expresses this notion in a 1529 response to Johann Koler, describing Koler's initial letter as one that "breathes a spirit of deep affection, which you could not have achieved by rhetoric alone. This is convincing proof to me that everything you write springs from a true and genuine heart. Ordinary love is a garrulous thing; a great love says less than it feels."[28] In other words, Erasmus is suggesting that genuine emotion can be expressed in a letter, but that it transcends words(!)—

---

25. CWE 28:441; see further also Manfred Hoffmann, *Rhetoric and Theology: The Hermeneutics of Erasmus* (Toronto: University of Toronto Press, 1994), 73–5.

26. Eden, *The Renaissance Rediscovery of Intimacy*, 85.

27. CWE 28:440.

28. CWE 15:349 (spiritus aliquid affectus eximii, quod oratione consequi non potueris ... te nihil non ex animo synceriissimo scribere. Loquax enim res est vulgaris amor, ingens minus eloquitur quam sentit).

not particularly easy advice to follow. Moreover, given the aforementioned quote from the *Ciceronianus*, we might suggest that an important way that early modern humanists like Erasmus themselves conceived of "self-fashioning," and thus of affective communication, was via a transformation of features of rhetorical style into self-expression. Rather than attempting either to discern Erasmus's genuine feelings or to dismiss his epistolary tactics as operating somehow above or outside of those feelings, we must be content to operate uncomfortably in a nebulous middle space when analyzing affective epistles.

Scheer also argues for conceptualizing emotional practices as "depending on historically and culturally specific habits and context," and while she is more interested in uncovering the embodied nature of emotions in history, her framework is, I would argue, applicable also to affective discourse as something learned, habituated, and practiced.[29] William Reddy had earlier suggested that naming our feelings is a feature of experiencing them, and thus Erasmus's expression of his emotions in letters can be appreciated as an emotional practice with "interiorizing effects."[30] While the ghost of authenticity raises its head here again, given the editing processes Erasmus was known to have undertaken when readying his letters for the courier or for the press, we can also appreciate *that* process too as an emotional practice whereby Erasmus's reflections upon his own expressed emotions and the subsequent modulating of them (one way or the other) can be imagined as a form of affective self-fashioning.

In the final analysis, we must admit that Erasmus's emotions, like most emotions, are both "constitutive and performative," to borrow a phrase from Nicholas Terpstra.[31] This allows us to approach Erasmus's correspondence while tacking between the approaches of the skeptics and those of the faithful, suspending judgment about sincerity except when it becomes an explicit concern of the letters themselves, or when there are other compelling reasons to consider Erasmus's emotional expression in relation to the events of his life. We are able to explore further the ways in which Erasmus's humanist commitments shaped his emotional discourse, which has been the subject of this book up to this point, in his correspondence. And we can evaluate the ways in which the humanist republic of letters might best be thought of as an example of what Jacqueline Van Gent— analyzing a different group of correspondents from another time and place—has called a "utopian emotional community of epistolary exchange," a gloss that also

---

29. That is not to suggest that the embodied and material aspects of letter writing are not salient features of the practice, or that they wouldn't be worth pursuing further, but we do not have the space to do so here. Indeed, Erasmus's body is often front and center in his letters, especially the later ones when it had become increasingly frail and subject to various ailments—these no doubt contributed (largely negatively, and often explicitly) to his emotional dispositions.

30. Scheer, "Are Emotions a Kind of Practice?" 212.

31. Giovanni Tarantino and Charles Zika (ed.), *Feeling Exclusion: Religious Conflict, Exile and Emotions in Early Modern Europe* (London: Routledge, 2019), 281.

helps to bring Jardine into conversation with Rosenwein. Or to paraphrase Susan Broomhall, also writing on a different context, Erasmus's letters "do emotion work, transcend distance, and sustain community in the absence of alternative forms of contact" between the author and his correspondents.[32] These models allow us to read the letters, paraphrasing Rosenwein, for what they tell us about "the evaluations that [Erasmus] makes about others' emotions; the nature of the affective bonds between" him and his correspondents, and "the modes of emotional expression that [Erasmus] expects, encourages, tolerates, and deplores."[33] With all this in mind, let us now turn to consider the emotions of Erasmus in exile.

Emotions in Exile: From Basel to Freiburg, 1528–30

Erasmus was, for most of his life, a man without a country, a sort of scholarly vagabond; like the students of the EU program that bears his name, he was perpetually studying abroad. He moved for patronage, for employment, for books. Emotion was always involved, of course, in some cases more explicitly than others. In only one case, though, did he consider himself an exile, a situation that gave rise to a constellation of feelings, most of them negative. In late 1528, tensions between the evangelicals and Catholics in Basel turned sour, resulting in a temporary agreement on January 5, 1529, that sermons should be preached only on the Bible, but that mass could still be celebrated once per day. A public disputation was set for May 30th, but on the 8th and 9th of February the Reformed iconoclasts jumped the gun, took to the streets and the churches, smashed all the icons and, according to Erasmus, gathered in the town square with cannons and bonfires. Virtually all university professors and Catholic city council members resigned, and the cathedral chapter left town. By April 1st, Basel had become formally Protestant. While the newly Protestant-city's leaders, including the once-Erasmian Johannes Oecolampadius, promised Erasmus he could stay there undisturbed, he nevertheless saw the writing on the wall and departed for the not-too-distant, but firmly Catholic, imperial city of Freiburg.[34]

Erasmus would become a religious refugee, if not a typical one given his extraordinary connections and, by this time, his substantial financial means. An examination of Erasmus's correspondence from this period reveals his feelings about moving into exile in particular, but also about his more general thoughts and attendant emotions about the religious conflict that was dividing Europe. Reading these letters as a test case, we are able to think more concretely about the questions raised above concerning authenticity as well as about humanist discourses of feeling in epistolography. A preliminary suggestion is that if Erasmus

---

32. Susan Broomhall, "Cross-channel Affections: Pressure and Persuasion in Letters to Calvinist Refugees in England, 1569–1570," in Tarantino and Zika, *Feeling Exclusion*, 38.

33. Paraphrasing Rosenwein, "Worrying about Emotions," 842.

34. See CWE 15:83n1 for more details.

was at one stage writing to construct an international humanist group through the affective bonds of correspondence, as Jardine demonstrated in analyzing his letters from the late 1510s and early 1520s, the severe disruptions of the Protestant break reveal feelings of deep uncertainty about the strength of those bonds, and they gave rise to a different set of feelings altogether. While Erasmus had never been an eternal optimist, hopeful feelings of a golden age of *bonae litterae* would be decidedly displaced by the Reformations and ultimately replaced with feelings of anxiety and despair.

In preparing to leave Basel, before the formal split with Rome, Erasmus sought out information about a number of potential places to move as regards their suitability. Friends likewise wrote to encourage and remind him that he wasn't short of options. Martinus Bovolinus, for example, wrote to Erasmus in February of 1529: "Have no fear: wherever you go, unless you travel to the Antipodes, you will never be a stranger."[35] But while Erasmus was indeed well connected, he also had plenty of enemies (real and perceived) in these divisive years. He even worried that leaving Basel itself would prove difficult, and he wrote to Bernard von Cles at the end of February to ask whether he could have King Ferdinand (Emperor Charles V's younger brother) write a letter of summons to get him out of town: "I hope I can leave here freely, and I have no obligations to anyone; nevertheless, such an arrangement would make me more secure about the move."[36] Despite his resolution to move, however, Erasmus could be picky, and for some time whatever actual fears he had of the Protestants were outweighed by anxieties about landing in an equally undesirable spot. In the same letter, he expresses reservations about Freiburg in particular, for fear of trading untenable evangelical fervor for popish conservativism, especially when it comes to the thing Erasmus might have feared most of all—eating fish:

> Freiburg is within easy reach, but it is a rather poor place and the people, I hear, are inclined to be narrow-minded. For a long time now the "scaly tribe" has not agreed with me. If I swallow even a mouthful, I am sick to death. Although I have better reason for not fasting than I would wish and have from the popes an official and unequivocal letter, yet there would be howls of protest from the ignorant mob, who sin as much by their narrow legalism as the other side sins by their arrogant disobedience. . . . These considerations have kept me here longer.

Erasmus found himself, in other words, in the very particular situation of being afraid to stay in Basel for fear of persecution by the Protestants, and afraid to move to Catholic Freiburg for fear of being castigated for not following the requisite dietary restrictions. These idiosyncrasies make clear as well the variegated nature of experiencing exile as a result of the sixteenth-century religious reformations and, at a very basic level, the benefit of historicizing emotions: while Erasmus could

---

35. CWE 15:94.
36. CWE 15:105.

loosely be thought to belong to a number of emotional communities of exile as a generalization, the specific nature of his feelings makes for a highly individualized story.

Relatedly, Erasmus's letters are laden with worries about his frail bodily disposition. It is something that preoccupied him constantly, and he was sensitive not only to specific foods, but to his surrounding environment. To Ludwig Baer, in March, Erasmus writes of a different kind of emotion toward more mundane objects which keeps him from moving back to the Low Countries, namely his hatred of German stoves. "Yesterday," he writes, "I received another letter from the archbishop of Palermo, who is the first chancellor of the imperial court at Brabant, promising favourable, even generous, treatment if I agreed to return. I would certainly do so, if all German stoves were put out, for I have an infernal hatred of those things."[37] (Elsewhere he says he hates castles and coal, both in the context of rejecting an offer to settle in Brabant.[38]) Erasmus continues with a common refrain, that he's afraid to move also because of his health, and what he considers to be his delicate constitution:

> I am also aware that wherever I go, the journey will not be without great danger to my life, for even the slightest thing—a change of wine, for example, or even a new coat—puts me at risk. But whatever the outcome, I must move somewhere. I would like to remain here until the booksellers return from Frankfurt, but I fear it may not be safe.[39]

Regarding wine, a persistent theme, sometimes his concerns do not conjure much sympathy: "This poor body of mine has many requirements, in particular it needs good wine."[40] Erasmus seems to have genuinely believe that only high-quality Burgundy did not cause him gastrological problems, which at first glance may seem like a blessing rather than curse—the malady of an oenophile's dreams. In fact, we learn in a later letter to Anton Fugger that as Erasmus's health declined, he diluted his Burgundy with water boiled with liquorice root (now an oenophile's

---

37. CWE 15:115.
38. Ep 2222 to Johann Von Vlatten (CWE 16:62–3).
39. CWE 15:115. One might wonder whether Erasmus needed some profits from the book fair for the move, but in a letter just a few days later Erasmus gives one of his trusted amanuenses, Talesius, a gift of 150 French *écus* (apropos of nothing), which was roughly equivalent to 1,400 days'—that is, four years'—wages for a master mason in Cambridge (see Ep 2113, and CWE 15:117n1). So probably he just wanted to conclude his ordinary seasonal business before leaving.
40. Ep 2327; CWE 16:329. See also Ep 2142 to François Bonvalot, where he writes: "I believe my letter reached you; it was absolutely barefaced about sending the wine. But need and shame 'go ill together and tarry not in the same place'" (CWE 15:194; the reference is to Ovid, *Metamorphoses* 2.846).

nightmare), which he admitted tastes like "some kind of medical potion".⁴¹ It might be noted that we are a good distance here from Erasmus's own advice to the imaginary refugee in his mock-consolatory-letter from the *De conscribendis epistolis*: "Poverty, exile, and war are not evils, but the occasion for virtue. For strength of mind thrives and is nurtured in adversity, like a holm-oak, which spreads its branches wider 'the harder it is hewn by the rugged axe.'"⁴²

While the sheer number of expressed worries about these and similar mundane matters reveal much about the ordinary anxieties of Erasmus facing exile, he ultimately had more serious concerns about the situation in Basel.⁴³ Several times Erasmus tells his correspondents that it is best that his messenger relay the story about the Basel iconoclasm in person, for fear of writing it down. Even worse, and despite reassurances he had received from Oecolampadius, Erasmus writes to Francisco de Vergara in mid-March, "I am afraid that what happened to those saints, both male and female [that is, the images that were destroyed], is an omen of what will happen one day to me also."⁴⁴ Despite the fact, he says, that he is erroneously associated with the evangelicals, "the more fanatical they are, the more they hate me. So to avoid this risk to my life, I must put my life at risk."⁴⁵ Erasmus's concerns shift from the mundane to the extraordinary in the months leading up to his decision to leave Basel. Whether he genuinely feared for his life is difficult to determine, but any paranoia would have had some foundation—Erasmus was acutely aware of the precarious nature of the politico-religious circumstances during these years, and his sometime correspondent and apologist Louis de Berquin would be burned in Paris right around the time Erasmus was departing for Freiburg.

We also gain potential insight into Erasmus's feelings about Basel from hindsight descriptions he wrote once he had relocated. Reflecting back on the situation from his new location, Erasmus wrote to Willibald Pirckheimer, recalling the iconoclastic riots and a near-pitch-battle in the middle of the town square: "When the worst of our fears had been removed and there was some reason to hope that no violent action would be taken against life or property . . . I began

41. CWE 15:343.
42. CE 22:154.
43. It was not only Erasmus who expressed his feelings about his own precarious situation. Erasmus Schets, the Antwerp banker who had managed Erasmus's affairs in England and the Low Countries, writes of the "grieved" locals who long for Erasmus's return to Holland, not without some melodrama: "Many are offering hospitality, board, and gifts, promising to provide Burgundy and anything else your beloved Basel has been able to supply. But to what purpose? For as long as you refuse to come, they pass their lives under this heavy burden and in semidespair [*semidesperati*]" (CWE 15:119). Erasmus responds sarcastically: "Between those cold-hearted friends and hot-headed critics [*inter istos frigidos amicos et calidos obtrecatores*] in your country I do not know what I could hope for. Report this to those friends who are ruining their eyes with weeping" (CWE 15:347).
44. CWE 15:139.
45. CWE 15:167.

to think of moving, even though I kept my intentions a secret . . . I worried that exile would turn out badly for me."[46] To Erasmus Schets, his banker, he wrote, "I changed my residence with great trepidation (*magno metu*) but without incident."[47] But sometimes his tune is slightly different. In a letter to Thomas More, his move was cast similarly in emotional terms, but not about his own fear:

> If I had remained in Basel, the theologians would have blazoned it abroad that I was in sympathy with the things that are going on there. Now they brag that I left because I was afraid. In fact my departure caused general disappointment, even among those whose teaching I frankly and openly detested. . . . But I preferred to risk my life rather than appear to approve a programme like theirs.[48]

Likewise, again to Pirckheimer: "I am glad I left Basel, although I left most reluctantly."[49] And a year later, he writes to Lorenzo Campeggi, further emphasizing mixed feelings: "My departure did not pain me overmuch. I was glad to leave such a city, though it grieves me that a famous and elegant city, whose hospitality I have enjoyed for so long, has been brought to such a state. If only this were the only one whose fate we mourn!"[50] Erasmus's emotional reporting shifts several times as his move became a more distant memory. Monique Scheer reminds us of the importance of taking such shifts into account: "In retrospect, emotional experiences can be reinterpreted and, in a sense, re-experienced, and sometimes it is only long after the fact that we 'understand' what our feelings 'actually' were."[51] With respect to Erasmus in exile, the question thus becomes not only whether he was articulating his emotions accurately in hindsight, but what his emotions were at a given time in relation to the events in question.

Reminding us again that he was no ordinary religious refugee, arriving in Freiburg Erasmus was put up in a residence originally built for the Emperor Maximillian I, and he enjoyed patronage from King Ferdinand, who was in Vienna. Unlike many religious refugees during the Reformation, Erasmus had options, and this must have at least partially assuaged the most serious worries (even if the plethora of options continued to entice Erasmus with another move, which seemed to perpetuate his anxiety). In one letter he writes,

> I am being lured to England with lavish promises. I have several times been invited to Trent by Bernhard, bishop of the city and supreme chancellor to King Ferdinand, with an offer of five hundred gold florins. King Ferdinand invites me to Vienna, offering four hundred on the sole condition that I live there. . . .

---

46. CWE 15:243.
47. CWE 15:347.
48. Ep 2211 to More; CWE 16:38.
49. CWE 15:352.
50. Ep 2327; CWE 16:328.
51. Scheer, "Are Emotions a Kind of Practice?" 213.

Anton Fugger sent his own messenger with an offer of one hundred gold florins for traveling expenses and an annual payment of the same amount, if I moved to Augsburg.[52]

These are significant sums—500 gold florins was the rough equivalent of about 13 years' salary for a master mason in Cambridge[53]—and it is testimony to Erasmus's financial security at this stage in his life that he turns down such lucrative offers.[54]

Nevertheless, Erasmus was never far away from complaining about something, and in September he wrote to William Blount: "Everything here is very expensive; moreover I have now lost the splendid advantages that the Froben press offered me." More seriously, again, and foreshadowing a shift in mood that would result from a more dramatic break between Protestants and Catholics: "I sadly fear that the gospel may involve us in a deadly war, so readily do men rush to arms."[55] From this perspective, Erasmus was also expressly worried about his friends back in Basel, such as Bonifacius Amerbach, and his letters are full of the language of anxiety: *sollicitus*, *cura*, *anxius*, and the like. Erasmus's initial optimism about settling in Freiburg becomes tempered by new fears of heightened religious conflict: "I think it safer to stay here for a while," he writes, "unless, as I sadly fear, the sudden onset of war should throw everything into confusion. Already there is a rumor that the citizens of Zurich have taken up arms."[56] (The Zurichers would, indeed, soon go to battle, where another one-time Erasmian turned Protestant, Ulrich Zwingli, would die on the battlefield in the Second Kappel War.) The fear that tensions between Catholics and Protestants would soon boil over into a war that would affect him directly increased as time went on, and not a year after he had arrived in Freiburg he was looking to move again. But where to? In Basel, the reformers made it so that every resident had to participate in their version of the Lord's Supper on penalty of exile, so a return to the comforts of Froben's press was out of the question.

Writing to Philip Melanchthon in mid-1530 about the imperial diet being held in Augsburg (which ultimately failed to resolve the question of religious division in the empire), Erasmus writes, "I have long been anxious to leave Germany, now I am compelled by necessity. Here we barely have anything to eat or drink; what would happen in time of war? And I don't see a safe haven for myself anywhere." He concludes, sarcastically, "The Gospel has given birth to this age in which we live."[57] In the same year he wrote to Pirckheimer, expressing similarly anxious feelings about needing to leave but having nowhere to go:

---

52. CWE 15:247–8.
53. See notes in CWE 15:248.
54. Ep 2192.
55. CWE 16:47.
56. CWE 15:283.
57. CWE 17:23.

> I am making preparations to escape with no sight of any safe and tranquil haven. What deters me from going to Italy is the long and dangerous journey. In France it seems that I am rid of the likes of Béda [Erasmus's most assiduous critic at the Sorbonne], but I am afraid that the flames of war will extend even there; what is more, I hardly dare to hope that Brabant will be free of warfare.[58]

So after a brief respite when he first arrived in Freiburg, Erasmus's nagging worries returned and he would never be as comfortable as he was in Basel before the Reformation spread. James Estes writes that the closest thing to a "single dominant theme" in this set of letters is Erasmus's "nagging anxiety, always present but not always at the forefront of discussion, about the conflicts and disorders of Europe and Germany."[59] I would only add that this anxiety is twofold: not only a concern for what those conflicts and disorders mean for the future of Christendom, but a palpable worry about how empire-wide political matters would affect him directly, all the way down to the wine in his glass.

A compelling feature of the letters from this period is, again, Erasmus's presentation of the inverse of what Jardine outlines in her analysis of the construction of a coherent and amiable Republic of Letters without borders. Examining the correspondence from the perspective of his feelings about being unmoored and exiled, we find that Erasmus paints a picture of an increasingly fragmenting Europe, of faraway lands not full of intimate friends, but populated by petty instigators, inimical to Erasmus himself and his love of learning. A key difference, of course, is that we have examined letters that directly report Erasmus's own emotional state, as opposed to considering letters for their broadly affective (rhetorical) force, although keeping both layers in mind is important for writing the history of emotions out of epistolary contexts. In the early 1520s, according to Jardine, collected volumes of letters "emphasised—or, possibly, deliberately constructed—Erasmus's connectedness with a number of European centres of learning, notably Cambridge, Germany, and the Low Countries."[60] By the end of the decade, Erasmus had enemies everywhere and nowhere to go. With more correspondents than ever, he depicts himself as alone—not leading a solitary and tranquil scholarly life, but persistently concerned his health and about war, accompanied with liquorice-flavored Burgundy.

A Burdensome Consoler

Erasmus's own despondent feelings about exile, which led to far more numerous expressions of anxiety-related emotions than have been detailed here, did not necessarily lead to him writing more compassionate letters to other refugees.

---

58. CWE 17:36.
59. CWE 16:xii.
60. Jardine, *Erasmus, Man of Letters*, 163.

Indeed, the descriptions of his own emotions provide an interesting contrast with his advice for others in a similar position. Exploring the differences allow for illumination of the slippage between theory and practice in Erasmus's ethics of emotion. In 1529, for example, he wrote a sort of backhanded consolatory letter to Johann von Botzheim, canon of the cathedral chapter at Constance, who had (along with the rest of the chapter) been forced to move to Überlingen after Constance succumbed to the Protestants: "Perhaps," Erasmus writes,

> you were expecting a letter of consolation from me; but at that time such was the state of affairs that I needed a physician myself. Finally, I was aware how that truly noble and truly Christian mind of yours could always rise above every blow of fortune. Until now Fortune has struck only at the least part of your happiness: she has just eaten away at your income; your reputation and your life remain unharmed.

He continues, as though Johann is responding:

> "But," you say, "what I am experiencing is a kind of exile." Suppose it is: yet it is not a harsh exile, and perhaps it will not last long. Is there a person alive who is so consistently favoured by Fortune as never to suffer anything unpleasant? It may be impossible to avoid or dispel misfortune, yet much of the pain will be eased if we bear it graciously. That will happen if each person says to himself (as is in fact the truth) that it is the hand of God that is scourging us for a time, not to destroy us but to correct us. If we calmly accept the blows of our physical parents, even sometimes when their rage is unreasonable, how much more calmly should we bear the hand of the Almighty, who is the father not only of our bodies but of our souls? How far we still are from the standard set by the blessed Job! The Babylonian exile afflicted the Israelites for seventy years, and they were restored to their temple as soon as it seemed good to the Lord. . . . Among all the remedies for sadness that speakers commonly devise, I know of nothing more effective than to reflect on these words: "It is the Lord: let him do what seems good in his eyes."[61]

The advice here, then, is to accept the scourge of God stoically like Job, but remember also that Erasmus defended himself for indulging in his own sadness by invoking the Apostle Paul.[62] Erasmus, then, did not always heed his own advice.

---

61. Ep 2205; CWE 16:7.
62. We referred to this passage from a letter to Alonso de Fonseca in the chapter on the New Testament above: "Sometimes [Paul's] letters are stained with tears, he tries to find comfort in the conversation of the pious, and prays to be spared the buffeting of Satan's minister. So is it surprising if I, who am no more a match for Paul's strong spirit than a worm crawling on the ground can match an eagle, feel in a human way?" (CWE 15:158).

Situating letters like this one alongside those considered in the previous section, and also in light of the advice Erasmus gives regarding consolatory correspondence in his manual for letter writing, allows us to appreciate the multifaceted nature of the rhetorics of consolation in the renaissance—and how Erasmus took advantage of the variety of strategies then available. As the work of George McClure has shown, there was a rich tradition of consolatory literature offered in the Italian renaissance, and much of Erasmus's advice can be traced to threads in that tradition as well as to ancient Rome.[63] Naama Cohen-Hanegbi suggests, additionally, that out of this tradition we might identify a new emotional regime, wherein "private and intellectual mourning practices" were privileged over excessive and public weeping, for example.[64] If Erasmus's humanist circle counts as an emotional community, the rhetorically rich traditions drawn upon in the renaissance literature of consolation makes for a multiform set of emotional practices associated with grieving.

Erasmus devotes about thirty pages to the subject of consolation in his expansive manual for letter writing, the *De conscribendis epistolis* of 1522. "Since the life of mortals," he writes, at the beginning of the grief-and-consolation section, "is full of misfortunes all around and few may be found who are not dissatisfied with their lot, no obligation arises more often than that of comforting our friends with consoling words."[65] In his advice (throughout the whole of the work) Erasmus eschews the rigid formalisms of the medieval *ars dictaminis* as well as the approach of the new Ciceronians of his own age, arguing that style, structure, and content should be determined by circumstance, subject, and correspondent, not by hard and fast rules. Erasmus also acknowledges that there are myriad occasions for grieving and thus as many for writing letters of consolation:

> Although consolation is reserved above all for cases of bereavement and exile, one may devise other themes on diverse matters that bring distress, such as bodily disease, poor and uncertain health, old age, an ill-omened marriage that it is useless to regret, the monastic order, the priesthood, or any other way of life which the person committed to it is becoming weary, family misfortune, inferior social standing, irksome poverty, unpopularity, the loss of property through some mischance, services rendered to an ungrateful person, children who dishonour their parents by a wicked life, plague, war, and countless other things.[66]

And so while each of these would require a tailor-made consolatory letter—at least in the fine-grained details—Erasmus does simplify matters by suggesting

---

63. George McClure, *Sorrow and Consolation in Italian Humanism* (Princeton, 1991).
64. "Mourning under Medical Care: A Study of a *Consilium* by Bartolomeo Montagnana," *Parergon* 31, no. 2 (2014): 44.
65. CWE 23:148.
66. CWE 23:155–6.

that there are more or less three types for all occasions: (1) the direct, wherein one argues forthrightly that the grieving person needs to take various steps to move past their dejection, offering "proofs to show that there is no reason to feel grief" ("we shall make use of strong medicines of this kind when we have a philosopher or a man of good sense [*viro cordato*] to deal with"—presumably von Botzheim was one such case); (2) the indirect, wherein one only glances at the problem at hand (for either "the weak in spirit" or "the noble-minded" person who would feel ashamed at being consoled); and (3) the lighthearted or humorous form, for either less serious situations, very close friends, or the most sturdy of sufferers. Erasmus even composes lengthy examples of each of these in the manual for his reader's benefit. But he had also composed such letters of his own, long before the publication of this manual.

In 1489 Erasmus had penned a letter to the bereaved daughters of Berta Heyen, a work which was eventually printed separately under the title *Oratio Funebris*. This was some three decades before the manual on letter-writing was first published (although the latter was originally conceived around the same time). The occasion was made more complicated by the fact that Erasmus imagined himself as a son of sorts to Berta—who often fed and cared for Erasmus and his fellow Augustinian monks—and so he was by no means an objective therapist. The letter is notable for its unrestrained expressions of grief, which we might compare usefully to the exile letters of the late 1520s, and also for Erasmus's descriptions of his own symptoms, however exaggerated they may be. The letter begins as follows:

> It has been a long time, my dearest daughters and sisters, since I decided to send you some pages with which you could soothe the grief (*dolorem*) inflicted upon you by the death of your mother. But whenever I take pen in hand in order to set down on paper the praises of our Berta, believe me, I immediately break out in tears, my fingers turn numb, my joints stiffen, my spirit swoons, and I am so overcome by sorrow (*moerore*) that I cannot even give a bit of serious reflection to your mother's virtues, let alone write about them. How often have I begun this speech, and how often have I thrown it down, overcome by sobbing and sorrow? How often have I taken it up again, stiffening my resolution and temporarily forcing back my tears, only to throw down again the task just resumed? How many times have I given it up altogether, and stubbornly tried yet again to take up the task? But just when I am making these efforts to apply a salve to the wound of your sorrow, I realize that I myself have been stricken by a much more painful blow; and just when I am beginning to examine your sores so that I may administer a healing ointment, my own wounds break open once again.[67]

---

67. CWE 29:15; LB VIII 551C-E: Iampridem quidem, filiae ac sorores charissimae, litterarum aliquid ad vos dare institueram, quibus dolorem, quo vos maternus affecit decessus, demulcere possetis. Sed (credite mihi) quotiens sumto calamo *Bertam* nostram celebraturus membranae manus admoveo, prorumpunt continuo lachrimae, stupent articuli, obrigent artus, elanguet animus, adeoque moerore conficior, ut non modo non

One gets the sense here that Erasmus, even though ostensibly writing a letter of consolation, is engaged in a form of writing as self-healing. Compared with his later works, and his advice in the letter-writing manual, Erasmus is indeed more effusive here (in line with Huizinga's claims), and so we might either take that as evidence of a genuinely distraught state in this particular case, as an early penchant for unchecked rhetorical flourish, *or* as an example of a specific rhetorical technique (or all three). He continues:

> And what wounds are these? I do not mean bodily ones, I assure you, but wounds much more serious than those, wounds in the spirit. For whenever I imagine the dear, sweet face of Berta, tears immediately burst forth from my eyes, like blood from a wounded soul, as it were; my sobbing is redoubled, I utter groans that reveal the gravity of the pain within, and a "chill trembling passes right through my bones," my face turns hideously pale, my tongue sticks in my throat, I am left breathless, and I am so completely seized by dread grief that I cannot bear it. Despite my shame, I confess my weakness; I am overcome by emotion, drowned in sorrow; I have no control over the tears my eyes shed.[68]

Erasmus's description here again raises the question of the location of the emotions in his anthropology. The wounds, he insists, are not corporeal, and yet they cannot help but make themselves known through bodily expression. All are signs of an *interior* suffering. Tears are blood from a wounded soul, groans reveal pain *within*. As Brian Cummings and Freya Sierhuis put it, describing early modern conceptions of emotion (or maybe *all* emotions), "while passions include bodily responses, it is precisely that they are not only bodily responses that makes them interesting."[69] A soul often manifests its pain in the body.

If the daughters of Berta found Erasmus's lamentations overwhelming, he would not have been surprised: "I fear that you may criticize me," he writes, "and fairly

---

scribere, verum ne cogitare quidem vel pauxillum de maternis virtutius liceat. Quotiens hanc adorsus sum oratiunculam, quotiens singultu moeroreque superatus rejeci e manibus, quotiens obfirmato animo, pressisque paulisper lachrimis, rejectam repetii, quotiens rursum repetitam rejeci, quotiens jam sepositam improbus adoriri conatus sum? Sed dum vestrae vulneri tristitiae medelam ferre contendo, ipse longe acerbiore plaga fauciatum me deprehendo, dumque ulcera vestra oleum infusurus rimari coepero, mea in me vulnera recrudescunt.

68. CWE 29:16. LB VIII 551E: Et quae vulnera? Non quidem corporea, sed longe corporeis atrociora, animi loquor. Quotiens enim subit animo meo *Berta* praedulcis imago, protinus ex oculis quasi quidam fauciae animae sanguis erumpunt lachrimae, ingeminantur singultus, prodeunt gemitus interni doloris indices, gelidusque per ima recurrit ossa tremor, informis ora pallor occupat, haeret faucibus lingua, elabitur spiritus, adeoque totum me dirus invadit dolor, ut ferre nequeam. Fateor (quanquam pudeat) imbecillitatem meam, vincor affectu, moerore absorbeor, luminibus imperitare nequeo.

69. *Passions and Subjectivity in Early Modern Culture* (London: Ashgate, 2013), 13.

too, in the words of the blessed Job: *You are a burdensome consoler.*"[70] But, he asks, "who in his right mind would think it shameful for a man to be stricken by human emotions? I do not deny that I am moved by human feelings, any more than I deny that I am human."[71] Nevertheless, he eventually does move on, writing, in a refrain that he will repeat forty years later to von Botzheim, "Although, therefore, I who wish to console you am myself in need of consolation, and I who am endeavoring to be a physician to you do myself need the attentions of a physician."[72] Erasmus prefaces the rest of the letter by noting that he is following the ancients who would offer lamentations in public for dead loved ones (citing Cicero on eulogy), and, more specifically Jerome, who did so in his letters. Thus, after recounting the virtues of Berta's life, at the end of the letter Erasmus comes around to what would become recognizable themes in later correspondence as well:

> How long will we go on indulging our tears and wasting away in useless grief [*vano moerore*]? Berta triumphs among the starry thrones in the gleaming ranks of heaven's residents, wreathed in sparkling garlands. And do we lament her death? . . . Clearly our lot is more to be lamented than hers. She has cast off the burden of mortal flesh and has entered her heavenly homeland. We are sojourners and visitors in this sad vale of tears, in this exile of misfortune and death, still weighed down by the burdensome load of the body. . . . So let us dry up our tears, cease our weeping, and put an end to grief.[73]

Christians may grieve (even excessively, per the early Erasmus), but not for too long. If Erasmus was a burdensome consoler for Berta's daughters, either he learned a few lessons by the time he came to put the finishing touches on the manual for letter writing thirty-odd years later, or it was a calculation on his part.

He writes of consolation in the *De conscribendis epistolis* that "we must perform the duty skilfully, lest like unskilled doctors we aggravate rather than alleviate a wound that is still raw and fresh."[74] But also, and, importantly, Erasmus actually describes something like burdensome consolation itself as a valid method in certain cases, thus foiling our attempts at adjudicating authenticity from the emotional effusiveness in the funeral oration for Berta. Describing the first approach to consolation, that is, when dealing with the "philosopher or man of good sense," he writes that "we shall give comfort in such a way as to transfer to ourselves the feelings of the person we wish to console, so adapting our language that we seem to

---

70. CWE 29:19.
71. CWE 29:17. LB VIII 552D: Deinde quis sanae mentis turpe ducat, hominem humanis pulsari affectibus. Non inficias eo humanis me agi passionibus, sicut nec me hominem diffiteor.
72. CWE 29:19.
73. CWE 29:29.
74. CWE 25:148.

wish rather to give into our own grief than to assuage their sorrow."[75] This, again, reflects a tendency in the consolation of von Botzheim. Moreover, it is not only useful in the case of grief, but for other forms of rhetorical *pathos* as well, for Erasmus cites Cicero's defense of Milo as an instance where Cicero "pretended to shift fear to himself [*ficte metum in se transfert*] so that he could remove fear from the minds of the judges." The *ficte* here reveals also the necessity of the consoler to *deceive* the bereaved, as it were, into overcoming their grief, for, as Erasmus writes, "persons plunged into grief must be treated in exactly the same way as those whose deranged state of mind leads them to believe that they have horns, or too long a nose, or are dead, or are made of clay. They dislike those who disagree with them, and like those who humour their fancy by dissembling."[76] Thus, Erasmus continues, "we shall say that we are not fit to give consolation ourselves, as we feel as much mental anguish as the person whom we ought to comfort."[77] This should sound familiar.

Relatedly, although Erasmus offers several examples of consolatory letters in the manual, in addition to additional formulae from Cicero's and Pliny's letters, he does not offer advice on how to write a letter expressing grief. But in addition to the oration for Berta, which was simultaneously such an expression as well as an elegy, he also writes a letter expressing his feelings at the death of his friend, patron, and printer Johann Froben in 1527. Erasmus, so ostensibly well versed in rhetorical coping strategies for grief, concludes in this instance that all the tools available at his disposal ultimately fail in their purpose:

> Although I have reached this advanced age, most virtuous friend, I have learned from experience that I am not yet sufficiently known to myself. Yes, and I thought that through the precepts of philosophy and the long and almost uninterrupted experience of enduring misfortunes I was sufficiently prepared for those common daily occurrences that we see can be borne with moderation even by little girls. But the unexpected death of my friend Johann Froben has so afflicted my spirit that no distraction has been able to free my heart from grief.[78]

Erasmus's storehouse of remedies for bereavement come up short—but then again, this is a formal letter that was printed in 1528 alongside the famous *Ciceronianus*, a dialogue in which Erasmus excoriates Ciceronian formalism of every stripe, and so one could reasonably make a case, however cynical, for rhetorical amplification. The letter is, either way, another eulogy, and not a talk-therapy session: Erasmus even appended to the letter two epitaphs—one in Latin, one in Greek—that he composed for Froben and which were engraved on his tomb.

---

75. CWE 25:149.
76. Ibid.
77. Ibid.
78. Allen Ep 1900; CWE 13:420–1.

Nonetheless, he continues in the letter to expand upon his own feelings and enumerate further the failure of methods he himself had advocated in that manual and which he had employed in his own consolatory letters. His expressed emotions cut against his prescriptions of restraint and decorum in the letter-writing manual, and include an implication that the rhetorics of consolation are in certain instances simply insufficient to the task. The following lengthy digression is illustrative:

> And time, which can assuage even the most grievous of sorrows, far from alleviating my distress, has made it increase a little more each day, as relentless as a slow and insidious fever that steals upon us unawares. There is nothing more irremediable, they say. A visceral anxiety consumed me despite my efforts to resist. How much more powerful are the bonds created by spiritual affinity and mutual sympathy than are those of nature! . . . Where now, I ask myself, is that rhetorician who with a brilliant display of words can ease or banish the sorrow of others? Where is that Stoic philosopher, the tamer of human emotions? Where the theologian who used to teach that the death of pious men should be accompanied not by tears and mourning but by congratulations and applause? . . . I am not angry at my sorrow, which is most justified, but I am exasperated that it is excessive and too prolonged.[79]

The emotional expansiveness of Erasmus in the *Funeral Oration* has returned with the death of Froben. If a difference exists, it is that he describes his own self-consciousness of such effusiveness at even greater length in the later letter. He knows all the tricks, but none of them work. A more balanced approach, perhaps, is offered in his treatise *On the Christian Widow*, dedicated to Mary of Hungary in 1528 after the death of her husband. Acknowledging how difficult it would be for such a young Mary to lose such a young husband, he writes there that the arbitrariness of the Fates should console us, or "at least help to set some limit to our grieving."[80] These texts, taken alongside his manual for letter writing and the consolatory letter to von Botzheim, demonstrate the range of modes of affective

---

79. CWE 13:421; Allen Ep 1900: Iam tempus, quod acerbissimis etiam doloribus mederi solet, adeo non leniit aegritudinem, ut paulatim magis ac magis increverit dolor, quemadmodum solet lentum et insidiosum quoddam febris genus obrepere. Quo non alid aiunt immedicabilius esse. Exedebat me reluctantem cura penitus medullis insita. Tanto potentius est quod conglutinavit animi inductio mutuaque benevolentia, quam quod natura coniunxit . . . Ubi nunc est, inquam, ille rhetor, qui splendidis dictis solet aliorum moerorem vel eximere vel obiurgare? ubi philosophus ille Stoicus, domitor humanorum affectum? ubi theologus, qui docere consuevit piorum hominum mortem non luctu lachrymisque, sed gratulationibus plausuque prosequendam esse? . . . Non irascor dolori meo nimirum iustissimo, sed immodicum nimisque diuturnum esse indignor.

80. CWE 66:186. Erasmus also gives a series of rather stereotypical assessments of grief along gendered lines in this text, with excessive weeping judged a feminine characteristic, and (by contrast) the virtuous Catherine of England described as containing "nothing in

rhetoric on offer for the humanist writing to alleviate grief, or seeking consolation. Regardless of the extent to which we believe they reflect the authentic innerworkings of Erasmus's heart, these texts provide historians with models of feeling taken out of specific historical and literary circumstances, and with further details of a Christian humanist emotional style.

Erasmus thought the familiar letter was an intrinsically affective genre, and his letters are riddled with affective language alongside descriptions of his own emotions, advice to others about feeling, and even short polemical treatises on the definition of *affectus* (as seen in the chapter on the New Testament). By utilizing insights from previous scholars' work on the significance of affective rhetoric in Erasmus's letters, coupled with some heuristic approaches from the history of emotions, I hope to have shed some further light on the importance of emotion in Christian humanist epistolography, and on the difficulties attendant to properly assessing it. A reconsideration of the epistles and epistolography of Erasmus, with close attention to the emotional language and descriptions of his letters, allows us to see some trends in what Jardine called Erasmus's "epistolary technology of affect." More specifically, I would suggest that describing his own emotional states is often part of Erasmus's rhetorical strategy of moving his interlocutors' emotions. A fuller way of conceiving of the inherent affectivity of Erasmus's correspondence is to recognize that it is, on the one hand, "rhetorical," in the sense of having a telos of moving and convincing his audience, but also that the letters reflect something of Erasmus's emotional experience. They are performative and constitutive with respect to the emotions they convey. Moreover, Erasmus's own prescribed strategies for consolation, for subduing grief-related emotions, are— by his own account—often inadequate for dealing with the upheaval caused by the death of a loved one, for example, or by being exiled from one's hometown in a religious revolution. In the next and final chapter, we will further consider Erasmus's feelings about the Reformation from a different angle, specifically by examining Erasmus's condemnations of Martin Luther's emotional temperament.

her that is like a woman, nothing indeed that is not masculine, except her gender and her body" (CWE 66:188).

Chapter 8

"ALWAYS BREATHING TRAGEDY"

LUTHER AND THE VIOLENT EMOTIONS

In a 1529 letter to Alonso de Fonseca, Erasmus recalls his feelings about the early days of what would become the Protestant movement, writing that he was "still uncertain what divine providence wanted to accomplish by means of Luther's ardour [*spiritus*]—for he still seemed to be a good man who, angered [*iratus*] by the vices of the world and inspired by religious zeal, acted with a passion [*zelo*] that was certainly excessive, but still controllable."[1] But then everything changed. Soon, Erasmus was parrying Luther's venomous darts (*toxica iacula*) and the converted Protestants in Basel were pursuing him with the most savage or cruel hatred (*atrocissimus odio*).[2] Any hopes Erasmus had about Luther's temperament being chastened were dashed; worse, his infectiously "angry" disposition was adopted by evangelicals across Europe, exacerbating the problem. Erasmus and Luther have long been set against each other as two early sixteenth-century psychological types: one moderate or, pejoratively, noncommittal and weak; the other determined or, worse, angry and hate-filled. One aim of this chapter is to consider the then-contemporary, primarily Erasmian, assessment of the ways in which emotion played a role in framing the early years of the Reformation. For historicizing the discourses of feeling in and around the disputes between Erasmus and Luther allows us to see, from another angle, how Erasmus felt about the rise of Protestantism.

Relatedly, recent research in the history of emotions has called on scholars to leave behind the "terminological ethnocentrism" of modern usage (primarily Anglophone) when describing the emotions of the past or those of other cultures

---

1. CWE 15:171; Allen, Ep 2134: Proinde quum reputarem Ecclesiam magna ex parte ad pharisaismum esse collapsam, quem ipsum tamen huic rerum confusioni anteposuerim; quum dubitarem quid divina prouidentia per Lutheri spiritum vellet agere—adhuc enim videbatur vir bonus qui viciis iratus pietatis zelo grassaretur, impotentius quidem sed ut cohiberi possit; adhaec cum meam imbecillitatem conferrem cum tot milibus theologorum, quos multorum annorum usus in hac palestra reddiderat absolutos, inter quos sunt aliquot Ecclesiastica dignitate praeminentes.

2. Ibid.

in the present. Regarding anger in particular, Thomas Dixon writes, "there is no agreement about which aspects of reality the term 'anger' properly refers to."[3] He argues further that there is a "crisis of definition" when it comes to emotion terms like "anger" and, on that basis, "we need to articulate what we think we are doing when we use those terms; to take greater care in explaining when we are, or are not, engaging in anachronism; and to articulate what, if anything, in human experience we think is shared across different emotional cultures."[4] As for Erasmus's feelings about Luther, and the feelings he ascribes to Luther, we might suggest similarly that a closer examination of the specific emotional language of his writings will shed light on the historically contingent and culturally specific nuances of the emotions and affective dispositions Erasmus was describing (and criticizing).

Another aim of this chapter, then, is to take Dixon's challenge seriously in order to look more closely at how Martin Luther's so-called anger is described in the works of Erasmus, who was frequently on the receiving end of whatever vehement emotions constituted Luther's temperament, and who—even before their debate over free will rendered their relationship truly irreconcilable—had diagnosed Luther and the wider Protestant movement as too beholden to violent emotions such as "anger" and "hatred." In doing so, the hope is to accomplish a few things: first, to continue untangling some of the mess attendant to writing a historical semantics of emotion, with sixteenth-century humanist discourse as the focal point; second, to illuminate Erasmus's ideal temperament by showing what he thought Christian affectivity should *not* look like; and, finally (especially in the epilogue after this chapter), to highlight Erasmus's use of the language and categories of tragedy which he employed to describe the Protestant movement because he thought it was a threat to the fledgling revival of the humanities. We will finish not far, then, from where we began: by describing a final Erasmian use of the distinction between the calm and violent emotions.

Lutheran Angers

Erasmus writes about Luther's temperament primarily in three types of sources: in his letters, in the treatises constituting Erasmus's half of the debate with Luther over free will, and in his 1534 response to a late attack by Luther called the *Purgatio*.[5]

---

3. Thomas Dixon, "What is the History of Anger a History of?" *Emotions: History, Culture, Society* 4 (2020): 2.

4. Ibid. For useful studies on anger in the sixteenth century, see, e.g., Karl Enenkel and Anita Traninger (eds.), *Discourses of Anger in the Early Modern Period* (Leiden: Brill, 2015); and Luisanna Sardu, "How Gaspara Stampa Challenged Classical Tradition and Conventional Notions of Women's Anger," *Emotions: History, Culture, Society* 3 (2019): 24–46.

5. The Erasmus–Luther dispute has much too large a bibliography to be reproduced here (and it is treated in virtually every history of the Protestant Reformation), but see,

The true enmity began with the famed debates over free will, which started when Erasmus finally capitulated to pressure to publish something against Luther: the *De libero arbitrio* of 1524, also known as the Διατριβή. Erasmus was generally allergic to theological disputation, especially given the vitriol that he knew often resulted from such engagements, and so he entered the fray reluctantly. Debating the specific topic of free will, he writes, had been "recently revived by Karlstadt and Eck (though their dispute was relatively moderate); more recently still it was violently stirred up by Martin Luther, who has written an *Assertion* on free will."[6] In proposing to contribute to the debate, Erasmus hopes that "[t]he debate will be carried on without abuse, both because this is more seemly for Christians, and because it is a surer way of discovering the truth, which is often lost in too much angry repartee."[7] He would be disappointed. Luther responded to Erasmus's *De libero arbitrio* with his own work, the *De servo arbitrio* in 1525, a relentless attack on Erasmus's person and his *ethos*. Erasmus's next two treatises in reply (the *Hyperaspistes* and *Hyperaspistes 2*) were thus preoccupied almost as much with Luther's vitriol and temper as they were with the substantive issues of faculty psychology and theological determinism.

Erasmus begins the *Hyperaspistes* with the rhetorical strategy of suggesting that some of the negative emotional tenor of Luther's treatise arose in fact not from Luther's own heart, but because he had been swayed by others toward vehemence—a tactic that might take some of the bite out of of Erasmus's criticisms. Erasmus even insinuates that the work was partly ghost-written. "Let's get down to business," he says, "without any proem or passion [Gk: παθῶν], as in Attic law." If Luther had done the same, Erasmus says, he would have saved everyone a lot of time. But "since you chose to follow the emotions [*affectibus*] of certain persons rather than your own judgment [*iudicio*], how much there is in your book that is completely off target, how much that is superfluous . . . how many tragical conclusions drawn from false distortions, and how much undeserved vociferation inspired by the conclusions!"[8] Luther, Erasmus continues, had "followed the

---

for example, Margaret Mann Phillips, *Erasmus and the Northern Renaissance* (London: Hodder and Stroughton, 1961), 150ff.; Marjorie O'Rourke Boyle, *Rhetoric and Reform: Erasmus's Civil Dispute with Luther* (Cambridge, MA: Harvard University Press, 1983); Brian Cummings, *Grammar and Grace: The Literary Culture of the Reformation* (Oxford: Oxford University Press, 2002); Erika Rummel, "Humanism and the Reformation: Was the Conflict Between Erasmus and Luther Paradigmatic?" in *Northern Humanism in European Context: From the "Adwert Academy" to Ubbo Emmius, 1469-1625*, ed. F. Akkerman et al. (Leiden: Brill, 1999), 187-97; and Arnoud Visser, "Irreverent Reading: Martin Luther as Annotator of Erasmus," *Sixteenth Century Journal* 48, no. 1 (2017): 87-109.

6. CWE 76:6. Luther had, a few years earlier, published a response to the condemnation of Leo X, the *Assertio omnium articulorum Martini Lutheri per bullam Leonis X novissimam damnatorum* (Wittenberg, 1520); WA 7 142-9.

7. CWE 76:7.

8. *Hyperaspistes 1*; CWE 76: 98, modified.

wishes of the 'brothers', among whom I know there are very many whose behavior is far removed from the evangelical message from which they boast they have taken their title. You have been too subservient to their desires [*cupiditatibus*], Luther, not without serious harm to the cause you are supporting."[9] Erasmus thus insinuates that Luther is doing someone else's bidding, in one sense, but also that meaningful reform of the Church is being sacrificed on the altar of vehement emotion and acerbic attacks.

Nevertheless, Erasmus continues by suggesting that the work was in fact *too mild* to be wholly Luther's: "I know the force of your style, which is like a torrent rushing down a mountain with a great roar and sweeping rocks and tree trunks with it. The language of this wordsmith flows more gently but carries more poison with it. I am not unaware of who he is."[10] The implication is, perhaps, that Phillip Melanchthon's more refined style has supplemented Luther's more direct one, although not in a way that truly ameliorates the offense. But Erasmus eventually gets around to laying the blame more firmly with Luther. Citing the many instances where Luther praises Erasmus in previous works, he writes, "But just as I was not taken in by those high-sounding praises, so too now I am not even the least bit disturbed by this vituperation [*vituperatione*] of yours. I knew that those praises were not truly meant, just as I knew this vituperation was dictated by hatred and anger [*odium et ira*]."[11] Erasmus deploys a copious range of terms to describe Luther's abusive rhetoric. Elsewhere throughout the *Hyperaspistes* Erasmus refers to Luther's "impetuous temperament" (*impetus animi*),[12] his "immoderate passion" (*immodica*), the "seditious wantonness of his pen,"[13] a "malicious eagerness to slander,"[14] and compares his "clamorous" spirit with the evangelical spirit of the Apostle Paul.[15] Moreover, in a theme that will also recur in his letters, he blames Luther's disposition for widespread and violent Protestant strife. Luther's vitriol

> not only hinders the cause you are working for—for you are engaged, as you affirm, in the business of recalling the gospel, which up till now has been buried all over the world—but this seditious wantonness of your pen also brings destruction down on all good things. The people are stirred up against the bishops and princes; magistrates are hard pressed to put down mobs eager to revolt; cities which once were joined by very close ties now quarrel among themselves with fierce hatred [*atrocibus odiis*], etc.[16]

---

9. *Hyperaspistes 1*; CWE 76: 99, modified.
10. *Hyperaspistes 1*; CWE 76: 103.
11. *Hyperaspistes 1*; CWE 76: 110; LB X 1255B.
12. *Hyperaspistes 1*; CWE 76: 139.
13. *Hyperaspistes 1*; CWE 76: 295; LB X 1333D.
14. *Hyperaspistes 1*; CWE 76: 283.
15. *Hyperaspistes 1*; CWE 76: 109.
16. CWE 76: 295.

The divisiveness and violent conflict of the early evangelical movement emerge from Luther's style. Luther's charisma, Erasmus continues, simultaneously attracts and corrupts his readers:

> At first these things [i.e., Luther's writings] have a certain titillation and we itch to read them, but when they gradually creep into the mind, they infect the sincerity and gentleness of the heart [*inficiunt sinceritatem et mansuetudinem pectoris*]. And although you see how many evils this ferocity [*ferocia*] of yours has brought into the world . . . still you continually get worse and worse, both uselessly drawing into danger those who commit themselves to your faith and alienating those whom you could have attracted to you . . . and finally preventing this worldwide uproar, however it arose, from ever bringing forth for us some degree of beneficent tranquillity.[17]

In other words, it is not an upright desire for reforming the Church that drives on the evangelicals, but Luther's forceful temperament and emotional writings, which are themselves ultimately reflected in physical violence. Luther's vehement style is attractive but deleterious, and *ferocia* in pamphlets gives rise to *ferocia* in the streets. This is all, again, written in a work whose ostensible purpose is to debate the issue of free will.

The contagiousness of Luther's excess is especially worrying to Erasmus, and letters from this period contain similar diagnoses. Erasmus had in fact warned about Luther's style at least as early as 1520. Then he wrote to George Spalatin, praying that "Christ almighty might moderate Luther's pen and his mind [*stilum et animum ita temperet*]." He continues, "How I wish Luther would take a rest for some time from these controversies, and treat simply the facts of the Gospel, with no personal feelings mixed in [*non admixtus affectibus*]!"[18] Writing later, in 1526 to Duke John of Saxony, Erasmus says, "[Luther] claims the inspiration of the spirit, but who can believe that the spirit of Christ dwells in a heart from which flow words of such arrogance, bitterness, savagery, malice, and abuse?"[19] In another letter from the same year, Erasmus equates Luther and his movement with God's wrath itself: Luther is—possibly—a violent scourge, but a temporary one, to cure the ills that cannot be healed with more moderate medicines.[20] This is an echo of something he wrote in the *Hyperaspistes* as well: "Finally, I sometimes thought to myself: what if it has pleased God to provide for the utterly corrupt morals of these times such a savage physician, who is to cure by cutting and cauterizing the wound he could not heal by potions and poultices?"[21] Perhaps there is a divine method to Luther's madness, although reluctantly Erasmus chooses to fight

---

17. CWE 76: 296; LB X 1334A.
18. Ep 1119; CWE 7:324.
19. Ep 1670; CWE 12:51.
20. See Ep 1672 to Johann Henckel.
21. *Hyperaspistes 1*; CWE 76:103.

against any potential scourge. To Reginald Pole, Erasmus writes, "I have always been a lover of peace and quiet, but now I am being forced to enter the arena, not just as a gladiator, but as a fighter against wild beasts."²² He accuses Luther, in another letter, of turning his "furious temper" against anyone he pleases (the Latin is *debacchatur*—to rage or rave wildly like Bacchus, a word he uses multiple times in the *Hyperaspistes*).²³ And to Mercurino Gattinara he complains of the *fremitus Luteranorum*—the growling or roaring or raging of the Lutherans.²⁴ These are, of course, superlative descriptions of Luther's personality, but Erasmus's repeated insistence that the emotional tenor of Luther's writings was extreme and dangerous makes clear that the ideal affective-discursive mode of Erasmian Christianity is one of mildness and concord, one that begets tranquility rather than violence.

Erasmus writes to Luther himself in 1526, responding to a now-lost letter. Luther seems, in that letter, to have conceded the point that he was emotionally immoderate: "You are a man," Erasmus recapitulates, "*as you wrote*, possessed of a violent temperament [*vehementi praeditus ingenio*]—and you are delighted to have such a remarkable excuse."²⁵ Erasmus continues, ascribing to Luther (not for the last time) the rhetorical penchant for δείνωσις, a Greek rhetorical term denoting vehemence, exaggeration, or forcefulness of speech.²⁶ In contrast with his own "moderate disputation," moreover, Erasmus writes to Luther that "because of your arrogant, insolent, and turbulent personality you cause a fatal dissension that unsettles the whole world, you expose good men and lovers of the humanities to the fury of the Pharisees, and you arm wicked and rebellious men for revolution."²⁷ Erasmus now lays the blame for the Europe-wide upheaval squarely on Luther's temperament. In his work against the "pseudevangelicals," Erasmus waxes literary and compares Luther to Até, the goddess of ruin, and Melanchthon to Litae, the personification of prayers offered in repentance who followed Até around, thus accusing Luther again of exacerbating the situation unnecessarily.²⁸ "You see," he writes, "how much Luther stood in the way of a cause that was at first not altogether bad, because of the animosity and violence of his writing. Now Melanchthon follows in his wake—just as prayers of repentance trail after an outburst of rage—diligently trying to set right what he threw into confusion."²⁹ Later, and somewhat less congenially, he writes, "True, Melanchthon

---

22. Ep 1675; CWE 12:76; Erasmus uses the Greek for "fighter against wild beasts": θηριομάχειν (a term used again in Ep 1678, lumping Cousturier in with Luther as a fellow wild beast).
23. Ep 1678; CWE 12:83.
24. Ep 1700.
25. Ep 1688; CWE 12:136, modified.
26. In the *De conscribendis epistolis* Erasmus cites Quintilian as describing *deinosis* as "among the chief excellences of speech," but he clearly disparages Luther's over-use of it.
27. Ep 1688; CWE 12:136.
28. CWE 78: 241; see note.
29. CWE 78: 240–1.

writes less violently [*minus violenter*], but he doesn't depart by a hair's breadth from the teachings of Luther; he is even, if I may say so, more Lutheran that Luther himself [*ipso Luthero lutheranior*]."[30] Luther's *furor* is, to Erasmus's mind, socially destructive, and his more mild-mannered colleagues are guilty by association.

To place this in the broader context of Erasmus's thoughts about a vehemently emotional style, we might point out that his criticisms of Luther are not unlike Erasmus's comments on the affective-rhetorical style of Seneca, whose Stoicism did not prevent him from indulging in heightened rhetoric for emotional effect. In the dedicatory epistle for Erasmus's second edition of Seneca's works (1529), addressed to Piotr Tomicki, Erasmus lays out the numerous criticisms of Seneca from antiquity. Suetonius, for example, writes that Nero preferred a simpler style, and criticized Seneca (his teacher) for being too unemotional (*lene*—gentle, or calm), while Erasmus disagrees: "Since Seneca is forceful in conveying tragic emotions [*affectibus tragicis vehemens*], I wonder why Suetonius thought him unemotional [*lenior*]."[31] And, later in the same letter, he continues:

> Seneca also goes astray in soliciting the emotions. Other writers lay the ground for these during the expository sections of their work and introduce them at the right moment. Learned critics do not approve the practice of playing constantly on the emotions; in fact some even reject the emotions altogether as tending to cloud the judgment. But Seneca at every point, even at the beginning of a work, does not so much stir the emotions as wring them from us, particularly those tragic emotions that the Greeks call πάθη. So when he has to deal with an imposing subject, as, for example, when writing about the universe, the nature of the gods, the Stoic sage, earthquakes, lightning, floods, the end of the world, contempt for death, suicide, it is as though he has been given his head and is now free to demonstrate his command of the grand style and breathe the tragic spirit.[32]

Too much indulgence in the tragic emotions is a rhetorical vice (even if vehemence itself isn't inherently problematic, as is evident when Erasmus describes Paul's writings thus), for it distracts from teaching in the same way that refusing to engage the emotions does. We may extrapolate these comments to cover Erasmus's

---

30. Ep 2911.
31. CWE 15:53; Allen Ep 2091.
32. CWE 15:53, modified; Allen Ep 2019: Neque nihil peccat in petendis affectibus, quos alii docendo praeparant suoque tractant loco. Nam passim agitare affectus adeo non probatum est a doctis, ut quidam affectus in totum submoverint velut officientes iudicio. At hos Seneca ubiuis et in ipso statim initio stimulat verius quam movet, et in his maxime tragicos, quae Graeci *pathē* vocant. Itaque quoties in grandes materias incidit, puta De universo, De natura deorum, De Stoico sapiente, De terrae motu, De fulmine, De diluuio, De fine mundi, De contemptu mortis, De mortibus spontaneis, veluti suum nactus campum, videtur ostentare grandiloquentiam suam, et nescio quid tragicum spirare.

criticism of Luther likewise—meaningful reform is hindered by the solicitation of tragic feeling and by excessive exaggeration for emotional effect.

While Erasmus's descriptions of the dispositions of other Protestant groups are dwarfed by his criticisms of Luther, Erasmus does offer commentary on how they too were emotionally intemperate. These usually have to do with his own experiences in Basel. Erasmus at times actually compares Luther favorably to the Basel reformers, as in a letter from 1529 to Justus Decius: "In my opinion, the things that Luther commends come quite close to the vigour of the gospel, if only they were treated temperately. But bitter sallies against images contribute very little to piety and much to division."[33] Erasmus is referring, of course, to the destruction of icons that occurred across the city only a few months earlier, and he goes on to lament the subsequent ban on the mass by Oecolampadius—events which forced Erasmus to ultimately leave Basel for Freiburg. In another letter written on the following day, Erasmus updates his correspondent with news from the frontlines: "It was only against the statues and pictures of the saints that [the evangelicals] vented their wrath, not stopping before total destruction."[34] Erasmus uses the same verb, *saevio*, multiple times in the letters he writes describing Swiss Protestants destroying images. It has the sense of venting one's rage, or raving furiously. To the preeminent banker Anton Fugger, Erasmus writes, recalling his fear of moving during the upheaval, "When the angry mob was venting their rage on the images [*saeviebat in imagines*], it was no time to move anywhere."[35] And later he remembers fearing that once the evangelicals in Basel had sufficiently "vented their rage" [*satis saevissent in divorum statuas*] against the statues of saints, they might turn to living people.[36]

More often, however, Erasmus maintains Luther's ultimate responsibility for exacerbating Protestant-Catholic tensions. In the *Spongia*, a treatise written against Ulrich von Hutten[37] in 1523 (a couple years before Erasmus and Luther had their formal falling out over free will), Erasmus had written:

> If from the outset Luther had explained his teachings in a candid and gentle [*mansuete*] way, refraining from the kind of language that is patently offensive, we would not have this tumult. Were he my brother three or four times over, and if I accepted all that he teaches, I must still vehemently reject the obstinacy with which he asserts his opinions and the harsh abuse he always has at hand. Nor have I been able to persuade myself that the spirit of Christ—than whom no one is more gentle [*mitius*]—dwells within a heart from which such bitterness

---

33. Ep 2175; CWE 15:286.
34. Ep 2176; CWE 15:290.
35. Ep 2192; CWE 15:346.
36. Ep 2249.
37. "Even Hutten does not deny that Luther lacks *modestiam ac lenitatem*" (ASD IX-1, 190).

[*amarulentia*] gushes forth. Would that I am deceived in what I suspect! yet the spirit of the gospel can also wax wrathful [*stomachum*]. Yes, but this is a wrath that never lacks the honey of charity to sweeten the bitterness of reproach.[38]

Erasmus here delineates two types of wrath: one which is destructive to no end, and one which has a form of correction as its aim (referring to Acts 8:20 where Peter denounces Simon, Erasmus suggests that while the apostles could get angry, the medicine was always sweetened with honey). Glossing the destructive anger, he goes on to compare Luther to "the wild Scyrian she-goat from the Greek proverb, who gives a pail of good milk, then kicks it over."[39] Contrasting further the "pseudevangelicals" with the New Testament apostles, he commends the character of the latter as showing "cheerful readiness in time of affliction, calmness in bearing injury, a heart simple and mild, thinking evil of no one and eager to deserve well of everyone" and so on, but condemns the fact that followers of the new gospel engage different passions, for example using the "crime of idolatry as a fright-producing pretext" (referring to iconoclasm), even though no one is actually so stupid as to believe that "there is sensation in pieces of stone and wood."[40] Of the same group Erasmus writes that they "yearn for a bloody conflict," and specifically in reference to Gerard Geldenhouwer, that he had written anti-Erasmian pamphlets "as if I [Erasmus] had run through with the sword his father, his mother, his grandfather, and both his grandmothers."[41] Even when they were not destroying icons, however, Erasmus found the converts to the new movement to bear the wrong sort of affective disposition: "I have never entered their churches, but I once saw a group of them returning from a sermon inspired, as it were, by an evil spirit. All their faces showed anger and astonishing ferocity [*vultibus omnium iracundiam ac ferociam miram*] . . . [but] who ever saw at their sermons anyone who wept, beat his breast, or groaned because of his sins?"[42] These all might be classed as vehement emotions, but *iracundia* and *ferocia* are not the pious feelings that a preacher ought to be eliciting.

θυμὸς ἀγήνορ: *The* Purgatio *of 1534*

Erasmus's accusations of Luther's anger and hatred toward him were corroborated by Luther himself. In a 1533 entry from the *Table-talk*, Luther is reported to have said to the theology students boarding with Luther and his wife, "By divine authority, I enjoin hatred of Erasmus upon all of you. . . . I have decided to slay

---

38. CWE 78:112.
39. CWE 78:112; Cf. *Adag.* I X 20.
40. CWE 78:230.
41. Ep 2358 to Melanchthon; CWE 17:4.
42. *Contra pseudevangelicos*; CWE 78:232.

him with my pen."⁴³ He then proceeded to do just that in a letter to Nikolaus von Amsdorf in 1534. Erasmus's shocked reply, the *Purgatio*, was published in the same year. The full title refers to Luther's letter as *non sobriam*, literally "drunken," or, by extension, intemperate or immoderate. The first line of the *Purgatio* runs thus: "Lo and behold, Martin Luther's θυμὸς ἀγήνορ is inflamed against me again. He has sent out a letter, completely unexpected, every line of which breathes a murderous hatred."⁴⁴ θυμὸς ἀγήνορ, translated in CWE as "proud spirit," is an epithet ascribed to a lion attacking cattle in Homer's *Iliad* as a comparison for Sarpedon, one of Zeus's sons and a Trojan warrior, as he fought against the Achaeans. It would perhaps be better rendered as something approximating "arrogant fury" in this context, and that would accord with the rest of the *Purgatio*, a work wherein Erasmus also compares Luther to the tragically violent figures of Orestes and Ajax. Erasmus has connected, if not identified, ancient Greek with sixteenth-century humanist understandings of a furious disposition, a strategy we explored in the second chapter, following Jessica Wolfe's heuristic of mythographic shorthand. It is worth emphasizing that the use of Greek descriptors for emotion terms in late medieval and early modern Latinate Europe represents a shift in the historical semantics of emotion, if a niche one, for it only becomes viable after the rise of the humanistic study of Greek texts toward the end of the fifteenth century.

Thomas Dixon's exegesis of anger terms from Homer's *Iliad* is useful for thinking about Erasmus's conceptualization of Luther's wrath as well, for he raises the question of whether we responsibly equate modern anger with that of Greek antiquity when, for example, we translate Homer's language of feeling into our own. Dixon writes, "Among the ancient Greek terms used in Homer's epic to describe the sorrowful fighting fury of Achilles, the terms μῆνις, θυμός and ὕπερθυμος referred to an energetic force, spirited ferocity, or hyper-fury. The blood-thirsty Achilles who slaughters the Trojans," he continues, "is driven by an unbearable, frenzied, grief which is not well captured by the relatively tame modern psychological term 'anger.'"⁴⁵ If Dixon is right to suggest a disconnect between these Homeric emotion terms and late modern "anger," what about early modern anger-like emotions? Is Erasmus's use of *ira* or *ferocia* to describe Luther closer to Homer's μῆνις or θυμός,

---

43. Qtd. in CWE 78:396, modified; Cf. WA Tr 1 446 for the longer passage: Qui Satanam non odit, amet tua carmina / Erasme, Atque idem iungat Furias et mulgeat orcum . . . Qui loquitur sophistice, dicunt, odibilis est, et Quintilianus monet vitandum, qui loquitur ambigue. Iam Erasmus studio et malitiose loquitur amphibola . . . Quare ego vobis mando autoritate divina odium Erasmi (hoc ad me dicebat)... Ego igitur contra eum scribam, etiamsi occidatur. "Let the one who does not hate Satan sing your song, Erasmus / Let him join the Furies and milk the orc . . . The one who speaks sophistically, they say, should be hated, and Quintilian suggests we shun the one who speaks ambiguously. Erasmus zealously and maliciously speaks with ambiguity . . . Thus with God's authority I order you to hate Erasmus. I will write against him, even if it kills him" (my translation).

44. CWE 78:412.

45. Dixon, "What is the History of Anger a History of?" 15.

or closer to our "anger"? I would suggest that even though Erasmus indulges in literary hyperbole and exaggeration, his invocation of rage-filled emotions to describe Luther are nearer to the Homeric original in their explicit associations with revenge and violence than to the tamer versions of anger offered by Dixon as more common to the late modern subject. At the same time, it would seem that Karl Enenkel and Anita Traninger go a bit too far in assessing early modern anger as "but a homonym" of its late modern counterpart.[46]

This becomes clearer in an analysis of Erasmus's consideration of Luther's emotions throughout the rest of the *Purgatio* and letters contemporaneous with it. Not long after Luther's letter to von Amsdorf appeared, but before Erasmus had written his response, Erasmus wrote to George Agricola: "I received Luther's absolutely furious [*simpliciter furiosa*] *Epistola* a while ago . . . What are people thinking when they commit their souls and their fortunes to a man subject to such emotions [*obnoxio affectibus*]?"[47] Likewise to Erasmus Schets: "Like a trumpeter of war, Luther has sent out a letter more furious than all the Furies [*furiis furiosiorem*], breathing a more than parricidal hatred [*parricidiale odium spirantes*], stuffed with slanders and lies."[48] To Erasmus's mind, Luther had gone well past the ordinary bounds of anger in his latest attack, and is firmly *furiosus*, raging with hatred. In the *Purgatio* itself, Erasmus offers a similar assessment: "the man is driven off course by uncontrolled hatred, the wish to domineer, and the promptings of those who incite him."[49] Hatred and fury rather than mere anger feature heavily in Erasmus's late descriptions of Luther's emotional disposition.

Erasmus also often uses the somewhat more idiosyncratic term *stomachus* to describe anger-like emotions. In the *Purgatio*, he writes, "Had I the opportunity to write to this man [i.e., Georg Witzel, who had written against Luther and ostensibly incited him against Erasmus, the latter whose ideas Witzel conveyed], I would have warned him not to attack Luther, or certainly not to indulge his anger [*indulgeret stomacho suo*],[50] which his letters demonstrated was easily sparked off [*satis exulceratem*]."[51] *Stomachus* is a difficult term, as we saw in Erasmus's exegesis of the Psalms, but it is often used by Erasmus in the sense of temper, or angry disposition, and frequently in his descriptions of Luther. In a 1526 letter to Pirckheimer, he writes that Luther claimed to have held or reigned in his temper in composing the *De servo arbitrio* (an idea Erasmus scoffs at), and the phrase

---

46. Enenkel and Traninger (eds.), *Discourses of Anger in the Early Modern Period*, introduction.

47. Ep 2918; CWE 20:265.

48. Ep 2924; CWE 20:274.

49. *Purgatio*, CWE 78:416; ASD IX-1, 446: impotens odium, regnandi libido et instigantium faces huc hominem transversum perpellunt.

50. Cf. Ep 2918. This phrase appears more than once in the *Purgatio*, and three times in Erasmus's letters, per the Brepols Library of Latin Texts. According to that database, there do not seem to be any instances of the phrase *indulgere stomachum* before Erasmus.

51. CWE 78:413.

Erasmus uses is *coercuisse stomachum*.⁵² It seems as though Erasmus uses the term to mean something more vehement than classical usage suggests, for the contexts in which he deploys it are more emotionally fraught than, for example, the Lewis and Short lexicon's gloss: "*distaste, dislike. . . displeasure, irritation, vexation, chagrin.*" One's chagrin is not usually described as "easily sparked off," as Erasmus describes Luther's *stomachus*, or as "boiling over" (*effervescenti*), as Erasmus writes of the same emotion when describing Agostino Steuco.⁵³ The deponent verb form *stomachor* (also used by Cicero and Terence, for example) is glossed by a sixteenth-century dictionary as *indignari ac turbari*, to despise or to throw into disorder, and this is closer to Erasmus's usage of the noun *stomachus*.⁵⁴ (And Erasmus was not entirely free from of this anger-like feeling himself: he recalls having "vented his anger at the Zwinglians" [*stomachatus sum in Zwinglianos*] to Melanchthon in 1530.⁵⁵)

Humanist allies of Erasmus unsurprisingly judged the dispute between Erasmus and Luther from a similar perspective, as Erika Rummel has documented. Rummel quotes Ulrich Zasius, the Freiburg jurist and eventual friend of Erasmus, as remarking on a "great difference of spirit: Erasmus is discreet as far as possible; Luther immodest, indeed full of impudent bragging; the latter creates enmities, strife, envy, anger, conflict, divisions, unpopularity, war; the former peace, gentleness, benignity, goodness, faith, meekness."⁵⁶ Zasius plays on the language of temperance in praising Erasmus's ability to use the rhetorical strategy of accommodation (Latin *temperamentum*) in arguing for free will, while also

---

52. Ep 1717.

53. See Ep 2465 to Steuco.

54. Erasmus uses the term (and, indeed, the phrase *indulgeret stomacho meo*) in a different sense in a letter to Sadoleto in 1531 (Ep 2443), where he writes that in expositing one of the Psalms, he "indulges his *stomachus* less (*parcius*)" because such a task calls for an attitude of pious reverence. It isn't clear to me exactly what he means here. The CWE translation reads: "I yield to emotion more sparingly," which seems straightforward enough and yet is still quite vague. In a Stephanus edition of Calepino's *Dictionarium*, after all the definitions related to the bodily organs of digestion, we find that "stomachus" may be used in place of *indignatione* and *iracundia*, with references to Cicero; and it can also be used *pro animo*, in place of the soul, for just as the stomach is easily moved by food whose nature it is averse to, thus the soul shrinks from those things whose nature runs contrary to its own ("quia quemadmodum stomachus facile eo cibo movetur, a quo natura abhorret: sic animus eas res maxime aversatur et abhorret, quas suae naturae contrarias esse sentit") (*Ambrosii Calepini Dictionarium, quarto et postremo ex R. Stephani Latinae linguae thesauro auctum*; Geneva, Robert Estienne: 1553, ad loc.). Erasmus does use the verb form in regards to Luther as well: "you were already angry (*stomachabaris*) with me for disagreeing with you over free will" (*Hyperaspistes 1*; LB 1266D).

55. Allen Ep 2365.

56. See Erika Rummel, *The Confessionalization of Humanism in Reformation Germany* (Oxford: Oxford University Press, 2000), 60–1.

handling the whole issue in a moderate (*temperasse*) manner.⁵⁷ Similar comments are made by Paul Volz, Boniface Amerbach, and Johann von Botzheim, as pointed out by Rummel. Thomas More also writes of Erasmus's *Hyperaspistes* that "in that volume you drew such a vivid picture of the beast and pointed your finger so precisely at the harsh spirit that drives him on that you unveiled for everyone to see a portrait of a fuming fiend from hell [*fumidum ac tartareum daemonem*], a sort of Cerberus dragged up from the underworld."⁵⁸ Leonard Cassembroot refers to Luther's "unbridled spirit" (*impotentissime spiritu*).⁵⁹ Johann Koler describes Luther as a "man given over to the Furies" in a letter about how Erasmus's *Purgatio* was too soft on Luther.⁶⁰ Hermann von Neuenahr, chancellor of the University of Cologne, writes to Erasmus that "Lutherans are so much the slaves of their passions that they make the situation utterly hopeless."⁶¹ In this correspondence we thus find further evidence of something like a humanist (or, perhaps, Catholic humanist) emotional community, whose emotional norms are shared, and whose affective identity is formed against another group, in this case intemperate Protestants like Luther.⁶²

Of course, if Erasmus and his Catholic-humanist cohort castigated Luther for his violent temperament, Luther's own followers venerated him.⁶³ Relatedly, Phillip Melanchthon, who tried occasionally to serve as mediator between Luther and Erasmus, uses similar language to describe the affective dispositions of other of Luther's enemies. In a 1530 letter to Erasmus, for example, he writes, "I would

---

57. Ibid.

58. Ep 1770; CWE 12:416. See also Ep 1697 to Wolsey on the violence of the emotions (*impotentes affectus*) of those who are trying to censure Erasmus and destroy the humanities, with reference to the problem of allowing the humanities to be usurped by the reformers.

59. Allen Ep 1720.

60. Ep 2937.

61. Ep 2137.

62. It should be noted that it is not only the Protestants, though, whom Erasmus finds immoderate in their emotions. In the same year (1526), Erasmus complains about Jacob Latomus's implacable hatred for him, and notes that if the princes are unable to reign in the unbridled emotions [*immoderatis affectibus*] of Erasmus's Catholic critics, and especially their hatred of the humanities, then they are playing into Luther's hands (Ep 1700; CWE 12:178–9). He repeats a trope, numerous times, that while he's engaged in battle with Luther (even in the enemy camp) he's being stabbed in the back by those he's trying to defend. Certainly an analysis of Erasmus's discourse of feeling in his many treatises against his Catholic critics would pay further dividends.

63. Some Protestants, though, lamented Luther's ferocity even as they largely agreed with his teachings. Conrad Pellican, the biblical humanist from Zurich, for example, wrote to Erasmus in 1525 that he also regretted Luther's "passionate nature and unbridled ferocity," and conceded that more people would have joined the Protestant cause had Luther had a "kindlier pen," and had he "expressed the same sentiments more temperately in a different style" (see Ep 1639; CWE 11:361–2).

never have believed that such ferocity [*ferociam*], such violence [*saevitiam*] could possess a man as I discern in Eck and some of his followers. The rulers themselves express fairly lenient and moderate [*clementes et moderatas*] opinions, but this band tries with incredible wiles to deflect them from their views."[64] Melanchthon goes on to ask Erasmus to continue appealing to rulers for peace. In his response, Erasmus writes that war seems inevitable, given that the "preludes of drama" (in Greek: τὰ τοῦ δρὰματος προίμια) have appeared, and implies that Luther could have avoided this result if he were not a "slave to his *ingenium*" (*Ille suo servit ingenio*), that is, his temper.[65] Whether the tendencies outlined here reflect two broadly construed emotional communities or, more simply, a series of rhetorical tropes used by multiple sides of the same dispute, is a compelling question that would require significantly more research. What we can say is that for Erasmus Luther was ruining his movement by his violent emotions, or at least inhibiting the possibility of reforming the church from within. From one perspective he was right: the church was never reunited; but from another perspective, Luther's approach proved to be successful, if dramatically so.

To move toward a conclusion it is worth noting that even if one does not share the full skepticism of Dixon regarding the possibility of rendering earlier emotion terms meaningful in modern parlance, it is clear that there is quite a lot to be gained from more nuanced considerations of discourses of feeling from the past—and, moreover, that something is lost in generalizing about affective attitudes and complex emotions with familiar and contemporary language and categories. On the other hand, perhaps "anger" is a useful term of designation for a cluster of related feelings (rather than merely as a descriptor of a single emotion), as Lisa Feldman Barrett has suggested, paraphrased by Dixon: it is a "'diverse population of experiences and behaviors' including bitterness, hostility, and rage, as well as wrath, grumpiness and scorn."[66] If the scope of "anger" is understood to include this wide range of emotions and dispositions, then it comes close to encapsulating the feelings of Erasmus's Luther.

Recent scholarship on Luther has also reckoned with his temperament. I still remember, twenty years later, my undergraduate religious studies professor, Mike Thompson, joking that he could count on one hand the number of people Luther *didn't* hate. While we do not have the space here to examine the manner in which Luther scholarship has engaged with the history of emotions, some recent work on Luther's emotional disposition supports Erasmus's earlier assessment. Susan Karant-Nunn writes of how Luther uses Latin anger terms to describe himself, even if they are milder (unsurprisingly) than those Erasmus ascribes to him. He writes in the *Table-talk*, for example, "I have no better medicine than anger [*iram*]. When I want to compose, write, pray, and preach well, I have to be angry [*oportet me esse iratum*], for [anger] refreshes my whole blood system, my understanding

---

64. Ep 2357; CWE 17:2.
65. Ep 2365.
66. Dixon, "What is the History of Anger a History of?" 8.

is sharpened, and all listless thoughts and temptations give way."[67] This tells us something about the emotional style that Luther envisaged himself to be working from, and it makes clear how it differs from that of his interlocutor. Moreover, as if paraphrasing Erasmus (although with no reference to him), Karant-Nunn writes that "the time has come to declare that Luther's own temperament, including his inclination toward outbursts of anger, did affect the Reformation" and that "Luther's anger at the outset could only have hindered the attainment of his goal."[68] Karant-Nunn then considers the early years of Luther's reform movement, noting that "the salient passages in his three signal treatises [of the year 1520] are well known and yet have been customarily treated for their ideation rather than their mood."[69] After tracing the vehement rhetoric in those formative works, she concludes, "It must be noted, too, that these treatises are not alone in their invective. A torrent of ad hominem and issue-directed prose flowed from Luther's pen almost simultaneously. The Wittenberg professor now abandoned all inhibitions in writing to his adversaries."[70] Erasmus, no doubt, would agree. As Karant-Nunn suggests, Luther's anger, while occasionally out-of-hand and inappropriate, was also a crucial feature of his charisma, especially insofar as it reflected a message of God's wrath.

Incidentally, another recent portrayal of an emotional Luther, namely, Lyndal Roper's description of Luther as a "grand hater," is closer to Erasmus's assessment in other ways.[71] Rather than characterizing Luther as angry, Roper, more like Erasmus, reflects on his "incendiary hostility" and the "full arsenal of hatred" that he unleashed on the papacy and against Jews and Judaism. Erasmus would perhaps diverge from Roper's portrait only by adding himself in as a key object of Luther's scorn. But despite compelling similarities with Erasmus in these two recent assessments of of Luther's emotions, it is important to acknowledge that

---

67. Trans. qtd. in Susan Karant-Nunn, "The Wrath of Martin Luther: Anger and Charisma in the Reformer," *The Sixteenth Century Journal* 48, no. 4 (2017): 918; "Ego nullum melius remedium habeo quam iram. Si bene scribere, orare, praedicare volo, tunc oportet me esse iratum; da erfrischt sich mein gantz geblut, et acuitur ingenium, et tentationes omnes cedunt" (WA Tr 2410b, 2:455–6). WA Tr 2410a, another account of the same episode, reads: "Nunquam mihi melius procedit orare, praedicare, scribere, quam cum irascor. Ira enim erfrischet mir mein gantz geblut, acuit ingenium, propellit tentationes" (WA Tr 2:455). For a broader treatment of Luther on the emotions, including his flexibility of terms for general affectivity (similar to that of Erasmus), see Simeon Zahl, "The Bondage of the Affections: Willing, Feeling, and Desiring in Luther's Theology, 1513–1525," in *The Spirit, the Affections, and the Christian Tradition*, ed. Dale Coulter and Amos Yong (South Bend, IL: University of Notre Dame Press, 2016), 181–205.

68. Karant-Nunn, "The Wrath of Martin Luther," 908–26.

69. Ibid., 914.

70. Ibid., 912.

71. For "grand hater," see Lyndal Roper, *Martin Luther: Renegade and Prophet* (Penguin, 2016), 383.

there still exist important differences when we consider Erasmus's denunciations of anger-like emotions in their renaissance literary context. That is, if we understand Erasmus's repeated associations of violent discourse with the literary genre of tragedy (explored further in the epilogue below) as *merely* a literary or rhetorical device, which itself is genealogically related to Aristotle's conception of anger as involving a desire for (usually violent) revenge, then meaningful literary-historical and semantic differences between his time and ours are too easily flattened out or erased. This is where Dixon's call to closely reassess past angers, and especially the languages and literary contexts of anger, pays off. Erasmus's repeated assertions that Luther's movement is a tragedy, and that Luther's violent emotions are a key character in the play, are rather different from glosses of Luther's emotional disposition using late modern psychological categories. While tragedy does not necessarily feature in modern understandings of anger,[72] it is impossible to understand Erasmus's Luther's anger—and, indeed, Erasmus's understanding of the Protestant Reformation—without it.

---

72. But cf. Martha Nussbaum, who argues for meaningful similarities (if not identity) between Aristotle's *orgē* and modern anger in *Anger and Forgiveness: Resentment, Generosity, and Justice* (New York: Oxford University Press, 2016).

Epilogue

"Philistines Foaming at the Mouth"

In 1525, Erasmus wrote to Germain de Brie:

> Here a cruel tragedy is being acted out; what the *dénoument* will be, I do not know. It seems to me that the world is sinking into a state of Scythian barbarity, with the total ruin of all liberal studies. For me the game is already over.... The old champions of the Muses are dying off everywhere: Longueil, who wrote a wonderfully polished oration against Luther, which I have here, has passed away at Bologna; Battista Casali died recently at Rome, Linacre in England and Deloynes near you; Dorp has passed away at Louvain: he had the courage to declare his support for liberal studies at a time when all the philistines were foaming at the mouth.[1]

While we explored in the previous chapter the ways in which Erasmus does not hesitate to criticize Luther for his vitriolic writings and abuse, he is also preoccupied with a larger-scale problem related to Luther's movement, but one not reducible to it. Erasmus saw how quickly he became associated with the evangelicals from the perspective of his more conservative Catholic critics, and he argued that this group would use Luther's heresies as a pretext for condemning the study of the humanities. If he could cope with Luther's personal slanders, he saw in the potential downfall of the liberal arts an assault on everything he had worked for. In the passage above, the tragedy Erasmus refers to is in fact the German Peasants' War, but he immediately ties it to the decline of the humanities—different symptoms of the same disease, or different acts in the same tragic play. That he described this problem repeatedly using the language of tragedy is not news. Margaret Mann Phillips, for example, in her 1949 book, *Erasmus and the Northern Renaissance*, entitled the penultimate chapter "The Lutheran Tragedy," and in it she draws a psychological contrast between the vitriolic Luther and the moderate Erasmus. By further examining the figurative language Erasmus uses to describe the fallout of the Luther movement, specifically the ways in which Erasmus invokes the affective category of the tragic emotions as well as tropes around the literary genre of tragedy itself, a clearer picture emerges of how Erasmus imagined Luther and

---

1. Ep 1598; CWE 11:241.

the potentially unintended consequences of his movement to be interlinked from an emotional perspective.

The arts (*studia humanitatis, bonae litterae, artes*) have affective import for Erasmus on multiple levels. As we have explored in various ways in this book, affectivity itself is organized in categories derived from the *ars rhetorica*, and according to the classical literary genres of tragedy and comedy. Erasmus considers *affectus* explicable via literary categories. Erasmus also used this heuristic framework to assess the emotionally charged atmosphere surrounding what he perceived to be a widespread attack on the arts during the early years of Protestant movement. His correspondence from the 1520s in particular evinces this rhetorical position. Erasmus's categorization of the emotions as derived from tragedy and comedy—or ultimately from Homer's "tragic" and "comic" epics respectively—was in the end not only useful for describing variations on human feeling, but was invoked to explain the consequences of religious upheaval. While the events in question, and the debates between Erasmus and his critics, have been well documented over decades of scholarship, we can add a new layer of analysis by paying close attention to the emotional aspects of Erasmus's characterizations. In this case, the "tragic" becomes multivalent, as it gives weight to Erasmus's conceptualization of the emotions themselves, of affective appeals in rhetorical discourse, and of Reformation-era attacks on the humanities.

Erasmus's relationship to the humanities had always been affectively laden. In a dedicatory letter to the *Antibarbari*, an apologia for the *bonae litterae* begun in the 1490s but not published until 1520, Erasmus recalls a formative moment from his youth, when "a sort of inspiration fired me with devotion to the Muses, sprung not from judgment (for I was then too young to judge) but from a kind of natural feeling." He continues, "I developed a hatred for anyone I knew to be an enemy of humane studies and a love for those who delighted in them."[2] This represents what would become Erasmus's lifelong disposition toward the humanities, but his defenses of the liberal arts would need to be strengthened in light of the rise of Protestantism. Not long after the inauguration of the evangelical movement, Erasmus finds himself forced to defend the arts more vigorously and to interpret attacks on the humanities in a new light. "The humanities were making pretty good progress everywhere," he writes in 1521, "had not this sad business of Luther arisen to throw everything into confusion."[3] From the beginning, conservative Catholics (as well as nascent Protestant-humanists, for that matter) connected Lutheranism to the Erasmian brand of Christian humanism which employed humanistic methods—specifically philological criticism and literary exegesis—to biblical scholarship, an approach which represented a departure from, and an affront to, the long-standing dialectical methods of the regnant university theologians, and which was also linked to the promotion of the translation of the Bible into vernacular languages (a hallmark of early Protestant efforts to democratize access

2. CWE 16:23.
3. CWE 8:312.

to scripture, which Erasmus had long called for as well). Thus was born the oft-repeated adage that Erasmus laid the egg which Luther hatched.

Erasmus mentions the proverbial egg in his first letter to Luther, which came in 1519. The letter is a cordial response to a letter from Luther, but Erasmus nonetheless tries to distance himself from the rising commotion:

> Even now it is impossible to root out from men's minds the most groundless suspicion that your work is written with assistance from me and that I am, as they call it, a standard-bearer of this new movement. They supposed that this gave them an opening to suppress both humane studies—for which they have a burning hatred, as likely to stand in the way of her majesty queen Theology, whom they value more than they do Christ—and myself at the same time, under the impression that I contribute something of importance to this outburst of zeal.[4]

Erasmus points out that some in England and even in Belgium support Luther (Erasmus was writing from Louvain), but says, "I keep myself uncommitted, so far as I can, in hopes of being able to do more for the revival of good literature. And I think one gets further by courtesy and moderation than by clamour."[5] But Erasmus's hopes for moderation would be short-lived, as we have seen, and his attempts to disassociate himself from the Protestant cause would never convince his most trenchant Catholic critics. Indeed, in contrast with his criticisms of Luther's own rage, Erasmus's descriptions of the wider Reformation as a tragedy are more concerned with attacks on the liberal arts, and these not by Protestants but by Catholic theologians and monks aligned with attempts by (for example) the Sorbonne to slander Erasmus's name and his mode of scholarship. In 1520, Erasmus wrote to another friend:

> Let me show you the criminal designs of some I could name, who hate me worse than they hate Luther himself!—not because I support him, which they know to be false, but because I support the humanities, with which they have been doing battle for a long time now, because I recall theologians to their sources, and because I point out to them where true religion has its roots.[6]

Though Erasmus would occasionally protest that his biblical scholarship was an innocent matter of correcting the text, and would claim not to be a theologian, moments like these reveal that he understood perfectly well what was at stake in editing and re-translating the New Testament.

The connection Erasmus makes between the violent emotions and Greek tragedy would appear in various forms in his diagnosis of the precarious place

---

4. Ep 980; CWE 6:392.
5. Ibid.
6. CWE 8:53.

the arts held in the impending schism in European Christendom. Again in 1520, Erasmus writes to Gerard Geldenhouwer: "I am filled with forebodings about that wretched Luther; the conspiracy against him is strong everywhere, and everywhere the ruling princes are being provoked against him, especially Pope Leo. . . . Hatred of liberal studies and the stupidity of monks—they were the prime sources from which the whole tragic story sprang."[7] In this case, the tragedy would seem to lie not in the fact that Luther has effected a schism, but in the energized philistinism of certain monks and theologians who both overreacted to Luther and associated his movement with the rise of the humanities. Erasmus was not just being paranoid. Noel Béda, who was the syndic of the Sorbonne theology faculty and one of Erasmus's most incorrigible critics, wrote to Erasmus as follows: "you will put us in your debt if you stand up to those enemies of religion with their show of Greek and their interest in the ancient tongues (you call them 'liberal studies')."[8] Writing to Pope Leo X, Erasmus complains about this unfortunate association: "I observe that, in order to strengthen their own faction, some have attempted to connect the cause of the humanities, Reuchlin's case, and my own with the case of Luther, although they have nothing in common."[9]

Of course, the movements had at least a few things in common, such as Luther's dependence on Erasmus's New Testament for his newfound understanding of penitence as repentance, a criticism of a similar set of abuses and hypocrisies of the Church, and a shared disdain for Aristotelianism in theology.[10] But Erasmus repeatedly expresses his exasperation at the discord that arose through abusive and over-passionate language in the Europe-wide disputes over Luther, in much the same way that he would eventually accuse Luther himself of writing with too much unbridled emotion. In contrast with Luther's impassioned diatribes, Erasmus calls for *mansuetudo* and *moderatio* (meekness and moderation), both components of *ethē*, or the calm *affectus*, in Erasmus's categorization of feeling.[11] "What could be more raving mad," he writes in a letter from 1521, "than to debate a question of such importance with scandalous pamphlets and lunatic uproar? . . . In this matter, the first point is that both sides have gone wrong, in my opinion, and that too

---

7. CWE 8:44.

8. Ep 1642; CWE 11:369.

9. CWE 8:50. The mention of Reuchlin shows the centrality of the study of original biblical languages in Erasmus's (and his critics') conception of the liberal arts. Johann Reuchlin was a Hebrew scholar who spent several years trying to ward off attempts by German Dominicans—led by Johannes Pfefferkorn—to confiscate and destroy all copies of the Talmud in an ill-guided attempt to convert Jews to Christianity.

10. The literature on this is massive, but see most recently David Whitford, "Erasmus Openeth the Way Before Luther," *Church History and Religious Culture* 96 (2016): 516–40.

11. Allen Ep 1225: Primus omnium admoniu hominem literis ut rem Evangelicam Evangelica mansuetudine moderationeque tractaret.

much emotion has been brought to bear in both directions."[12] In the same letter, he complains that even if Luther had borrowed from *his* books, that was no fault of his own, although he concedes that he (Erasmus) might

> have phrased some things more cautiously, had I seen that a different time was coming as fraught with tragedy as the present. . . . In the points which are condemned in Luther's book I find nothing in which he agrees with me, except perhaps that what I have stated with moderation [*moderate*] and in its proper context, he utters without restraint [*immodice*].[13]

In the end, Erasmus writes, again invoking dramatic technique, "Personally, I see no way out, unless Christ himself, like some god from a machine [in Greek: *apo mêchanês*], gives this lamentable play [*infelici fabulae*] a happy ending."[14] Later in the year, writing to Wolfgang Capito, Erasmus more explicitly lays blame on the Lutherans for their abusive language: "Luther's party are crazier and more insolent and more self-assertive in everything; they fix their teeth on anyone, no matter whom, and abuse everyone to his face with barbarous impertinence. . . . I begged them not to be so *violent* in everything and so grossly offensive in maintaining their cause." The violence (*vehementem*) of Lutheran anti-papal discourse is thus tragic on several levels, not only because it contributes to the demise of the humanities, but also because it avoids the *moderatio* that Erasmus prefers.

Erasmus prays to be rescued from the tragedy and extricated from the modern *Iliad* with its violent emotions: "This business of Luther," he writes to the archbishop of Canterbury, William Warham, in 1521,

> far removed as it is from liberal studies, even so burdens the work of people like myself with considerable unpopularity. There is an element of chance in this: before Luther arose, I had long been fighting a bitter campaign against the sort of people who are now Luther's chief opponents. . . . And now they all vie with one another in attacking Luther, as the Greeks of old attacked Hector when he was down.

---

12. Ep 1225: Nunc quid furiosius quam rem tantam maledicis libellis et insanis clamoribus agi?

13. CWE 8:200; Allen Ep 1225: Scripsi eo seculo quae tum videbantur ad bonos mores conducere: fortasse quaedam scripturus circumspectius, si praescissem exoriturum hoc seculum plusquam tragicum . . . In his articulis qui damnantur in Lutheri libris, nihil video quod illi mecum conveniat, nisi forte quod a me moderate suoque loco dictum est, ille dicit immodice.

14. That Erasmus doesn't always use *fabula* metaphorically is shown in his 1534 response to Luther, where he defends using the phrase *fabula salutifera* in his *Explanatio symboli* (CWE 78:424, and 38n5).

Erasmus would prefer to be acting in the Ür-comedy, the *Odyssey*: "We must avoid [Luther] like Scylla," he continues, "and yet make sure we are not swept into Charybdis."[15] The middle course of Ulysses made Erasmus unpopular with both sides, and he was doubly criticized for his refusal to either call Luther a heretic or denounce the Pope. Ironically, as Rummel has noted, Girolamo Aleandro, a staunchly anti-Lutheran cardinal, referred to Erasmus as "the director of the Lutheran tragedy."[16] Erasmus himself also saw that attacks on his refusal to choose sides would themselves weaken his attempts to instantiate the humanities as foundational, as is evident in a colorful passage from his 1523 apologia against Ulrich von Hutten, where Erasmus fictionally paraphrases the Catholics who would be happy to see an anti-papist such as Hutten doing their work for them:

> Do us a favor, do away with that Erasmus who attacks us with strange tongues and new ways of writing, and shakes the foundations of our kingdom. Onward! More books like this will make those so-called good letters distasteful to princes and studious youth, letting them see the virulence within them, and that they are good for nothing but calumniating decent folk and inciting rebellion. Pull back the curtain on those lewd poetic mysteries; spit, blow snot, piss, and shit into the well-spring of the Muses so that no one will ever again want to drink there.[17]

Hutten, though an occasional supporter of Luther, had relocated to Zwingli's Zurich for asylum, and Erasmus dedicates his response to Hutten's treatise (which response is called the *Sponge*) to Zwingli himself, warning him against maintaining safe harbor for such a vitriolic personality, especially because his treatises are "exactly what the enemies of good literature enjoy and hope for."[18]

A few years later Erasmus thought, briefly, that the situation might improve. In 1525, he writes,

> The squabbles of comedy usually end with a marriage, at which point a sudden calm descends on the whole scene. Nowadays the tragedies acted out by our princes often have the same ending.... It looks as though the Luther tragedy will end in a similar way. He has married a wife, a religious like himself. Evidently the marriage began under good auspices, for within a fortnight of the singing of the wedding hymn, the bride went into labour. Luther is now becoming more moderate. There is nothing so wild that it cannot be tamed by a wife.[19]

---

15. Ep 1228; CWE 8:286.
16. Erika Rummel, *The Confessionalization of Humanism in Reformation Germany* (Oxford: Oxford University Press, 2000), 27.
17. CWE 78:139, modified.
18. CWE 78:30.
19. CWE 11:393.

Alas, the rumor of a shotgun wedding proved false, and Erasmus writes several times that his hopes that marriage would mitigate Luther's vitriol did not come to fruition, and he reverts to pessimism: "I see death and starvation hanging over the humanities and all who practice them."[20] By 1528, Erasmus, who had seen that there was to be no *deus ex machina*, and who had by then been involved in the protracted debate with Luther over free will, modified the terms in his narrative. Writing to Thomas More, he casts himself not in a Greek tragedy, but in a plague-grade biblical epic: "Many things have led me to believe that God is the director of this turbulent drama," he writes. "He has set loose upon us for our just deserts these beetles, dog-flies, and locusts."[21] Erasmus's woes had become even more personal, as we saw in the chapter on his correspondence, and his isolation was more deeply felt as a result of being caught in the middle:

> The majority of the Lutheran faction is convinced that I am the only obstacle to the conversion of all of Germany to the gospel ... others hope that, exhausted by the endless show of hatred directed at me by certain monks and theologians, I will desert to their camp. That is my position with the Lutherans. Now the other side is striving with every ounce of energy to knock my books from men's hands. This could be tolerated, but the pretext they devised to camouflage the rashness of their actions cannot and ought not to be tolerated. From this first step they would go on to do away with good letters altogether.[22]

One gains insight from these comments into the difficult position Erasmus imagined himself to be in. Decried then and after as a lukewarm fence-sitter, if we take seriously Erasmus's assiduous arguments for *moderatio* in and reform of the emotions of Christendom, it is easier to see how his disaffection resulted from a turbulent period that he judged too immoderate to fully engage with.

The violent *pathē* often result from vehement rhetorical *pathos*, and this sort of affective style was, to Erasmus's mind, detrimental to Christian concord, and he continues to condemn the venomous tendencies of religious disputation until the end of his life. He comes to understand Luther's movement specifically as tragic and violent. Not only does Quintilian's distinction between the comic and tragic emotions come into play in the *Purgatio* of 1534, but, as we noted in the previous chapter, Erasmus writes that Orestes (from Aeschylus's tragedy) was saner than Luther, and that Luther is as bad as Ajax, who attacks livestock thinking they are Greek soldiers in Sophocles's play bearing his name.[23] Toward the end of the *Purgatio*, Erasmus again condemns Luther's penchant for rhetorical vehemence, in a passage that ties together Erasmus's association of the Reformation, which had unintentionally dragged the humanities in as collateral damage, with literary tragedy: "Rhetoricians must first of all teach using arguments,

---

20. Ep 1635; CWE 11:341.
21. Ep 1804; CWE 18:18.
22. Ep 1804; CWE 18:18.
23. CWE 78:437, 453.

then, if the matter demands, stimulate the emotions, but must not rashly excite the violent feelings known as πάθη. But never to stop being δεινόν, never to cease thundering truly tragic words, this is lunacy rather than eloquence."[24] In the same section, Erasmus writes that Luther was guilty, too, of a related affective-rhetorical vice, namely πλήκτης, the tendency to be pugnacious or contentious, literally a "striker." The Apostle Paul had denounced a penchant for πλήκτης as something to beware of in bishops at 1 Timothy 3:3, and Erasmus uses the term elsewhere as an undesirable emotional disposition that results in violence and is linked to tragedy, as in the *Lingua* of 1525:

> Paul is eager that a bishop above all should be remote from this vice [of slander] when he says: "I do not want a striker [*percussorem*]," that is, πλήκτης in Greek. For a violent tongue has brought sudden death to many without any wound to the body. There are even men who wield their tongues against their brother with the purpose of killing him. I count in this category men who stir up quarrels on any trivial pretext and brew tragic dramas [*suscitant tragoedias*] about mere goat's wool.[25]

Paul himself becomes a conduit for thinking through the emotional implications of tragic discourse, an Erasmian model of moderation. And the comic Erasmus compares himself emotionally one last time to the tragic Luther, combining the language of Paul, characters from classical myth, and ancient literary categories, in what feels like an appropriate way to conclude our own story about Erasmian emotion: "I confess that I am by natural inclination rather given to jesting, both in my writings and in my conversations with friends.... But since no person is free of every fault, I prefer to seem slightly foolish to some than a kind of harsh, πλήκτης, Procrustean character, always breathing tragedy."[26]

---

24. CWE 78:458–9, modifed; ASD IX-1, 479–80: Rhetorum est, primum docere argumentis, deinde si res postulet solicitare affectus, atroces autem illos, quos πάθη vocant, non temere movere. Verum nusqum non esse δεινόν, nusquam non intonare voces plusquam tragicas, dementiae verius est quam eloquentiae.

25. CWE 29:339. In his *Annotationes* on the New Testament, Erasmus glosses the term πλήκτης at 1 Tim. 3:3 as violence not of the hand, but of the tongue: "non pertinet ad violentiam manuum, sed acerbitatem linguae, ne saeuus et improbus sit obiurgator" (*Novum Testamentum omne*... [Basel: Froben, 1540], 671, ad loc.).

26. CWE 78:458; ASD IX-1, 478: Verum quando nullus hominum vacet omni naevo, malo quibusdam videri ineptior quam truculentus πλήκτης ac Procrustes quispiam ubique tragicum spirans.

BIBLIOGRAPHY

The Renaissance of Feeling: Erasmus and Emotion, by Kirk Essary

Primary Sources

Aristotle. *The Complete Works of Aristotle: The Revised Oxford Translation*, edited by Jonathan Barnes. Princeton: Princeton University Press, 1984.
Cicero. *De oratore*, translated by E. W. Sutton and H. Rackham. Loeb Classical Library. London and Cambridge, MA: Harvard University Press, 1942.
Cicero. *Tusculan Disputations 3 and 4*, edited and translated by Margaret Graver. Chicago: University of Chicago Press, 2002.
Dictionariolum puerorum, edited by Robert Estienne. London, 1552.
Dictionarium latinarum e greco pariter dirivantium, edited by Ambrogio Calepino et al. Basel, 1512.
Erasmus. *Collected Works of Erasmus*, 72 vols. Toronto: University of Toronto Press, 1974–.
Erasmus. *De libero arbitrio ΔIATPIBH sive collatio*. Basel: Froben, 1524.
Erasmus. *Novum testamentum . . . cum annotationibus*. Basel: Froben, 1540.
Erasmus. *Opera omnia*, edited by J. Leclerc, 10 vols. Leiden: Pieter van der Aa, 1703–06.
Erasmus. *Opera omnia*, 9 vols. in parts. Amsterdam: North-Holland, 1969–.
Erasmus. *Opus epistolarum*, edited by P. S. Allen, 12 vols. Oxford: Clarendon Press, 1906–58.
Erasmus. *Paraclesis*. In *Desiderius Erasmus Roterodamus, Ausgewälte Werke*, edited by Hajo Holborn and Annemarie Holborn. Munich: Beck, 1933.
Erasmus. *Ratio seu compendium verae theologiae*. Basel: Froben, 1519.
Erasmus. *The Praise of Folly*, translated by Clarence H. Miller. New Haven: Yale University Press, 1979.
Erasmus. *Tomus primus paraphraseon D. Erasmi Roterodami*. Basel: Froben, 1524.
Erasmus. *Tomus secundus continens Paraphrasim D. Erasmi Roterodami*. Basel: Froben, 1532.
Lexicon graeco-latinum, seu Thesaurus linguae graecae, edited by Guillaume Bude et al. Geneva: Crespin, 1554.
Lexicon theologicum complectus vocabulorum descriptiones, edited by Johann Altenstaig, 1517.
Luther, Martin. *D. Martin Luthers Werke: Kritische Gesamtausgabe*, 68 vols. Weimer: Hermann Böhlau, 1883–1999.
Migne, J. P., ed. *Patrologiae cursus completus latina*. 221 vols. Paris, 1844–64.
Migne, J. P., ed. *Patrologiae cursus completus graeca*. 162 vols. Paris, 1857–66.
Plato. *Timaeus*, edited and translated by Marsilio Ficino. London, 1563.
Quintilian. *Institutio oratoria*, translated by Donald A. Russell. Loeb Classical Library, 5 vols. Cambridge, MA: Harvard University Press, 2002.
Titelmans, Francis. *Collationes quinque super Epistolam ad Romanos beati pauli Apostoli*. Antwerp: Vorstermanm, 1529.

Valla, Lorenzo. *Antidoti in Pogium*. In *Opera omnia I*, edited by Eugenio Garin. Torino: Bottega d'Erasmo, 1962.

Vives, Juan Luis. *De ratione dicendi*, edited by David Walker. Leiden: Brill, 2018.

Secondary Sources

Augustijn, *Erasmus: His Life, Works, and Influence*. Toronto: Toronto University Press, 1991.

Bailey, Merridee. "Early English Dictionaries and the History of Meekness." *Philological Quarterly* 98, no. 3 (2019): 243–72.

Baker-Smith, Dominic. "Erasmus as Reader of the Psalms." *Erasmus of Rotterdam Society Yearbook* 20, no. 1 (2000): 1–18.

Baker-Smith, Dominic. "Tranquillitas Animi: Erasmus and the Quest for Spiritual Reassurance, 1533-43." In *Erasmus and the Renaissance Republic of Letters*, edited by Stephen Ryle, 383–97. Turnhout: Brepols, 2014.

Baker-Smith, Dominic. "Uses of Plato by Erasmus and More." In *Platonism and the English Imagination*, edited by Baldwin and Hutton, 86–101. Cambridge: Cambridge University Press, 1994.

Barclay, Katie. *Caritas: Neighbourly Love and the Early Modern Self*. Oxford: Oxford University Press, 2021.

Barclay, Katie. "State of the Field: The History of Emotions." *History* 106 (2021): 456–66.

Béné, Charles. *Érasme et Saint Augustin*. Geneva: Droz, 1969.

Bernat, Chrystel and Frédéric Gabriel, eds. *Émotions de Dieu: Attributions et Appropriations Chrétiennes (XVIe-XVIIIe Siècle)*. Turnhout: Brepols, 2019.

Boquet, Damien. *L'Ordre de l'affecte au Moyen Âge*. Caen: CRAHM, 2005.

Boquet, Damien and Piroska Nagy. *Sensible Moyen Âge: Une histoire des émotions dan l'Occident médiéval*. Paris: Le Seuil, 2015.

Bouwsma, William. "The Two Faces of Humanism: Stoicism and Augustinianism in Renaissance Thought." In *Itinerarium Italicum: The Profile of the Italian Renaissance in the Mirror of Its European Transformations*, edited by Heiko Oberman and Thomas Brady, 3–60. London: Brill, 1975.

Broomhall, Susan, ed. *Authority, Gender and Emotions in Late Medieval and Early Modern England*. London: Palgrave Macmillan, 2015.

Broomhall, Susan. "Cross-channel Affections: Pressure and Persuasion in Letters to Calvinist Refugees in England, 1569–1570." In *Feeling Exclusion: Religious Conflict, Exile and Emotions in Early Modern Europe*, edited by Giovanni Tarantino and Charles Zika, 27–43. London: Routledge, 2019.

Broomhall, Susan, ed. *Gender and Emotions in Medieval and Early Modern Europe: Destroying Order, Structuring Disorder*. Routledge, 2015.

Cairns, Douglas and Laura Fulkerson, eds. *Emotions Between Greece and Rome*. BICS Supplement 125. London: University of London, 2015.

Carrera, Elena. "Anger and the Mind-Body Connection in Medieval and Early Modern Medicine." In *Emotions and Health, 1200–1700*, edited by Elena Carrera, 95–146. Leiden: Brill, 2013.

Carrera, Elena. "Augustinian, Aristotelian, and Humanist Shaping of Medieval and Early Modern Emotion: *Affectus, affectio*, and "affection" as Traveling Concepts." In *Before Emotion: The Language of Feeling in Europe, 400-1800*, edited by Juanita Feros Ruys, Michael Champion and Kirk Essary, 170–84. London: Routledge, 2019.

Carrera, Elena. "The Emotions in Sixteenth-Century Spanish Spirituality." *Journal of Religious History* 3 (2007): 235–52.
Caston, Ruth Rothaus. "Pacuvius hoc melius quam Sophocles: Cicero's Use of Drama in the Treatment of the Emotions." *Bulletin of the Institute of Classics Studies* 125 (2015): 129–48.
Champion, Michael. "From *affectus* to Affect Theory and Back Again." In *Before Emotion: The Language of Feeling, 400-1800*, edited by Juanita Feros Ruys, Michael Champion, and Kirk Essary, 240–56. London: Routledge, 2019.
Chomarat, Jacques. *Grammaire et Rhetorique Chez Erasme*, 2 vols. Paris: Les Belles Lettres, 1981.
Cohen Hanegbi, Naama. *Caring for the Living Soul: Medicine and Penance in the Late Medieval Mediterranean*. Boston: Brill, 2017.
Cohen Hanegbi, Naama. "Mourning under Medical Care: A Study of a *Consilium* by Bartolomeo Montagnana," *Parergon* 31, no. 2 (2014): 35–54.
Colish, Marcia. "Juan Luis Vives on the Turks." In *Medievalia et Humanistica: Studies in Medieval and Renaissance Culture no. 35, Scales of Connectivity*, edited by Paul Maurice Clogan, 1–15. Lanham, MD: Rowman and Littlefield, 2009.
Copeland, Rita. *Emotion and the History of Rhetoric in the Middle Ages*. Oxford: Oxford University Press, 2022.
Cummings, Brian. "Encyclopaedic Erasmus." *Renaissance Studies* 28, no. 2 (2014): 183–204.
Cummings, Brian. "Erasmus and the Colloquial Emotions." *Erasmus Studies* 40, no. 2 (2020): 127–50.
Cummings, Brian. "Erasmus and the Invention of Literature." *Erasmus of Rotterdam Society Yearbook* 33 (2013): 22–54.
Cummings, Brian. *Grammar and Grace: The Literary Culture of the Reformation*. Oxford: Oxford University Press, 2002.
Cummings, Brian and Freya Sierhuis. *Passions and Subjectivity in Early Modern Culture*. Ashgate, 2013.
Crocker, Holly. "Medieval Affects Now." *Exemplaria* 29, no. 1 (2017): 82–98.
Cytowska, Maria. "Erasme et la philosophie antique." *Ziva antika. Antiquité vivante* 26 (1976): 451–62.
Cytowska, Maria. "Érasme de Rotterdam et Marsile Ficin son maître." *Eos* 63 (1975): 165–79.
Dealy, Ross. *Stoic Origins of Erasmus's Philosophy of Christ*. Toronto: University of Toronto Press, 2017.
Dixon, Thomas. *From Passions to Emotions: The Creation of a Secular Psychological Category*. Cambridge: Cambridge University Press, 2004.
Dixon, Thomas. "What is the History of Anger a History of?" *Emotions: History, Culture, Society* 4 (2020): 1–35.
Dreyer, Elizabeth. "The Transformative Role of Emotion in the Middle Ages." In *The Spirit, the Affections, and the Christian Tradition*, edited by Dale Coulter and Amos Yong, 113–42. South Bend, IN: University of Notre Dame Press, 2016.
Eden, Kathy. *Hermeneutics and the Rhetorical Tradition*. New Haven: Yale University Press, 1997.
Eden, Kathy. *The Renaissance Rediscovery of Intimacy*. Chicago: Chicago University Press, 2012.
Enenkel, Karl and Anita Traninger, eds. *Discourses of Anger in the Early Modern Period*. Leiden: Brill, 2015.

Essary, Kirk. "Annotating the Affections: The Philology of Feeling in Erasmus' New Testament and Its Reception in Early Modern Dictionaries." *Erasmus Studies* 37, no. 2 (2017): 193–216.

Essary, Kirk. "Clear as Mud: Metaphor, Emotion, and Meaning in Early Modern England." *English Studies* 98, no. 7 (2017): 689–703.

Essary, Kirk. *Erasmus and Calvin on the Foolishness of God: Reason and Emotion in the Christian Philosophy*. Toronto: University of Toronto Press, 2017.

Essary, Kirk. "Milk for Babes: Erasmus and Calvin on the Problem of Christian Eloquence." *Reformation and Renaissance Review* 16, no. 3 (2014): 246–65.

Essary, Kirk. "Passions, Affections, or Emotions? On the Ambiguity of 16th-Century Terminology." *Emotion Review* 9, no. 4 (2017): 367–74.

Essary, Kirk. "Rhetorical Theology and the History of Emotions." In *The Routledge History of Emotions in Europe, 1100–1700*, edited by Susan Broomhall and Andrew Lynch, 86–101. London: Routledge, 2020.

Essary, Kirk. "'The Bloody Sweat of Our Minds': (Dis)embodied Emotions in Erasmus, More, and Calvin." *Parergon* 38, no. 1 (2021): 41–64.

Essary, Kirk. "The Renaissance of *affectus*? Biblical Humanism and Latin Style." In *Before Emotion: The Language of Feeling in Europe, 400-1800*, edited by Juanita Feros Ruys, Michael Champion, and Kirk Essary, 156–69. London: Routledge, 2019.

Fantazzi, Charles. "The Erasmus-Vives Correspondence." In *Erasmus and the Renaissance Republic of Letters*, edited by Stephen Ryle and Lisa Jardine. Turnhout: Brepols, 2014.

Fantazzi, Charles. "The Evolution of Erasmus's Epistolary Style." *Renaissance and Reformation* 13, no. 3 (1989): 263–88.

Farmer, Craig. *The Gospel of John in the Sixteenth Century*. Oxford: Oxford University Press, 1997.

Feros Ruys, Juanita. "Before the Affective Turn: *Affectus* in Heloise, Abelard, and the Woman Writer of the *Epistolae duorum amantium*." In *Before Emotions: The Language of Feeling, 400-1800*, edited by Juanita Feros Ruys, Michael Champion, and Kirk Essary. London: Routledge, 2019.

Fox, Cora. *Ovid and the Politics of Emotion*. London: Palgrave MacMillan, 2009.

Frevert, Ute et al., *Emotional Lexicons*. Oxford: Oxford University Press, 2014.

Fumaroli, Marc. *L'Age de l'éloquence*. Geneva: Droz, 1980.

Gammerl, Benno. "Emotional Styles—Concepts and Challenges." *Rethinking History* 16, no. 2 (2012): 161–75.

Ginzburg, Carlo. *Threads and Traces*. Berkley, CA: University of California Press, 2001.

Gomez Gil, Javier. "La Retorica del Vir Bonus: El Ethos del Orador y Los Lenes Adfectus en el De Oratore de Ciceron." PhD dissertation, Universidad Zaragosa, 2015.

Graver, Margaret. *Cicero on the Emotions: Tusculan Disputations 3 and 4*. Chicago: University of Chicago Press, 2009.

Havu, Kaarlo. *Juan Luis Vives: Politics, Rhetoric, and Emotion*. London: Routledge, 2022.

Hoffmann, Manfred. "Erasmus on Language and Interpretation." *Moreana* 28 (1991): 1–20.

Hoffmann, Manfred. "Erasmus: Rhetorical Theologian." In *Rhetorical Invention and Religious Inquiry*, edited by Walter Jost and Wendy Olmsted, 136–61. New Haven: Yale University Press, 2000.

Hoffmann, Manfred. *Rhetoric and Theology: The Hermeneutics of Erasmus*. Toronto: University of Toronto Press, 1994.

Huizinga, Johan. *Erasmus*. New York: C. Scribner's Sons, 1924.

Jager, Eric. *The Book of the Heart*. Chicago: Chicago University Press, 2000.

Jardine, Lisa. *Erasmus, Man of Letters: The Construction of Charisma in Print*. Princeton: Princeton University Press, 1993.
Jost, Jean E. "Spirituality in the Late Middle Ages: Affective Piety and the Pricke of Conscience." In *Mental Health, Spirituality, and Religion in the Middle Ages and Early Modern Age*, edited by Albrecht Classen, 387–405. Berlin, DE: De Gruyter, 2014.
Karant-Nunn, Susan. *The Reformation of Feeling: Shaping the Religious Emotions in Early Modern Germany*. Oxford: Oxford University Press, 2010.
Karant-Nunn, Susan. "The Wrath of Martin Luther: Anger and Charisma in the Reformer." *The Sixteenth Century Journal* 48, no. 4 (2017): 909–26.
Kilcoyne, Francois and Margaret Jennings. "Rethinking "Continuity": Erasmus' *Ecclesiastes* and the *Artes Praedicandi*." *Renaissance and Reformation / Renaissance et Reforme* XXI, no. 4 (1997): 5–24.
King, P. "Late Scholastic Theories of the Passions: Controversies in the Thomist Tradition." In *Emotions and Choice from Boethius to Descartes*, edited by H. Lagerlund and M. Yrjönsuuri, 229–58. New York: Springer, 2002.
Knuuttila, Simo. *Emotions in Ancient and Medieval Philosophy*. Oxford: Oxford University Press, 2004.
Kraye, Jill. "Stoicism in the Renaissance from Petrarch to Lipsius." *Grotiana* 22, no. 1 (2001): 21–45.
Leo, Russ. "Affective Physics: *Affectus* in Spinoza's *Ethica*." In *Passions and Subjectivity in the Early Modern Era*, edited by Brian Cummings and Freya Sierhuis, 33–49. London: Ashgate, 2013.
Leushuis, Reinier. "Poetics or Homiletics? Hearing and Feeling the New Testament in Erasmus's *Paraphrases*." *Erasmus Studies* 40, no. 2 (2020): 101–26.
Leushuis, Reinier. "The Paradox of Christian Epicureanism in Dialogue." *Erasmus Studies* 35, no. 2 (2015): 113–36.
Lynch, Andrew, Stephanie Downes, and Katrina O'Loughlin, eds. *Emotions and War: Medieval to Romantic Literature*. London: Palgrave MacMillan, 2015.
Mack, Peter. *A History of Renaissance Rhetoric (1380-1620)*. Oxford: Oxford University Press, 2001, 98–103.
Mack, Peter. "Quintilian in Northern Europe during the Renaissance, 1479-1620." In *The Oxford Handbook to Quintilian*, edited by Marc van der Poel et al., 379–97. Oxford: Oxford University Press, 2022.
Mack, Peter. "Twenty-fourth Annual Margaret Mann Phillips Lecture: Erasmus' Contribution to Rhetoric and Rhetoric in Erasmus' Writing." *ERSY* 32 (2012): 27–45.
MacPhail, Eric. "The Mosaic of Speech: A Classical Topos in Renaissance Aesthetics." *Journal of the Warburg and Courtauld Institutes* 66 (2003): 249–64.
Marsh, David. "Erasmus on the Antithesis of Body and Soul." *Journal the History of Ideas* 37, no. 4 (1976): 673–88.
McCarthy, Michael. "Augustine's Mixed Feelings: Vergil's 'Aeneid' and the Psalms of David in the 'Confessions'." *Harvard Theological Review* 102, no. 4 (2009): 453–79.
McGowan, Matthew. "The *Nux* Attributed to Ovid and Its Renaissance Readers: The Case of Erasmus." In *Constructing Authors and Readers in the Appendices Vergiliana, Tibulliana, and Ovidiana*, edited by Tristan E. Franklinos and Laurel Fulkerson, 262–75. Oxford: Oxford University Press, 2020.
McNamer, Sarah. *Affective Meditation and the Invention of Medieval Compassion*. Philadelphia: University of Pennsylvania Press, 2010.
Meek, Richard. *Sympathy in Early Modern Literature and Culture*. Cambridge: Cambridge University Press, 2023.

Meek, Richard and Erin Sullivan, eds. *The Renaissance of Emotion: Understanding Affect in Shakespeare and His Contemporaries*. Manchester: University of Manchester Press, 2015.

Monfasani, John. "Erasmus and the Philosophers." *Erasmus of Rotterdam Society Yearbook* 32 (2012): 47–68.

Nagy, Piroska. "Émotions de Dieu au Moyen Âge." In *Émotions de Dieu: Attributions et Appropriations Chrétiennes (XVIe-XVIIIe Siècle)*, edited by C. Bernat et al., 67–88. Turnhout: Brepols, 2019.

Newman, Barbara. "*Affectus* from Hildegard to Helfta." In *Before Emotion: The Language of Feeling in Europe, 400-1800*, edited by Juanita Feros Ruys, Michael Champion and Kirk Essary, 97–107. London: Routledge, 2019.

Norena, Carlos. *Juan Luis Vives and the Emotions*. Carbondale, IN: University of Southern Illinois Press, 1980.

Nussbaum, Martha. *Anger and Forgiveness: Resentment, Generosity, and Justice*. New York: Oxford University Press, 2016.

Nussbaum, Martha. *Upheavals of Thought: The Intelligence of Emotions*. Cambridge: Cambridge University Press, 2001.

Oberman, Heiko. "The Reorientation of the Fourteenth Century." In *Studi sul XIV secolo in memoria di Anneliese Maier*, edited by A. Maierù and A. Paravicini Bagliani, 513–30. Rome: Raccolta di Studi e Testi, 1982.

O'Malley, John. "Erasmus and the History of Sacred Rhetoric: The *Ecclesiastes* of 1535." *ERSY* 5 (1985): 1–29.

O'Rourke Boyle, Marjorie. *Erasmus on Language and Method in Theology*. Toronto: University of Toronto Press, 1977.

O'Rourke Boyle, Marjorie. *Rhetoric and Reform: Erasmus's Civil Dispute with Luther*. Cambridge, MA: Harvard University Press, 1983.

Palmer, Ada. "The Recovery of Stoicism in the Renaissance." In *The Routledge Handbook of the Stoic Tradition*, edited by John Sellars, 117–32. London: Routledge, 2016.

Payne, J. B. "Towards a Hermeneutics of Erasmus." In *Scrinium Erasmianum II*, edited by J. Coppens, 13–30. Leiden: Brill, 1969.

Peyroux, Catherine. "Gertrude's *furor*." In *Angers Past: The Social Uses of an Emotion in the Middle Ages*, edited by Barbara Rosenwein, 36–56. Ithaca, NY: Cornell University Press, 1998.

Phillips, Margaret Mann. *Erasmus and the Northern Renaissance*. London: Hodder and Stoughton, 1961.

Pitkin, Barbara. "Erasmus, Calvin, and the Faces of Stoicism in Renaissance and Reformation Thought." In *The Routledge Handbook of the Stoic Tradition*, edited by John Sellars, 145–59. Routledge, 2016.

Pontani, Filippomaria. "From Bude to Zenodotus: Homeric Readings in the European Renaissance." *International Journal of the Classical Tradition* 14, no. 3/4 (2007): 375–430.

Raeburn, Gordon. "Erasmus and the Emotions of Death." *Erasmus Studies* 40, no. 2 (2020): 157–73.

Reddy, William. "Sentimentalism and Its Erasure." *The Journal of Modern History* 72 (2000): 109–52.

Robinson, Benedict. "Disgust, *c.* 1600." *ELH* 81, no. 2 (2014): 553–83.

Rosenwein, Barbara. "Emotion Words." In *Le sujet des émotions au Moyen Âge*, edited by Piroska Nagy and Damien Boquet, 93–106. Paris: Beauchesne, 2008.

Rosenwein, Barbara. *Generations of Feeling: A History of Emotions, 600-1700*. Cambridge: Cambridge University Press, 2016.
Rosenwein, Barbara. "Worrying About Emotions in History." *The American Historical Review* 107, no. 3 (2002): 821-45.
Rummel, Erika. *Erasmus as a Translator of the Classics*. Toronto: University of Toronto Press, 1985.
Rummel, Erika. *Erasmus on Women*. Toronto: University of Toronto Press, 2000.
Rummel, Erika. *The Confessionalization of Humanism in Reformation Germany*. Oxford: Oxford University Press, 2000.
Ryrie, Alec. *Being Protestant in Reformation Britain*. Oxford: Oxford University Press, 2013.
Sardu, Luisanna. "How Gaspara Stampa Challenged Classical Tradition and Conventional Notions of Women's Anger." *Emotions: History, Culture, Society* 3 (2019): 24-46.
Sartori, Paolo. "La controversia neotestamentaria tra Frans Titelmans ed Erasmo da Rotterdam (1527-1530 ca): Linee di siviluppo e contenuti." *Humanistica Lovaniensia* 52 (2003): 77-135.
Scheer, Monique. "Are Emotions a Kind of Practice (and Is That What Makes Them Have A History)? A Bourdieuian Approach to Understanding Emotion." *History and Theory* 51, no. 2 (2012): 193-220.
Scheer, Monique. "Topographies of Emotion." In *Emotional Lexicons*, edited by Ute Frevert et al., 32-61. Oxford: Oxford University Press, 2014.
Scott, Anne. "The Role of *Exempla* in Educating Through Emotion: The Deadly Sin of 'lecherye' in Robert Mannyng's *Handlyng Synne* (1303-1317)." In *Authority, Gender and Emotions in Late Medieval and Early Modern England*, edited Susan Broomhall, 34-50. London: Palgrave Macmillan, 2015.
Screech, M. A. *Ecstasy and the Praise of Folly*. London: Duckworth, 1980.
Shuger, Debora. *Sacred Rhetoric: The Christian Grand Style in the English Renaissance*. Princeton: Princeton University Press, 1988.
Shuger, Debora. "The Philosophical Foundations of Sacred Rhetoric." In *Religion and Emotion: Approaches and Interpretations*, edited by John Corrigan, 115-32. Oxford: Oxford University Press, 2004.
Smith, James K. A. "Redeeming the Affections: Deconstructing Augustine's Critique of Theatre." In *The Spirit, the Affections, and the Christian Tradition*, edited by Dale Coulter and Amos Yong, 41-64. South Bend, IN: University of Notre Dame Press, 2016.
Spencer, F. Scott, ed. *Mixed Feelings and Vexed Passions: Exploring Emotions in Biblical Literature*. Atlanta, GA: Society of Biblical Literature Press, 2017.
Stearns, Peter N. and Carol Z. Stearns. "Emotionology: Clarifying the History of Emotions and Emotional Standards." *American Historical Review* 90 (1985): 813-36.
Strier, Richard. "Against the Rule of Reason: Praise of Passion from Petrarch to Luther to Shakespeare to Herbert." In *Reading the Early Modern Passions*, edited by Gail Kern Paster, 29-58. Chicago: University of Chicago Press, 2004.
Sullivan, Erin. *Beyond Melancholy: Sadness and Selfhood in Early Modern England*. Oxford: Oxford University Press, 2016.
Teubner, Jonathan. "The Failure of *Affectus*: *Affectiones* and *constantiae* in Augustine of Hippo." In *Before Emotion: The Language of Feeling in Europe, 400-1800*, edited by Juanita Feros Ruys, Michael Champion and Kirk Essary, 9-25. London: Routledge, 2019.

Tilmouth, Christopher. "Passion and Intersubjectivity in Early Modern Literature." In *Passions and Subjectivity in Early Modern Culture*, edited by Brian Cummings and Freya Sierhuis, 13–32. London: Ashgate, 2014.

Trinkaus, Charles. *In Our Image and Likeness: Humanity and Divinity in Italian Humanist Thought*, 2 vols. South Bend, IN: University of Notre Dame Press, 1995.

Van Dijk, Mathilde. "The *Devotio Moderna*, the Emotions and the Search for Dutchness." *BMGN: Low Countries Historical Review* 129, no. 2 (2014): 20–41.

Vessey, Mark, ed. *Erasmus on Literature: His Ratio or 'System' of 1518/1519*. Toronto: University of Toronto Press, 2021.

Visser, Arnoud. "Irreverent Reading: Martin Luther as Annotator of Erasmus." *Sixteenth Century Journal* 48, no. 1 (2017): 87–109.

von Moos, Peter. "Literary Aesthetics in the Latin Middle Ages: The Rhetorical Theology of Peter Abelard." In *Rhetoric and Renewal in the Latin West 1100–1540*, edited by C. Mews, C. J. Nederman, and R. M. Thomson, 81–98. Turnhout: Brepols, 2003.

Vredeveld, Harry. "The Ages of Erasmus and the Year of His Birth." *Renaissance Quarterly* 46, no. 4 (1993): 754–809.

Weiss, James. "Ecclesiastes and Erasmus: The Mirror and the Image." *Archiv für Reformationsgeschichte* 65 (1974): 83–108.

White, Carolinne. "Allegory and Rhetoric in Erasmus' Expositions of the Psalms." In *Meditations of the Heart: The Psalms in Early Christian Thought and Practice: Essays in Honour of Andrew Louth*, edited by Casiday et al., 257–76. Turnhout: Brepols, 2011.

Whitford, David. "Erasmus Openeth the Way Before Luther." *Church History and Religious Culture* 96 (2016): 516–40.

Wierzbicka, Anna. "The 'History of Emotions' and the Future of Emotion Research." *Emotion Review* 2 (2010): 269–73.

Zahl, Simeon. "On the Affective Salience of Doctrines." *Modern Theology* 31, no. 3 (2015): 428–44.

Zahl, Simeon. "The Bondage of the Affections: Willing, Feeling, and Desiring in Luther's Theology, 1513–1525." In *The Spirit, the Affections, and the Christian Tradition*, edited by Dale Coulter and Amos Yong, 181–206. South Bend, IN: University of Notre Dame Press, 2016.

Zahl, Simeon. *The Holy Spirit and Christian Experience*. Oxford: Oxford University Press, 2020.

INDEX

1 Thessalonians   58 n.43, 93
1 Timothy   101 n.88, 210
2 Timothy   148

Abraham   82, 86
accommodatio   39, 101, 109, 126–7, 140–1, 155–61, 198
Achilles   30, 33, 52, 94, 196
Acts of the Apostles   195
Aeneas   32, 39
affective piety   7, 15, 17–18, 78, 150, 157
affectus   9–21, 29–32, 38, 41–3, 49, 53–6, 59, 72–5, 88, 95–100, 110–16, *see also* emotion(s)
Agricola, George   197
Agricola, Rudolf   29, 95
Agricola, George   197
Ajax   196, 209
Amerbach, Bonifacius   177, 199
amor   32, 54, 56 n.30, 69, 85–6, 99 n.82, 151 n.77, 170 n.28
Andromache   32–3
anger   18, 39, 50, 53–4, 63, 73, 114
   divine   74, 84–6, 101, 125–9
   and gender   46 n.82
   as a goad to virtue   92, 144, 154, 160
   and the humors   55, 65, 67, 128
   Martin Luther's   188–202
   Paul on   102–6
   Stoics on   51, 71–2
   and tragedy   35
   unbridled   54, 57, 69
   as a vice   58–9, 80, 94, 117, 120–2
anxiety   36, 122, 173, 176–8, 185
apatheia   22, 52, 61–4, 71–4, 99
Aquinas, Thomas   2, 10, 15, 52, 69, 79, 138
Arachne   38
Aristophanes   2, 120
Aristotle   2, 6, 22, 28–30, 51, 79, 81, 92, 137, 153 n.85, 159 n.117, 202

Athena (Pallas)   33, 38, 52
Athenodorus   120
Augustine   2, 11, 16, 20, 90, 95 n.68, 105, 113, 114 n.23
   on the Psalms   122, 125, 128–30
   on rhetoric and emotion   135 n.7, 145, 149–51
Augustus   120
Aulus Gellius   2, 61–2

Bacchus   38, 192
Basel   172–8, 187, 194
Bernard of Clairvaux   16, 100
Bible   4, 21, 62, 80, 86, 101, 107–9, 121, 127, 145, 152, 154, 172, 204
Boleyn, Anne   107, 112
Boleyn, Thomas   107, 112
Bracciolini, Poggio   4 n.8
Bucer, Martin   63 n.65, 64

Calvin, John   64
Campeggi, Lorenzo   176
Caracciolo, Roberto   157
caritas   10, 29, 85, 87, 92 n.55, 94 n.61, 104–5, 118 n.37
Christ, *see* Jesus
Chrysostom, John   136, 155
Cicero   6, 20, 25 n.3, 28–30, 138, 144, 183–4
   emotional language of   54, 71–2, 85 n.27, 95, 97, 128, 198
   Hortensius   151
   Tusculan Disputations   55 n.28, 71
Circe   34, 37
Clytemnestra   43–4
Colet, John   39, 60–5, 133
compassion   16, 54, 83, 125, 154, 156–7, 178, *see also* pity
consolation   57, 108, 112, 165, 179–86

Daphne 38
de Berquin, Louis 175
de Vergara, Francisco 167 n.17, 175
deinosis (δείνωσις) 156, 157, 192
despair 45–6, 70, 106, 108, 173
devotio moderna 16
dictionaries (lexicons) 18, 20 n.72, 30, 198
Dido 32, 35

ecstasy 57–8
 as madness 74
emotion(s)
 and affectation 17, 137–8, 153, 157–60, 164, 166
 calm *vs.* violent 1, 22, 28–9, 31, 32, 71, 88, 90, 148, 188, 193, 206
 comic *vs.* tragic (of comedy and tragedy) 22, 26–32, 38, 41–2, 47, 153, 204, 208–10
 as corresponding to body(flesh)/soul/spirit 13, 20 n.72, 56–9, 64–5, 74, 91, 93–4, 98–9, 115–16, 118, 123
 and death 30, 45, 53, 60–5, 68, 85, 101, 108, 181–6
 and facial expression 91, 127, 157–9, 195
 and gender 40, 45–6, 56, 185 n.80
 and gesture 134, 136–7, 157–9
 as goads to virtue 10, 67, 72–3, 92, 102, 112, 144, 162
 and iconoclasm 175, 194–5
 language/semantics of 17–21, 55, 94 n.65, 95, 99, 102, 128, 146, 188, 196, 198
 and medicine 66–70, 115
 mixed 33, 37, 176
 and myth 22, 25–7, 33, 35–48, 82, 92, 196, 210
 neutral (morally) 35, 58–61, 86, 93, 113, 116, 119
 and the Old Testament 100–1, 107–9, 125, 127–8, 161
 and preaching 141–61
 and reason 11, 12, 22, 33–5, 39, 49–56, 59, 61, 64–74, 77, 91–4, 97–8, 105 n.101, 110, 119, 144–5

 religious 9–17, 35, 75, 87–8, 107, 112, 143, 147, 187
 and/as sin or vice 12, 13, 19–21, 26, 39, 53–61, 74, 81, 86, 89, 94, 103, 105, 120, 193
 taxonomy of 22, 27, 29, 31, 42, 55 (*see also affectus*)
 and teaching/pedagogy 10, 15, 25 n.3, 27, 31, 34, 41, 49, 73, 79–82, 86–8, 109, 112–13, 135–9, 143–54, 160–2, 193–4
emotional community 7, 18, 46, 55, 63, 95, 152, 169, 171, 199
emotional lexicon(s) 17–20, 55, 95
emotional style 3–6, 14, 70, 80, 89, 95, 145, 186, 193, 201
emotives 10
envy 26, 36–7, 53–9, 67, 73, 92, 94, 103, 120, 156, 198
Ephesians 83 n.23, 89, 102
epic 22, 26, 28, 32, 39, 196, 204
Epicurean(ism) 56–7
Erasmus, works of
 Adages 22–3, 26–9, 32–3, 36–7, 40, 51–2, 135–40, 150, 195 n.39
 Annotations on the New Testament 22, 78, 84–5, 93 n.60, 95–103, 113, 145 n.45, 210 n.25
 Antibarbari 49, 204
 On the Christian Widow 185–6
 Ciceronianus 15 n.48, 23, 69, 72, 135, 138–9, 143, 145 n.45, 169–71, 184
 Colloquies 36 n.46, 37 n.49, 67 n.72, 69, 91 n.52, 135–6
 Commentaries on the Psalms 9, 18, 80, 100–32
 Commentary on Ovid's Nux 22, 40–7
 Contra pseudevangelicos 192, 195
 Correspondence 11–12, 52–3, 62, 79, 88, 89 n.48, 97–101, 133–4, 163–85, 191–9, 205
 De conscribendis epistolis 31 n.26, 167, 175, 180–5, 192 n.26
 De copia 22, 25–34, 153
 De preparatione ad mortem 61 n.53, 107
 De pueris instituendis 26, 32 n.30, 34, 45 n.82

De ratione studii 22, 31
De recta pronunciatione 140
De taedio Iesu 19 n.69, 22, 39, 50–1, 58, 60–7, 70, 72, 83, 85, 98, 126, 131
Diatribe de libero arbitrio 93, 189
Ecclesiastes 1, 7, 23, 29 n.15, 30 n.22, 31 n.26, 32, 34, 38, 55 n.28, 82, 90, 101 n.88, 109, 112, 122 n.56, 127, 133–62
Enchiridion 9, 11–14, 18, 22, 25, 49–60, 62, 64, 67, 69–74, 86, 91, 93, 98, 119, 131, 161
Hyperaspistes 189–92, 198 n.54, 199
Hyperaspistes 2, 12, 35, 58 n.44, 91–2, 115, 189
Methodus 77–8, 81 n.13
Novum Instrumentum 9 n.23, 37, 77
Novum Testamentum 78, 94 n.65, 95–100, 103 n.94, 210 n.25
Oratio Funebris 181, 183, 185
Panegyricus 33
Paraclesis 9 n.23, 49 n.2, 77
Paraphrase of 1 Corinthians 148
Paraphrase of 1 Thessalonians 93 n.60
Paraphrase of 2 Timothy 148
Paraphrase of Colossians 113 n.21
Paraphrase of Ephesians 89, 102–4
Paraphrase of Galatians 90
Paraphrase of James 80
Paraphrase of John 15, 85–6, 139
Paraphrase of Matthew 83–4, 88, 107
Paraphrase of Romans 96
Paraphrase of Valla's Elegantia 97 n.74
Praise of Folly 22, 37, 40, 50, 51, 58, 70–5
Purgatio 127, 188, 195–200, 209–10
Ratio verae theologiae 9, 22, 39, 78–88
Sermon on the Child Jesus 15
Spongia 194
Estienne, Robert 20 n.72
ethē/ethos (ἤθη) 1, 2, 22, 28, 30, 54, 81, 116, 153, 155, 206
Euripides 2, 29 n.15
Eurycleia 33
Eve 39

fear 34, 36, 46, 69, 79, 87, 99, 105–6, 117, 119, 120, 130, 144, 153 n.87, 158–9, 164, 173–7, 182–4
of death 60–6, 85
of disgrace 54
Erasmus's 173–7, 182–4, 194
of God or the gods 38–9, 105, 107–8, 147
feeling, *see* emotion(s)
Ficino, Marsilio 18, 54–5, 71
Freiburg 172–8
Froben, Johann 89, 177, 184–5
Fugger, Anton 37, 174, 177, 194

Galatians 90–1, 94
Galen 6, 36, 66–7, 115
Geldenhouwer, Gerard 195, 206
Genesis 1, 39
Gerson, Jean 2 n.5, 20 n.72, 160
Gethsemane/Mount of Olives 39, 61–5, 86
Gilles, Pieter 13, 74, 97, 99
God/gods 57, 72, 84, 120, 122, 124, 134, 143, 150, 192–3
contemplation of 73
emotions of 38, 110, 125–30
fear of (*see* fear)
incarnate 77
as instigator/shaper of human emotions 39, 85, 89, 100, 114, 117, 151
love of/pious feelings for 11, 74, 97, 119, 160
voice of 101, 139, 161
wrath of 100, 103, 191, 201, 209 (*see also* emotion(s) of God)
grief 19, 30, 33, 63, 68–70, 74, 85, 99, 101, 114, 117, 125, 159, 180–6, 196

habitus 28 n.12, 30–2, 69, 85, 160, 169
happiness 33, 39, 49, 57, 120, 123, *see also* joy
hatred 29 n.17, 36, 53, 59, 63, 69, 102, 104, 117, 120–2, 127, 144, 156, 160, 174, 187–90, 195–201, 206
heart
as moral center 53, 81, 103, 129
as organ of feeling 23, 33, 35, 57, 62, 68, 71, 80, 88–91, 102, 112, 117,

120–1, 134, 137–51, 166, 170, 184, 189, 191, 195
  as physical organ   105, 126, 128
Hector   32, 207
Hercules   36–7
Hildegard of Bingen   112 n.18
Hippocrates   67 n.72
Holbein, Hans the Younger   37
Homer   1, 2, 6, 22, 27, 34, 37–9, 70, 204
  Battle of Frogs and Mice   40
  Iliad   28, 196–7
  Odyssey   28, 32, 33
hope   19, 26, 37–9, 54, 69, 74, 99, 107–8, 113 n.21, 114, 119, 123, 159, 175
Horace   32, 95, 121
Hume, David   29
humanities   151, 188, 192, 199, 203–10
humors/humoral theory   36, 55, 66–70, 114–15
hypotyposis   156–7

Ino   36

Jerome   37, 94 n.65, 136, 165–6, 183
Jesus   12, 70, 99, 103–4, 107, 114, 143, 152, 192–4
  agony of   85
  anger of   84, 85 n.27, 103
  as consoler   108
  his fear of death   60–1
  human emotions of   61–5, 74, 83, 86, 99
  as model and teacher of emotions   22, 34, 58 n.41, 84–8, 94 n.65, 139, 148
  sorrow of   85, 86
  suffering of   7, 16, 39
  wept   86
Job   124, 179, 183
John (Gospel of)   15, 77, 83, 85–6, 139, 150
John the Baptist   128, 150
Jonas, Justus   133
joy   19, 33, 37–8, 57, 58 n.41, 63, 65, 68–9, 74–5, 87 n.38, 94, 99, 119, 125–6, 159
Juno   39
Jupiter   37, 38, 71

Koler, Johan   90 n.48, 170, 199

laughter   32 n.34, 33, 65, 74, 89, 126, 129
Lazarus   64, 83, 86
Lefèvre d'Etaples, Jacques   131
Lernaean Hydra   36
love   55, 59, 98–9, 127, 130 n.83, 150–1, 153, 159, 170
  divine   150
  familial   29, 54, 58, 73, 86, 118
  religious   65, 74–5, 85–7, 100, 104, 112, 137–8, 144, 147, 160
  romantic/passionate   32, 67, 69, 112
Lucian   29 n.15, 36, 120
Luke (Gospel of)   2, 86, 155
lust   54, 57, 59, 69, 71, 73, 80, 94–5, 120, 156
  for revenge   46
Luther, Martin   3, 12, 18, 27, 35, 58 n.44, 78, 90–4, 98, 107, 114, 127, 149, 187–210

Macrobius   2
Mark (Gospel of)   83–4, 86, 103
Matthew (Gospel of)   31, 54 n.23, 83, 86, 88, 107, 155
Medea   32, 36, 37, 40
melancholy   70, 89
Melanchthon, Phillip   6, 177, 190, 192, 195, 198–200
metaphor   36, 40, 46, 54, 68, 80, 88, 110, 114–17, 125–9, 139, 146, 149–51, 155
More, Thomas   176, 199, 209
Moses   2, 39, 108, 147
movere   79, 109, 142, 147, 162

Neoplatonism   51
New Testament   1, 4, 13, 83, 87, 96, 100, 101, 103, 108–10, 123, 128, 131, 195
  Erasmus's scholarship on   18, 74–5, 77–8, 95, 99, 106, 113, 205–6

Odysseus/Ulysses   33–5, 38, 208
Odyssey, see Homer
Oecolampadius, Johannes   172, 175, 194
Old Testament   1, 9, 100, 101, 106–9, 125, 127–8, 130, 161

Oppian 45
Orestes 43, 44, 196, 209
Origen 6, 58 n.43, 118, 160
Ovid 6, 22, 27, 36, 39, 121
   Metamorphoses 37, 174 n.40
   Nux 40–7

Pan 38
passio 18–21, 63, 66, 95–8
pathē/pathos (πάθη) 1, 2, 22, 28, 30, 64, 72, 81, 93, 96, 97 n.75, 99 n.82, 116, 153, 155, 160, 209
Paul 35, 115–16, 128, 134, 149, 154, 190
   affective rhetorical style of 31, 87, 141, 160–1, 194
   on anger and Psalm 2, 100–4
   on emotion 56, 64, 81, 83 n.23, 88–94, 96–8, 148, 210
   as emotional model 22, 99, 140–1, 179
   letters of 78, 80
Peripatetic 10, 55–6, 92, 144
Phaedra 32
philosophy 10–12, 21–2, 26, 31, 33–5, 48–52, 64, 66, 72–3, 77–8, 87, 90, 109, 113, 119, 133, 136, 142, 146, 149–51, 166, 184
Pirckheimer, Willibald 175–7, 197
pity 32, 42–5, 73, 74, 83, 84, 99, 125, 130, 143, 154, 156, 160, *see also* compassion
Plato 18, 22, 51, 54–5, 59, 62, 71, 73, 92, 122, 151
Plautus 32, 70
Pliny the Elder 2
Pliny the Younger 137
Plutarch 50, 70
Protestant(s) 3, 14, 23, 41, 63–4, 130, 172–3, 177, 187–8, 190–1, 194, 199–210
Proteus/protean 39
Proverbs 26, 36–7
Psalm(s) 57, 59, 68, 88, 100–4, 109–25, 127, 129, 130, 150
Pythagorean 46

Quintilian 1, 2, 4, 22, 26–31, 41, 54, 72, 95, 97, 112, 134–5, 147, 153–4, 196, 209

rage 40, 87, 105, 106, 127, 148, 179, 192, 194, 197, 200, 205
Reformation(s) 28, 63 n.65, 186, 187, 191
   of Basel 172–8
   as tragedy 201–10
Revelation 103, 114
rhetoric 21, 30–1, 45, 47, 81, 90, 109, 113, 133–5, 139, 147–8, 155, 170, 184–6, 204
   classical 15, 22, 28–31, 42, 72, 137, 145, 161, 193
   criticism of 11
   against dialectic 6, 77
   and philosophy 50
   and theology 10, 78–9, 88, 141–8
   violent/vehement 94, 201, 209–10
Romans (Paul's letter) 58 n.43, 94–7, 128–9

sadness 19, 54, 56, 60, 67, 70, 90, 159, 179
Savonarola, Girolamo 157
Schets, Erasmus 175–6, 197
scholastic/scholasticism 6, 11–15, 17, 20, 30, 49, 64, 77–9, 114, 135, 138, 145–6
Scotus, Duns 12, 15, 133
Seneca 5, 50, 51, 72, 89–90, 193
Shakespeare 2, 6, 120
shame 43, 65, 80, 87, 91, 95–6, 144, 157, 163, 181–3
sincerity 138, 149, 153, 164–71, 191
Sisyphus 37
Socrates 55, 69, 119, 139
sorrow 36–7, 65, 85–6, 90, 119–20, 122, 181–2, 184–5, 196
Stoicism 6, 12, 19, 22, 34, 49–52, 55–7, 61–74, 92, 99, 105, 120, 143–4, 157, 163, 179, 185, 193
stomach 22, 80, 107, 110 -11, 114–15, 146–7
stomachus 18, 110–11, 115, 146, 197–8
Suetonius 193
suicide 122, 193
synderesis 35, 91–2
synecdoche 22, 107, 110, 125, 128–30

Tantalus 36, 73, 81
tears 1, 33, 65, 74, 78, 85, 90–1, 117, 123–4, 152, 179, 181–3, 18′

Terence   31, 120, 198
terror   38, 40, 73, 108, 112, 130
Titelmans, Francis   12–13, 20, 64, 96–9
tragedy   1, 2, 23, 26, 28–9, 31–2, 187–8, 202–10
tragicomic   29, 40–2, 47

Ulysses, *see* Odysseus

Valla, Lorenzo   20, 30, 31, 51, 64, 95–7
Virgil   2, 6, 22, 26, 39–40, 57
Vitrier, Jean   133–5, 138, 152
viva vox   90, 112–13, 135–7
Vives, Juan Luis   6, 13, 30, 95, 100, 166
Volz, Paul   11, 52–3, 62, 199

von Amsdorf, Nikolaus   196–7
von Botzheim, Johann   179, 181, 183–5, 199
von Hutten, Ulrich   194, 208
Vulgate   18, 20, 68, 83–5, 88, 94–6, 102, 105, 129

Warham, William   207
weeping, *see* tears
Weyer, Johann   5
will   12, 92–4, 98, 100

zeal   56, 84, 86, 133, 144, 151–2, 187, 196, 205
Zeus, *see* Jupiter